The Advisory Function of the International Court of Justice 1946–2005

Mahasen M. Aljaghoub

The Advisory Function of the International Court of Justice 1946–2005

Springer

Professor Mahasen M. Aljaghoub
University of Jordan
PO Box 941958
11194 Amman
Jordan
e-mail: mahasen@ju.edu.jo

ISBN 978-3-642-07140-9 e-ISBN 978-3-540-35734-6

Springer is part of Springer Science+Business Media

springer.com

Printed in Germany

Cover: Erich Kirchner, Heidelberg

To my wonderful husband, Munther, for all his love, support and encouragement. He has always been my inspiration, my great mentor and my best friend in the whole world. With him by my side I have found all that I ever wanted.

Foreword

I am pleased to write these words by way of a foreword to Dr. Mahasen Aljaghoub's book "The Advisory Function of the International Court of Justice". I do so with a sense of pride in the achievement of a fellow countrywoman and, metaphorically speaking, a sister in law.

My pride is coupled with hope and a nascent optimism that she – and a group of young Jordanian academics, mostly recent graduates of universities in the United Kingdom – will contribute further and significantly to the teaching and dissemination of international law in Jordan and, if I do not strain hope by hoping too much, in a region in which, notwithstanding its past glory, the culture of law has for too long been superceded by the logic of power politics and unbridled raison d'état.

My only hesitation in writing this foreword is that a particularly heavy Court schedule has permitted me only a chance at a perusal of the contents of the book. A perusal which, whilst more than casual, falls short of the serious study that it deserves. Yet, I can unhesitatingly concur with the verdict of the internal and external examiners who praised Dr. Aljaghoub's thesis (as it then was) for "its thoroughness, detail and authoritativeness on this important area of international law". I would only add to this sentence, which sums up an objective assessment of the book, the further observation that Dr. Aljaghoub's book is closely argued and draws reasonable conclusions. These are all features that commend her work as an important reference that updates previous academic work on the Advisory jurisdiction of the Court, all the more timely in view of the more recent advisory opinions emanating from the Court.

Edward Hambro, when once asked to write an introduction to a book, did so with the following words: "A good book needs no introduction; a bad one deserves none". This statement is certainly witty and often true but not always. Good books written by new authors deserve to be introduced and praised and I have no doubts that Dr. Aljaghoub's book falls into this category.

The Hague, May 2006

Awn Al-Khasawneh
Vice-President
International Court of Justice,
Peace Palace, The Hague

Foreword

It gives me great pleasure to write this brief foreword for Dr Aljaghoub's book. Her rigorous and comprehensive text fills a gap in the literature as comparatively little scholarly attention has been paid to the Court's advisory jurisdiction since the early 1970s when no less than three monographs were published on the subject. In the intervening period there have been several important advisory opinions of the ICJ touching on issues including self-determination and the legality of the threat or use of nuclear weapons, and culminating in the politically sensitive and high-profile *Advisory Opinion on the Legal Consequences of the Construction of a Wall in the Occupied Palestinian Territory*. The need for a new book, such as this, on the Court's advisory jurisdiction has become increasingly apparent.

Dr Aljaghoub provides a thoughtful and careful analysis of the structure and procedure of the Court and of its wide-ranging opinions which have contributed to the development of international law in numerous fields. Her book also offers a fascinating account of the historical background to the development of the Court's advisory jurisdiction. In addition, it considers the thorny question of why greater use has not been made of the Court's capacity to give advisory opinions. Since its inception, after World War II, the Court has delivered only twenty five such opinions.

Dr Aljaghoub's deep commitment to international law and, in particular, to the role of judicial settlement in the resolution of international disputes is apparent throughout this book. Her idealism (which in the longer-term may come to be recognised as level-headed pragmatism) is commendable, particularly at a time when international law is being flouted by certain powerful states.

Dr Aljaghoub wrote the PhD that formed the basis of this book while also caring for a young and growing family in an unfamiliar environment. Her tenacity, optimism and capacity for unrelenting hard work – as well as her good-humoured ability to juggle the innumerable demands made on her – have elicited my admiration as her supervisor.

Warwick, May 2006

Professor Istvan Pogany
Director, Legal Research Institute,
School of Law,
University of Warwick

Preface

This book originated as a thesis submitted in 2005 for the Doctor of Philosophy at the University of Warwick, United Kingdom. My first and very great thanks go to my doctoral supervisor Professor, Istvan Pogany. I owe him a great depth of gratitude for his incredible support, encouragement, and patience in reading successive drafts and for his invaluable guidance in the development of my work throughout my years of study. Without his vigorous and detailed comments, which were always constructive, helpful and appropriate, the writing of this book would not have been possible.

I am also grateful to the staff of the library at the University of Warwick, especially those in charge of the legal materials on the fourth floor. For the past four years of my research I have witnessed with admiration their professionalism, helpfulness and dedication.

I would like also to thank Dr. Gerard Sharpling, of CELTE at the University of Warwick, and Dr. Frank Griffith Dawson, a life Fellow of Hughes Hall, University of Cambridge, for reading this work in draft. They helped me to avoid numerous grammatical errors, and suggested many ways in which the quality of the English might be improved. This work also benefited greatly from Dr. Dawson's valuable comments, encouragement and suggestions. In addition, I would like to thank the staff of Springer Press, especially, Brigitte Reschke, Senior Editor in Law, for their care in the preparation of this book.

My thanks also go to my parents, brothers and sisters, who have displayed ceaseless support and love and whom I can never repay in full.

Above all, I am greatly indebted to Munther Hattab, my husband, to whom I dedicate this book. He shouldered a great deal of the burden and encouraged me to persevere at all times. Words cannot adequately express my appreciation to him for the great and countless sacrifices that he has made, which have not gone unappreciated. My thanks go to him for always being there for me. Our two little sons, Rashid and Mohammad, also helped to sustain my strength and motivation and were a much needed source of comfort and encouragement. Their understanding and their amiable tolerance of their mother's long days and late nights of work, which I hope I can make up to them, have been an inspiration throughout.

Finally, I am deeply grateful to Judge Awn Shawket Al-khasawneh, the Vice President of the International Court of Justice, for kindly consenting to write foreword for this book.

Amman, May 2006 | Mahasen Aljaghoub

Table of Contents

CHAPTER TWO

The Advisory Jurisdiction of the ICJ: Compliance with Requests and the Court's Discretion in Giving Advisory Opinions 35

CHAPTER THREE

The Role of the ICJ as the Principal Judicial Organ of the UN and the Implications of This Role for the Court's Advisory Function 69

CHAPTER FOUR

The Judicial Character of the ICJ's Advisory Function and the Problem of Consent 95

CHAPTER FIVE

Procedural Aspects of the Advisory Function of the ICJ 123

CHAPTER SIX

The Contribution of Advisory Opinions to the Development of the Law of International Institutions and to Public International Law 155

CHAPTER SEVEN

The Attitude of United Nations Member States Towards the Use of the Advisory Procedure 201

CHAPTER EIGHT

The Reception of Advisory Opinions 223

CONCLUSION

The Advisory Function of the ICJ: Concerns, Limitations and Future Role 237

List of Abbreviations

The following abbreviations are used in this work.

AJIL	American Journal of International Law
BYIL	British Yearbook of International Law
CJEC	Court of Justice of European Community
Diss. Op.	Dissenting Opinion
Doc(s)	Document(s)
ed.	Editor
eds.	Editors
EC	European Community
ECHR	The European Court of Human Rights
ECOSOC	Economic and Social Council
e.g.	exempli gratii
et al.	et alii
EPIL	Encyclopaedia of Public International Law
GAOR	General Assembly Official Records
HILJ	Harvard International Law Journal
HLR	Harvard Law Review
IACHR	The Inter-American Court on Human Rights
IAEA	International Atomic Energy Organization
ICJ	International Court of Justice
ICJ Pled.	International Court of Justice, Pleadings
ICJ Rep.	International Court of Justice, Reports of Judgments, Advisory Opinions and Order
ICJYB	Yearbook of the International Court of Justice
ICCPR	International Covenant on Civil and Political Rights
ICESCR	International Covenant on Economic, Social and Cultural Rights
ICLQ	International and Comparative Law Quarterly
IGO	Intergovernmental Organization
ILAC	Informal Inter-Allied Committee on the Future of the Permanent Court of International Justice
ILA	International Law Association

ILC	International Law Commission
ILM	International Legal Materials
ILO	International Labour Organization
ILOAT	International Labour Organization Administrative Tribunal
IMCO	Intergovernmental Maritime Consultative Organization
IMO	International Maritime Organization
JAIL	Japanese Annual of International Law
LJIL	Leiden Journal of International Law
LNTS	League of Nations Treaty Series
NGO	Non-Governmental Organization
ONUC	United Nations Force in the Congo
PCA	Permanent Court of Arbitration
PCIJ	Permanent Court of International Justice
PLO	Palestine Liberation Organization
Sep. Op.	Separate Opinion
Ser.	Series
SG	Secretary General
Supp.	Supplement
UK	United Kingdom
UN	United Nations Organization
UN Doc.	United Nations Documents
UNAT	United Nations Administrative Tribunal
UNCIO	United Nations Conference on International Organization
UNEF	United Nations Emergency Force
UNESCO	United Nations Economic, Social and Cultural Organization
UKTS	United Kingdom Treaty Series
UNTS	United Nations Treaty Series
UNYB	United Nations Year Book
UPLR	University of Pennsylvania Law Review
UPU	Universal Postal Union
US	United States
USSR	Union of Socialist Soviet Republics
VCLT	Vienna Convention of the Law of Treaties
VJIL	Virginia Journal of International Law
WHO	World Health Organization
YLJ	Yale Law Journal

Glossary of Terms

ad hoc judge	Judge appointed to a specific case for a specific purpose.
Amicus curiae	A person permitted to present arguments bearing upon issues before a tribunal yet not representing the interests of any party to the proceedings.
audi alteram partem	The right to a fair hearing before a decision is made.
Audiatur et altera pars	One should not be condemned without being heard.
Compétence de la compétence	The power of the Court to decide on its own jurisdiction *de facto.*
de Jure	Existing by law.
Dicta	A statement of law stated by tribunals or by individual members of tribunals; propositions not directed to the principal matters in issue.
erga omnes	Opposable to, against 'everyone.'
ex aequo et bono	Principle in international law for deciding on the basis of fairness and justice.
ex officio	By virtue of the authority implied by office.
fait accompli	Established fact.
Forum prorogatum	If there is no explicit consent to the Court's jurisdiction, the parties may be thought to have acquiesced to the jurisdiction if they participate in the proceedings.
infra legem	Application of rules of law using principles of equity.
inter alia	Among other things.
intra vires	Action taken within the scope of body's authority. Contrast with ultra vires.
jura novit curia	The Court is not restricted to the law presented by the parties, but is free to take its own research.
jus cogens	Peremptory norms of international law that no one can derogate from.
lex specialis	A law with a specific application.
locus standi	The power to apply to a tribunal for a particular remedy; more specifically, the existence of a sufficient legal interest in the matter in issue.

non liquet	A situation when a court is unable to give a legal decision because of the lack of relevant rules.
Prima facie	Presumptively.
Proprio motu	Acting on its own motion.
Ratione materia	By reason of the subject matter.
Ratione personae	Determined by the status and dignity of the person or entity as such.
res judicata	The principle that an issue decided by a court should not be reopened.
stare decisis	The principle that a tribunal should follow its own previous decisions and those of other tribunals of greater authority.
terra nullius	Land which belongs to no one because it has not been claimed by a nation, yet it might be subject to such a claim.
Travaux préparatoires	Preparatory works; the documents and proceedings of the meetings where a treaty is drafted.

Table of Cases

ICJ Advisory Opinions

1. *Conditions of Admission of a State to Membership in the United Nations (Article 4 of the Charter)*, ICJ Reports 1948, p. 57
2. *Reparation for Injuries Suffered in the Service of the United Nations*, ICJ Reports 1949, p. 174
3. *Competence of the General Assembly for the Admission of a State to the United Nations*, ICJ Reports 1950, p. 4

4. & 5. *Interpretation of Peace Treaties with Bulgaria, Hungary and Romania*, ICJ Reports 1950, First Phase p. 65; Second Phase p. 221

6. *International Status of South-West Africa*, ICJ Reports 1950, p. 128
7. *Reservations to the Convention on the Prevention and Punishment of the Crime of Genocide*, ICJ Reports 1951, p. 15
8. *Effects of Awards of Compensation made by the United Nations Administrative Tribunal*, ICJ Reports 1954, p. 47
9. *Voting Procedure on Questions Relating to Reports and Petitions Concerning the Territory of South-West Africa*, ICJ Reports 1955, p. 67
10. *Admissibility of Hearings of Petitioners by the Committee on South West Africa*, ICJ Reports 1956, p. 23
11. *Judgments of the Administrative Tribunal of the International Labour Organisation Upon Complaints Made Against the United Nations Educational, Scientific and Cultural Organisation*, ICJ Reports 1956, p. 77
12. *Constitution of the Maritime Safety Committee of the Inter-Governmental Maritime Consultative Organization*, ICJ Reports 1960, ICJ Reports 1960, p. 150
13. *Certain Expenses of the United Nations (Article 17, Paragraph 2, of the Charter)*, ICJ Reports 1962, p. 151
14. *Legal Consequences for States of the Continued Presence of South Africa in Namibia (South West Africa) Notwithstanding Security Council Resolution 276* (1970), ICJ Reports 1971, p. 16
15. *Application for Review of Judgment No. 158 of the United Nations Administrative Tribunal*, ICJ Reports 1973, p. 166
16. *Western Sahara*, ICJ Reports 1975, p. 12
17. *Interpretation of the Agreement of 25 March 1951 Between the WHO and Egypt*, ICJ Reports 1980, p. 73

18. *Application for Review of Judgment No. 273 of the United Nations Administrative Tribunal*, ICJ Reports 1982, p. 325
19. *Application for Review of Judgment No. 333 of the United Nations Administrative Tribunal*, ICJ Reports 1987, p. 18
20. *Applicability of the Obligation to Arbitrate Under Section 21 of the United Nations Headquarters Agreement of 26 June 1947*, ICJ Reports 1988, p. 12
21. *Applicability of Article VI, Section 22, of the Convention on the Privileges and Immunities of the United Nations*, ICJ Reports 1989, p. 177
22. *Legality of the Use BY a State of Nuclear Weapons in Armed Conflict*, ICJ Reports 1996, p. 66
23. *Legality of the Threat or Use of Nuclear Weapons*, ICJ Reports 1996, p. 226
24. *Difference Relating to Immunity From Legal Process of a Special Rapporteur of the Commission on Human Rights*, ICJ Reports 1999, p. 62
25. *Legal Consequences of the Construction of a Wall in the Occupied Palestinian Territory,* 2004. Available at: http://www.icj-cij.org/icjwww/idocket/imwp/imwpframe.htm

PCIJ Advisory Opinions

1. *Status of Eastern Carelia*, PCIJ Series B, No. 5, July 23rd, 1923
2. *Exchange of Greek and Turkish Populations (Lausanne Convention VI, January 3oth, 1923, Article 2)*, PCIJ Series B, No. 10, February 21st, 1925
3. *Interpretation of Art. 3, Para. 2, of the Treaty of Lausanne (Frontier Between Turkey and Iraq)* [referred to as the Mosul case], PCIJ Series B, No. 12, November 21st, 1925
4. *Interpretation of Greco-Turkish Agreement of December 1st, 1926 (Final Protocol, Article IV),* PCIJ Series B, No. 16, August 28th, 1928

ICJ Contentious Cases

1. *Nottebohm case (Liechtenstein v. Guatemala) Second Phase*, Judgment of April 6th, 1955: ICJ Reports 1955, p. 4
2. *South-West Africa cases (Ethiopia v. South Africa; Liberia v. South Africa) Second Phase,* Judgment of July 18th, 1966: ICJ Reports 1966, p. 6
3. *Case Concerning Questions of Interpretation and Application of the 1971 Montreal Convention Arising From the Arial Incident at Lockerbie (Libya Arab Jamahiriya v. United Kingdom),* Provisional Measures, Order of April 14th, 1992: ICJ Reports 1992, p. 3

4. *Case Concerning Questions of Interpretation and Application of the 1971 Montreal Convention Arising From the Arial Incident at Lockerbie (Libya Arab Jamahiriya v. United States of America),* Provisional Measures, Order of April 14th, 1992: ICJ Reports 1992, p. 114
5. *Corfu Channel (United Kingdom v. Albania),* Judgment of April 9th, 194: ICJ Reports 1949, p. 4
6. *Asylum case (Colombia/ Peru),* Judgment of November 20th, 1950: ICJ Reports 1950, p. 266
7. *Bercelona Traction, light and Power Company, limited (New Application) (Belgium v. Spain),* Judgment of February 5th, 1970: ICJ Reports 1970, p. 3

Table of Treaties and Other International Instruments

American Convention on Human Rights, 22 November 1969, San Jose, PAULTS 36; 9 ILM (1970) 673; 65 AJIL (1971) 679.

Charter of the United Nations, 26 June 1945, San Francisco, UKTS 67 (1946) Cmd. 7015; 1 UNTS 16; 39 AJIL (1945) Supp. 190.

Constitution of the World Health Organization, 22 July 1946, 14 UNTS 185; UKTS 43 (1948), Cmd 7458.

Convention for the Establishment of the Intergovernmental Maritime Consultative Organization, 6 March 1948, 289 UNTS 48; UKTS 54 (1958)

Convention for the Suppression of Unlawful Acts against the Safety of Civil Aviation (Montreal Convention), 23 September 1971, 974 UNTS 177; UKTS 10 (1974), Cmnd 5524; 66 AJIL (1972) 455.

Convention on the Law of the Sea, 10 December 1982, 21 ILM (1982) 1261.

Convention on the Prevention and Punishment of the Crime of Genocide, United Nations, 9 December1948, 78 UNTS 277; 45 AJIL (1951) Supp. 7.

Convention on the Privileges and Immunities of the Specialized Agencies of the United Nations, 21 November 1947, 33 UNTS 261; UKTS 69 (1959), Cmnd 855.

Convention on the Privileges and Immunities of the United Nations (the General Convention), 13 February 1946, London, 1 UNTS 15; UKTS 10 (1950) Cmnd. 7891; 43 AJIL (1949) Supp. 1.

Covenant of the League of Nations, Versailles, 28 June 1919, in force 10 January 1920, UKTS 4 (1919); 13 AJIL (1919) Supp. 128, 361.

Egypt-World Health Organization (WHO), Agreement and Exchange of Notes on Status of WHO in Egypt, 25 August 1950, 92 UNTS 39.

European Convention for the protection of Human Rights and Fundamental Freedoms, Council of Europe, 4 November 1950. Rome, UKTS 71 (1953) Cmd. 8969; 213 UNTS 221; 45 AJIL (1951) Supp. 24.

Geneva Convention (IV) Relative to the Protection of Civilian Persons in Time of War, 12 August, 1949. 75 UNTS 287; UKTS 39 (1958).

Headquarter Agreement between the United Nations and the United States of America, 26 June 1947, 11 UNTS 11.

International Convention on Civil and Political Rights, New York, 16 December 1966, Annex to UN GA Resolution 2200 (XXI) GAOR, 21st Sess. Supp. 16, p. 49; UKTS 6 (1977) Cmnd. 6702; 6 ILM (1967) 368.

International Covenant on Economic Social and Cultural Rights, 16 December 1966, New York, Annex to UN GA Resolution 2200 (XXX) GAOR, 21st Sess. Supp. 16, p. 49; UKTS 6 (1977) Cmnd. 6702.

Statute of the International Court of Justice, 26 June 1945, San Francisco, UKTS 67 (1946) Cmd. 7015; 1 UNTS 993, 59 Stat. 1031; 39 AJIL (1945) Supp. 215n.

Statute of the Permanent Court of International Justice, 16 December 1920, PCIJ, Ser. D, No. 1 (2nd edn), 7

The Rio Declaration on Environment and Development, 1992.

Treaty on European Union (Maastricht Treaty), 7 February 1992, 31 ILM (1992) 247.

Universal Declaration of Human Rights, United Nations, 10 December 1948, UN Doc. A/811.

Vienna Convention on the Law of Treaties, 23 May 1969, UN. Doc. A/Conf. 39/27, 63 AJIL, 875-903; UKTS 58 (1980) Cmnd. 7964.

Vienna Convention on the Law of Treaties between States and International Organization or between International Organizations, 21 March 1986, 25 ILM (1986)

Introduction

1 Origin and Purpose of the Advisory Function

The International Court of Justice (ICJ) was established as the principal judicial organ of the United Nations (UN),[1] with an organisation and powers broadly similar to those of its predecessor, the Permanent Court of International Justice (PCIJ).[2] As the UN's principal judicial organ the Court is therefore part of the UN system.

In addition to its function of settling disputes between States in its contentious jurisdiction, the Court may also give non-binding advisory opinions on legal questions submitted to it by certain bodies. Thus, Article 65 of the Court's Statute provides that "the Court may give an advisory opinion on any legal question at the request of whatever body may be authorized by or in accordance with the Charter of the United Nations to make such a request." Article 96 of the Charter notes that in addition to the General Assembly and Security Council, other organs of the UN and specialised agencies where so authorised by the Assembly may also request such opinions on legal questions arising within the scope of their activities. The Court's latter function is the subject-matter of this study.

Authorising advisory opinions at the international level was first provided for in Article 14 of the League Covenant, which declared the PCIJ competent to give advisory opinions upon any dispute or question referred to it by the Council or by the Assembly.[3] The experience of the PCIJ proved to be of greater value than was anticipated at its inception.[4] As a result, at the San Francisco Conference two landmark decisions were taken of relevance to this study. First, in the light of the successful experience of the advisory function of the PCIJ, it was decided that an advisory capacity should be retained and even extended for the PCIJ's successor, the ICJ. Second, the ICJ became the principal judicial organ of the UN, sharing collectively with the other UN organs in the fulfilment of the tasks stated in the provisions of the Charter.[5] It has been suggested that the deci-

---

1 See Article 92 of the UN Charter which complements Article 7(1) of the Charter.

2 This point will be discussed in Chapter One, *infra*.

3 See Chapter One, *infra*.

4 Hudson, Manley, O., *The Permanent Court of International Justice, 1920-1942: A Treaties*, New York: The Macmillan Company, 1943, pp. 513-524.

5 A detailed analysis of the evolution of the advisory function of the ICJ is provided in Chapter One, *infra*.

sion to establish the Court as a principal organ of the UN was the most important innovation made by the UN's founders since it meant that the Court's decisions had to be closely geared to the requirements of the political community which it was designed to serve.[6]

The advisory function of the ICJ underlines the 'organic connection' between the Court and the UN and, therefore, its role and contribution as one of the Organisation's principal organs, as well as the principal judicial organ. The position of the Court within the UN and its integral relationship within the Organisation has largely been reflected in the way the Court has viewed its advisory jurisdiction.[7] The practice and dicta of the Court have emphasised this relationship by affirming that the delivery of an opinion represents the participation of the Court in the work of the UN, and so, in the absence of compelling contrary reasons, a request for an opinion ought not to be refused.[8] One should also remember that in the dicta of the Court there has always been the presumption of validity as regards resolutions adopted by the UN political organs, if such resolutions are appropriate for the achievement of the UN purposes.[9]

On the other hand, the practice of the UN organs, and more specifically of the political organs, sometimes reveals a cautious attitude towards the Court. One cannot but notice that the political organs are, for various reasons, reluctant to seek an advisory opinion from the Court when it might be needed.[10] This attitude of the political organs is partly reflected in the matters that did not come before the Court for advisory opinions.[11] Many different reasons might explain this limited recourse to the advisory jurisdiction.

In light of the above, many inaccurate and divergent views, assumptions, and unfulfilled expectations about the nature and purpose of the advisory jurisdiction, and indeed the advisory role of the ICJ, have been voiced. Hence, two major interrelated questions will be of immediate concern. First, what exactly is the nature of the advisory function of the ICJ, and what are its peculiar characteristics? Second, how has the Court reconciled its role as a court of law and as a principal organ of the UN? Both questions are also intimately related to other, wider questions that I hope to examine in this study.

---

6 Rosenne, Shabtai, *The Law and Practice of the International Court, 1920-1996*, The Hague; London: Martinus Nijnhoff Publishers, vol. 1, 1997, pp. 162-163.

7 A detailed analysis of this point is provided in Chapters Two, Three, Five of this book.

8 See Chapter Four, *infra.*

9 See Chapter Two, *infra.*

10 The reasons behind this cautious attitude of the political organs will be analysed in Chapters Seven and Nine, *infra.*

11 See the discussion in Chapter Nine, *infra.*

2 General Features of the Existing Literature

While the ICJ, more generally, has already received extensive scholarly treatment, the advisory function has not received proportional attention from international lawyers, a fact which has partly influenced my choice of this subject.[12] The comparatively little literature that is available on the ICJ advisory function may be criticised on several grounds: First, the studies are somewhat dated so that a new, fresh approach is required. Second, most of the studies tend to examine the advisory function in terms of both the PCIJ and the ICJ.[13] Third, some studies have misconceived the status of the Court as the "principal judicial organ of the United Nations" and conclude that the Court-political organs relationship is a "client-lawyer" relationship,[14] while others looking at the Court as an "academy of jurists" have concluded that the Court should be responsive to the sensitivities of the General Assembly.[15] Fourth, the existing literature has paid little attention to the

[12] The three major studies on this subject are Keith, Kenneth J., *The Extent of the Advisory Jurisdiction of the International Court of Justice*, Leyden: A. W. Sijthoff, 1971; Pratap, Dharma, *The Advisory Jurisdiction of the International Court of Justice*, Oxford: Clarendon Press, 1972; Pomerance, Michla, *The Advisory Function of the International Court in the League and U.N Eras*, Baltimore; London: John Hopkins University Press, 1973. On the other hand, there are some non-exclusive studies which took the advisory function of the ICJ as part of the complete study on the Court as a whole, examples of those studies are many: Amr, Mohamed S., *The Role of the International Court of Justice as the Principal Judicial Organ of the United Nations*, The Hague: Kluwer Law International, 2003; Oduntan, Gbenga, *The Law and Practice of the International Court of Justice [1945-1996]: A Critique of the Contentious and Advisory Jurisdictions*, Enugu: Fourth Dimension Publishers, 1999; Rosenne, Shabtai, *The Law and Practice of the International Court, 1920-1996*, The Hague; London: Martinus Nijnhoff Publishers, 4 Vols., 1997; Rosenne, Shabtai., *The World Court: What it is and How it Works,* Dordrecht, London: Martinus Nijhoff Publishers, 1994; Oda, Shigeru, "The International Court of Justice Viewed from the Bench 1976-1993", 244 *RCADI*, 1993, pp. 9-190; Fitizmaurace, Gerald G., *The Law and Procedure of the International Court of Justice*, Cambridge: Grotius Publications limited, 2 Vols., 1986; Gross, Leo, (ed.), *The Future of the International Court of Justice*, Dobbs Ferry, New York: Oceana Publications, 1976; Lissitzyn, Oliver J., *The International Court of Justice: Its Role in the Maintenance of International Peace and Security*, New York: Carnegie Endowment for International Peace, 1951.

[13] This is perhaps for two reasons: first, the ICJ is the continuation of the PCIJ as the Statute and Rules of the ICJ are essentially that of its predecessor. Secondly, the available cases were too few in numbers to merit an exclusive study for the ICJ advisory opinions.

[14] Pomerance, *supra* note 12. This view seems to underestimate the peculiar characteristics of a court-of-law, and implies that the weight of the Court's pronouncement is "advisory" rather than "authoritative".

[15] Falk argues that the Court has to be a much more genuine judicial arm of the UN, sensitive to the way the Organisation has evolved. In effect he claims that "what the world

contribution of the advisory opinions to UN law and to International Law.[16] Fifth, some of the available literature has overlooked the role of the advisory function in clarifying the law and providing guidance for future action by the UN organs, and has consequently called for applying the principle of consent as a condition for giving an advisory opinion on questions relating to disputes pending between States.[17] Sixth, a sizable amount of literature has concentrated on ways and means to increase the use of the advisory function through expanding the number of bodies authorised to request the Court's opinion, while overlooking methods which would not require constitutional changes.[18] Lastly, some studies have gone further to compare the ICJ with the European Court of Justice, ignoring the fact that such a comparison is between two judicial bodies which are entirely dissimilar.[19]

Court should become is an academy of jurists, responsive primarily to the prevailing normative sensitivities of the General Assembly, although maintaining as well a more principled and long-range view on the overall global agenda. It should be an academy of jurists that seeks to persuade a non-professional audience of individuals concerned about global policy that in the Court's view deserves respect." See Falk, Richard, *Reviving the World Court*, Charlottesville: University Press of Virginia, 1986, pp. 186- 191.

16 A handful of writers have addressed this subject, although as part of the Court's total contribution. See Amr, *supra* note 12; Schwebel, Stephen M., "The Contribution of the International Court of Justice to the Development of International Law", in: Heere, Wybo p. (ed.), *International law and the Hague's 750th Anniversary*, T.M.C, Asser Press, 1999, p. 405. Lauterpacht, Hersch, *The Development of International Law by the International Court*, London: Stevens and Sons Ltd, 1958; Lauterpacht, Elihu, "The Development of the Law of International Organization by the Decisions of International Tribunals", 152 *RCADI*, 1976, pp. 377-478; Higgins, Rosalyn, "The International Court of Justice and Human Rights", in: Wellens, Karel, (ed.), *International Law: Theory and Practice: Essays in Honour of Eric Suy*, The Hague; Boston; London: Martinus Nijhoff Publishers, 1998, pp. 691-706; Rosenne, Shabtai, "The Contribution of the International Court of Justice to the United Nations", 35 *Indian Journal of International Law*, 1995, pp. 67-76.

17 See Pomerance, Michla, "The Advisory Role of the International Court of Justice and its 'Judicial' Character: Past and Future Prisms, in: Muller, A.S. & Raic, D. *et al* (eds.), *The International Court of Justice: Its Future Role After Fifty Years*, The Hague; Boston; London: Martinus Nijhoff Publishers, 1997, pp. 271-323; Greig, D. W., "The Advisory Jurisdiction of the International Court of Justice and the Settlement of Disputes between States", 15 *ICLQ*, 1966, pp. 325-368.

18 Gross, Leo, "The International Court of Justice: Consideration of Requirements for Enhancing it Role in the International Legal Order" in: Gross, (ed.), *The Future of the International Court of Justice*, Dobbs Ferry, New York, Oceana Publications, 1976, pp. 22-105; Schwebel, Stephen M., "Authorizing the Secretary-General of the United Nations to Request Advisory Opinion", 78 *AJIL*, 1984, pp. 869-879.

19 Schwebel, Stephen, "Preliminary Rulings by the International Court of Justice at the Instance of National Courts", 28 *VJIL*, 1987- 88, pp. 495-506; Rosenne, Shabtai, "Preliminary Rulings by the International Court of Justice at the Instance of National Courts: A Reply", 29 *VJIL*, 1989, pp. 401-413; McLaughlin, William T., "Allowing Federal

On the whole, the literature available centres on a rather narrow evaluation of the role, scope and contribution of the advisory function, and, consequently, on the unfulfilled expectations of the international legal community. This limited approach is regrettable.

The importance of the advisory function stems from the fact that it affects the general interpretation of International Law for the international community rather than simply for the particular States or entities directly affected by an individual opinion. Thus, advisory opinions of the Court if properly implemented cannot only guide the requesting organ but also may serve the interests of the whole international community. Many International Law principles which are now taken for granted, such as self-determination, international legal personality of certain international organisations, implied powers, and the object and purpose of the Convention principle, were born out of advisory opinions.[20]

To my knowledge this study is the first one, in English, since 1973 that seeks to provide a comprehensive analysis of the advisory role of the ICJ in the light of its jurisprudence over more than fifty-five years. It attempts to update the previous work and also to reanalyse the function of the advisory opinion in light of the more recent opinions of the Court. This analysis is carried out by examining the nature, object, scope, contribution, and limits of the role of the advisory function of the Court. This study hopes to bring some elements of clarification to, and fresh insight into, a rather confused yet important subject.

The basic argument of this study is that the advisory function should be understood as a two-sided process involving the interplay between other UN organs and the ICJ. In other words, the requesting for and giving of an advisory opinion is a collective coordinated process involving more than one organ or part of the Organisation. Consequently, each must be mindful of the need for some degree of restraint. The genuine need for legal advice must be the only motive for requesting advisory opinions, but the Court must always be mindful of the need to protect its judicial character and not to sacrifice its independence in order to satisfy the interests of the requesting organ.

The study concludes that the Court's role as participant in the UN's activities is circumscribed by its duty to act judicially. In practice, the Court has succeeded to establish a balance between its role as a principal organ of the UN and its position as a judicial institution with a duty to administer justice impartially. Still, many practical and theoretical issues regarding the advisory role of the Court remain unsettled. From the proper perspective of the function which was designed originally to clarify the law and to participate in the Organisation's work but not to settle, at least directly, international disputes, the Court has not only achieved the expectations of its founders but it has contributed to the progressive development of International Law.

Courts Access to International Court of Justice Advisory Opinion: Critique and Proposal", 6 *Hastings International and Comparative Law Review*, 1983, pp. 745-772.

20 This will be discussed in Chapter Six, *infra*.

Lastly, it must be emphasised that the framework of analysis that this study uses does not call into question the Court's role as a judicial body or undermine the authority of its opinions as authoritative statements of law. Moreover, it does not detract from, or contradict, the literature available on the Court or its function. On the contrary, it is hoped that this study will help to increase awareness of the role of the advisory function by stimulating and provoking academic discussion.

3 The Contemporary Relevance of the Advisory Function

The advisory process if invoked at the right time can be an effective instrument of preventative diplomacy or it can make a substantial contribution to resolving an existing dispute.[21] It is to be hoped that the Court's most recent advisory opinion, the *Legal Consequences of the Construction of a Wall in the Occupied Palestinian Territory,* will have such an effect.[22]

The Israeli-Palestinian conflict constitutes a serious threat to international peace and security.[23] Rightly or wrongly, many statesmen and experts assume that its resolution would be the key to lasting stability in the Middle East. However, since the inception of the UN, years of debates and countless resolutions have not brought the problem any closer to a permanent solution. Until the *Wall* Case, no UN organ had ever succeeded in requesting the Court to voice its views on this conflict, which had preoccupied the international community for such a long time. In the *Wall* Case, for the first time, the Court was given the chance to give an opinion on legal issues relating to the status of the Palestinian People, their right to self-determination, the status of Israeli settlements on the West Bank and in East Jerusalem, Israel's acquisition of territory in those areas, and the applicability of the laws of war in the Occupied Territories.[24]

It is now up to the international community to utilise this landmark advisory opinion with the seriousness it deserves, and to treat the Court's findings in helping to achieve a just and peaceful solution to the Israeli-Palestinian conflict.

The Court's Opinion, much like its Opinion on Namibia,[25] strengthens the position of the global community as it seeks to enforce International Law on reluctant

---

[21] Bedjaoui, Mohammed, "The Contribution of the International Court of Justice Towards Keeping and Restoring Peace", in: *Conflict Resolution: New Approaches and Methods*, UNESCO Publishing, 2000, p. 13.

[22] Advisory opinion of 9 July 2004. Available at: http://www.icj-cij.org/icjwww/idocket/imwp/imwpframe.htm (accessed 21 October 2004).

[23] For a historical background of the Arab-Israeli conflict, see Pogany, Istvan, *The Security Council and the Arab-Israeli Conflict*, Aldershot: Gower, 1984; Cotran, Eugene & Mallat, Chibli, (eds.*), The Arab-Israeli Accords: Legal Perspective*, Kluwer Law International, 1996.

[24] See Chapter Six, *infra.*

[25] Discussed in Chapter Six, *infra.*

States, and to assert International Law as a basis for resolving protracted or difficult problems.[26] It is necessary that both sides, Palestine and Israel, should accept their responsibilities under International Law. Although it is perhaps too early to predict the effect of the *Wall* Opinion, it nevertheless illustrates vividly the contemporary relevance of the advisory function.

4 The Structure of the Work

This book is divided into nine Chapters reflecting the controversies, questions and concerns that have long animated legal studies on the advisory function. The starting point is Chapter One, which examines the historical evolution of the function, along with the associated surrounding political atmosphere at the inception of the advisory function. This Chapter sheds light upon the history of the advisory function of the present Court and the circumstances in which the function was adopted and, consequently, the reasons behind the taking up or rejection of certain proposals. Moreover, some consideration is given to the institutional status of the two Courts, the PCIJ and the ICJ.

Chapter Two examines the advisory jurisdiction of the Court, along with the Court's compliance with requests for advisory opinions. This is followed by an examination of those UN organs which are empowered to request advisory opinions, and the prerequisites to do so. An analysis of the Court's jurisdiction *ratione personae* and jurisdiction *ratione materiae,* accompanied with a detailed examination of the Court's dicta in dealing with these requirements. Lastly, the discretion of the Court to render or to refrain from rendering an advisory opinion is discussed.

Chapter Three identifies the effect of the 'organic relationship' between the Court and the UN upon their views of the advisory function. This Chapter argues that the success of the advisory function depends on a process of interaction which can be characterised as coordination between the UN and the Court, within the boundaries of duties and restraints imposed on each actor. Because the Court does not act *proprio motu,* it can only contribute to the development of UN law if it is given the opportunity to do so. Therefore, this Chapter concludes that the advisory opinion rendered by the Court could be used as a suitable guide for UN organs in future actions or as a device to control their actions. The last part of the Chapter argues that coordination among UN organs by requesting an opinion upon the compatibility of certain acts with law might create certain kinds of control over the acts of UN political organs, thereby helping to protect the Organisation's institutional life.

---

26 See Quigley, John & Akram, Susan , "A Reading of the International Court of Justice Advisory Opinion on the Legality of Israel's Wall in the Occupied Palestinian Territories" available at: http://www.palestinecenter.org/cpap/pubs/update_on_wall_072004.pdf (accessed 21 October 2004).

Chapter Four pays particular attention to the Court's duty to act judicially. It addresses the question of reconciliation of the Court's role as a principal UN organ and its duty to adhere to its judicial character, and examines in detail the Court's dicta concerning these two obligations.

Chapter Five further stresses the judicial character of the advisory function by shedding light on the Court's procedure in exercise of its advisory jurisdiction. A true gauge of the quality of the law administered by a court of law is its procedure, as the law administered by the Court is reflected, at least in part, in the procedures employed. The Court's advisory procedures are highly assimilated to the procedures in contentious cases. The Chapter highlights at least two important issues: First, the implications of the assimilation of the advisory proceedings to contentious proceedings where appropriate, including the question of *ad hoc* judges, and the equality of parties. Second, the process of decision making, which includes the choice of law, deliberation and reading the opinion.

Besides providing an extensive examination of the origins, nature, and procedure of the advisory function, Chapter Six deals at length with the actual practice of the Court and its contribution to the development of International Law through the exercise of its advisory jurisdiction. This Chapter shows how the Court has been mindful of the evolving nature of International Law and acknowledges that the real measure of the function's role could not be determined exclusively in terms of the number of advisory opinions handed down. Of more importance is the Court's contribution to providing authoritative statements of law, thus aiding the development of International Law in a wide variety of areas, such as the law of international organisations, the law of treaties, human rights law, international humanitarian law and international environmental law.

The attitude of States towards adjudication and International Law in general, along with the attitude of UN member States toward the advisory function in particular, provide the subject matter of Chapter Seven. In trying to understand the reasons why States tend not to invoke the advisory function of the Court, one must look at the general attitude of States towards law and adjudication. Therefore, the Chapter examines two important issues: first, it analyses States' attitude towards adjudication by examining not only the place of law in international society, but also the factors which determine its place, second, it reviews the frequently cited reasons for the reluctance of States to use the Court.

Chapter Eight examines the attitude of the requesting organ on receiving the opinion. This Chapter also emphasises that the primary motive for most advisory opinions rendered so far has been for law clarification and guidance for future action, rather than judicial legitimation of decisions already taken.

The concluding Chapter discusses some of the concerns that have been raised about the advisory jurisdiction and its limitations, while also considering the future role of the advisory procedure. Finally, the Chapter suggests certain ways to improve the Court's advisory function.

5 Methodology and Methodological Issues

This study is based primarily on an analysis of primary and secondary texts. The ICJ's jurisprudence, together with some selected PCIJ cases which have had an important impact on the ICJ, provide rich insights as well as useful tools for an overview of the advisory function. This jurisprudence of the ICJ is examined for four purposes: First, to show how the advisory function marks the role of the Court as a principal organ of the UN.[27] Second, to demonstrate that the ICJ has conceived of its advisory function as a judicial one and that in exercising this function it has kept within the limits which characterise its judicial role.[28] Third, to consider the impact of the advisory opinions on facilitating the work of the Organisation, and on the development of International Law. Last, to illustrate how the judicial reasoning of the Court in advisory opinions affects the authoritativeness of the opinion and the degree of compliance.

Due to the limited number of advisory opinions, this study has dealt with all the cases rendered up to 2004, including the most recent advisory opinion rendered on seventh of July 2004, the *Legal Consequences of the Construction of a Wall in the Occupied Palestinian Territory*. This study also provides some statistical data as one method of illustration of the role and use of the advisory function. Although such an examination yields quantitative rather than qualitative results, it helps to illustrate the attitude of UN member States towards the advisory function.

The documents used in this study are first, ICJ and PCIJ publications, pertinent *ad hoc* agreements, and UN documents. In addition, a wide variety of scholarly monographs and articles on the advisory function, on the ICJ and other legal studies on related issues are examined. All translations from Arabic Language texts, unless specified to the contrary, are those of the author. Emphasis has been placed, in particular, on the more recent scholarly publications related to the subject of this study.

Moreover, in this study references are made to several branches of knowledge outside public International Law: sociology; philosophy; as well as literature on general management theory. To sum up, the data collected from all the above sources, primary and secondary, has been employed to answer questions and concerns about the role of the advisory function of the ICJ. While this was the goal, I hope that the result of this study will contribute, in some small measure, towards a better understanding of the Court's advisory function.

---

[27] See Chapter Three.

[28] Hudson, *supra* note 4, p. 511.

CHAPTER ONE

The Advisory Function of the International Court of Justice in an Historical Context

1 Introduction

Article 14 of the League Covenant gave the PCIJ competence to render advisory opinions "upon any dispute or question referred to it by the Council or by the Assembly." This provision introducing the advisory function at the international level was a controversial innovation in International Law. Article 14 of the League Covenant stated:[1]

> *The Council shall formulate and submit to the Members of the League for adoption plans for the establishment of a Permanent Court of International Justice. The Court shall be competent to hear and determine any disputes of an international character which the parties thereto submit to it. The Court may also give an advisory opinion upon any dispute or question referred to it by the Council or by the Assembly.*

However, the advisory function cannot be discussed in the abstract. Its historical evolution, together with the surrounding political environment at its inception, must be considered. This Chapter explores the history of the advisory function of the PCIJ and the ICJ, and the circumstances in which the function was adopted and, consequently, the reasons behind the adoption or rejection of certain proposals. Moreover, some consideration will be given to the institutional status of the two Courts, the PCIJ and the ICJ.

---

1 See Hudson, Manley O., *World Court Reports: A Collection of the Judgements, Orders and Opinions of the Permanent Court of International Justice, 1922-1926*, vol. 1, p. 3; Miller, David H., *The Drafting of the Covenant*, New York: G.P. Putnam's Sons, 1928, Vol. 2, p. 331; available also at: http://www.yale.edu/lawweb/avalon/leagcov.htm, (accessed 9 December 2004).

2 Advisory Opinions in General

An advisory opinion has been defined as "an authoritative but non-binding explanation of a question or issue."[2] A tribunal does not have the authority when exercising its advisory jurisdiction to order judicial sanctions to impose duties or obligations on any State.[3] However, although an advisory opinion cannot create legal obligations, it nevertheless can be said to enjoy "legal value and moral authority."[4] Pasqualucci argues that advisory opinions may be more influential than judgements in contentious cases because they affect the general interpretation of International Law for all States rather than just for the parties to an individual opinion.[5]

The need for an advisory function to help the Council and Assembly of the League of Nations was realised and accepted almost immediately by the League's member-States.[6] However, it seems that the difficulties of putting this function into practice were not fully appreciated and, indeed, the function came to be regarded with scepticism if not suspicion.[7] One could say that this attitude seems to persist, even today, though to a lesser degree.

The power of an international tribunal to give advisory opinions must normally be expressly stated in the constitutive instrument of that tribunal and not thought of as inherent to its judicial status.[8] This raises two questions: how could the PCIJ

---

2 See Pasqualucci, Jo M., *The Practice and Procedure of the Inter-American Court of Human Rights*, Cambridge: Cambridge University Press, 2003, p. 29; *Interpretation of Peace Treaties with Bulgaria, Hungary and Romania* Advisory Opinion, ICJ Rep., 1950, p. 71.

3 Hudson, Manley, *The Permanent Court of International Justice, 1920-1942: A Treatise*, New York: The Macmillan Company, 1943, p. 512.

4 See Diss. Op. of Judge Koroma in the *Legality of the Threat or Use of Nuclear Weapons* Advisory Opinion, ICJ Rep., 1996, p. 930. Hudson also noted that advisory opinions are "advisory not legal advice in the ordinary sense, not views expressed by the counsel for the guidance of client, but pronouncements as to the law applicable in given situations formulated after deliberation by the Court", Hudson, Manley, "The Effect of Advisory Opinions of the World Court", 42 *AJIL*, 1948, p. 630.

5 Pasqualucci, Jo M., *supra* note 2, p. 30; Heffernan, Liz, "The Nuclear Weapons Opinions: Reflections on the Advisory Procedure of the International Court of Justice", 28 *Stetson Law Review*, 1998, p. 133.

6 Dunne, Michael, *The United States and the World Court, 1920-1935*, London: Pinter, 1988. ; It was the organs of the League of Nations that were expected to feel the need for advisory opinions, and was not intended for States to be entitled for such requests. Thirlway, Hugh, "The International Court of Justice" in: Evans, Malcolm D. (ed.), *International Law*, Oxford University Press, 2003, p. 582.

7 See the views of Judges Elihu Root and Moore who maintained a negative attitude towards empowering the Court an advisory jurisdiction at the time of drafting the PCIJ Statute. See Sugihara, Takane, "The Advisory Function of the International Court of Justice", 17 *Japanese Annual of International law*, 1973, pp. 26-27.

8 Amerasinghe, Chittharanjan F., *Jurisdiction of International Tribunals*, The Hague; London: Kluwer Law International, 2003, p. 503.

begin to exercise its advisory jurisdiction absent expressly stated relevant provisions in its Statute? And, can other tribunals possess such jurisdiction?

Keith has pointed out that the absence of express provisions in the treaty establishing the PCIJ had raised two important questions: whether the Court was competent to give advisory opinions, and whether the Court had an obligation to answer requests for opinions.[9] The answer to the first question seems to emerge from President Loder's[10] statement that, by virtue of Article 1 of the PCIJ Statute the Court was established in accordance with Article 14 of the Covenant, therefore Article 14 could be regarded as an integral part of the Statute.[11] As for the obligation of the Court to answer a request, Judge Moore, in his memorandum of 18 February 1922, concluded that the Court was under no unconditional obligation to accept a request for an advisory opinion and this view was not challenged by other judges.[12] In 1922, there was a proposal for a provision in the Rules to be adopted stating that "the Court reserves the right to refrain from replying to questions put to it which require an advisory opinion on a theoretical case."[13] However this was not adopted.

The question now is whether an advisory jurisdiction can be given to tribunals of a non-permanent, non-general and regional nature, unlike the PCIJ and the ICJ. Although one must assert that the advisory jurisdiction of the ICJ is unique, due to the nature of the Court, it seems that in theory other tribunals can possibly have an advisory jurisdiction.[14] At present there are a number of regional tribunals with advisory jurisdiction expressly stated in their constitutive instruments. These are: the Court of Justice of the European Communities (CJEC)[15], the European Court of Human Rights (ECHR)[16], the Inter-American Court on Human Rights

---

9 Keith, Kenneth, *The extent of the Advisory Jurisdiction of the International Court of Justice*, Leyden: A.W, Sijthoff, 1971, p. 14.

10 Judge Loder was the first President of the PCIJ.

11 PCIJ, Ser. D, No. 2, p. 502.

12 PCIJ, Ser. D, No. 2, 1922, p. 383.

13 See draft Article 63 a., PCIJ Ser. D, No. 2, 1922, p. 308.

14 Thirlway notes that since the purpose of international arbitral tribunals is to give a binding settlement to a dispute, the possibility of giving advisory opinions seems to be unlikely. Thirlway, Hugh, "Advisory Opinions of International Courts", in: Bernhardt, R. (ed.), *Encyclopedia of Public International Law*, vol. 1, 1992, p. 38.

15 Article 300 (ex 228) of the Treaty of European Union states: "[t]he Council, the Commission or a Member State may obtain the opinion of the Court of Justice whether an agreement envisaged is compatible with the provisions of this Treaty. Where the opinion of the Court of Justice is adverse, the agreement may enter into force only in accordance with Article 48 of the Treaty on European Union."

16 Articles 47 and 48 of the Convention of ECHR provides: 47(1): "[t]he Court may, at the request of the Committee of Ministers, give advisory opinions on legal questions concerning the interpretation of the Convention and the protocols thereto." Article 48: "[t]he Court shall decides whether a request for an advisory opinion submitted by the Committee of Ministers is within its competence as defined in Article 47. See the present European Convention for the Protection of Human Rights and Fundamental Freedoms, signed in Rome, 4 November 1950, and as amended by Protocol No. II. See Brownlie, Ian, *Basic Documents in International Law*, Oxford University Press, 5th edition, 2002, p. 244.

(IACHR).[17] Lastly, the Sea-Bed Disputes Chamber of the International Tribunal for the Law of the Sea also has advisory jurisdiction .[18]

It is worthy of note that the jurisprudence developed by the ICJ, which is, in broad lines, a continuation of the PCIJ, sets the standards which may apply to the advisory jurisdiction of other tribunals in appropriate cases.[19] As a result the advisory function has become widely accepted in International Law. It has been argued that "advisory opinions contribute to an international common law and to the resolutions of doctrinal differences. They also provide an alternative non-confrontational means to resolve international disputes."[20]

3 The Advisory Function Prior to the Inception of International Courts[21]

The advisory function was used at the national level before the establishment of the League of Nations. The genesis of such a function may be traced back to the twelfth century when the King of England used to call upon judges to seek legal advice as to the state of the law. This consultation with the judges was done in the King's capacity as the fountain of justice.[22] Contrary to the position in England,

---

17 Article 64 of the American Convention on Human Rights provides that: 1. The member states of the Organization may consult the Court regarding the interpretation of this Convention or of other treaties concerning the protection of human rights in the American states. Within their spheres of competence, the organs listed in Chapter X of the Charter of the Organization of American States, as amended by the Protocol of Buenos Aires, may in like manner consult the Court. 2. The Court, at the request of a member State of the Organization, may provide that state with opinions regarding the compatibility of any of its domestic laws with the aforesaid international instruments. See American Convention on Human Rights, 22 November 1969, 9 ILM, 1970, p. 673.

18 Article 191of the Law of the Sea Convention of 10 December 1982 which entered into force on 16 November 1994 provides that the Sea-Bed Disputes Chamber of the International Tribunal for the Law of the Sea "shall give advisory opinions at the request of the Assembly or the Council on legal questions arising within the scope of their activities. Such opinions shall be given as a matter of urgency." See The Law of Sea Convention of 10 December 1982, UN A/CONF. 62/122, 21 ILM, 1982, p. 1261.

19 Amerasinghe, *supra* note 8, p. 505.

20 Pasqualucci, Jo M., *supra* note 2, p. 31.

21 On the advisory function of national courts in general see Hudson, Manley, "Advisory Opinions of National and International Courts", 37 *HLR*, 1924; Wright, Q., "Advisory Opinions" in: *Encyclopaedia of the Social Science*, Vol. 1, 1953, pp. 475-478.

22 The King could seek judicial advice not only in his capacity as a dispenser of justice, but also in his executive capacity. Judges did not attend the Concilium Regis, which was an administrative body. However, the King could require their presence as necessary. See Baldwin, James F., "The King's Council in England During the Middle Ages", 1913, p. 301, cited in: Beg, Mirza A., *The Attitude of United Nations Members Towards the Use of Advisory Opinion Procedure: 1945-1963*, Ph.D. thesis, Columbia University, 1965, p. 8.

the framers of the US Constitution rejected proposals to confer specifically upon the executive and Congress the right to request opinions from the Supreme Court.[23] Therefore, when President Washington turned to the judges of the Supreme Court for an advisory opinion, the judges declined to comply.[24]

It is worth noting that the constitutions of many States embody provisions for advisory opinions to be given by their respective supreme courts.[25] Finally, the advisory function as developed in practice by the PCIJ was different from the advisory function of national courts in some States.[26] Pomerance argues that advisory opinions of national courts were normally "served with reference to proposed administrative or legislative measures, without reference to actual litigants or specific sets of facts.[27] Hudson also concluded that "in view of the history of Article 14 ... it cannot be said that the provision ... was due to the experience of national courts", but that "this experience may have been in the minds of the draftsmen."[28]

4 The Advisory Function and the Permanent Court of International Justice

The PCIJ's advisory function raised serious questions regarding the jurisprudence and jurisdiction of the Court.[29] Judge Moore claimed that "[n]o subject connected with the organization of the Permanent Court of International Justice has caused so much confusion and proved to be so baffling as the question whether and under what conditions the Court shall undertake to give 'advisory' opinions."[30]

It was arguable whether this function was suitable for a court of law, whose primary function is deciding disputes brought voluntarily by the contending

---

23 See Wright, Q, *supra* note 21, p. 476.

24 Wright, Q, *supra* note 21, p. 476.

25 For the experience of the domestic legal system with advisory opinions see De Wet, Erika, *The Chapter VII Powers of the United Nations Security Council*, Oxford; Portland Oregon: Hart Publishing, 2004, pp. 25-26.

26 For the difference between the two experiences, see Pomerance, Michla, *The Advisory Function of the International Court in the League and UN Eras*, Baltimore; London: John Hopkins University Press, 1973, p. 9; Goodrich, Leland, "The Nature of the Advisory Opinions of the Permanent Court of International Justice", 32 *AJIL*, 1938, pp. 738-758.

27 Pomerance, Michla, "The Advisory Role of the International Court of Justice and its 'Judicial' Character: Past and Future Prisms, in: Muller, A.S., *et al.*, (eds.), *The International Court of Justice: Its Future Role After Fifty Years*, Martinus Nijhoff Publishers, the Hague; Boston; London: Martinus Nijhoff Publishers, 1997, p. 272.

28 Hudson, *supra* note 3, p. 458.

29 See Eyffinger, Arthur, *The International Court of Justice 1946-1996*, The Hague; London: Kluwer Law International, 1996, p. 146; Rosenne, Shabtai, *The World Court: What it is and How it Works*, Dordrecht, London: Martinus Nijhoff Publishers, 1995, pp. 106-107.

30 Memorandum of 18 February 1922, PCIJ, Ser. D, No. 2, p. 383.

States. Moreover, the League of Nations' "Great Powers" as well as the US feared that this function could become a back-door for compulsory jurisdiction. The US government was also concerned that advisory opinions could be used to legitimise the League's policies[31] thereby committing the US government, (as a potential member of the League) to such policies.[32] Another point of concern for the US government was the protection of its domestic jurisdiction from foreign judicial scrutiny, a concern which still exists.[33]

Indeed, there was great uncertainty about how the advisory function would work in practice.[34] This resulted in numerous draft proposals and counter proposals, and even the demand by the US government for a veto power on the exercise of the advisory jurisdiction by the PCIJ.[35] Many attempts were made to create a clear, distinct differentiation between the contentious and the advisory jurisdictions of the Court but were unsuccessful.[36]

5 The Advisory Function at the Drafting Stage

Article 14 of the Covenant gave the League Council responsibility for formulating plans for the establishment of the PCIJ.[37] However, the term "advisory opinion" was only introduced for the first time in the final draft of Article 14, in the third sentence.[38] Although some earlier drafts of Article 14 had made reference

---

[31] Dunne, *supra* note 6, p. 104.

[32] Ibid, p. 9.

[33] Dunne, ibid, p. 39. For details about the attitude of the great power States at the time of the League of Nations see Section 2 in Chapter Seven, *infra.*

[34] Pomerance, *supra* note 27, p. 272.

[35] Between 1926-29 the US Government and the League were at an impasse over this point. Dunne, *supra* note 6, p. 4.

[36] Pomerance, *supra* note 27, p. 272. The argument against a clear distinction that, if the advisory opinions were to be regarded as provisional with uncertain status, that may be reversed by a subsequent contentious proceedings, then this would render the whole function "self– stultifying", lacking in authority and hence effectiveness. See Dunne, *supra* note 6, p. 38.

[37] Resulting on a meeting between Wilson, Cecil, Smits, and Miller on January 31, 1919, it was decided that "a general provision might be inserted for the creation of a permanent Court." See Miller, *supra* note 1, vol. 1, p. 67.

[38] The original draft of this Article contained no reference to the advisory opinion. The Hurst – Miller draft which presented to the Commission on the League of Nations by President Wilson provided for the creation of the PCIJ with no reference to the idea of an advisory function. Article 12 of the draft provided "[t]he Executive Council will formulate plans for the establishment of a Permanent Court of International Justice, and this Court will be competent to hear and determine any matter which the parties recognize as suitable for submission to it for arbitration under the forgoing Article". See Miller, ibid, vol. 2, p. 234.

to the Court's competence to answer questions referred to it by some specific organs,[39] none of those drafts had directly used the term "advisory opinion." The British Draft Convention of 20 January 1919, in Article 7, might be considered to refer indirectly to advisory opinions. This draft provided:[40]

> *Where the Conference or the Council finds that the dispute can with advantage be submitted to a court of international law, or that any particular question involved in the dispute can with advantage be referred to a court of international law, it may submit the dispute or the particular question accordingly, and may formulate the questions for decision, and may give such directions as to procedure as it may think desirable. In such case, the decision of the Court shall have no force or effect unless it is confirmed by the Report of the Conference or Council*

On 18 March 1919, Lord Robert Cecil and President Wilson proposed an addition to an early draft of Article 14.[41] This gave the Court competence to hear and determine "any issue referred to it by the Executive Council or Body of Delegates."[42] A similar amendment was also proposed by France, on March 24, to the effect that the Court would be competent to hear and determine "any matter which is submitted to it by the Body of Delegates or the Executive Council."[43] The broad language of these proposed drafts, however, were believed to have implied the "idea of obligatory arbitration."[44]

Miller, the American legal advisor, wrote to Colonel House that: "[i]t seems to me that still more objection will be raised in the Senate to the addition to Article 14. This goes the whole length of permitting the Executive Council or the Body of Delegates to compel arbitration."[45] Hurst and Miller met again to draft a text that

---

39 Article 5 of the French Ministerial Commission of 8 June 1918; Article 7 of the British draft of 20 January 1919; Article 14 of the Italian draft of 3 February 1919; and Article 10 of the Colonel House draft of 16 July 1918. See Miller, ibid, vol. 2, p. 239, 111, 250, and 8 respectively.

40 Miller, ibid, vol. 2, p. 111.

41 The early draft of Article 14 stated that: "[t]he Executive Council shall formulate plans for the establishment of a Permanent Court of International Justice and this Court shall, when established, be competent to hear and determine any matter which the parties recognize as suitable for submission to it for arbitration under the forgoing Article." See Miller, vol. 2, p. 311.

42 Miller, ibid, vol. 2, p. 585.

43 Ibid, vol. 1, p. 391; vol. II, p. 585.

44 Ibid, vol. 1, p. 391and p. 290.

45 Ibid, vol. 1, p. 290.

could satisfy Miller.[46] While the new formulation met Miller's objection regarding compulsory arbitration, Miller considered that this formulation could have been construed "to make the Court the legal advisor of the Council and of the Assembly, a duty which its function of rendering advisory opinions does not involve."[47] Eventually, Miller accepted the draft, and the words "Executive Council" were replaced by the word "Council".

It is quite clear that Miller's objections were intended to exclude the possibility of compulsory jurisdiction developing in accordance with this provision.[48] Eventually, the Drafting Committee, in its final draft[49] of Article 14 introduced the term "advisory opinion" in a separate sentence, and the phrase "give an advisory opinion" was used instead of the term "advice". Miller argued that this substitution was made to indicate that "the function to be exercised is a judicial one."[50]

The uncertainty and doubt associated with adopting the advisory function led to the omission of any reference to such opinions in the original Statute of the PCIJ.[51] Therefore, "[t]he matter, implied from Article 14 of the Covenant, was initially left to the governance of the Court."[52]

In 1920 an Advisory Committee of Jurists (ACJ) was established to draft a Statute for the Court.[53] Article 36 of their draft provided that the Court shall give an advisory opinion upon any question or dispute of an international nature referred to it by the Council or the Assembly. Thus, it distinguished between two kinds of advisory opinions, namely, advisory opinions on a "question" and advi-

---

46 Hurst had proposed this draft: "[t]he Executive Council shall formulate plans for the establishment of a permanent Court of International Justice. The Court shall be competent to hear and determine any dispute or difference of an international character which the parties thereto may submit to it and also advise upon any legal questions referred to it by the Executive Council or the Body of Delegates". See Miller, ibid, vol. 1, p. 391.

47 Miller, ibid, vol. 1, pp. 391-392.

48 Wright, Q., *supra* note 21, p. 479. Miller's point of view was that the establishment of the PCIJ "would make compulsory arbitration depend solely upon the vote of the Executive Council, a vote from which the parties to the dispute would be presumably excluded." See Miller, vol. 1, p. 290.

49 Report of 5 April of 1919 of the Drafting Committee.

50 Miller, *supra* note 1, vol. 1, p. 406. Thus Article 14 then read: "[t]he Court may also give an advisory opinion upon any dispute or question referred to it by the Council or by the Assembly."

51 Pomerance, *supra* note 26, p. 277. The Statute that was issued, in its first form, contained no provisions concerning advisory opinions.

52 Rosenne, Shabtia, *The Law and Practice of the International Court. 1920-1996*, The Hague; London: Martinus Nijnhoff Publishers, vol. 1, 1997, p. 280.

53 This Committee was appointed by the League Council to draft a Statute of the PCIJ. See PCIJ, Ser. D, No. 2, 1936, p. 838.

sory opinions on an existing "dispute"[54] The draft article was controversial. The French jurist, M. De Lapradelle maintained that a "question" was a theoretical matter, while a "dispute" was a practical one.[55] Therefore, a limited panel of judges should respond to a question, while, in contrast, the plenary full Court should deal with a dispute.[56]

On the other hand, Root, an American jurist, totally opposed giving the PCIJ any right to give advisory opinions affecting disputes. In his view this right would be "a violation of all juridical principles"[57], and therefore the League Assembly removed the entire Article from the draft.[58] The opinion was expressed that "[t]he Covenant, in Article 14, contained a provision in accordance with which the Court could not refuse to give advisory opinions". It "was therefore unnecessary to include a rule to the same effect in the Constitution of the Court."[59] Pomerance observed that the ambiguity of the criterion for distinguishing the two types of advisory opinions, in addition to the "desire not to bind the Court in an area which had no international past and an uncertain international future,"[60] led the Assembly to omit Article 36 from the Statute as finally adopted.

However, the conflict regarding the usefulness of the advisory function and its compatibility with the function of a court of law was resolved quickly by the PCIJ itself which did not doubt its competence to render advisory opinions. In fact, the first decision that the Court rendered was under its advisory jurisdiction.[61] Meanwhile, the Court in 1922 adopted its own Rules of procedure as permitted by Arti-

---

54 This draft Article provided: [w]hen the Court shall give an opinion on a question of an international nature which does not refer to any dispute that may arise, it shall appoint a special commission of three to five members. When it shall give an opinion upon a question which forms the subject of an existing dispute, is shall do so under the same conditions as if the case had been actually submitted to it for decision. See League of Nations, Advisory Committee of Jurists 1920, 27th meeting, p. 584.

55 Permanent Court of International Justice Advisory Committee of Jurists, *Procés-Verbaux of the Proceedings of the Committee* (1920), 27th meeting p. 584.

56 Ibid, p. 584.

57 Ibid.

58 The Sub-Committee was of the view that the opinions in every case should be given by the same quorum of judges as judgments as many practical difficulties would result in making this distinction. See League of Nations, Records of the first Assembly, Third Committee, 9th meeting, p. 401.

59 Records of the First Assembly, Meeting of the Committees, I, p. 401; Hudson, *supra* note 3, p. 483.

60 Pomerance, *supra* note 26, p. 274. Goodrich was of the view that the omission might be due to "the authority of certain of the Court's opinions would be weakened thereby." See Goodrich, *supra* note 26, p. 740.

61 The first case which the PCIJ dealt with was the *Designation of the Worker's Delegate for the Netherlands at ILC*, PCIJ, Ser. B, No. 1, 1922.

cle 30 of its Statute, and these set out in detail, in Article 71-74, the procedure to be followed in advisory opinions.[62]

It is interesting to note that during the discussion of the Rules, Judge Moore once again in his memorandum on "the question of advisory opinions", which was submitted to the Court, proposed omitting any reference to advisory opinions. They were not "an appropriate function of a Court of Justice", he wrote, because:[63]

A Court of Justice, whether national or international, is essentially a judicial body, whose function is to end disputes by deciding them. The maintenance of the character, reputation and usefulness of such a Court is inextricably bound up with the obligatory force and the effective performance of its decisions or judgments.

This memorandum, although submitted to the Court, was not put to the vote.[64] Judge Altamira then submitted a draft proposal that would have distinguished between an opinion related to an existing dispute from one related to a question.[65] Another proposal regarding the Rules of the Court suggested granting the Court the right to give secret advice.[66] Judges Moore and Finalay had opposed this proposal on the grounds that secret advice would be incompatible with the Statute and "would be a death blow to the Court as a judicial body."[67]

In the end, all these proposals were rejected and Articles 71-74 of the Rules were adopted. Furthermore, it was decided that advisory opinions should always

---

62 Articles 71-74 of 24 March 1922 Rules of the Court stated:

Article 71: *Advisory opinions shall be given after deliberation by the full Court. The opinions of dissenting judges may, at their request, be attached to the opinion of the Court.*

Article 72: *Questions upon which the advisory opinion of the Court is asked shall be laid before the Court by means of a written request, signed either by the President of the Assembly or the President of the Council of the League of Nations, or by the Secretary–General of the League under instructions from the Assembly or the Council.*

The request shall contain an exact statement of the question upon which an opinion is required, and shall be accompanied by all documents likely to throw light upon the question.

Article 73: *The Registrar shall forthwith give notice of the request for an advisory opinion to the members of the Court, and to the Members of the League of Nations, through the Secretary-General of the League, and to the States mentioned in the Annex to the Covenant.*

Notice of such request shall also be given to any international organizations which are likely to be able to furnish information on the question.

Article 74: *Any advisory opinion which may be given by the Court and the request in response to which it was given, shall be printed and published in a special collection for which the Registrar shall be responsible.*

It is to be noted that these Rules were revised in 31 July 1926, 21 February 1931, and 11 March 1936. See Hudson, *World Court Report*, *supra* note 1, vols. I and IV.

63 Memorandum of Judge Moore, of 18th February 1922, *The question of advisory opinions*, PCIJ, Series D, No. 2, 1922, pp. 383-398.

64 Sugihara, Takane, *supra* note 7, p. 29.

65 PCIJ, Ser. D, No. 2, p. 280.

66 This proposal was submitted by Judge Anzilotti. See PCIJ, Ser. D, No. 2, 1922, p. 160. To avoid the possibility of secrecy Article 74 provided that the opinions "should be read out at a public meeting of the Court."

67 Ibid.

be given by the full Court.[68] In fact, the Rules as finally adopted aimed to attribute a judicial character to advisory opinions.

When the Court revised its Rules in 1926 any distinctions between the advisory and contentious jurisdictions were eliminated. The revision, indeed, reflected the practice of assimilating the advisory to the contentious function which the Court demonstrated in 1923 in the *Eastern Carelia* Case.[69] Here the League Council requested an advisory opinion over the objection of Soviet Russia, but the Court declined to answer the question on the ground that "[a]nswering the question would be substantially equivalent to deciding the dispute between the parties." Since the question submitted to the Court concerning a pending dispute between two States (Soviet Union and Finland), the consent of the two States was required by the Court in order to render its opinion.[70]

Moreover, during the revision of the Rules, a proposal to admit a national judge in advisory cases in certain circumstances was also rejected.[71] However, in 1927 the Court reversed its earlier position, adding a new paragraph to Article 71 of the Rules adopting judges *ad hoc* to its proceedings.[72] By adding this provision the Court enhanced the assimilation of the advisory jurisdiction to the contentious in cases related to existing disputes.

Once again the Court never doubted its competence to render advisory opinions even absent any reference to this function in its Statute.[73] An amendment to the Statute, which came into force in February 1936, clarified the legal position by adding four Articles concerning Advisory Opinions. Articles 65-68 reaffirmed the provisions of the Rules of the Court of 1926, that is to say Articles 71-74. However, Article 68 of the Statute was new, and provides that "[i]n the exercise of its advisory function, the Court shall further be guided by the provisions of the present Statute which apply in contentious cases to the extent to which it recognizes them to be applicable. To correspond to this new addition, the Court on 11 March 1936 added Article 82 to its Rules.[74]

---

68 PCIJ, Ser. D, No.2, p. 98.

69 PCIJ, Ser. B, No. 5, 1923, pp. 27-29.

70 PCIJ, ibid.

71 PCIJ, Ser. E, No. 4, p. 73.

72 This added paragraph provided "[o]n a question relating to an existing dispute between two or more States or Members of the League of Nations, Article 31of the Statute shall apply. In case of doubt, the Court shall decide."

73 The legal basis of the Court's power to give advisory opinions embodied in Article 14 of the Covenant.

74 Article 82 of the 1936 Rules provided "[i]n proceedings in regard to advisory opinions, the Court shall, in addition to the provisions of Chapter IV of the Statute of the Court, apply the provisions of the articles hereinafter set out. It shall also be guided by the provisions of the present Rules which apply in contentious cases to the extent to which it recognizes them to be applicable, according as the advisory opinion for which the Court is asked relates, in the terms of Article 14 of the Covenant of the League of Nations, to a "dispute" or to a "question." See PCIJ, Ser. D, No. 1.

The history of the drafting of the Covenant, Statute and the Rules of the Court, demonstrates that the doubts and uncertainty initially associated with Article 14 of the Covenant gradually diminished and that the Court adopted "the essential principle that advisory procedure before a Court of Justice could not differ from judicial procedure."[75]

6 The PCIJ Advisory Opinions and the Nature of the Requests for Advisory Opinions

During the PCIJ's short life it rendered twenty-seven advisory opinions.[76] Nineteen were on questions relating to existing disputes and eight on questions not so related.[77] Hudson opined that in no cases, including cases relating to the competence of the ILO,[78] was the Court requested to give an opinion on a purely hypothetical question.[79]

Some questions were deemed improper for submission to the Court such as: questions of a general theoretical nature with abstract formulations and without practical interest[80] because this might lead to legislation or policy determination;[81] questions calling for determining the law of the future, which is considered as an act of legislation; questions that undermine the voluntary nature of international litigation, where the request constituted a back-door for compulsory jurisdiction;[82] questions related to Covenant interpretation in the abstract, since this could lead to de facto amendments that should be reserved for the Covenant signatories,[83] and questions related to domestic jurisdiction.[84]

---

75 Judge Anzilotti, PCIJ, Ser. D, No.2, p. 189.

76 See Oda, Shigeru, "The International Court of Justice Viewed from the Bench 1976-1993", Chapter III, "The Advisory Function of the Court", 244 *RCADI*, 1993, pp. 90-91.

77 Oda, ibid, p. 91; Goodrich, *supra* note 26, pp. 744-745.

78 However, requests related to the provisions of the ILO constitution were "framed in more generalized and abstract terms", See Pomerance, *supra* note 26, p. 50.

79 Hudson, *supra* note 3, p. 496.

80 League of Nations Official Journal, 1923, pp. 585-586, pp. 667-670.

81 Pomerance, *supra* note 26, p. 216.

82 Hudson, *supra* note 3, p. 497.

83 Pomerance, *supra* note 26, p. 216.

84 Article 15(8) of the Covenant stated that the Council "[i]f the dispute between the parties is claimed by one of them, and is found by the Council, to arise out of a matter which by international law is solely within the domestic jurisdiction of that party, the Council shall so report, and shall make no recommendation as to its settlement." See the Covenant of the League of Nations, Hudson, *supra* note 1.

7 Sources of Requests for Advisory Opinions During the League Era

Although Article 14 of the League Covenant authorised both the Council and the Assembly to request advisory opinions, in fact, the Council submitted all of the twenty-seven requests for opinions during the period 1922 – 1935. One must not draw any distinction between the competence of the League Council and that of the Assembly with respect to the capacity to request advisory opinions.[85]

In its recourse to the Court, the Council did not always act in the same capacity. Pomerance noted that the Council frequently served simply as the avenue of access to the Court for other international bodies or for States involved in a dispute.[86] The Council requested advisory opinions on behalf of the ILO[87] and other international bodies such as the Mixed Commissions for the Exchange of Greek and Turkish Populations.[88] It is interesting to note that agreements by interested States for requesting an advisory opinion were sufficient for initiating a request by the Council.[89]

8 Assimilation of the Advisory Procedure to the Contentious Procedure Before the PCIJ

As stated earlier, the uncertainty associated with the advisory jurisdiction in the drafting of the original PCIJ Statute in 1920, which led to its deletion, extended to the drafting of the Rules governing the advisory function in 1922. The distinction between the subject matter of the request as involving disputes or questions, which would in turn have involved different procedures for handling the requests, was not adopted. The judicial character of the function was emphasised, and the 1922 Rules included Articles 71-74 to that effect.[90] Sugihara observed that the most striking feature in the advisory practice of the PCIJ was "the close assimilation of advisory procedures to the Court's contentious procedures."[91] The consent of the

---

85 It seems that once the Council refused a request, this refusal did not exclude the Assembly from lodging a request, provided that the matter was not expressly reserved to the Council.

86 Pomerance, *supra* note 26, p. 47.

87 The rendered opinions in relation to the internal procedures of international organisations were all related to the function of the ILO. Oda suggests that this is natural due to the fact that between the two World Wars the ILO was the first if not the only international organisation playing an important role in the international community. See Oda, *supra* note 76, pp. 90-91.

88 Pomerance, *supra* note 26, p. 47.

89 Ibid.

90 See *supra* note 62.

91 Sugihara, *supra* note 7, p. 31.

interested States was required in the great majority of advisory cases dealt with by the PCIJ.[92]

In 1927 a further step towards assimilating the advisory to the contentious procedure was taken when the Court allowed the admission of judges *ad hoc* in certain advisory proceedings where the submitted question related to an existing dispute.[93] This marked the Court's acceptance of the dichotomy between requests relating to 'questions' and others relating to 'disputes', and meant that the latter should be assimilated as closely as possible to contentious procedures. The rationale behind assimilating the advisory procedure to the contentious, when the request involved a dispute, was out of concern on how to protect the moral authority and prestige of the Court while executing its advisory function.[94]

Goodrich claimed that the Court's refusal to give an opinion in the *Eastern Carelia* Case was due, *inter alia,* to the Court's practice of assimilating its advisory to its contentious procedure.[95] The Court had considered the lack of the Soviet consent,[96] along with the USSR failing to furnish the necessary facts of the case, as grounds to turn down the request. However, it is important to note that when a question submitted to the Court dealt with the competence of the Council, rather than the actual merits of a dispute, the Court did not consider consent as important for exercising its advisory jurisdiction. Hence, in the opinion requested in the *interpretation of Article 3, paragraph 2, of the Treaty of Lausanne (Frontier between Turkey and Iraq*) Case,[97] the Court held that answering the request would not equate to deciding the dispute since the request "referred not to the merits of the affair but to the competence of the Council."[98] Due to this assimilation it was thought that the advisory function exercised by the PCIJ was to a large extent, "of substantially the same kind as that performed where there were contentious proceedings."[99]

---

92 Ibid.

93 PCIJ, Ser. C, No. 15, p. 250. Before adopting this amendment, the question of Judge ad hoc arose in the *Exchange of Greek and Turkish populations* case in 1925 and in the *Mosul* Case in 1925. The Court decided in the two cases that Article 31 of the Statute did not apply to the advisory procedure, therefore, no national judge could be appointed.

94 Goodrich, *supra* note 26, p. 739.

95 Ibid, p. 742.

96 Consent is the principle for establishing the Court's jurisdiction in the contentious procedure. See the discussion in Chapter Four, *infra.*

97 In this case the Court gave an opinion despite the absence of Turkey's consent.

98 PCIJ, Ser. B, No. 12, 1925, p. 18.

99 Sugihara, *supra* note 7, p. 39.

9 Voting in the League Council and Assembly to Request Advisory Opinions

It was unclear to members of the League whether voting in the Council or the Assembly must be unanimous. In addition, Article 5(1) of the Covenant provides that "except where otherwise expressly provided in this Covenant or by the terms of the present treaty, decisions at any meeting of the Assembly or of the Council shall require the agreement of all the members of the League represented at the meeting." Moreover, Article 5(2) of the Covenant provides that:[100]

> *All matters of procedure at meetings of the Assembly or of the Council, including the appointment of Committees to investigate particular matters,... may be decided by a majority of the Members of the League represented at the meeting.*

The question remains as to whether a request for an advisory opinion is a matter of procedure or otherwise. Proposals to refer the nature of the vote required to the PCIJ for advisory opinions were always rejected.[101] In practice, the Council developed a practice whereby requesting the Court's opinion may only occur on the base of a unanimous vote.[102]

10 The PCIJ and the ICJ: Their Institutional Status

Prior to studying the advisory function in the ICJ era it is pertinent to investigate the institutional status of the two Courts. This is necessary for two reasons: first, the historical dimension of the study will not be complete without such a study, especially in view of the fact that the institutional setting could have an effect on the advisory jurisdiction of the Court. Second, the determination of the institutional setting could, perhaps, pave the way for understanding the institutional role of the two Courts.

The PCIJ was not established as a formal part of the League. Indeed, its Statute was independent of the League Covenant and the Members of the League were not *ipso facto* parties to the PCIJ Statute. This contrasts with the position of the ICJ within the UN. Nevertheless, there was a strong relationship between the PCIJ and the League, as demonstrated by several facts: at the outset, the PCIJ was established under the auspices of the League;[103] the League Council and Assembly elected the members of the PCIJ bench;[104] expenses of the PCIJ were borne by the

---

[100] See Hudson, *supra* note 1; Walters, F.R., *A History of the League of Nations*, Oxford University Press, 1952, p. 46.

[101] Pomerance, *supra* note 26, p. 213.

[102] For exceptions to this rule see Pomerance, *supra* note 27, p. 277 (note 22).

[103] See Article 14 of the Covenant, *supra* note 1.

[104] See Articles 4, 8 and 10 of the PCIJ Statute.

League;[105] States other than members of the League and those States mentioned in the Annex to the Covenant could access the Court in accordance with conditions determined by the Council;[106] the Court's main function, which coincided with the conceived purpose of the League,[107] was to assist in resolving international disputes and the Council and the Assembly had the right to request advisory opinions from the PCIJ. In this regard, it is interesting to note that the PCIJ was regarded as one of the organs of the League of Nations.[108] President Loder, the first elected president of the PCIJ, in his inaugural speech stated:[109]

> *The Court is one of the principal organs of the League, and at the same time it exercises its powers in full and sovereign independence. It occupies within the League of Nations a place similar to that occupied in many States by the Judicature, which is an integral part of the State, and depends upon the national legislature as regards all that concerns its constitution, its organization, its powers, its maintenance, but which recognises no master in the exercise of its duties, in regard to which it enjoys absolute liberty and is bound only by the law which is its task to apply.*

League Secretary General Sir Eric Drummond in the Court's inaugural speech stated:[110]

> *The definite establishment of the Court completes the organizations of the League as laid down under the Covenant. It is clearly the greatest and will, I believe, be the most important creative act of the League ... an international judicial body ... which is entirely free from all political control and entirely unfettered as to its decisions by political bodies. Although it derives its authority from the League, its judgments are in no way subject to advice or revision by the Council or Assembly.*

A closer look at the practice of the PCIJ discloses that the Court functioned as part of the League system, although the Court's Statute did not formally constitute an "integral part" of the League Covenant. The Court's concern to cooperate with the

---

105 See Articles 32 and 33 of the PCIJ Statute.

106 Article 35 of the PCIJ Statue.

107 Article 14 of the Covenant.

108 See League of Nations Official Journal, March 1920, p. 37. Hudson, *supra* note 3, p. 111. Contrary to this view Kelsen was of the opinion that the PCIJ was not an organ within the League of Nations, but that it was an independent organisation. Kelsen, Hans, *The Law of the United Nations: A Critical Analysis of its Fundamental Problems*, London: Stevens and Sons Ltd, 1951, p. 465.

109 PCIJ, Ser. D, No. 2, 45, (minute of inaugural meeting), Annex 36, p. 326.

110 Minutes of PCIJ inaugural meeting of 15 February 1922, Annex 33, Speech of Sir Eric Drummond, League Secretary-General. Ser. D, No. 2, 45 (minutes), Annex 33, p. 320.

League Council manifested itself through the Court's attitude towards the Council when the request was deemed urgent.[111] In more than one case the Court declared its readiness to accelerate its procedures whenever the Council needed the Court's opinion.[112]

By contrast, the organic connection between the ICJ and the UN is much clearer. Article 92 of the UN Charter states that the Court is the "principal judicial organ" of the UN and that the Statute is an "integral part" of the Charter. This means that all Members of the UN are *ipso facto* parties to the Statute of the ICJ, as further confirmed by Article 93 of the Charter.[113] Moreover, the Charter has extended accessibility to the Court and made it possible for authorised organs, other than the General Assembly, Security Council and the UN specialised agencies, to request advisory opinions on legal questions arising within the scope of their activities,[114] thereby allowing the Court a broader participation in the activities of the UN. These facts lead to the conclusion that the ICJ is a new Court and that it "operates in a political and legal environment entirely different from that of the Permanent Court."[115]

As for the Statute being an "integral part" of the Charter, the Charter and the Statute should be read together as one instrument without implying that the Statute is subordinate to the Charter.[116] First, the provisions of the Statute are to be interpreted in the light of the Charter[117] and, secondly, the provisions of the Charter which are of general applicability to the Organisation as a whole, as well as to its individual organs, are applicable to the Court.[118] Thirdly, and most, importantly, this could be extended to permitting the Court "to extract from the Charter all that it can in order to strengthen itself for its role in international life.[119]

It is clear that the position of the PCIJ in the League of Nations was different from that of the ICJ in the UN. As the ICJ is the main judicial organ of the UN, this new status of the ICJ has largely affected the way in which the ICJ has exer-

---

[111] Keith, *supra* note 9, p. 144.

[112] For instance by invoking extraordinary sessions or by fixing the time limit and gave the request priority over a matter which preceded it on the list. For example this happened in the case *of Polish War Vessels in the Port of Danzig.* See Keith, ibid.

[113] Article 93 provides: (1) "All Members of the United Nations are ipso facto parties to the Statute of the International Court of Justice. (2) A state which is not a Member of the United Nations may become a party to the Statute of the International Court of Justice on conditions to be determined in each case by the General Assembly upon the recommendation of the Security Council".

[114] See the full text of Article 96(2) of the Charter below.

[115] Rosenne, *supra* note 52, p. 106.

[116] Rosenne, ibid, p. 109.

[117] Simma, Bruno, *et al.*, (eds.) *The Charter of the United Nation: A Commentary*, Oxford University Press, Vol. 2, 2002, p. 1147.

[118] Rosenne, *supra* note 52, p. 109.

[119] Ibid, p. 110.

cised its advisory jurisdiction. This new status has enabled the Court to embrace the principle that, as a principal organ of the UN, giving an advisory opinion represents its participation in the work of the Organisation, as will become clearer throughout the study.

11 The Advisory Function of the ICJ: How Much Is It Changing?

It is an undisputed fact that the advisory function of the ICJ is based to large extent on the experience of its predecessor, the PCIJ, as will be made clear in the following pages.

12 The Drafting Stage

The uncertainty and scepticism which surrounded the adoption of the advisory function of the PCIJ had to some degree diminished by the time the provisions of the Charter and the Statute relating to advisory opinions were drafted.[120] Article 96 of the Charter has been, to some extent, built on the League's experience with the advisory function. Indeed, the efforts at the San Francisco Conference centred primarily on ways and means of enhancing the usefulness of this function.[121] Even the US, despite its previous attitude towards the advisory opinions of the PCIJ, consented to such a function being entrusted to the new Court.

The advisory function of the ICJ is broadly similar to that of the PCIJ, and the ICJ Statute is based on the Statute of the PCIJ. This is confirmed in Article 92 of the UN Charter which provides "[i]t shall function in accordance with the annexed Statute, which is based upon the Statute of the Permanent Court of International Justice ... "The ICJ, therefore, has generally been regarded as a continuation of its predecessor.[122] However, the UN Charter departed from Article 14 of the Covenant

---

[120] Even though, some of the members of the Inter –Allied Committee were inclined to think that the Court's jurisdiction to give advisory opinions was "anomalous and ought to be abolished" it was argued that the existence of this function tended to encourage using the court as an instrument to settle, political issues. See para. 65 of the Report of the Informal Inter –Allied Committee on the Future of the PCIJ, 39 *AJIL*, 1945, p. 20.

[121] This was exemplified by extending the number of bodies authorised to request an advisory opinion.

[122] Judge Read observed in his dissenting opinion in *the Interpretation of Peace Treaties* Case that: "[t]he provisions of Article 92 of the Charter discloses the intention of the United Nations that continuity should be maintained between the Permanent Court of International Justice and this Court. There can be no doubt that the United Nations intended continuity in jurisprudence, as well as in less important matters." See Diss. Op. of Judge Read, ICJ Rep., 1950, pp. 232-233.

by making the Court one of "the principal organs of the United Nations",[123] and more specifically "the principal judicial organ of the United Nations".[124] Although this change introduced by the Charter did not relate specifically to the advisory function, it has influenced the Court's view of its advisory role.[125]

Prior to the San Francisco Conference, many proposals were made and committees charged with preparing drafts for consideration by the Conference.[126] Earlier, the Informal Inter-Allied Committee on the future of the PCIJ,[127] held in London in 1943, adopted a liberal approach in considering the usefulness of the advisory function. The majority believed that this function ought to be retained and even extended,[128] while at the same time proposing safeguards to prevent misuse.[129] Except for authorising States to request advisory opinions of the Court, the recommendations of the Inter Allied Committee were adopted at San Francisco. In effect, this adoption rejected the Dumbarton Oaks proposals that the right to request advisory opinions should be limited to the Security Council. In the end, the Conference resolved that both the General Assembly and the Security Council

123 See Article 7 of the UN Charter.

124 See Article 92 of the UN Charter.

125 Pomerance, *supra* note 26, p. 25.

126 The most important proposals were formulated by the Informal Inter Allied Committee, The Dumbarton Oaks and Washington Committee of Jurists.

127 The Inter Allied Committee commenced its deliberations in 1943 to consider "the question of the Permanent Court of International Justice". Early in 1943, the UK invited a number of experts to London to constitute an informal Inter-Allied Committee to examine the matter. This Committee, under the chairmanship of Sir William Malkin held 19 meetings, which were attended by jurists from 11 countries. In its report, which was published on 10 February 1944, it recommended that the Statute of any new international court should be based on that of the Permanent Court of International Justice; that advisory jurisdiction should be retained in the case of the new Court; that acceptance of the jurisdiction of the new Court should not be compulsory; and that the Court should have no jurisdiction to deal with essentially political matters. See Report of the Informal Inter-Allied Committee, *supra* note 120, pp. 1-42.

128 In its report the Committee, by way of replying to the objections raised by some of the members about the compatibility of this function with the proper function of a court of law, stated that "it is not correct to say that the jurisdiction of an 'advisory' nature is inconsistent with the proper function of a court of law." See para. 66 of the Report, *supra* note 120, p. 21.

129 For instance, the questions referred to the Court were not to be "of a merely general or abstract character", but were to "relate to some definite issue and circumstance," the Court was not to be used "for making pronouncements on political issues, or in a semi-legislative capacity." Moreover, in order to avoid a species of indirect compulsory jurisdiction and to ensure that the Court proceeded on "an agreed basis of fact", *Ex parte* should not be permitted. On the whole, the Committee had found it desirable to leave the necessary control to be exercised by the Court itself. See Report of Inter – Allied Committee, *supra* note 120, paras. 69–75.

may request advisory opinions on any legal question as well as other UN organs and specialised agencies through authorisation by the Assembly.

It was decided also, to insert a new paragraph into Article 65 of the Statute, making explicit provision for the Court to give an advisory opinion at the request of certain bodies. Thus Article 96 of the UN Charter states:

> *(1) The General Assembly or the Security Council may request the International Court of Justice to give an advisory opinion on any legal question.*
>
> *(2) Other organs of the United Nations and specialized agencies, which may at any time be so authorized by the General Assembly, may also request advisory opinions of the Court on legal questions arising within the scope of their activities.*

This was incorporated into Article 65 of the ICJ Statute as "[t]he Court may give an advisory opinion on any legal question at the request of whatever body may be authorised by or in accordance with the Charter of the United Nations to make such a request." The following pages go on to discuss the drafting stage of the provisions pertaining to advisory opinions.

12.1 The Rights of the General Assembly and the Security Council to Request an Advisory Opinion

It was mentioned above that the Dumbarton Oaks proposals would have given the Security Council the exclusive right to request advisory opinions. Chapter VIII of Section A, paragraph 6 of the proposals stated:[130]

> *Justiciable disputes should normally be referred to the international court of justice. The Security Council should be empowered to refer to the court, for advice, legal questions connected with other disputes.*

Schwebel maintains that, this "regressive approach" of confining the right to request advisory opinion to the Security Council, reflected the preoccupation of the United States with the exclusive role of the Security Council in the maintenance of international peace and security.[131] Despite this, the Washington Committee of Jurists, which was convened prior to the opening of the San Francisco Conference and was

---

[130] UNCIO, Vol. 14. It is to be noted that the word "justiciable" had been recognized at the San Francisco Conference, in Committee III/2, it was suggested that the word "legal" rather than "justiciable" described more accurate the category of disputes which was in question. UNCIO, 12, summary Report of eleventh Meeting of Committee III/2, Document, 674, III/2/24, p. 97.

[131] Schwebel, Stephen, "Was the Capacity to Request an Advisory Opinion Wider in the Permanent Court of International Justice than it is in the International Court of Justice" in: Schwebel, Stephen, *Justice in International Law*, Cambridge University Press, 1994, p. 55.

charged with preparing a draft of the Court's Statute for the consideration of the Conference[132] proposed that, the General Assembly, as well as the Security Council, should have the right to request advisory opinions.[133] At San Francisco, the delegates supported the view that the General Assembly as well as Security Council should have the right to ask the Court for an advisory opinion.[134] The representative of China argued that, in view of the relationship of the Assembly to the Economic and Social Council and the former's function of co-ordinating the policies of the specialised agencies, the Assembly could be called upon to consider juridical questions.[135]

The San Francisco Conference approved the recommendations of the Committee of Jurists and extended to the General Assembly the right to request advisory opinions. It was also agreed, as mentioned above, to add to the UN Charter the provisions of Article 96(2), and a new paragraph to Article 65 of the Statute granting the Court the right to give advisory opinions to certain authorised organs.[136]

The provisions as adopted have given both the General Assembly and the Security Council the right to ask for an advisory opinion "on any legal question", while paragraph 2 of Article 96 permits the General Assembly to authorise other organs of the UN and specialised agencies to request an advisory opinion on a legal question arising within the scope of their activities. Paragraph 2 of Article 96 of the UN Charter, as finally adopted "was an innovation, having no counterpart in the League Covenant."[137] Moreover, the San Francisco Conference authorised UN specialised agencies to seek advisory opinions although this was restricted to intergovernmental agencies brought into relationship with the UN.[138]

---

[132] This Committee, under the chairmanship of G. H. Hackworth (United States), was entrusted with the preparation of a draft Statute for the future International Court of Justice, for submission to the San Francisco Conference. The draft Statute prepared by the Committee was based on the Statute of the PCIJ. The Committee nevertheless left a number of questions open which it felt should be decided by the San Francisco Conference such as should a new court be created; in what form should the court's mission as the principal judicial organ of the United Nations be stated; should the court's jurisdiction be compulsory and, if so, to what extent; and how should the judges be elected. Available at: http://www.icjcij.org/icjwww/igeneralinformation/ibbook/Bbookframepage.htm, (accessed 24 October 2004).

[133] Despite the earlier attitude of the US at Dumbarton Oaks, in confining the right to request advisory opinion only to the Security Council, in the Committee of Jurists, the Chairman of the Committee said that the US did not object to the authorization of the Assembly. See UNCIO, vol. 14, The United Nations Committee of Jurists, 45, G/34, p. 178.

[134] The Delegations of Australia, Belgium, Netherlands, Norway, and many other Members. See UNCIO, 14, The United Nations Committee of Jurists, 45, G/34, pp. 178-179.

[135] Ibid, p. 177.

[136] For the full texts of those Articles see Section 6.1 above.

[137] Pomerance, *supra* note 26, p. 33.

[138] UNCIO, vol. 9, 161-162. See also UNCIO, vol. 13, p. 298. For details see discussion in Chapter Two, *infra.*

Another major difference between Article 14 of the Covenant and Article 96 of the Charter concerns the Court's jurisdiction *ratione materiae* in its advisory capacity. In San Francisco, the term "any legal question" was introduced instead of the former term, "any dispute or question". This change has raised a number of questions which will be discussed in the following Chapter.[139]

12.2 Proposals That Were Not Adopted

It is pertinent before ending this discussion to refer to some proposals put forward during the drafting stages which were not adopted. These were geared towards authorising States and international organisations to request advisory opinions.

The question of empowering States to request advisory opinions arose during the League's era.[140] At San Francisco it was again proposed that States should be authorised to request advisory opinions of the Court directly. Here, the UK representative pointed out that disputes which might otherwise lead to litigation could be prevented if States, by agreement among themselves, obtained the Court's advice on their position in the matters involve dispute at an early stage.[141] The Belgian representative put forward a most provocative proposal to enable individual States to request advisory opinions, upon a recommendation or decision of the Security Council, on matters which affected their essential rights.[142] These proposals were rejected on the grounds that the Court should not be treated as a general adviser to Member States and that it should not become overloaded with work. In addition, States could get the Court's advice indirectly through the General Assembly.[143] This indirect access to the Court had many applications in the practice of the two Courts.[144]

---

[139] See Chapter Two, *infra.*

[140] While drafting Article 36 of the PCIJ Statute, the representative of Argentina proposed that such a power should be given to States. Moreover, there was another proposal by the International Labour Organization to the same effect. Those proposals were rejected by the subcommittee because such proposals "would involve a considerable extension of the duties of the members of the Court and might lead to consequences difficult to calculate in advance." See Records of the First Assembly, Meeting of the Committees, I, p. 534.

[141] UNCIO, vol. 14, p. 319.

[142] UNCIO, 12, p. 48. This proposal was withdrawn on the grounds that, if adopted it would weaken the authority of the Security Council and cause delay when action was needed. See ibid, p. 49.

[143] Ibid, p. 181. See also, Keith, *supra* note 9, p. 23.

[144] For instance, the advisory opinion of the PCIJ in the *Nationality Decrees issued in Tunisia and Morocco* Case. PCIJ, Ser. B, No. 4, 1923. In the present Court, The *Applications for Review of Judgment No. 273of the United Nations Administrative Tribunal* Case, ICJ Rep., 1982, p. 325. In this latter case the application was presented by the US for review of an Administrative Tribunal judgment.

The majority of delegates at San Francisco agreed that only States could be parties to a contentious case before the Court.[145] International organisations were not given *locus standi* as parties before the Court, neither in the League nor in the UN eras. Therefore, the only access to the Court for international organisations has been through the medium of advisory opinions. The authorisation of international organisations was hardly in question at San Francisco. However, the point under consideration was the form of authorisation, whether direct or indirect. In the Committee of Jurists, the UK representative argued that international organisations should be given direct access to the Court.[146] On the other hand, some members favoured indirect access.[147] Eventually, the Committee of Jurists did not adopt the UK proposal because the question of allowing international organisations the right to request an advisory opinion was a policy matter best left to the San Francisco Conference to decide. While considering the matter at San Francisco, Committee IV/I unanimously adopted the UK proposals[148] which stated "[s]uch other organs of the Organization, and such specialized agencies brought into relationship with it, as may at any time be authorised thereto by the General Assembly, may also request advisory opinions of the Court on questions of constitutional or juridical character arising within the scope of their activities."[149] International organisations other than UN organs and UN specialised agencies were thus denied the right to request advisory opinions.

---

[145] UNCIO, 13, p. 282. This became paragraph (1) of Article 34 of the ICJ Statute, which provides "only states may be parties in cases before the Court." This principle has its roots in Article 34 of the Statute of the PCIJ which provided that "only States or Members of the league of Nations may be parties in cases before the Court". However, two paragraphs were added to Article 34 of the ICJ's Statute on the recommendation of the Washington Committee of Jurists, namely, paragraphs (2) and (3) of Article 34. The second paragraph of Article 34 of the new Statute provides that "[t]he Court, subject to and in conformity with its Rules, may request of public international organizations information relevant to cases before it, and shall receive such information presented by such organizations on their own initiative." Paragraph (3) provides "[w]henever the construction of the constituent instrument of a public international organization or of an international convention adopted thereunder is in question in a case before the Court, the Registrar shall so notify the public international organization concerned and shall communicate to it copies of all the written proceedings."

[146] UNCIO, 14, p. 319. See also, by the same token, the views of the representatives of Venezuela and France, ibid, pp. 179-180.

[147] See, for instance, the view of the Australian representative, ibid, p. 182.

[148] UNCIO, 13, p. 233.

[149] UNCIO, 13, p. 513.

13 Concluding Remarks

In the early years of the League of Nations the concept of an "advisory opinion" was a "controversial innovation" because jurists could not agree as to whether it was proper for a court of law to render advisory opinions.[150] As a consequence of some of the early doubts about the judicial character of advisory opinions, the PCIJ was inclined to interpret its jurisdiction narrowly, refusing to give an advisory opinion on a legal dispute actually pending between two or more States without the consent of the States concerned.[151] The drafting stage of the Covenant and the Statute indicate that the prime concern of the drafters was to protect the judicial character of the Court. This was exemplified by the proposals put forward during the drafting of the original Statute to distinguish between a request related to a "dispute" and one related to a "question".[152]

The concept of advisory opinions has become well established. The advisory function of the ICJ is largely based on that of its predecessor and on the experience of the League of Nations. Few alterations were introduced. The most important of these is paragraph 2 of Article 96 of the UN Charter which extends the range of organs empowered to seek the Court's opinion. More drastic alterations were introduced by Article 92, pursuant to which the Court was established as the "principal judicial organ of the United Nations". This innovation has made the Court more inclined to participate in the work of the UN. In the final analysis, the advisory function is now recognised and accepted in international law, and its existence is no longer in question.

---

150 Rosenne, *supra* note 52, p. 107.

151 The principle of Eastren Carelia. For further details on this principle, see Section 2.1.2 in Chapter Four, *infra*.

152 For the drafting of the original Statute in 1920, see discussion above.

CHAPTER TWO

The Advisory Jurisdiction of the ICJ: Compliance with Requests and the Court's Discretion in Giving Advisory Opinions

1 Introduction

As noted in Chapter One, the ICJ may provide advisory opinions to certain UN organs and agencies upon their request. This jurisdiction was primarily designed to assist UN organs and agencies in deciding on the course of action that they should follow. When the Court is seised of a request for an advisory opinion, it must first determine whether the request is within its jurisdiction, both *ratione personae* and *ratione materiae*. In other words, the Court's first concern as to determine the standing of the organ requesting the opinion and the subject matter of the requested opinion.

Having established its jurisdiction, the Court can then consider its 'discretionary power' to render or to refrain from rendering the requested opinion. The Court is not bound to give an advisory opinion even if the requesting organ is acting fully *intra vires* in requesting the question.[1] However, the Court's case law demonstrates that it will not refuse a request unless there are 'compelling reasons' to do so. Before discussing these issues in some detail, it will be pertinent to describe briefly the ICJ's jurisdiction in general, and the difference between jurisdiction and competence.

2 The Jurisdiction of the ICJ

In its broadest sense the Court's jurisdiction refers to its power "to do justice between the litigating States, to decide the case before it with final and binding force on those States."[2] The ICJ enjoys two different types of jurisdiction. On the one

---

1 Bowett, Derek W., "The Court's Role in Relation to International Organizations" in: Lowe, Vaughan & Fitzmaurice, Malgosia, (eds.), *Fifty Years of the International Court of Justice: Essays in Honour of Sir Robert Jennings*, Cambridge: Grotius Publications, 1996, p. 186.

2 Rosenne, Shabtai, *The Law and Practice of the International Court, 1920-1996*, The Hague; London: Martinus Nijhoff Publishers, 1997, p. 536.

hand, it possesses a contentious jurisdiction to decide disputes between States in accordance with Article 36(1) of the Statute.[3] The exercise of this jurisdiction depends on the consent of the States parties to the dispute and is known as 'consensual jurisdiction.'[4] Once consent has been given, the Court is under a duty to fulfil its judicial function unless a gap in International Law forces it to make a finding of *non liquet*.[5] Contentious cases produce judgments binding on the parties to the case.

On the other hand, the Court has another type of jurisdiction which permits it to give an advisory opinion upon a request by certain international organisations. This latter jurisdiction is set out in Article 65(1) of the ICJ Statute, which is parallel to Article 96 of the UN Charter.[6] Rosenne pointed out that Article 65 is incomplete as it indicates just two elements of the advisory jurisdiction, namely that the request must be made by a duly authorised organ *(ratione personae)*, and that the question posed to the Court for an opinion must be a 'legal question.' However, the ICJ Statute and even the UN Charter pass in silence over the third element, namely the addressee of the opinion.[7] Rosenne has argued that this silence over the third element of jurisdiction entitles the Court "to act independently of any formal expression of consent on the part of States individually."[8]

2.1 Distinction Between Jurisdiction and Competence

The interchangeable and inconsistent use of the terms 'jurisdiction' and 'competence' when referring to the Court's power to give advisory opinions has caused some confusion.[9] Rosenne has pointed out that the Statute has used the term "jurisdiction" mostly in a contentious context while the term 'competence' is more frequently found in advisory opinions with an occasional use of the term 'jurisdiction.'[10] Moreover, he states that the difference between the two terms is not of major importance, maintaining that 'jurisdiction' is a stricter concept and relates to the Court's capacity to decide cases before it with binding force while 'compe-

---

3 Article 36(1) provides: "[t]he jurisdiction of the Court comprises all cases which the parties refer to it and all matters specially provided for in the Charter of the United Nations or in treaties or conventions in force."

4 Rosenne, *supra* note 2, pp. 563-603.

5 Bedjaoui, Mohammed, "Expediency in the Decisions of the International Court of Justice", 71 *BYIL*, 2000, p. 11.

6 For the full text of both Articles see Chapter One, *supra*.

7 Both Articles 96 of the Charter and 65 of the Statute use the verb 'give' in a general way, which is theoretically open to several interpretations. Rosenne, *supra* note 2, pp. 988-989.

8 Rosenne, *supra* note 2, p. 989. This will be discussed in detail in Chapter Four, *infra*.

9 Paratap, Dharma, *The Advisory Jurisdiction of the International Court of Justice*, Oxford: Clarendon Press, 1972, p. 113.

10 Rosenne, *supra* note 2, p. 536.

tence' includes both jurisdiction and elements of propriety when the Court is exercising its function.[11]

At any rate, the Court's practice does not provide a definite answer to the above question and it appears that the Court does not distinguish between the two terms.[12] Caution must be taken here as the risk of differentiating between the Court's powers in advisory and contentious cases might lead to the suggestion that the advisory function is less judicial.[13] Therefore, Sir Gerald Fitzmaurice, amongst others, has suggested that the term 'jurisdiction' should preferably be used for both, contentious and advisory functions, while 'competence' should be used only when referring to the capacity of an organ to request an opinion.[14]

2.2 The Court's *compétence de la compétence*[15]

It is a generally accepted rule that courts are competent to decide on their own competence.[16] The ICJ in the exercise of the principle of *compétence de la compétence* may determine whether it has jurisdiction to give an advisory opinion or a judgement in a contentious case. This principle is embodied in Article 36(6) of the Court's Statute which provides that "in the event of a dispute as to whether the Court has jurisdiction, the matter shall be settled by the decision of the Court."[17] As far as the advisory function is concerned, the Court's power to decide upon its advisory jurisdiction is conferred by Article 68 of the Court's Statute which provides that the Court shall be guided in advisory cases by the Statute's provisions which apply in contentious proceedings.

In its jurisprudence the Court has examined its own jurisdiction *proprio motu,* even if no objections were raised by interested parties. In the *Judgments of the Administrative Tribunal of the ILO upon Complaints made against UNESCO*

---

[11] Ibid.

[12] Paratap, *supra* note 9, pp. 114-115.

[13] Ibid, p. 115.

[14] Fitzmaurice, Gerald, "The Law and Procedure of the International Court of Justice, 1951-4: Questions of Jurisdiction, Competence and Procedure", 43 *BYIL*, 1958, p. 8-9; Pratap, *supra* note 9, p. 115.

[15] This principle means the power of the Court to decide on its own jurisdiction. The origins of the principle can be traced back to the 1794 *Jay Treaty*; the 1797 *Betsy Case* and the 1872 *Alabama* Case. See Rosenne, *supra* note 2, pp. 846-862; Shihata, Ibrahim, *The Power of the International Court to Determine its Own Jurisdiction*, The Hague: M. Nijhoff, 1965, pp. 11-24.

[16] Shihata, ibid.

[17] In the *Nottebohm* Case (Liechtenstein v. Guatemala), the Court stated that "[s]ince the *Alabama* case, it has been generally recognized, following the earlier precedents, that, in the absence of any agreement to the contrary, an international tribunal has the right to decide as to its own jurisdiction and has the power to interpret for this purpose the instruments which govern that jurisdiction. See ICJ Rep., 1953, p. 119.

Case,[18] none of the interested parties challenged the Court's jurisdiction. Yet, the Court considered at the outset its right to exercise jurisdiction in this case *ex officio* and held that:[19]

> *The Court will consider at the outset whether it should comply with the request for an opinion. The question put to the Court is a legal question. It arose within the scope of the activities of UNESCO when the Executive Board had to examine the measures to be taken as a result of the four judgments. The answer given to it will affect the result of the challenged raised by the Executive Board with regard to these judgments. In submitting the request for an opinion the Executive Board was seeking a clarification of the legal aspects of a matter with which it was dealing.*

Based on the above, it seems that the Court has the power to decide upon its own jurisdiction, its *compétence de la compétence*, and, if it finds that it has no jurisdiction because of the absence of the required elements, namely jurisdiction *ratione personae* or jurisdiction *ratione materiae,* it may refrain from giving the requested opinion.

In the following pages the conditions which are required to establish the Court's jurisdiction in advisory cases will be examined to illustrate the attitude of the Court towards challenges to its jurisdiction. In general terms the Court, when determining its own jurisdiction in advisory cases, has adopted a liberal approach when it has received a request from the political organs of the UN. Yet, the Court has been more restrictive and cautious when it has received requests for advisory opinions from specialised agencies. In the latter cases, the Court has adopted a narrow interpretation of the purposes and functions of the requesting agencies and seems to not have accorded them discretion comparable to that which it has accorded to the political organs.[20]

3 The Elements of Jurisdiction to Give an Advisory Opinion

The ICJ, in accordance with Articles 96 of the UN Charter and 65 of the Court's Statute, may give an advisory opinion upon requests submitted to it by the General Assembly, Security Council and by other UN organs and specialised agencies authorised by the General Assembly.[21] By contrast the PCIJ could only respond to requests for advisory opinions on 'disputes' or 'questions' referred by the Council or the Assembly of the League of Nations.[22]

---

18 Hereinafter cited as: "the *ILO Administrative Tribunal* Case", ICJ Rep., 1956, p. 77.

19 Ibid, p. 84.

20 See discussion in Section ii below.

21 For the full texts of Articles 96 of the Charter and 65 of the Statute, see Section 6.1 in Chapter One, *supra.*

22 See Article 14 of the League Covenant in Chapter One, *supra.*

As mentioned above, there are at least two legal conditions to be met before requesting an advisory opinion.[23] The first is that the request must emanate from a body authorised by or under Article 96 of the Charter i.e. jurisdiction *ratione personae*. The second is that the advisory opinion requested must be related to a 'legal question' within the meaning of the UN Charter and the ICJ's Statute, i.e. jurisdiction *ratione materiae.* In this respect the Court in its advisory opinion of July 2004, in the *Legal Consequences of the Construction of a Wall in the Occupied Palestinian Territory*[24] cited its findings in the *Application for Review of Judgement No. 273 of the United Nations Administrative Tribunal* Case, held that:[25]

> *It is . . . a precondition of the Court's competence that the advisory opinion be requested by an organ duly authorized to seek it under the Charter, that it be requested on a legal question, and that, except in the case of the General Assembly or the Security Council, that question should be one arising within the scope of the activities of the requesting organ.*

Moreover, the Court in its advisory opinion in the 1996 *Legality of Threat or Use of Nuclear Weapons* Case stated that:[26]

> *For the Court to be competent to give an advisory opinion, it is thus necessary at the outset for the body requesting the opinion to be "authorized by or in accordance with the Charter of the United Nations to make such a request." The Charter provides in Article 96, paragraph 1, that: "The General Assembly or the Security Council may request the International Court of Justice to give an advisory opinion on any legal question*

In the 1975 *Western Sahara* Case the Court explained that legal questions are "framed in terms of law and rais[ing] problems of international law ... are by their very nature susceptible of a reply based on law ...[and] appear ... to be questions of a legal character."[27]

The absence of either of the aforementioned conditions may lead the Court to decline to render an advisory opinion. On the other hand, it may be inferred from Article 65 of the Court's Statute which provides that the Court "may give" advisory opinions, that the Court has 'discretion' to give or to refrain from giving an opinion requested even when the aforementioned prerequisites are satisfied.

---

[23] In the view of some scholars there is another condition relating to the consent of the parties to a dispute. This condition is not expressly embodied neither in the Charter nor the Statute of the ICJ. See Section 2.1 in Chapter Four, *infra.*

[24] Hereinafter cited as: "the *Wall* Case", available at: http://www.icjcij.org/icjwww/idocket/imwp/imwpframe.htm (accessed 21 October 2004).

[25] ICJ Rep., 1982, para. 21, pp. 333-334.

[26] ICJ Rep., 1996, para. 11, p. 232.

[27] Cited in the ICJ Rep., 1996, para. 13, p. 233.

3.1 Jurisdiction *ratione personae*

The General Assembly and the Security Council have an 'original' right under Article 96(1) of the UN Charter to request an advisory opinion on 'any legal question', while other UN organs and specialised agencies have a 'derivative' right that may be conferred by the General Assembly.[28] The following pages shed light on those organs authorised by or in accordance with the Charter to request advisory opinions and on the Court's attitude towards objections made to the competence of the requesting organs.

3.1.1 Organs with an 'Original Right' to Request Advisory Opinions: The General Assembly and the Security Council

Article 96(1) of the UN Charter authorises the General Assembly and the Security Council to request advisory opinions on any 'legal question.'[29] This Article has prompted international lawyers to debate the intended meaning of the term 'any legal question.' Some maintain that both organs have an absolute right to request an advisory opinion 'on any legal question' without limits. Judge Schwebel has argued that the term 'any legal question' is a broad term which "would entitle the General Assembly to serve as a conduit (though a conditional rather than a 'mere' conduit) for requests to the Court from national courts to answer international legal questions arising in the Course of national judicial proceedings."[30]

This view is based on the permissive wording of paragraph 1 of Article 96 which provides that both organs may request advisory opinions on 'any legal question.' This reading of the term is enhanced by paragraph 2 of Article 96 which imposes restrictions on other UN organs and specialised agencies by limiting the legal question to those that are within the organ's range of activities. Rosenne rejects such views and argues that "[n]o organ, including the General Assembly and the Security Council, can decide to request an advisory opinion except within the scope of its activities."[31] Moreover, Kelsen argued that:[32]

> *The determination of any organ's jurisdiction implies the norm not to act beyond the scope of its activity as determined by the legal instrument instituting the organ. It is not very likely that it was in-*

---

[28] See Bowett, Derek W., *The Law of International Institutions*, London: Stevens and Sons, 1982, p. 277; Sands, Philippe & Klien, Pierre, *Bowett's Law of International Institutions*, London: Sweet and Maxwell, 2001, p. 364.

[29] For the full text of Article 96 of the UN Charter see Chapter One, *supra*.

[30] Schwebel, Stephen, "Relations between the International Court of Justice and the United Nations" in: *Justice in International Law: Selected Writings of Stephen M. Schwebel*, Cambridge: Grotius Publications, 1994, pp. 18-19.

[31] Rosenne, Shabtai, *The Law and Practice of the International Court of Justice*, Dordrecht; Lancaster: Martinus Niijhoff, 1985, p. 660.

[32] Kelsen, Hans, *The law of the United Nations: A Critical Analysis of Its Fundamental Problems*, London: Steven and Sons Ltd, 1951, p. 546.

tended to enlarge, by Article 96, paragraph 1, the scope of the activity of the General Assembly and the Security Council determined by other articles of the Charter. Hence, the words "arising within the scope of their activities" in paragraph 2 of Article 96 are redundant.

Judge Higgins more recently observed that the General Assembly practice in regard to the *Alvarez-Machain* Case indicates that even the General Assembly and the Security Council cannot decide to request an advisory opinion unless the request relates to their activities. Higgins emphasised that although the phrase 'any legal question' may be wider than the formulation in Article 96(2), it must at least refer to a legal question under consideration within the UN.[33]

One can conclude that Article 12(1) of the Charter restricts the General Assembly's power to ask for an advisory opinion.[34] It could also be argued that the broad scope of the term 'any legal question' may be construed to reflect the broad competence of the General Assembly and the Security Council.[35]

In its jurisprudence the Court has adopted a wide interpretation of the powers and activities of the political organs of the UN.[36] It has been argued in several cases that the requesting organ lacked competence to seek an advisory opinion as it acted *ultra vires* in making the request, claming powers that it did not possess.[37]

---

[33] In this case most of the General Assembly's Latin American members, in addition to Spain, Portugal and Iran proposed a draft resolution to ask the ICJ for an advisory opinion in regard to the findings of the Supreme Court of the US that the abduction of Mr. Alvarez from Mexico, and his transfer to the US to stand trial, did not violate the extradition treaty between Mexico and the US and as a consequence render the US courts without jurisdiction. It should be noted that this draft resolution was formulated in abstract terms avoiding reference to Mr. Alvarez and the dispute between Mexico and the US. On the recommendations of the Sixth Committee this draft resolution was turned down. See Higgins, Rosalyn, "A comment on the current health of Advisory Opinions", in: Lowe, Vaughan & Fitzmaurice, Malgosia (eds.), *Fifty Years of the International Court of Justice: Essays in honour of Sir Robert Jennings*, Cambridge: Grotius Publications, 1996, p. 580.

[34] This Article provides: "[w]hile the Security Council is exercising in respect of any dispute or situation the functions assigned to it in the present Charter, the General Assembly shall not make any recommendations with regard to that dispute or situation unless the Security Council so requests."

[35] The powers of the General Assembly are broadly stated in chapter IV of the UN Charter and include the power to "discuss any question or any matter within the scope of the present Charter."

[36] See Section 5 in Chapter Five, *infra*. In the *Reservations* Case the Court stated that Article 96 of the Charter conferred upon the General Assembly and the Security Council in general terms the "right" to request the Court to give an advisory opinion on any legal question. ICJ Rep., 1951, p. 20.

[37] Ciobanu observed that difficulties in raising the *ultra vires* objection to the jurisdiction of UN political organs are due to the fact that under the law of the UN, these organs are not, in principle, required to state the reasons for their resolutions. See Ciobanu, Dan, *Preliminary Objections Related to the Jurisdiction of the United Nations Political Organs*, The Hague: Nijhoff, 1975, p. 73.

In the *Wall* Advisory Opinion, Israel contended that due to the active engagement of the Security Council with the Palestinian question, the General Assembly had acted *ultra vires* under the Charter when it requested this advisory opinion because the request was in breach of Article 12(1) of the Charter.[38]

In reply the Court stated that a request for an advisory opinion was not in itself a 'recommendation' by the General Assembly "with regard to [a] dispute or situation" within the meaning of Article 12.[39] However, thc Court after examining Article 12 and relevant Articles such as Article 24 of the Charter,[40] together with the practice of the General Assembly and Security Council[41] with regard to interpreting and applying Article 12, concluded that the General Assembly in requesting that advisory opinion "did not contravene the provisions of Article 12, paragraph, 1, of the Charter."[42]

In submissions to the Court in the *Interpretation of Peace Treaties* Case,[43] which concerned the interpretation of the 1947 peace treaties with Bulgaria, Hungary, and Romania, it was contended that:[44]

> *[T]he Request for an Opinion was an action ultra vires on the part of the General Assembly because, in dealing with the question of the observance of human rights and fundamental freedoms in the [concerned States], it was "interfering" or "intervening" in matters essentially within the domestic jurisdiction of States.*

The Court rejected this argument because the object of the request was directed at obtaining from the Court a legal clarification of the applicability of the procedure

---

38 The question of the General Assembly was "[w]hat are the legal consequences arising from the construction of the wall being built by Israel, the occupying Power, in the Occupied Palestinian Territory, including in and around East Jerusalem, as described in the report of the Secretary-General, considering the rules and principles of international law, including the Fourth Geneva Convention of 1949, and relevant Security Council and General Assembly resolutions?"

39 See para. 25 of the Court's opinion, *supra* note 24.

40 Article 24 of the Charter provides that the Security Council has "primary responsibility for the maintenance of international peace and security." Therefore, the Court held that Article 24 refers to a primary, but not necessarily exclusive, competence. Thus the Court emphasised that the General Assembly does have the power, *inter alia*, under Article 14 of the Charter, to "recommend measures for the peaceful adjustment" of various situations. See *Expenses* Case, ICJ Rep., 1962, p. 163.

41 The Court concluded that, "both the General Assembly and the Security Council initially interpreted and applied Article 12 to the effect that the Assembly could not make a recommendation on a question concerning the maintenance of international peace and security while the matter remained on the Council's agenda". See para. 27 of the Opinion, *supra* note 24.

42 See paras. 26-28 of the *Wall* Opinion.

43 Hereinafter cited as: "the *Peace Treaties* Case", ICJ Rep., 1950, p. 65.

44 Ibid, p. 70.

for dispute settlement provided for in the Peace Treaties. This purpose did not constitute a question within the domestic jurisdiction of a State, but was a question of International Law which lay within the Court's jurisdiction.[45]

The 1962 *Certain Expenses of the United Nations (Article17, paragraph 2, of the Charter)* Case,[46] arose out of the refusal of some member States, most notably the former Soviet Union and France, to pay their share of the costs of the UN Emergency Forces in the Middle East (UNEF) and the UN Force in the Congo (ONUC).[47] The contesting States' view was that peace-keeping operations should only be taken under the exclusive powers of the Security Council. Therefore, the General Assembly decision to set up the peace-keeping operations was *ultra vires*. To this objection the Court stated that:[48]

> *[W]hen the Organization takes action which warrants the assertion that it was appropriate for the fulfilment of one of the stated purposes of the United Nations, the presumption is that such action is not* ultra vires *the Organization.*
>
> *If it is agreed that the action in question is within the scope of the functions of the Organization but it is alleged that it has been initiated or carried out in a manner not in conformity with the division of functions among the several organs which the Charter prescribes, one moves to the internal plane, to the internal structure of the Organization. If the action was taken by the wrong organ, it was irregular as a matter of that internal structure, but this would not necessarily mean that the expense incurred was not an expense of the Organization. Both national and international law contemplate cases in which the body corporate or politic may be bound, as to third parties, by an* ultra vires *act of an agent.*

In the 1971 Legal Consequences for States of the Continued Presence of South Africa in Namibia (South West Africa) notwithstanding Security Council Resolution 276 (1970) Case,[49] South Africa did not contend that the Security Council had acted ultra vires.[50] However, it alleged that the Security Council resolution which

---

45 ICJ Rep., 1950, pp. 70-71.

46 Hereinafter cited as: "the *Expenses* Case", ICJ Rep., 1962, p. 151.

47 The Soviet Union declined to pay its share to UNEF and to the ONUC, while France declined to contribute to the latter. The UNEF was established by the General Assembly in 1956. See Res. 1000 (ES-1) of 5 November 1956 and 1001 (ES) of 7 November 1956. As for ONUC, it was established by the Security Council in 1960.

See SC Res. 143 of 14 July 1960; Res. 145 of 22 July 1960 and lastly Res. 146 of 9 August 1960.

48 ICJ Rep., 1962, p. 168.

49 Hereinafter cited as: "the *Namibia* Case", ICJ Rep., 1971, p. 16.

50 South Africa contended that General Assembly Resolution 2145 (XXI) which terminated South Africa's mandate in South West Africa was *ultra vires*. For further details See Section 6.3.3 in Chapter Three, *infra*.

requested an advisory opinion was invalid because two permanent members had abstained from voting on the draft resolution requesting an opinion.[51] The Court stated that: "[a] resolution of a properly constituted organ of the United Nations which is passed in accordance with that organ's rules of procedure, and is declared by its President to have been so passed, must be presumed to have been validly adopted."[52]

Lastly, in the *Legality of the Threat or Use of Nuclear Weapons* Case, in a positive response to the General Assembly's request for an advisory opinion, the Court stated that:[53]

> *Some States which oppose the giving of an opinion by the Court argued that the General Assembly and Security Council are not entitled to ask for opinions on matters totally unrelated to their work. They suggested that, as in the case of organs and agencies acting under Article 96, paragraph 2, of the Charter, and notwithstanding the difference in wording between that provision and paragraph 1 of the same Article, the General Assembly and Security Council may ask for an advisory opinion on a legal question only within the scope of their activities.*
>
> *In the view of the Court, it matters little whether this interpretation of Article 96, paragraph 1, is or is not correct; in the present case, the General. Assembly has competence in any event to seise the Court. Indeed, Article 10 of the Charter has conferred upon the General Assembly a competence relating to "any questions or any matters" within the scope of the Charter. Article 11 has specifically provided it with a competence to "consider the general principles ... in the maintenance of international peace and security, including the principles governing disarmament and the regulation of armaments." Lastly, according to Article 13, the General Assembly "shall initiate studies and make recommendations for the purpose of ... encouraging the progressive development of international law and its codification."*

The Court's practice throughout its history bears out that allegations of *ultra vires* in regard to actions taken by the two political organs are difficult to sustain. This is due to the broad competence of the General Assembly and Security Council. Moreover, the Court's case law has established that the Court will not refuse a request for an advisory opinion unless there are 'compelling reasons' for it to do so. Therefore the Court applies a presumption that requests by the political organs for an advisory opinion as *intra vires*.

---

51 For further details about this case see Chapters Three and Six, *infra*.

52 ICJ Rep., 1971, para. 20, p. 22.

53 ICJ Rep., 1996, para. 11, pp. 232-233.

On the other hand, one could argue that the Security Council and the General Assembly are special cases and that the ICJ would not make a comparable assumption with respect to requests from other UN organs and specialised agencies. This argument is supported by the Court's findings upon the WHO's request in the *Legality of the Use by a State of Nuclear Weapons* Case. At any rate, as Judge Elihu Lauterpacht has observed, "although there have been quite a number of allegations of unlawful or *ultra vires* action by the Organisation, these allegations and the episodes in the context of which they were made, have not led to the formation of any general theory about the effect of such acts."[54]

3.1.2 Organs with a "Derivative Right" to Request Advisory Opinions: Other UN Organs and the Specialised Agencies

Paragraph 2 of Article 96 of the UN Charter expressly gives the General Assembly the power to authorise other organs of the UN and specialised agencies to request advisory opinions on 'a legal question arising within the scope of their activities.'[55] As far as the nature of such an authorisation given by the General Assembly is concerned, one might ask if it is of a general or of an *ad hoc* character. The answer may be found in General Assembly practice. When the General Assembly dealt with the request of ECOSOC to be authorised to request an advisory opinion from the Court, the Soviet Union argued that the authorisation should have an *ad hoc* character. However, this view was rejected by the General Assembly and instead it gave ECOSOC authorisation of a general character.[56]

One can conclude that the practice of the General Assembly on this issue suggests that authorisations have not been confined to a given case or a group of cases, but have been given either generally 'within the scope of the activities' of an organisation or agency, or as far as legal questions arising from a convention are concerned.[57] However, it is widely accepted that an authorisation may be revoked unilaterally at any time by the General Assembly.[58]

---

[54] Lauterpacht, Elihu, "The legal Effect of Illegal Acts of International Organisations", in: *Cambridge Essays in International Law: Essays in Honour of Lord McNair*, London: Stevens, 1965, p. 100; Gowlland-Debbas Vera, "The Relationship between the International Court of Justice and the Security Council in the light of the Lockerbie case", 88 *AJIL*, 1994, p. 670; and Osieke, Ebere, "The Legal Validity of *Ultra Vires* Decisions of International Organization", 77 *AJIL*, (1983), p. 239.

[55] For the full text of para. 2 of Article 96 see Chapter One, *supra*. It is obvious from this paragraph that the General Assembly is the sole organ that is empowered to give such an authorisation. In contrast, Stone argued that both the General Assembly and the Security Council can give such authorisation. See Stone, Julius, *Legal Controls of International Conflict: A Treaties on the Dynamics of Disputes- and War-Law*, Sydney: Maitland Publications, 2nd Impression, 1959, p. 120.

[56] See GA Res. 89 (1), 11 December 1946.

[57] Simma, Bruno, *et al.*, *The Charter of the United Nations: A Commentary*, Oxford University Press, vol. 2, 2002, p. 1184.

[58] Ibid.

(i) Authorised Organs

As indicated above, the General Assembly in accordance with Article 96(2) of the Charter may authorise other UN organs and specialized agencies to request advisory opinions on 'legal questions' arise within the scope of their activities. The term 'other organs' raises a question as to whether they are restricted to the other principal organs indicated in Article 7(1) and 96(2) of the Charter, namely ECOSOC, the Trusteeship Council and the Secretariat, or whether it can be extended to 'subsidiary organs' established under the provisions of the Charter.[59] One view asserts that paragraph 2 of Article 96 does not empower the subsidiary organs to request advisory opinions from the Court. This view is based on the argument that Article 65 of the ICJ Statute and 96 of the UN Charter give the right to request an opinion solely to organs and specialised agencies which already exist and have a legal personality of their own.[60]

The practice of the General Assembly indicates that "other organs of the United Nations" includes both the principal organs established in accordance with Article 7(1) and subsidiary organs established in accordance with Articles 7(2), 8, 22, 29 and 68 of the UN Charter.[61] The General Assembly has authorised two subsidiary organs to request advisory opinions on a 'legal question' within their sphere competence. These were the Interim Committee of the General Assembly[62] and the Committee for Applications for Review of Judgments of the Administrative Tribunals.[63]

---

59 The Charter gives the authority to the General Assembly and the Security Council by virtue of Articles 22 and 29 of the Charter to establish subsidiary organs as it deems necessary for the performance of their functions. There are also provisions authorising other organs of the UN to establish their own subsidiary organs. Article 68 authorises the Economic and Social Council (ECOSOC) to set up commission in economic and social fields and for the promotion of human rights, and any commissions that is necessary to perform its functions.

It is interesting to note that Judge Hackworth defined the term 'subsidiary organ' in his dissenting opinion in the Effect of Awards of Compensation Made by the United Nations Administrative Tribunal Case, where he stated that:

[t]he term "subsidiary organ" has a special and well recognized meaning. It means an auxiliary or inferior organ; an organ to furnish aid and assistance in a subordinate or secondary capacity. This is the common acceptation of the meaning of the term.

See Diss. Op. of Judge Hackworth, ICJ Rep., 1954, p. 79.

60 This view was cited in the dissenting opinion of Judge De Castro in the *Application for Review of Judgment No.158 of the United Nations Administrative Tribunal* Case, ICJ Rep., 1973, p. 276.

61 See Amr, Mohamed S., *The Role of the International Court of Justice as the Principal Judicial Organ of the United Nations*, The Hague: Kluwer Law International, 2003, p. 63.

62 This Committee was established by the General Assembly under Resolution 196(III), 30 December, 1948.

63 This Committee was established by the General Assembly under Resolution 957, November, 1955 and is composed of the representatives of all member States of the most

The latter subsidiary organ had requested three advisory opinions of the Court before abandoning this procedure in 1995.[64] One of these three advisory opinions raised an important question regarding the relationship between the principal organ and its subsidiary, the authority that a principal organ exercises over its subsidiary body and whether decisions of a subsidiary organ can in any case bind the principal organ which created the subsidiary.

The Court, in the 1954 *Effects of Awards of Compensation Made by the UNAT* Case was asked to determine whether the General Assembly is legally entitled to refuse to give effect to an award of compensation made by the Administrative Tribunal properly constituted and acting within the limits of its statutory competence.[65] The Court, after examining the relevant provisions of the Statute of the Tribunal, took the view that the decisions of the Tribunal did bind the General Assembly, the creator of the Tribunal.[66] Therefore, the Assembly must comply with an award granting compensation to a staff member. The fact that the Tribunal was established as a judicial body to exercise judicial functions which the General Assembly did not itself possess led the Court to deliver that the Tribunal was established "not as an advisory organ or a mere subordinate committee of the General Assembly, but as independent and truly judicial body pronouncing final judgments without appeal within the limited field of its functions."[67] The Court found that a principal organ which establishes a subsidiary organ to exercise powers that it cannot itself exercise cannot change decisions of its subsidiary which are an exercise of those powers and functions. In this respect Sarooshi has argued that if the Court acted otherwise "the principal organ would in effect be performing the very functions which it does not itself possess under the Charter."[68]

As far as other principal organs are concerned, these organs are ECOSOC, the Trusteeship Council and the Secretariat.

---

recent regular session of the General Assembly. See Rosenne, *supra* note 2, p. 335; and Amr, *supra* note 61, p. 354. In the words of the Court in the *Fasla* Case this Committee "is an organ of the United Nations, duly constituted under Articles 7 and 22 of the Charter, and duly authorized under Article 96, paragraph 2, of the Charter to request advisory opinions of the Court for the purpose of Article 11 of the Statute of the United Nations Administrative Tribunal." ICJ Rep., 1973, p. 175.

64 See Section 4.4 in Chapter Five, *infra.*

65 ICJ Rep., 1954, p. 51.

66 Contrary to the Court's opinion, Judge Hackworth was of the view that "[t]he whole idea of the Charter was that the role of subsidiary organs should be, as the name implies, to assist and *not* to control the principal organ. Any other view, if accepted, would render extremely hazardous the creation of subsidiary organs, unless their powers were severely circumscribed. The principal organ must continue to be the principal organ with authority to accept, modify or reject, the acts or recommendations of the subordinate organs if the former is not to become *functus officio* in any given field." See Diss. Op. of Judge Hackworth, ICJ Rep., 1954, p. 79 (emphasis in original).

67 ICJ Rep., 1954, p. 53.

68 Sarooshi, Danesh, "The Legal Framework Governing United Nations Subsidiary Organs", 67 *BYIL*, 1996, p. 452.

(a) The Economic and Social Council (ECOSOC)

On 21st December 1946, ECOSOC adopted Resolution 15(III) requesting the General Assembly to authorise it to request advisory opinions "on all legal questions within its scope, including legal questions concerning mutual relations of the United Nations and Specialised Agencies"[69] in order to discharge its co-ordinating responsibility under Chapter X, and more particularly under Article 63 of the Charter.[70] The request was discussed in the Sixth Committee which resulted in the resolution 89(I), on 11 December 1946, authorising ECOSOC to request advisory opinions. ECOSOC has twice used this power.

The first request was in 1989, relating to the Applicability of Article VI, section 22, of the Convention of the Privileges and immunities of the United Nations,[71] while the second was in 1999 in the Difference relating to immunity from legal process of a special Rapporteur of the commission on human rights.[72]

(b) The Trusteeship Council

In 1947, the General Assembly, upon its own initiative, authorised the Trusteeship Council to request advisory opinions on legal questions arising within the scope of its activities conferred upon it by Chapters XII and XIII of the Charter.[73] However, the Trusteeship Council has never requested an advisory opinion.

Indeed, the aims of the trusteeship system have now been fulfilled because all trust territories have now attained self-government or independence either as separate States or by joining neighbouring independent countries.[74] The Trusteeship Council is no longer operative following the emergence of Palau as an Associate State of the United States, in 1994, and its admission to the UN.[75]

---

[69] Rosenne, *supra* note 2, p. 327.

[70] Article 63(2) of the UN Charter provides that the ECOSOC, "may co-ordinate the activities of the specialized agencies through consultation with and recommendations to such agencies and through recommendations to the General Assembly and to the Members of the United Nations."

[71] Hereinafter cited as: "the *Mazilu* Case", ICJ Rep., 1989. For the facts of this case see Section 4 in Chapter Six, *infra.*

[72] Hereinafter cited as: "the *Cumaraswamy* Case", ICJ Rep., 1999. For the facts of this case see Section 4 in Chapter Six, *infra.*

[73] See GA Res. 171(I), 14 November 1947. Rosenne, *Supra* note 2, p. 332. This authorisation for the Trusteeship Council was due to the Trusteeship functions and responsibilities in accordance with chapters XII and XIII of the Charter.

[74] See http://www.un.org/documents/tc.htm (accessed 24 October 2004). The Trusteeship Council has discharged successfully all the functions entrusted to it under the Charter: see *UN Yearbook Special Edition: UN Fiftieth Anniversary*, The Hague; Boston; London: Martinus Nijhoff Publishers, 1945-1995, 1995, p. 212.

[75] Rosenne, *supra* note 2, p. 332. See GA Res. 51/209, 17 December 1996, where the General Assembly initiated a review of the role of the Trusteeship Council.

(c) The Secretariat

Pursuant to Article 7(1) of the Charter, the Secretariat is one of the principal organs of the UN. The Secretary General is "the chief administrative officer of the Organization."[76] Nevertheless, the Secretariat is the only principal organ which has not been authorised to request advisory opinions from the Court. The question which is frequently raised is whether the Secretariat, acting through the Secretary-General, is legally entitled to be authorised to request advisory opinions with regard to any legal question within the scope of its activities and if so whether there is any reason for such an authorisation.[77]

The Secretariat, as one of the principal organs, may be authorised by the General Assembly to request an advisory opinion. It has been suggested that Paragraph 2 of Article 96, which provides that 'Other organs of the United Nations and specialised agencies, which may at any time be so authorised by the General Assembly', does not relate to the scope of UN organs that may be authorised to request advisory opinions, but to the scope of legal questions that they may put to the Court. The Secretary-General, then, is legally in a position to seek such an authorisation,[78] and he has not hesitated on several occasions[79] to seek a general right to request an opinion on his own initiative.

In his 1950 report on whether the Commission of Human Rights could be authorised to request advisory opinions from the Court, the Secretary-General argued that as the Commission had no right under Article 96(2) to be granted such authorisation, it would be appropriate if he himself could be granted such an authorisation to consider suggestions of the Commission in regard to requesting advisory opinions arising out of that Commission's work.

Again, in 1955, the Secretary-General asked to be authorised to request advisory opinions on legal questions concerning the Administrative Tribunals' Judgements. The last attempt to seek an authorisation was in his 1992 report "An agenda for peace: preventive diplomacy, peace making and peace keeping" where the Secretary-General sought authorisation to seek advisory opinions from the Court.[80] These suggestions have not yet been accepted.

However, the Secretary-General may seek an advisory opinion through the General Assembly or the Security Council. In practice, there is no instance where

---

76 See Article 97 of the UN Charter.

77 Schwebel, Stephen, "Authorizing the Secretary-General of the United Nations to Request Advisory Opinions of the International Court of Justice", 78 *AJIL*, 1984, p. 869.

78 Schwebel, ibid, p. 870.

79 See Judicial Review of United Nations Administrative Tribunal Judgments, working paper submitted by the Secretary-General: UN Doc. A/AC.78/L.1and corr. 1 (1955); Annual Reports of the Secretary-General: UN Doc. A/45/1, part III.

80 See Para. 38 of the Agenda for Peace: A/47/277; S/2411, 17 June 1992, which provides that "I recommend that the Secretary-General be authorized, pursuant to Article 96, paragraph 2, of the Charter, to take advantage of the advisory competence of the Court." available at http://www.un.org/Docs/SG/agpeace.html,(accessed 12 December 2004).

the Secretary-General has requested the General Assembly to ask for an advisory opinion on a specific issue confronting him while carrying out his duties and was denied permission.[81] One might try to imagine a situation where a genuine need arising from the duties of the Secretary-General for direct authorisation really exist. If so, what are the possible consequences of such an authorisation? These consequences could, in fact, be the reasons behind withholding authorisation.

The role of the Secretary-General encompasses administrative as well as "so-called" political functions,[82] which flow from Articles 98 and 99 of the Charter.[83] In view of the Secretary-General's broad functions and duties it would be undoubtedly helpful for him to be able to request advisory opinion from the Court. A wide range of international lawyers believe that he should be accorded such an authority.[84]

However, Judge Bedjaoui has observed that if the Secretary-General is authorised to request advisory opinions on legal questions arising within the scope of his activity, it is only to be expected that he will not confine himself to putting questions related to the running of the Secretariat as his activities are wide and include every sector of the Organisation's work. Therefore, authorising the Secretary-General to request an advisory opinion of the Court might encourage him to compete with the Security Council or the General Assembly.[85] Bowett maintains that

---

81 The requests by the General Assembly for advisory opinions in the *Reparations* Case; *Reservations* Case, *UNAT* Cases were made on behalf of the Secretary-General. Moreover, on the conditions determined by the Headquarters agreement between the UN and the US, the Secretary-General may ask the General Assembly to make a request.

82 Simma, *supra* note 57, p. 1196.

83 The range of the groups of functions that the Secretary-General can perform is large: Administrative, technical, financial, representational, and political. See Simma, ibid, p. 1207. For example: the Secretary-General participates in the meetings of all principal organs of the UN except the Court, and he also may be entrusted by the General Assembly, Security Council, ECOSOC and Trusteeship Council with some functions (Article 98 Charter). He has the right to convoke special sessions of the General Assembly and to bring to the attention of the Security Council any issue that in his opinion may threaten peace and security (Article 99 Charter): Also, Article 12(2) Charter requests him, with the consent of the Security Council, to notify the General Assembly of matters relating to the maintenance of peace and security that being dealt with by the Security Council. UN organs have frequently asked the Secretary-General or his official representative for advice on procedural and legal questions. See Simma, ibid, p. 1209.

84 See Schwebel, *supra* note 77; Szasz, Paul, "Enhancing the Advisory Competence of the World Court" in: Gross, Leo, *The Future of the International Court of Justice*, Dobbs Ferry, New York, Oceana Publications, 1976, vol. 2, pp. 531-532; Bedjaoui, Mohammed, *The New World Order and the Security Council: Testing the Legality of its acts*, Dordrecht, London: Martinus Nijhoff Publishers, 1994, p. 78.

85 Bedjaoui, *supra* note 84, p. 78. In contrast to this argument, Schwebel argues that "there is no reason to believe that, if the Secretary-General were accorded the authority to request advisory opinions of the Court, he would exercise the authority incautiously". Schwebel, *supra* note 77, pp. 876-878.

the argument for authorising the Secretary-General to request advisory opinions presupposes that the Security Council and the General Assembly are not prepared to make that request. In such circumstances, it would be very likely that the Secretary-General would lack the support of the political organs for making such a request. Therefore, Bowett concludes that such an authorisation might "heighten the risk of conflict between the Secretary-General and those main organs, and this may be too high a price to pay for the advantage gained."[86] Bedjaoui has stated that another reason behind withholding authorisation from the Secretary-General is fear that the Secretary General "would be politically over-strengthened if he were able to obtain from the Court opinions that might encourage him to exercise greater autonomy in his action vis-à-vis the Security Council or the General Assembly."[87]

Lastly, the Secretary-General's authorisation to request advisory opinions might embarrass the Security Council or the General Assembly if he referred a legal question to the Court where the Council or the Assembly, for political reasons, did not desire such a referral. Because of the above considerations it is doubtful, at least in the near future, that the Secretary-General will be authorised to request advisory opinions directly.

(ii) Specialised Agencies

Specialised agencies are international organisations of limited competence linked to the UN by special agreements under Article 57(1) and 63 of the Charter.[88] They may request advisory opinions from the ICJ on legal questions within the scope of their activities if authorised by the General Assembly to do so.[89] Provisions for such authorisation are contained in the agreements between the UN and the specialised agencies.[90] So far there are sixteen specialised agencies authorised by the

---

86 Bowett, *supra* note 1, pp. 187-188.

87 Bedjaoui, *supra* note 84, p. 78.

88 Sands & Klein, *supra* note 28, p. 77. The Convention on the Privileges and Immunities of the specialised agencies provides that specialised agencies means specifically agencies mentioned in the Convention, and any other agency brought into relationship with the UN in accordance with Article 57 and 63 of the UN Charter. This Convention was approved by the General Assembly on 21 November 1947, Res. 197 (III), Article 1. See also Article 57 and 63 of the Charter.

89 Article 96 (2) of the UN Charter.

90 For instance, Article 76 of the WHO constitution; Article 66 of the IMO constitution. See ICJ Yearbook, 2000, No. 54, p. 96. Article 9 of the agreement with the ILO provides: "[t]he General Assembly authorises the International Labour Organisation to request advisory opinions of the International Court of Justice on legal questions arising within the scope of its activities other than questions concerning the mutual relationships of the Organisation and the United Nations or other specialised agencies.

Such request may be addressed to the Court by the Conference or by the Governing Body acting in pursuance of an authorisation by the Conference.

General Assembly to request advisory opinions,[91] in contrast to the Universal Postal Union which has not been authorised in this manner.[92]

Specialised agencies cannot request advisory opinions beyond their sphere of competence, and each agency has a broad discretion to determine whether its request falls within its activities. As the Court stated in the 1996 *Legality of the Use by a State of Nuclear Weapons in Armed Conflict* Case[93] "each organ must, in the first place at least, determine its own jurisdiction."[94] However, it is ultimately within the powers of the Court to determine whether the subject matter of a request is within the legitimate sphere of activities of a particular organ.[95]

The Court generally interprets the scope of a specialised agency's activities in a restrictive manner. In order to illustrate this, the Court's finding in the *WHO Legality* Case is illustrative. Here the Court was asked whether the danger to health that would result from States using nuclear weapons would breach their international obligations, including those set forth in the WHO constitution.[96] The cardinal objections raised were whether the WHO was competent to request an advisory opinion on the legality of the use of nuclear weapons and whether the advisory

---

When requesting the International Court of Justice to give an advisory opinion the International Labour Organisation shall inform the Economic and Social Council of the request".

It is interesting to note that all the agreements between the UN and the specialised agencies which grant the authority to request an advisory opinion of the Court require that the organisation shall inform the ESOSOC, with the exception of the agreement with UNESCO. See Hambro, Edvard, "The Jurisdiction of the International Court of Justice", 76 *RCADI*, 1950, p. 149; Jenks, Wilfred C., *The Prospects of International Adjudication,* London: Stevens and Sons, 1964, p. 197.

91 Those specialised agencies are: International Labour Organisation (ILO), Food and Agriculture Organisation of the United Nations (FAO), United Nations Educational, Scientific and Cultural Organisation (UNESCO), World Health Organisation (WHO), International Bank for Reconstruction and Development (IBRD), International Finance Corporation (IFC), International Development Association (IDA), International Monetary Fund (IMF), International Civil Aviation Organisation (ICAO), International Telecommunication Union (ITU), World Meteorological Organisation (WMO), International Maritime Organisation (IMO), World Intellectual Property Organisation (WIPO), International Fund for Agricultural Development (IFAD), United Nations Industrial Development Organisation (UNIDO), International Atomic Energy Agency (IAEA). See ICJ Yearbook 1990-1991, pp. 63-68.

92 Article 32 of the constitution of the UPU refers disputes directly to arbitrators.

93 Hereinafter cited as: "the *WHO Legality* Case". ICJ Rep., 1996, p. 66.

94 ICJ Rep., 1996, para. 29, p. 82.

95 Pasqualucci, Jo M., *The Practice and Procedure of the Inter-American Court of Human Rights*, Cambridge: Cambridge University Press, 2003, p. 40.

96 The WHO question was: "[i]n view of the health and environmental effects, would the use of nuclear weapons by a State in war or other armed conflict be a breach of its obligations under international law including the WHO constitution?

opinion requested related to a question arising "within the scope of [the] activities"[97] of that Organisation in accordance with Article 96/2 of the Charter. The Court, however, refused to render an opinion on the ground that the WHO's request was *ultra vires*:[98]

> *It has thus been argued that World Health Assembly resolution WHA46.40, having been adopted by the requisite majority, "must be presumed to have been validly adopted" ... The Court would observe in this respect that the question whether a resolution has been duly adopted from a procedural point of view and the question whether that resolution has been adopted* intra vires *are two separate issues. The mere fact that a majority of States, in voting on a resolution, have complied with all the relevant rules of form cannot in itself suffice to remedy any fundamental defects, such as acting* ultra vires, *with which the resolution might be afflicted.*

The Court stated that in order to delineate the field of activity or the area of competence of an international organisation it is necessary to refer to the relevant rules of the organisation and in the first place, to its constitution.[99] According to the "well-established rules of treaty interpretation"[100] expressed in Article 31 of the 1969 Vienna Convention of the Law of Treaties, the terms of treaties must be interpreted "in their context and in the light of its object and purpose."[101] Therefore, the Court concluded that in the light of the object and purpose of the WHO constitution, as well as of the practice followed by the Organisation, the question put to the Court did not relate to the effect of the use of nuclear weapons on health, but to the legality of the use of such weapons in view of the health and environmental effects arising from their use. According to the Court, the functions listed in Article 2 "may be read as authorising the Organisation to deal with the effects on health of the use of nuclear weapons, or of any other hazardous activity, and to take preventive measures aimed at protecting the health of populations in the event of such weapons being used or such activities engaged in."[102]

The Court's opinion was that the question before it did not relate to the "*effects* of the use of nuclear weapons on health, but to the *legality* of the use of such weapons *in view of their health and environmental effects*."[103] The Court, after defining the WHO's functions listed in Article 2 of its constitution, concluded that

---

97 ICJ Rep. 1996, para. 18, p. 74.

98 The "*Legality of the Use by a State of Nuclear Weapons in Armed Conflict* Case", ICJ Rep., 1996, para. 29, p. 82.

99 Ibid, para. 19, p. 74.

100 Ibid.

101 Ibid, para. 19, p. 75.

102 ICJ Rep., 1996, para. 21, p. 76.

103 Ibid , para 21, p. 76, (emphasis in original).

none of these functions had a sufficient connection with the question before it and that "the legality or illegality of the use of nuclear weapons in no way determines the specific measures, regarding health or otherwise (studies, plans, procedures, etc.), which could be necessary in order to seek to prevent or cure some of their effects."[104]

The Court's view was that, whether nuclear weapons were used legally or illegally their effects on health would be the same, and the competence of the WHO to deal with those effects would not depend upon the legality of the acts that caused them.[105] The Court also pointed out that international organisations do not possess a general competence but are governed by the "principle of speciality":[106]

> *The Court need hardly point out that international organizations are subjects of international law which do not, unlike States, possess a general competence. International organizations are governed by the "principle of speciality", that is to say, they are invested by the States which create them with powers, the limits of which are a function of the common interests whose promotion those States entrust to them.*

The Court also held that:[107]

> *[T]o ascribe to the WHO the competence to address the legality of the use of nuclear weapons ... would be tantamount to disregarding the principle of specialty; for such competence could not be deemed a necessary implication of the Constitution of the Organization in the light of the purpose assigned to it by its member States.*

Furthermore, interpreting the term "wide international responsibilities" in Article 57 of the UN Charter, the Court held that those responsibilities are necessarily restricted to the sphere of public health and cannot encroach on the responsibilities of other parts of the UN system.[108] Therefore, the WHO was not competent to deal with the question of the legality of nuclear weapons.

The Court's decision provoked controversy. While the Court declined jurisdiction, it must be remembered that the Court has asserted on various occasions that only "compelling reasons" should lead it to refuse to give an advisory opinion when requested.[109] With this background, were there any compelling reasons for the Court to refuse to render an advisory opinion for the WHO?

---

[104] Ibid, para. 22, p. 77.

[105] Ibid, para. 22, pp. 76-77.

[106] Ibid, para. 25, p. 78.

[107] ICJ Rep., 1996, para. 25, p. 79.

[108] Ibid, para. 26, p. 80.

[109] See Chapters Three and Four, *infra.*

The WHO is one of the UN specialised agencies within the meaning of Articles 57 and 63 of the Charter and is entrusted with wide responsibilities related to health and, therefore, issues that affect peoples' health globally.[110] According to the Court, the question of the legality of the use of nuclear weapons did not fall within the WHO mandate. It held that the Organisation was only authorised to "deal with the effects on health of the use of nuclear weapons, or of any hazardous activity and to take preventive measures aimed at protecting the health of populations in the event of such weapons being used or such activities engaged in."[111]

Despite this finding by the Court, one can still argue that the question was within WHO's sphere of activities and that it was directly relevant to it. The question submitted was not devoid of a relevant object and purpose, and an answer by the Court would have given important guidance to the WHO in discharging its duties. Also, an opinion would have helped to develop International Law in relation to environmental and health matters. Indeed, the purpose of the Court's advisory jurisdiction is to provide an authoritative legal opinion to the requesting body and is a means of participating in the UN activities.[112] On the other hand, if we are to suppose that the question was improperly formulated and led the Court to misconstrue the question, the Court nevertheless should have felt called upon to accept the task of assisting the UN and should not have declined to give an opinion. The Court in such cases should utilise its discretion to reformulate the question in order to overcome abstractness, speculation or any other shortcoming.[113]

Moreover, the Court has applied the doctrine of implied powers in the absence of express provisions in the constituent instrument of an organisation in regard to its competence.[114] Such competence might be assumed if considered an essential for the promotion of its function. Indeed, one might wonder why the Court did not deduce from WHO practice that the WHO was attempting to exercise its implied powers to further its duties towards promoting peoples' health when the WHO requested the advisory opinion.

One might also disagree with the Court's findings, because the WHO is entitled to propose conventions, agreements and regulations, and also to make recommendations with respect to international health matters by virtue of Article 2(K) of its constitution. Akande argues that it seems logical that the WHO should have com-

[110] By virtue of Article 1 of the WHO's constitution, the objective of the Organisation is "the attainment by all peoples of the highest possible level of health." At the same time, Article 2 (V) provides that the Organization may "generally ... take all necessary actions to attain the objective of the Organization."

[111] ICJ Rep., 1996, para. 21, p. 76.

[112] See Chapter Three, *infra*.

[113] Such discretion was applied in the *Application for Review of Judgment No. 273 of the United Nations Administrative Tribunal* Case. Indeed, in this case the Court noted several irregularities in the way the request had been formulated. Despite such irregularities the Court did not decline to give the opinion requested. See Chapter Five, infra.

[114] For discussion on the doctrine of implied powers, see Section 2.2 in Chapter Six, *infra.*

petence as regards actions affecting the legality of activities affecting health since the WHO has the right to propose treaties dealing with things that are known to damage human health.[115] Nevertheless, the Court held that the WHO was not empowered to seek an opinion on the interpretation of its constitution in relation to matters outside the scope of its function.

Judge Weeramantry in a dissenting opinion rightly argued that there is an inconsistency between an agency having the power to seek advisory opinions on a question of law, while at the same time having no power to seek an interpretation of its constitution.[116]

3.2 Jurisdiction *ratione materiae*, or Subject Matter Jurisdiction

Even if the question posed for an advisory opinion falls within the scope of the requesting organ and is therefore admissible, the question must still be a "legal" one. This follows from Articles 96 of the UN Charter and 65 of the ICJ Statute.[117] It has been argued that if a question is entirely political in character, the Court in theory has no jurisdiction[118] and should refuse to give an opinion. In the *Expenses* case the Court held that it "can give an advisory opinion only on a legal question. If a question is not a legal one, the Court has no discretion in the matter; it must decline to give the opinion requested."[119]

The Court in its case law has adopted the principle that the question would have a legal character if it were framed in terms of law and raised problems of International Law, even if it had political or factual elements. In the *Admission of a State to the United Nations (Charter, Article 4)* Case,[120] the *Peace Treaties* Case,[121] the *Western Sahara* Case,[122] the *Interpretation of Agreement of 25 March 1951 between the WHO and Egypt* Case,[123] the *Legality of the Use by a State of Nuclear Weapons in Armed Conflict* Case,[124] the *Legality of the Threat or Use of Nuclear*

---

115 Akande, Dapo, "The Competence of International Organizations and the Advisory Jurisdiction of the International Court of Justice", 9 *EJIL*, No. 3, 1998, pp. 458 *ff.*

116 See Diss. Op. of Judge Weeramantry, ICJ Rep., 1996, p. 129.

117 See Articles 96(1) of the Charter and 65 of the Statute. The characterization of the legality of the question by the requesting organ is not binding on the Court. See Amerasinghe, Chittharanjan F., *Jurisdiction of International Tribunals*, The Hague; London: Kluwer Law International, 2003, p. 521.

118 Gerig, D. W., "The Advisory Jurisdiction of the International Court and the Settlement of Disputes between States", 15 *ICLQ*, 1966, p. 339.

119 See the *Expenses* Case, ICJ Rep., 1962, p .155.

120 Hereinafter cited as: "the *Admissions* Case", ICJ Rep., 1948, p. 61.

121 ICJ Rep., 1950, p. 65.

122 ICJ Rep., 1975, p. 18.

123 Hereinafter cited as: the "*WHO/Egypt* Case", ICJ Rep., 1980, p. 88.

124 ICJ Rep., 1996, pp. 71-72.

Weapons Case,[125] and lastly in the *Wall Case*[126] the Court had the opportunity to identify what constitutes a 'legal question.' The Court's consistent practice illustrates that it has always been able to answer questions placed before it, even if these were intermixed with political and factual issues or even if the drafting of the request was unclear.

Thus, the Court emphatically held in the *Wall* Case that "lack of clarity in the drafting of a question does not deprive the Court of jurisdiction. Rather, such uncertainty will require clarification in interpretation, and such necessary clarifications of interpretation have frequently been given by the Court."[127] The Court observed that throughout its jurisprudence there had been cases where the wording of a request for an advisory opinion did not correspond to the "true legal question" under consideration,[128] or that "the question put to the Court was, on the face of it, at once infelicitously expressed and vague."[129] Consequently, the Court stated that it had often been required to broaden, interpret and even reformulate questions put to it.[130] The Court concluded that, in the case under consideration, the Court would only have to do what it had often done in the past, namely "identify the existing principles and rules, interpret them and apply them …, thus offering a reply to the question posed based on law."[131]

Some scholars have also contributed to defining what constitutes a 'legal question.' Lissitzyn argued that in advisory cases the request must be "capable of being adequately answered by the application of judicial techniques within the existing framework of law."[132] Judge Dillard has noted that "[t]he notion that a legal question is simply one that invites an answer "based on law" appears to be question-begging and it derives no added authority by virtue of being frequently repeated."[133]

Before ending the discussion on the meaning of a 'legal question', it is important to recall that while the provisions of Article 96 of the UN Charter and Article 65 of the ICJ Statute have limited the scope of the request to a 'legal question', Article 14 of the Covenant of the League covered "any legal dispute or

---

[125] ICJ Rep., 1996, pp. 233-234.

[126] See the *Wall* Opinion at: http://www.icj-cij.org/icjwww/idocket/imwp/imwpframe.htm (accessed 21 October 2004).

[127] The *Wall* Opinion, ibid, para. 38.

[128] See the *WHO/Egypt* Case, ICJ Rep., 1980, paras. 34-36, pp. 87-89.

[129] See the *Application for Review of Judgement No. 273 of the United Nations Administrative Tribunal* Case, ICJ Rep., 1982, para. 46, p. 348.

[130] See the *Admissibility of Hearings of Petitioners by the Committee on South West Africa* Case, ICJ Rep., 1956, p. 25; the *Expenses* Case, ICJ Rep., 1962, p. 162.

[131] The *Legality of the Threat or Use of Nuclear Weapons* Case, ICJ Rep., 1996, para. 13, p. 234.

[132] Lissitzyn, Oliver, *The International Court of Justice: Its Role in the Maintenance of International Peace and Security*, New York: Carnegie Endowment for International Peace, 1951, p. 30.

[133] Sep. Op. of Judge Dillard, ICJ Rep., 1975, p. 117.

question."[134] However, the phrase 'legal question' would seem to be wider than 'dispute' and would even seem to include the latter. In this regard Hambro has pointed out that "any legal question" does not seem to allow for any restrictive interpretation.[135]

At any rate, despite the deletion of any reference to the term "dispute" in Article 96 of the UN Charter, the Rules of the Court contain provisions relating to the procedure to be followed in advisory requests concerning inter-States disputes, including the possibility of appointing a judge *ad hoc*. Article 102 of the Rules (1978 rules as amended in 2000) reads:

> 1. *In the exercise of its advisory functions under Article 65 of the Statute, the Court shall apply, in addition to the provisions of Article 96 of the Charter and Chapter IV of the Statute, the provisions of the present Part of the Rules.*
> 2. *The Court shall also be guided by the provisions of the Statute and of these Rules which apply in contentious cases to the extent to which it recognizes them to be applicable. For this purpose, it shall above all consider whether the request for the advisory opinion relates to a legal question actually pending between two or more States.*

Article 102(3) of the Rules provides that if the requested opinion relates to a legal question actually pending between States, Article 31 of the Statute shall apply.[136] As will be made clear in Chapter Four, the Court's case law indicates that the deletion of the word 'dispute' from the provisions pertaining to the advisory procedure does not prevent UN organs from requesting advisory opinions in respect of legal disputes between two States, or between a State and the Organisation as long as the question is a 'legal question' and of interest to the UN.

3.2.1 The Political Nature or Motivation of Questions Referred for Advisory Opinions

Objections to the Court's jurisdiction to give advisory opinions based on the political implications of a question have been frequently raised and justified on the grounds that these implications would risk politicising the Court. In the *Admissions* Case, the Court replied to the contention that the question submitted to it was political

---

[134] The jurisprudence of the PCIJ drew a distinction between "disputes" and "questions". The latter was meant to be the request for an opinion "to obtain authoritative guidance on a question of a legal nature arising during the activities of the Council or the Assembly of the League of Nations" while an opinion on a "dispute" was meant to be a legal dispute actually pending between two or more states. See Rosenne, *supra* note 2, p. 280.

[135] Hambro, *supra* note 90, p. 192.

[136] This Article deals with provisions relating to appointing of Judges *ad hoc*.

and that the Court therefore lacked competence to render an advisory opinion by stating:[137]

> *It has nevertheless been contended that the question put must be regarded as a political one and that, for this reason, it falls outside the jurisdiction of the Court. The Court cannot attribute a political character to a request which, framed in abstract terms, invites it to undertake an essentially judicial task, the interpretation of a treaty provision. It is not concerned with the motives which may have inspired this request, nor with the considerations which, in the concrete cases submitted for examination to the Security Council, formed the subject of the exchange of views which took place in that body. It is the duty of the Court to envisage the question submitted to it only in the abstract form which has been given to it; nothing which is said in the present opinion refers, either directly or indirectly, to concrete cases or to particular circumstances.*

In the *Expenses* Case, the Court again rejected contentions that it should refuse to give an opinion simply because "the question put to the Court is intertwined with political questions."[138] The Court's view was reiterated in the *WHO/Egypt* Case, which arose from a request by the WHO Assembly for an advisory opinion on whether transfer of its Regional Office would be covered by Section 37 of the 1951 Agreement between the WHO and Egypt.[139] In this case doubts were raised concerning the legal character of the question. The Court held that its jurisprudence "establishes that if, as in the present case, a question submitted in a request is one that otherwise falls within the normal exercise of its judicial process, the Court has not to deal with the motives which may have inspired the request."[140]

The Court has reaffirmed its settled jurisprudence on this issue in the *Legality of the Threat or Use of Nuclear Weapons* Case, which arose out of a request for an advisory opinion by the General Assembly, when it held that "the political nature of the motives which may be said to have inspired the request and the political implications that the opinion given might have are of no relevance in the establishment of its jurisdiction to give such an opinion".[141]

One could say that the Court regards all questions submitted to it as "legal" regardless of their political implications as long as the requested question can be answered by the application of legal rules. Scobbie observes that "[i]t has been a prominent feature of the Court's jurisprudence that the possible political ramifica-

---

[137] The *Admission of a State to the United Nations* Case, ICJ Rep., 1948, p. 61.

[138] *The Expenses of the United Nations* Case, ICJ Rep., 1962, p. 155.

[139] For further details about this Case see Section II in Chapter Four, *infra*.

[140] ICJ Rep., 1980, para. 33, p. 87.

[141] The *Legality of the Threat or Use of Nuclear Weapons* Case, ICJ Rep., 1996, para. 13, p. 234.

tions of an advisory opinion do not compromise its judicial character and thus involve no impropriety."[142]

In the final analysis, because all questions necessarily have a political background, attempting to draw a clear distinction between legal and political questions would be futile. However, the whole purpose of such an endeavour is to determine justiciability. The fact that the Court has a duty to clarify the law is paramount and should supersede other considerations. Indeed, the Court has a wide discretionary power. Therefore, it can reformulate questions put to it in order to highlight the legal points contained within the question. In general States try to avoid having to refer their vital interests to the decision of a third party.[143] This consideration can lead them to argue that the question referred to the Court is essentially political in character. In this regard it is important to cite the eloquent statement of the former United Nations Secretary-General, Javier Perez de Cuellar in the introduction to his last report, which provides:[144]

> *[E]ven those disputes which seem entirely political (as the Iraq-Kuwait dispute prior to invasion) have a clearly legal component. If, for any reason, the parties fail to refer the matter to the Court, the process of achieving a fair and objectively commendable settlement and thus defusing an international crises situation would be facilitated by obtaining the Court's advisory opinion.*

The Court at any rate must decide whether to take into account the political motives behind the request and subsequently decline to respond, or to answer the request in accordance with its duty as the principal UN judicial body, entrusted with responsibilities for coordinating with other organs of the UN in order to achieve its goals. The practice of the Court in dealing with the subject matter of the questions posed for advisory opinions is in harmony with the spirit of the UN Charter that places great emphasis on full coordination amongst the UN organs.[145] Finally, the fact remains, as Bowett has argued that "refusal to give an opinion ought never to be based on the ground that the question at issue is a "political" one: the distinction between "legal" and "political" questions has many meanings and should not be used as a *jurisdictional* criterion."[146]

---

142 Scobbie, Iain, "Legal Consequences of the Construction of a Wall in the Occupied Territory: Request for an advisory opinion, An Analysis of issues Concerning Competence and Procedure", available at: http://www.soas.ac.uk/lawpeacemideast/papers/1scobbie.pdf (accessed 23 October 2004), p. 18.

143 Higgins, Rosalyn, "The Place of International Law in the Settlement of Disputes by the Security Council", 64 *AJIL*, 1970, p. 14.

144 UN Doc. A/41/1, 1991, p. 8.

145 See Chapter Three, *infra*.

146 Bowett, Derek W., *supra* note 28, p. 278. (Emphasis in original).

3.2.2 Factual Questions

Following several requests for advisory opinions some States objected to the requests on the grounds that the question was factual question rather than legal. However, such arguments have never caused the Court to decline to render an opinion requested. In the *Namibia* Case the Court held:[147]

> *In the view of the Court, the contingency that there may be factual issues underlying the question posed does not alter its character as a "legal question" as envisaged in Article 96 of the Charter. The reference in this provision to legal questions cannot be interpreted as opposing legal to factual issues. Normally, to enable a Court to pronounce on legal questions, it must also be acquainted with, take into account and, if necessary, make findings as to the relevant factual issues.*

The Court rejected the notion that where factual matters require clarification a legal issue cannot be said to arise. In the Court's view, factual and legal questions may coexist. The Court reaffirmed this view in the *Western Sahara* Case where it was argued that "the questions posed by the General Assembly are not legal, but are either factual or are questions of a purely historical or academic character."[148] The Court dismissed this argument and stated that "a mixed question of law and fact is nonetheless a legal question."[149] The Court's case law on this issue is in line with that of its predecessor. In the *Status of Eastern Carelia* Case the PCIJ stated that:[150]

> *The Court does not say that there is an absolute rule that the request for an advisory opinion may not involve some enquiry as to the facts, but, under ordinary circumstances, it is certainly expedient that the facts upon which the opinion of the Court is desired should not be in controversy, and it should not be left to the Court itself to ascertain what they are.*

3.2.3 Abstract Questions

It has been mentioned in Chapter One that the PCIJ was never asked to give an opinion on an abstract question in the sense that the question was "purely hypothetical."[151] The ICJ's view in this respect has been manifested on various occasions. In the *Wall* Advisory Opinion the Court did not consider allegedly the ab-

---

[147] ICJ Rep., 1971, para. 40, p. 27.

[148] *Western Sahara* Case, ICJ Rep., 1975, para. 16, p. 19.

[149] *Western Sahara*, ibid; see also Elias, Taslim O., "How the International Court of Justice Deals with Requests for Advisory Opinions" in: Makarczyk, Jerzy, (ed.), *Essays In International Law In Honour of Judge Manfred Lachs*, The Hague; Boston; Lancaster: Martinus Nijhoff Publishers, 1984, p. 356.

[150] PCIJ, Ser. B, No. 5, 1923, p. 28.

[151] Hudson, Manley, *The Permanent Court of International Justice, 1920-1942: A Treatise*, New York, The Macmillan Company, 1943, p. 497.

stract nature of the question posed to it as raising an issue of jurisdiction. The Court observed that the contention that it should not deal with a question couched in abstract terms was "a mere affirmation devoid of any justification" and that "the Court may give an advisory opinion on any legal question, abstract or otherwise."[152] The Court in the *Wall* Opinion followed its own previous case law[153] and stated that the question posed was not an abstract one.

An abstract question need not necessarily be a vague one. Article 65 of the Statute provides that a request for an advisory opinion should contain "an exact statement of the question upon which an opinion is required." This requirement should suffice to limit the vagueness of the questions asked. In this connection Judge Azevedo in his Separate Opinion in the *Peace Treaties* case stated:[154]

> *No doubt it is always possible to discern at the base of any abstract opinion a specific situation which is alluded to remotely or indirectly; for, apart from any factitious attitude of mere curiosity, there is always a fact underlying any question. But it is necessary to refrain from too deep or too searching an effort for its discovery, not from a vain desire to create purely artificial situations, but to promote the usefulness of the advisory function by reducing the difficulties.*

It was feared by some States in the *Legality of Nuclear Weapons* Case that the abstract question posed might lead to hypothetical answers outside the scope of the Court's legal function. In this regard the Court stated:[155]

> *Certain States have however expressed the fear that the abstract nature of the question might lead the Court to make hypothetical or speculative declarations outside the scope of its judicial function. The Court does not consider that, in giving an advisory opinion in the present case, it would necessarily have to write "scenarios", to study various types of nuclear weapons and to evaluate highly complex and controversial technological, strategic and scientific information. The Court will simply address the issues arising in all their aspects by applying the legal rules relevant to the situation.*

Ideally the presence of elements of concreteness is desirable in a request. Judge Zoričić, in the *Admissions* Case, correctly stated that:[156]

---

[152] See the *Wall* Case para. 44.

[153] See ICJ Rep., 1996, p. 236, para. 15, referring to *Conditions of Admission of a State to Membership to the United Nations (Article 4 of the Charter)*, ICJ Rep., 1948, p. 61; *Effect of Awards of Compensation Made by the United Nations Administrative Tribunal* Case, ICJ Rep., 1954, p. 51; and *Legal Consequences for States of the Continued Presence of South Africa in Namibia (South West Africa) notwithstanding Security Council Resolution 276 (1970)* Case, ICJ Rep., 1971, p. 27, para. 40.

[154] Sep. Op. of Judge Azevedo, ICJ Rep., 1950, p. 85.

[155] ICJ Rep., 1996, para. 15, p. 237.

[156] Diss. Op. of Judge Zoričić, ICJ Rep., 1947-1948, p. 96.

> *In human life, all activity is based on concrete considerations or facts. To attempt to judge and explain such acts in the abstract would be to misconstrue the intentions, to work in vacuum, and to misunderstand the meaning of real life. This is still more evident in the case of a Court of Justice whose first duty is to decide whether certain acts are in accordance with law.*

In the final analysis, the Court's position towards abstract questions is clear, and objections advanced by the States regarding the abstract nature of a question cannot consequently lead the Court to decline to give the requested opinion.[157] One must take into account that, to a significant extent, International Law is interpreted and applied in the light of the case law of the ICJ.

Therefore in drafting a request for an advisory opinion a balance between abstractness and elements of factuality should be present. The question offered should not be narrowly defined and confined to a very specific point. On the other hand, the question should be phrased in such a way as to produce a broad answer not confined to the case initiating the question but also applicable to future cases. Indeed, this view is compatible with what was suggested by Judge Azevedo in his Separate Opinion in the *Admissions* Case that "it is quite fitting for an advisory body to give an answer *in abstracto* which may eventually be applied to several *de facto* situations: *minima circumstantia facti magnam diversitatem juris.*"[158]

4 The Advisory Jurisdiction as Subject to the Court's Discretion

Judicial discretion has been defined by Barak as "the power the law gives the judge to choose among several alternatives, each of them being lawful."[159] In this connection, Judge Bedjaoui has pointed out that "[w]hen a legal norm gives courts the choice between two or more solutions, all of them are legal ones therefore, it

---

[157] The tendencies of the Court, in general, seems to treat questions submitted to it for an advisory opinion as an abstract question. See Rosenne, *supra* note 2, p. 1004.

[158] Sep. Op. of Judge Azevedo, ICJ Rep., 1948, p. 74. (Emphasis in original). In the same context see the statement of the UK representative, where he stated that the requests were "specific legal questions" and that they "were of a general character, strictly legal in nature and limited in scope, and were designed to illicit the maximum guidance from the Court without calling upon it actually to retry the cases which had been adjudicated by the Administrative Tribunal." UN General Assembly, 8th session, 5th committee, official records, 425th meeting, p325. The statement of the UK representative in the fifth committee where the Court was requested to render an opinion on the obligation of the Assembly to give effect to an award of compensation made by the United Nations Administrative Tribunal.

[159] Barak, Aharon, *Judicial Discretion*, New Haven: Yale University Press, 1989, p. 7.

gives them latitude or freedom of decision, whence comes what is termed their discretion or discretionary power."[160]

One may wonder whether 'discretionary power' is inevitable. Roscoe Pound's answered this question by stating that "in no legal system, however, minute and detailed its body of rules, is justice administered wholly by rule and without any recourse to the will of the judge and his personal sense of what should be done to achieve a just result in the case before him. Both elements are to be found in all administration of justice."[161]

As far as the ICJ is concerned, the Court's power to determine its jurisdiction is distinct from its power to exercise its discretion when considering the merits of a case with which it has been seised.[162] When its jurisdiction to render an opinion is challenged, the Court will first consider whether it is competent to decide the case before it. If it finds that it has the requisite jurisdiction, the Court will then determine whether it will exercise that jurisdiction or whether to decline to do so. In the *Wall* Advisory Opinion the Court stated that "when seised of a request for an advisory opinion, it must first consider whether it has jurisdiction to give the opinion requested and whether, should the answer be in the affirmative, there is any reason why it should decline to exercise any such jurisdiction."[163] In *the WHO Legality* Case where the Court eventually declined jurisdiction, the Court stated:[164]

> *[V]arious arguments have been put forward for the purpose of persuading the Court to use the discretionary power it possesses under Article 65, paragraph 1, of the Statute, to decline to give the opinion sought. The Court can however only exercise this discretionary power if it has first established that it has jurisdiction in the case in question; if the Court lacks jurisdiction, the question of exercising its discretionary power does not arise.*

The constitutional basis of the ICJ's discretionary power in its advisory function is to be found in the terms of the permissive language of Article 65(1) of the Statute which provides that "the Court may give an advisory opinion."[165] The Court has

---

[160] Bedjaui, *Supra* note 5, p. 3.

[161] Roscoe Pound, Jurisprudence, Saint Paul, Minn. : West Publishing, vol. II, 1959, p. 355.

[162] For the power of the Court to decide upon its own jurisdiction see discussion above.

[163] See para. 13 of the Court's opinion.

[164] The *Legality of the Use by a State of Nuclear Weapons in Armed Conflict* Case, ICJ Rep., 1996, para. 14, p. 73.

[165] The term "may give" which is contained in Article 65 of the present Statute is deeply rooted in Article 14 of the Covenant of the League of Nations. However, this term has been subject to controversies during the League period, because Article 14 of the League Covenant, in its French version used the word "*donnera*" which means shall or will give, while the English version reads may give. The French version conveys a duty on the Court to answer the question. In this connection Judge Moore went on to say that "the contradiction between two provisions can consider that a difference in formulation." See Memorandum to the PCIJ, 18 February 1922, p. 385.

repeatedly made it clear, whenever confronted with a request for an advisory opinion that the language of Article 65 is permissive in character. In the *Peace Treaties* Case the Court stated that "Article 65 of the Statute is permissive. It gives the Court the power to examine whether the circumstances of the case are of such a character as should lead it to decline to answer the request."[166] Thus, in the *Western Sahara* Case the Court stated:[167]

> *In exercising this discretion, the International Court of Justice, like the Permanent Court of International Justice, has always been guided by the principle that, as a judicial body, it is bound to remain faithful to the requirements of its judicial character even in giving advisory opinions. If the question is a legal one which the Court is undoubtedly competent to answer, it may non the less decline to do so.*

The Court has taken a similar view in its advisory opinions in other cases. In the 1951 *Reservations* Case;[168] the 1956 *ILO Administrative Tribunal* Case;[169] the 1962 *Expenses* Case;[170] the 1973 *Application for Review of Judgment No. 158 of the United Nations Administrative Tribunal* Case;[171] the 1989 *Mazilu* Case;[172] the 1996 *legality of the Threat or use of nuclear weapons* Case;[173] the 1999 *Cumaraswamy* Case,[174] and lastly the 2004 *Wall* Case.[175]

This being said, the Court has repeatedly emphasised that, as the principal judicial organ of the UN, its opinion on a legal question posed by the UN or its specialised agencies ought not to be refused unless there are 'compelling reasons' to the contrary. In the *Wall* Case, where the Court reiterated its statements in earlier cases, the Court observed that "the reply of the Court, itself an 'organ of the United Nations', represents its participation in the activities of the Organisation, and, in principle, should not be refused."[176]

In the *Legality of the Use of Nuclear Weapons* Case, the Court, citing statements in several earlier cases, stated that only "compelling reasons" could lead it to refuse to give an opinion requested.[177] The Court explained that there had been

---

166 ICJ Rep., 1950, p. 72.

167 ICJ Rep., 1975, para. 23, p. 21.

168 ICJ Rep., 1951, p. 19.

169 ICJ Rep., 1956, p. 86.

170 ICJ Rep., 1962, p. 155.

171 ICJ Rep., 1973, p. 175 para 24.

172 ICJ Rep., 1989, p. 189 ff.

173 ICJ Rep., 1996, p. 234.

174 ICJ Rep., 1999, p. 78.

175 See http://www.icj-cij.org/icjwww/idocket/imwp/imwpframe.htm, (accessed 24 October 2004).

176 See para. 47 of the *Wall* Opinion.

177 ICJ Rep., 1996, para.14, p. 235.

no refusal in its history based on its 'discretionary power' to act upon a request for an advisory opinion, and that its refusal in the *WHO Legality* Case to give the opinion requested was justified by its lack of jurisdiction.[178]

Arguably there is no doubt that a literal interpretation of Article 65 of the Statute gives the Court a 'discretionary power' to reply or refrain from replying to a request for an advisory opinion. However, the judicial policy of the Court in exercising its advisory jurisdiction can be summed up in its tendency to respond affirmatively to requests unless there are 'compelling reasons' to decline.[179] As the principal judicial organ of the UN designed to serve the UN in its work, the Court's primary role is to uphold the aims and objects of the Organisation while at the same time preserving its own autonomy.

Whilst discussing the 'discretionary power' of the ICJ in advisory cases, it is important to note that Judge Abi Saab in a recent work[180] observed that there is an apparent contradiction between the Court's statement in the *Western Sahara* Case that: "[i]f the question is a legal one which the Court is undoubtedly competent to answer, it may non the less decline to do so,"[181] and its statement in the same opinion that "the reply of the Court, itself an organ of the United Nations, represents its participation in the activities of the Organization and, in principle, should not be refused."[182]

Judge Abi Saab observed that the Court on the one hand, said that because its power is 'discretionary' it can decline to give an opinion even if it is competent to do so. On the other hand, because it is 'the principal judicial organ' of the UN, the delivery of an opinion represents its participation in the work of the UN and so, in the absence of compelling contrary reasons it cannot refuse to give an opinion.[183] Judge Abi Saab examined the issue of whether the Court could exercise an unfettered discretion when exercising its advisory function. He concluded that the discretion in question is very far from being unfettered, and that it is in fact reduced to:[184]

---

178 Ibid, p. 235.

179 Although the Court did not declare these compelling reasons, it has been suggested that the Court might refuse to give an opinion if it found that rendering an opinion might complicate the matter or create difficulties for the UN in discharging its duties or that such rendered opinion would effect the Court's judicial character as a court of law. See Amr, *supra* note 61, pp. 108-109.

180 Abi Saab, Georges, "On Discretion: Reflections on the Nature of the Consultative Function of the International Court of Justice" in: Boisson De Chazournes, Laurence & Sands, Philippe, (eds.), *International Law, The International Court of Justice and Nuclear Weapons*, Cambridge University Press, 1999, pp. 36-51.

181 ICJ Rep., 1975, para. 23, p. 21.

182 Ibid.

183 Abi Saab, supra note 180, pp. 42-43.

184 Ibid, p. 45. See also the written statement of the League of Arab States in *Wall* Case. available at http://www.icj-cij.org/icjwww/idocket/imwp/imwpframe.htm, (accessed on 9 December 2004), p. 19.

> *[A]special duty of vigilance for the Court lest in any advisory proceedings (but also in any contentious proceedings) be trespassed those "inherent limitations" of the judicial function 'which are none the less imperative because they may be difficult to catalogue.'*
>
> *In other words, the 'discretionary power' of the Court comes down to no more than a wider margin of appreciation of the general considerations of admissibility('recevabilité générale' in French) of requests for advisory opinions, considerations whose default would mean that answering the question would be incompatible with the judicial function and not merely 'inopportune' or 'inconvenient' for the Court or for any other instance, and would thus constitute one of those "compelling reasons" which alone "should lead [the Court] to refuse to give the requested opinion."*

It is argued here that due to the place of the ICJ within the UN and its particular responsibility to share collectively with the other UN organs in the fulfilment of the tasks enumerated in the Charter's provisions, the Court does not enjoy unfettered discretion in terms of its advisory jurisdiction. It has a duty to give an advisory opinion whenever possible in order to assist the UN in its future course of action. However, the Court's 'discretionary power' is "circumscribed by the overriding principle of the Court's duty."[185] This 'discretionary power' is then subject to the test of what is compatible with the proper judicial function, namely the consideration of 'propriety', but it is not at all an unfettered power. Therefore, it has been rightly stated that the apparent meaning of the discretionary language of Article 65 is significantly offset by other Charter articles that oblige the organs of the United Nations to cooperate with each other.[186]

5 Concluding Remarks

The potential importance of the advisory function led the drafters of the UN Charter to extend the number of bodies authorised to request an advisory opinion, as compared with the PCIJ. Some twenty organs and agencies may ask the ICJ for advisory opinions. Although the Secretary-General has not hesitated on various occasions to insist upon his right to request an advisory opinion, he has not succeeded for reasons suggested earlier.

The Court's jurisprudence illustrates that, in giving advisory opinions, it is concerned about its position and role within the UN as its principal judicial organ. In general terms, the Court, when determining its jurisdiction in advisory cases, has adopted a liberal approach when the request emanates from UN political organs.

---

185 Amr, *supra* note 61, p. 106.

186 Memorandum of Egypt in the *Wall* Advisory Opinion p. 15. Available at http://www.icj-cij.org/icjwww/idocket/imwp/imwpframe.htm (accessed 16 November 2004).

However, the Court has been more restrictive and cautious when the request for an advisory opinion has come from a specialised agency.

The Court's case law also illustrates that, in exercising its 'discretionary power', it accepts its status as a "major participant in the activities of the Organisation and has acted accordingly, notwithstanding the permissive nature of Article 65 (1) of its Statute."[187] The Court's discretion is always circumscribed by its duty to act judicially and to preserve its autonomy *vis-à-vis* the UN organs.

Judge Ruda, in his Separate Opinion, in the *Review of Judgement No. 273* Case, was conscious to the Court's role and responsibility to the UN system:[188]

> *The main purpose of the advisory competence of the Court is precisely to assist, on legal questions, organs of the United Nations and the specialized agencies in the fulfillment of their functions; such assistance partakes of the very nature of the advisory competence. But, as the Court has always remembered, and as it does also in the present instance, such competence is discretionary, according to the clear terms of Article 65 of the Statute. The discretionary power to give or not to give an advisory opinion could have only one purpose, to leave to the Court the power to fix by itself the limits of the assistance to be given. Discretionary power means also, by its very nature, that there are limits beyond which the assistance should not be given.*

The next two Chapters continue the legal analysis by addressing the following questions: the effect of the 'organic relationship' between the Court and the UN on the processes of interaction and coordination between them, and the effect of such a link on the judicial Character and integrity of the Court.

---

[187] Weissberg, Guenter, "The Role of the International Court of Justice in the United Nations System: the First Quarter Century", in: Gross, Leo, (ed.), *The Future of the International Court of Justice*, 1976, p. 137.

[188] ICJ Rep., 1982, p. 377.

CHAPTER THREE

The Role of the ICJ as the Principal Judicial Organ of the UN and the Implications of This Role for the Court's Advisory Function

1 Introduction

The Court like other UN organs is bound by the purposes and principles of the Charter,[1] as Judge Schwebel writes:[2]

> *In reaching its judgments and advisory opinions, it [the Court] shall take account of the generally applicable provisions of the United Nations Charter, particularly its Purposes and Principles. That requirement does not detract from the Court's judicial character, not only because of the content of those Purposes and Principles (which speak,* inter alia, *of "conformity with the principles of justice and international law") but because the States and international organizations which plead before the Court in any event are obliged to take account of those Purposes and Principles.*

Both commentators and the Court have stressed the Court's institutional status, arguing that its integration within the Organisation structure has had, or should have, primary impact on its advisory function. The stress laid by the Court on its institutional status has taken the form of assertions that the delivery of an advisory opinion represents the participation of the Court in UN activities. Therefore, in the

---

1 The overarching purpose of the Organisation is the maintenance of international peace and security. This is to be achieved by "peaceful means and in conformity with the principles of justice and international law." See Article 1(1) of the UN Charter. See also Shaw, Malcolm N., "*The Security Council and the International Court of Justice: Judicial Drift and Judicial Function*" in: Muller, Sam A., *et al.*, (eds.), *The International Court of Justice: Its Future Role After Fifty Years*, The Hague; Boston; London: Martinus Nijhoff Publishers, 1997, p. 237; Keith, Kenneth, *The Extent of the Advisory Jurisdiction of the International Court of Justice*, Leyden: A.W. Sijthoff, 1971, p. 146.

2 Schwebel, Stephen, "*Relations Between the International Court of Justice and the United Nations*" in: Virally, Michael M. (ed.), *Le Droit International Au Service de la Paix, de la Justice et du Développement*, Paris: A. Pedone, 1991, p. 434.

absence of compelling reasons, an opinion ought not to be refused.[3] Similarly, commentators assert that the Court is *prima facie* under a duty to cooperate with UN organs by giving requested advisory opinions unless there are compelling reasons to the contrary.

This study contends that the exercise of the advisory function is essentially a two-sided process involving "coordination" between other UN organs and the Court.[4] Each actor must be mindful of the need to achieve the UN's purposes, and at the same time acknowledge the necessity for some degree of self-restraint. It follows, therefore, that the coordination envisaged emerges from the organisational relationship between the Court and other UN organs and should be based on the respective organs' sense of responsibility towards realising the purposes of the Organisation in accordance with the Charter and International Law. By requesting advisory opinions, the UN organs demonstrate they are concerned about the lawfulness of their acts, and by responding to such a request the Court exercises its judicial function. The Court coordinates with other organs either by issuing legal opinions, thus helping the UN organs to execute their duties, or by evaluating through a type of "judicial review", the lawfulness of UN organs' acts which have been already taken.

This Chapter introduces readers to a variety of questions raised by the Court's view of its advisory function, and thus provides a comprehensive background against which subsequent Chapters can unfold.

2 Organisations in General: A Theoretical Perspective

Depending upon the background and interests of researchers concerned with the dynamics of organisations, the emphasis on the dimensions and characteristics of organisations varies greatly. Nevertheless, scholars agree that organisations generally develop as instruments for attaining specific goals.[5] Parsons, for example, distinguishes organisations from other social collectives by noting that an organisa-

---

[3] See discussion below.

[4] Schwebel argues that "the fact that the Court is a principal organ of the Organization may influence its readiness to participate in the work of the Organization particularly insofar as it is requested by other organs to render advisory opinions." See Schwebel, *supra* note 2, p. 434.

[5] See Pfeffer, Jeffrey & Salancik, Gerald R., *The External Control of Organizations: A Resource Dependence Perspective*, Stanford, California: Stanford University Press, 2003, pp. 23-24; Zedeck, Sheldon & Blood, Milton R., *Foundations of Behavioral Science Research in Organizations*, Monterey, California: Wadsworth Publishing Company, 1974, pp. 25-32; Perrow, Charles, *Organizational Analysis: A Sociological View*, Great Britain: Tavistock Publications, 1970, p. 133; Parsons, Talcott, *Structure and Process in Modern Societies*, The Free Press of Glencoe, 3rd Printing, 1964, pp. 17-19; Bedeian, Arthur G., *Organizations: Theory and Analysis*, The Dryden Press, 2nd edition, 1984, pp. 2-3.

tion possesses some purpose or goal. Parsons argues that "primacy of orientation to the attainment of a specific goal is used as the defining characteristic of an organization which distinguishes it from other types of social systems."[6]

Sociologists and administrative scientists have argued that, as the environment in which an organisation functions becomes more complex, the organisation becomes more specialised.[7] Thus, each unit within the organisation is given its own task which should contribute to the overall shared purpose. This development consequently gives rise to the concept of interdependence between the various units of the organisation.[8]

Thompson suggests that both the "natural-system and rational models of complex organizations assume interdependence of organizational parts."[9] He goes on to argue that:[10]

> *To assume that an organization is composed of interdependent parts is not necessarily to say that each part is dependent on, and supports, every other part in any direct way. ... Yet they may be interdependent in the sense that unless each performs adequately, the total organization is jeopardized; failure of any one can threaten the whole and thus the other parts.*

This argument underlines the importance of coordination between the various parts of an organisation in pursuit of their common goals. The UN is no exception.

3 The United Nations Organisation

The delegates at San Francisco provided the UN with a decentralised structure laid out in the Charter. Thus, the UN is made up of the following principal organs: the General Assembly, the Security Council, the ECOSOC, the Trusteeship Council, the Secretariat and the ICJ. These are called the principal organs of the UN and usually comprise a number of committees, subsidiary organs and *ad hoc* bodies.

---

6 Parsons, *supra* note 5, pp. 17-19.

7 Rogers, David L., et al., *Interorganizational Coordination: Theory, Research, and Implementation*, Ames: Iowa State University Press, 1982, p. 11.

8 The recognition of each unit's domain (domain consensus) leads to interdependence between the various units. See Rogers, ibid, p. 10. Thompson argues that "[d]omain consensus defines a set of expectations both for members of an organization and for others with whom they interact, about what the organization will and will not do. It provides, although imperfectly, an image of the organization's role in a larger system, which in turn serves as a guide for the ordering of action in certain directions and not in others." See Thompson, James D., *Organizations in Action: Social Science Bases of Administrative Theory*, New York: McGraw-Hill Book Company, 1967, p. 29.

9 Thompson, ibid, p. 54.

10 Ibid.

All UN organs are expected to act within the framework of functions and powers conferred on them by the Charter.[11]

The term 'UN system' often refers both to the UN principal organs and the various specialised agencies connected to the UN by relationship agreements. Article 57(1) of the Charter defines specialised agencies as international organisations that have been established by treaties between States and that have been brought into relationship with the UN in accordance with the provisions of Article 63 of the Charter. The specialised agencies form a decentralised system. They perform global functions as defined in their respective basic instruments. At present, there are sixteen specialised agencies which have entered into agreements with the UN which determine their degree of closeness to and dependence on the Organisation.[12]

Judge Bedjaoui has argued that in general the UN is governed by four principles:[13]

- First, a specialisation principle whereby all UN organs are expected to act within the framework of functions and powers conferred on them by the Charter. Although the Charter delimits the functions and powers for each organ, there still exists some overlapping of those functions and powers.
- Second, a non-subordination principle between the principal organs. Although the Charter has delimited the functions and powers for each organ, there is no hierarchical order between the principal organs. Each enjoys autonomy while carrying out its special mission.[14]
- Third, the competence principle including the *Kompetenz-Kompetenz* concept. This is the logical consequence of the organs' autonomy which is derived from the above specialisation and non-subordination principles. Hence each organ may inevitably interpret from day to day those provisions of the Charter which concern its activities.[15]

Judge Bedjaoui further maintains that out of this system emerges a fourth principle, a coordination principle, which is in turn a logical consequence of the above three principles. Judge Bedjaoui argues that Coordnation principle obligates the organs to achieve the overall purposes of the UN.[16]

---

11 Idris, Kamil & Bartolo, Michael, *A Better United Nations for the New Millennium*, The Hague; London: Kluwer Law International, 2000, p. 16.

12 For the full names of the specialised agencies see Section II in Chapter Two, *supra*; See also Simma, Bruno, et al., (eds.) *The Charter of The United Nations: A Commentary*, Oxford University Press, 2002, pp. 947-950.

13 Bedjaoui, Mohammed, *The New World Order and the Security Council: Testing the Legality of its Acts*, Dordrecht, London: Martinus Nijhoff Publishers, 1994, pp. 12-13.

14 Thirlway, Hugh, "The Law and Procedure of the International Court of Justice: 1960-1989" Part Eight, 67, *BYIL*, 1996, p. 39.

15 UNCIO, 13, p. 831.

16 Bedjaoui, *supra* note 13, p. 13.

Before discussing what "coordination" might mean in the UN context, it might be useful to first summarise what has been written about "coordination" in the field of managerial studies.

4 Coordination: A Theoretical Perspective

Robbins defines an organisation as "a consciously coordinated social entity, with a relatively identifiable boundary, that functions on a relatively continuous basis to achieve a common goal or set of goals."[17] He went on to explain that the words 'consciously coordinated' imply management, and the term 'social entity' indicates that it is made up of people or groups of people who interact with each other within the organisation in premeditated patterns.[18] Robbins explained that:[19]

> *[B]ecause organizations are social entities, the interaction patterns of their members must be balanced and harmonized to minimize redundancy yet ensure that critical tasks are being completed. The result is that ... the need for coordinating the interaction patterns of people.*

In general terms coordination[20] is the act of working together and thus is a collective response involving more than a single unit.[21] The origin and necessity for coordination derives from the process of functional differentiation (or specialisation), and integration,[22] and is frequently suggested as a way to make the UN system function better.[23] It has been argued that, in the organisational context, coordination can be split up into *intra* and *inter* organisational coordination.[24] Dijkzeul claims that "[i]ntra-organizational coordination concerns the control and fine-

---

17 Robbins, Stephen p.°, *Organization Theory: Structure, Design, and Applications*, Prentice-Hall International, 3rd edition, 1990, p. 4.

18 Ibid.

19 Ibid.

20 To coordinate has been defined as meaning "to place or arrange things in proper position relatively to each other and to the system of which they form parts; to bring into order as parts of a whole." See Chisholm, Donald W., *Informal Organization and the Problem of Coordination*, Ph.D. dissertation, University of California, Berkeley, 1984, p. 14.

21 Rogers, David L., *et al.*, *supra* note 7, p. 179.

22 Dijkzeul, Dennis, *The Management of Multilateral Organizations*, Boston: Kluwer Law International, 1997, p. 64. This really points to dividing the organisation's goal among its units and how to obtain integration within it. See Lawrence, Paul R. & Lorsch, Jay W., "*Organizations and Environment: Managing Differentiation and Integration*" in: Brinkerhoff, Merlin B. & Kunz, Phillip R. (eds.), *Complex Organizations and Their Environments*, Dubuque, Iowa: WM. C. Brown Company Publishers, 1972, pp. 249-250.

23 Dijkzeul, *supra* note 22, p. 61.

24 Ibid, p. 64; See also Rogers, David, *et al.*, *supra* note 7, p. 11.

tuning of the internal work flows of one organization."[25] This fine tuning takes into consideration the shared task between the involved units, which is to be realised in accordance with created and/or existing decision rules established to deal collectively with the shared task.[26]

Despite the unique aspects which distinguish coordination from other forms of interaction, coordination has sometimes been seen as synonymous with, or defined in terms of cooperation.[27] However, specialists have shown that cooperation and coordination differ in terms of, first, the existence of decision rules (in the case of coordination) and, second the kind of goals that are emphasised. It has been suggested that the goals involved in cooperation are likely to be comparatively vague and the tasks less clearly delimited. Moreover, the outcomes of coordination and cooperation are different. With cooperation, participants seek to accomplish respective individual goals. Moreover, cooperation is more likely to be characterised by informal trade offs and attempts to establish reciprocity in the absence of rules.[28] With coordination the outcomes might be different to the initially preferred ones. Coordination is usually more formal than cooperation and may involve contractual agreements. Dijkzeul argues that "[c]oordination is more limited, it concerns systematically ordered forms of cooperation. Hence it often becomes more formalized than most other forms of cooperation."[29]

To sum up: cooperation has been defined as "[b]ehaviors that occur when it is perceived that the goals of the self and others are compatible and in which individuals believe they are benefiting both themselves and others."[30] By contrast, coordination differs from cooperation in two important aspects: first, the decision rules (or agreement) can be developed by the participants or mandated by a third party and second, the participants decisions are made with regard to their shared task environment and the focus is upon the attainment of collective goals, not those of the individual participants.

The above discussion suggests several requisites for achieving successful coordination. First, the various units involved in coordination are not expected to be competitors or mutually antagonistic.[31] Second, common purposes and shared goals are fundamental to the coordination process. Third, the existence of an agreement in which formal rules and joint goals are stated is usually a fundamental requirement.[32]

---

25 Dijkzeul, *supra* note 22, p. 64.

26 Rogers, David, *et al.*, *supra* note 7, pp. 12-13.

27 Deware, Robert & Aiken, Michael, *et al.*, *Coordinating Human Services*, San Francisco, London: Jossey-Bass Publishers, 1975, pp. 7-16; Rogers, David *et al.*, *supra* note 7, p. 12.

28 Schermerhorn, John R., "Determinants of Interorganizational Cooperation", 18 *Academy of Management Journal*, 1975, pp. 846-856.

29 Dijkzeul, *Supra* note 22, p. 64.

30 Greenberg, Jerald & Baron, Robert A., *Behavior in Organizations*, Prentice Hall, 8th edition, 2003, p. 412.

31 Rogers, *supra* note 7, p. 7.

32 Ibid, p. 13.

Scholars agree that coordination can be accomplished through several strategies,[33] and that the use of possible coordination mechanisms is contingent on the practical situation.[34] Moreover, the kind of mechanisms and the timing of their use "will constitute an important variable in the explanation of the degree and success of coordination."[35] At any rate, various forms of coordination mechanism can be applied simultaneously and in different combinations.[36] The major factor which may impede or hamper coordination is the need for mutual adjustment between the coordinating units. Coordination necessarily implies a loss of autonomy and therefore a loss of power for participants.[37] The strategic implication of placing a high value on autonomy results in an implicit hierarchy of preferred alternative strategies where the most preferred are proprietary ones because "these maintain possession and control over resources and protect boundaries."[38] On the other hand, it has been suggested that the quest for survival by an organisation is the prime factor motivating coordination.[39] This includes situations in which an organisation seeks to forestall or prevent future crisis which may imperil its success or even continuation.[40]

Approaching the ICJ for an advisory opinion represents one of the coordination strategies between UN organs. Both the requesting organ and the Court are concerned about achieving UN goals and the proper functioning of the Organisation, in conformity with the Charter and the principles of general International Law. It is suggested that the institutional relationship between the Court and the other UN organs should facilitate coordination among them to achieve the overall purposes of the UN. However, it is at the same time expected that UN political organs might view a request for an advisory opinion as a threat to their autonomy. Judge Bedjaoui has argued that for the political organs, and especially for the Security Council, consulting the Court would be incompatible with their autonomy to determine their own powers.[41] In general, the political organs may consider that reference to the Court would make them subordinate to an outside organ.[42] This is because of doubts concerning the effect of such a request upon their capacity or competence to continue to consider, or seek to resolve, a particular issue.

33 Ibid, pp. 17-26.

34 Dijkzeul, *supra* note 22, p. 71.

35 Ibid, p. 71.

36 Ibid, p. 66.

37 Ibid, p. 65.

38 Rogers, *supra* note 7, p. 11, 27.

39 Rogers, *supra* note 7, p. 54.

40 Ibid, p. 54.

41 Bedjaoui, *supra* note 13, p. 19.

42 Ibid.

5 The Organisational Relationship Between the ICJ and the UN: Its Implications for the Court's Readiness to Participate in the UN Activities[43]

As indicated in Chapter One, the relationship of the ICJ to the UN differs from that of its predecessor to the League because the PCIJ was not an organ of the League. By contrast, the ICJ is the UN's principal judicial organ.[44] It functions in accordance with the terms of its Statute, and "forms an integral part of the present Charter." The legal relationship between the ICJ and the UN is regulated not only by the provisions of the Charter but also by interorganisational agreements concluded in accordance with those provisions.[45]

For Keith, the 'organic relationship' between the Court and the UN is important because it highlights the closeness of the connection of the Court to the remainder of the UN structure. He argues that the closer this connection is, the more likely it is that the Court would give an opinion where it would be of great value to the Organisation, despite the Court's absolute discretion under the Statute.[46] This relationship strongly inclines the Court to answer a request for an opinion. Simma and others claim that "the advisory function of the ICJ, even more than its activities in contentious disputes, marks its role as one of the principal organs of the UN."[47] The Court, through its advisory function, has demonstrated its willingness to carry

[43] This Section is only concerned with the effect of this relationship on the Court's advisory function.

For a detailed discussion about the consequences of the institutional relationship upon both the Court and the UN, see Amr, Mohamed S., *The Role of the International Court of Justice as the Principal Judicial Organ of the United Nations*, The Hague: Kluwer Law International, 2003, pp. 26-41.

[44] See Articles 7 and 92 of the UN Charter and Article 1 of the Statute.

[45] See Articles 34(1), 34(2), 92, 93, 94, and 96 of the UN Charter. See also the relationships agreements between the UN and the Specialised Agencies especially clauses providing for furnishing information to be provided to the ICJ. However, all the agreements except that with the Universal Postal Union authorise the agency to request advisory opinion of the ICJ on any legal question arising within the scope of their activities. See Sands, Philippe & Klein Pierre, *Bowett's Law of International Institutions*, London: Sweet & Maxwell, 5th edition, 2001, pp. 78-81.

[46] Kieth, *supra* note 1, p. 146. Fitzmaurice argued on behalf of the United Kingdom in the *Peace Treaties* Case that the Court is organically and constitutionally linked to the UN. Therefore the Court is the organ to which the UN and other organs are entitled to refer for purposes of legal advice. This is "subject, therefore, to the inherent right of the Court as a court, and therefore as independent, and as the highest international tribunal in the world, to decline to give an opinion in a case where the Court itself considered that it would be wrong for it to do so, I respectfully submit, subject to those reservations, that the Court has unquestionably a right, and (with the same limits) an obligation, to give an opinion if it possibly can." ICJ Pled., 1950, p. 306.

[47] Simma, Bruno *et al.* (eds.), *supra* note 12, p. 1182.

out its task of assisting the UN by complying with duly made requests.[48] Judge Bedjaoui suggests that the Court has been assisting the political organs by rendering advisory opinions which take "into account its preoccupations or difficulties of the moment and by selecting, from all possible interpretations of the Charter, the one which best serves the actions and objectives of the political organ concerned."[49]

Klabbers, moreover, upholds the view that "[w]ithout having the needs of the organization in view, advocacy of the implied powers doctrine simply falls flat, and has little to offer: its attraction resides precisely in its being hooked up with a normative proposition."[50] He went on to state that the concept of functional necessity "is biased in favour of international organizations, and therewith based on the view that international organizations are a good thing."[51] This view is clearly asserted in the *Application for Review of Judgment No. 273 of the United Nations Administrative Tribunal* Advisory Opinion where the Court stated:[52]

> *The stability and efficiency of the international organizations, of which the United Nations is the supreme example, are however of such paramount importance to world order, that the Court should not fail to assist a subsidiary body of the United Nations General Assembly in putting its operation upon a firm and secure foundation.*

Nevertheless, as will be made clear throughout this study,[53] the Court while responsive to the needs of the Organisation has not been subordinate to any external authority in the exercise of its judicial function.[54]

The Court in several advisory opinions has emphasised its perception of its role as the UN's principal judicial organ.[55] In its most recent advisory opinion the, *Le-*

---

[48] Ibid, p. 1182.

[49] Bedjaoui, *supra* note 13, p. 22.

[50] Klabbers, Jan, *An Introduction to International Institutional Law*, Cambridge: Cambridge University Press, 2002, p. 41; For the discussion of the implied powers doctrine see Section 2.2 in Chapter Six, *infra.*

[51] Klabbers, ibid, p. 37.

[52] The *Application for Review of Judgment No. 273 of the United Nations Administrative Tribunal* Case, ICJ Rep., 1982, p. 347. Along the same theme Schwarzenberger suggested that in the advisory opinion on *Reparations for Injuries,* the Court resisted the suggestion to base the competence of the United Nations to bring international protection to its officials on the grounds of diplomatic protection, and based such competence on the more secure ground of the interpretation of the Charter. Schwarzenberger, Georg, *International Law as Applied by International Courts and Tribunals*, London: Stevens & Sons, 1957, p. 64.

[53] The following three Chapters deal extensively with the impact of the institutional link on the Court's view of its advisory function.

[54] Rosenne, Shabtai, *The Law and Practice of the International Court, 1920-1996*, The Hague, London: Martinus Nijhoff Publishers, 1997, p. 139.

[55] See Chapters Two, Three, Four and Five of this book.

gal Consequences of the Construction of a Wall in the Occupied Palestinian Territory,[56] the Court reiterated its view of its role as an organ of the UN. It was contended that the Court should decline to give the requested advisory opinion on the basis, *inter alia,* of the *Status of Eastern Carelia* Case. The Court however, stated that:[57]

> *The consent of States, parties to a dispute, is the basis of the Court's jurisdiction in contentious cases. The situation is different in regard to advisory proceedings even where the Request for an Opinion relates to a legal question actually pending between States. The Court's reply is only of an advisory character: as such, it has no binding force. It follows that no State, whether a Member of the United Nations or not, can prevent the giving of an Advisory Opinion which the United Nations considers to be desirable in order to obtain enlightenment as to the course of action it should take. The Court's Opinion is given not to the States, but to the organ which is entitled to request it; the reply of the Court, itself an 'organ of the United Nations', represents its participation in the activities of the Organization, and, in principle, should not be refused.*

In the above passage the Court made five important points:[58] first, it declared that "the reply of the Court, itself an 'organ of the United Nations' represents its participation in the activities of the Organization", second, the reply "in principle, should not be refused", third, the reply "is only of an advisory character: as such, it has no binding force", fourth, it follows that "no State, whether a Member of the United Nations or not, can prevent the giving of an Advisory Opinion which the United Nations considers to be desirable in order to obtain enlightenment as to the course of action it should take." Lastly, that while the consent of States, parties to a dispute, is the basis of the Court's jurisdiction in contentious cases, the situation is different with advisory proceedings.

Relying on the Court's dicta and on the fact that the Court is a principal organ of the UN and, consequently, has a duty to attain the UN goals, Rosenne, Azvedo, Kieth and Pomerance have argued that the Court, in its advisory procedure, must cooperate with fellow organs unless there are compelling reasons to the contrary. Rosenne has argued that the Court, in exercising its judicial function of deciding a dispute or in giving an advisory opinion, must "co-operate in the attainment of the aims of the Organization and strive to give effect to the decisions of other principal

---

[56] Hereinafter cited as: "the *Wall* Case", available at: http://www.icj-cij.org/icjwww/idocket/imwp/imwpframe.htm, (accessed 21 October 2004).

[57] See Para. 47 of the Court's Opinion. For the facts of the *Eastern Carelia* Case, See Chapter Four, *infra.*

[58] For a similar line of discussion see Gross, Leo, "The International Court of Justice and the United Nations", 120 *RCADI*, 1967, p. 339.

organs, and not to achieve results which would render them inconsequential."[59] Judge Azevedo, in the *Peace Treaties* Case, pointed out that "the Court, which has been raised to the status of the principal organ and thus more closely geared into the mechanism of the U.N.O, must do its utmost to co-operate with the other organs with a view to attaining the aims and principles that have been set forth."[60] Keith also suggested that "[t]he Court as a principal organ of the Organization is under a general obligation to cooperate whenever possible with the other organs and with member States in the attempted attainment of their objects."[61] Pomerance argues that the status of the Court as the principal UN judicial organ "would significantly influence the way the Court viewed its advisory task; it would provide the basis for judicial 'duty –to-co-operate' doctrine."[62]

A careful study of the commentators' views indicates that the UN purposes, as a shared goal for all the UN organs including the Court itself, means that the Court is under a 'duty to cooperate' with the other UN organs. However, one could argue that 'cooperation' may not be the proper expression to use.[63] The foregoing analysis of the concept of coordination suggests that when some legal writers state that the Court must cooperate with the other UN organs in attaining the Organisation's aims, they really mean coordination.

It is submitted that UN organs must coordinate in order to achieve the interests of the Organisation even if this interest clashes, on occasion, with the interest of the individual organ. On the other hand, the Court, if circumstances so require, ought to coordinate with the other organs in attaining the Organisation's objects, especially if giving an opinion would contribute to the smooth running of the Organisation. Therefore, international organisations should make full use of the advisory function, taking into account the safeguards recommended at San Francisco. Coordination among UN member States and between the organs themselves will give the Court the chance to meet the demands of the international community by either clarifying important legal issues for future courses of action or by ensuring the lawfulness of UN decisions. The latter aspect of the Court's coordination constitutes the material of the following Section.

6 "Judicial Review" as a New Direction

Despite the wide powers with which the Charter entrusts the two principal political organs, and despite the assertion in the Charter that Security Council measures

---

59 Rosenne, *supra* note 54, p. 112.

60 Sep. Op. of judge Azevedo, ICJ Rep., 1950, p. 82.

61 Kieth, *supra* note 1, p. 146.

62 Pomerance, Michla, "*The Advisory Role of the International Court of Justice and its 'Judicial' Character: Past and Future Prisms*", in: Muller, Sam A. *et al* (eds.), *The International Court of Justice: Its Future Role After Fifty Years*, The Hague; Boston; London: Martinus Nijhoff Publishers, 1997, p. 290.

63 See discussion above.

should be compatible with UN purposes and principles, the Charter and the Statute of the Court lack any mechanism to determine compatibility.[64] Of course, as the great majority of scholars agree,[65] the UN organs, including the Security Council, are limited by law and by the purposes and principles of the UN.[66] The ICJ, for its part has also asserted that the powers of the political organs are limited by the Charter. In the *Admissions* Case, and in replying to the argument put before the Court that the General Assembly and the Security Council have complete freedom in regard to the admission of new members to the Organisation, the Court stated:[67]

> *[T]he political character of an organ cannot release it from the observance of the treaty provisions established by the Charter when they constitute limitations on its powers or criteria for its judgment. To ascertain whether an organ has freedom of choice for its decisions, reference must be made to the terms of its constitution.*

Therefore, the issue examined in the following Section is not whether the UN is bound by the law or the Charter, rather the focus is on the Court's role in determining the compatibility of the UN organs' acts with International Law and with the Charter.

---

64 It was suggested that in the absence of any express provision authorising "judicial review", this power cannot be implied. See Skubiszewski, Krzysztof, "The International Court of Justice and the Security Council" in: Lowe, Vaughan, & Fitzmaurice, Malgosia (eds.) *Fifty Years of the International Court of Justice*: *Essay in Honour of Sir Robert Jennings*, Cambridge University Press, 1996, p. 623.

65 Bedjaoui, *supra* note 13, p. 35; Brownlie, Ian, "*The Decisions of Political Organs of the United Nations and the Rule of Law*" in: Macdonald, R. (ed.) *Essays in Honour of Wang Tieya*, Dordrecht; London: M. Nijhoff Publishers, 1994, p. 102; Shaw, *supra* note 1, p. 225; Judge Fitzmaurice also argued that the limitations on the powers of the Security Council "are necessary because of the all too great ease with which any acutely controversial international situation can be represented as involving a latent threat to peace and security, even where it is really too remote genuinely to constitute one. Without these limitations, the functions of the Security Council could be used for purposes never originally intended." See Diss. Op. of Judge Fitzmaurice in the *Namibia* Case, ICJ Rep., 1971, p. 294. Contrary to these views, see D'Angelo who argued that the Security Council must have absolute freedom to take the appropriate resolutions without "impediment" as any review by the Court frustrates the purposes of the UN. D'Angelo, Deborah, "The 'Check' on International Peace and Security Maintenance: The International Court of Justice and Judicial Review of Security Council Resolutions", *Suffolk Transnational Law Review*, 2000, p. 590.

66 See Article 1(1) concerning the purposes of the UN which provides that one of the aims of the Organisation is "to bring about by peaceful means in conformity with the principles of justice and international law, adjustment or settlement of international disputes or situations which might lead to a breach of the peace." Article 24(2) of the UN Charter which provides that the "Security Council shall act in accordance with the Purposes and Principles of the United Nations."

67 ICJ Rep., 1948, p. 64.

6.1 The Complexities of 'Judicial Review'

The extent to which the Court may exercise a judicial review function is the subject of extensive debate. Although the ICJ enjoys a very special status within the UN, it functions in accordance with its Statute which is annexed to the Charter and forms "an integral part" of it, however, there are no express provisions in the Statute authorising the ICJ to review the decisions of the UN's political organs. The San Francisco Conference rejected Belgium's suggestion that the ICJ should be granted the power of 'judicial review', and decided instead that each organ of the UN would be responsible for interpreting the provisions of the Charter applicable to its particular function.[68]

Rosenne asserts that proposals for judicial review must consider the following questions: the meaning of the expression,[69] who is to initiate review proceedings and who might be the respondent. Rosenne argues that the Court's Statute does not permit the Court to become a 'constitutional court' as "[i]t is neither in a position of superiority nor in one of inferiority in relation to the others."[70] Indeed, one must recognise that the UN Charter is not a constitution with a system of checks

---

68 UNCIO, 13, 1945, pp. 709-710; Watson, Geoffrey R., "Constitutionaism, Judicial Review, and the World Court", 34 *HILJ*, 1993, p. 13. In the same context, the Court has also asserted, on more than one occasion, that it is not a constitutional court. In the *Expenses* Case, the Court asserted the fact that proposals made during the drafting of the Charter to place the ultimate authority to interpret the charter in the ICJ were not accepted. See, ICJ Rep., 1962, p. 168. The Court has asserted the same meaning in the *Namibia* Case, ICJ Rep., 1971, p. 45; Sep. Op. of Judge De Castro, ICJ, Rep., 1971, p. 180.

69 The concept of judicial review, in general, has been defined by Kaikobad as:

[T]he power of a court or a system of courts to examine an act of either a constitutional organ of government, or of a statutory body or official thereof, with a view to determining whether or not the act is consistent with the provisions of the constitutions, a statue or statues or other sources of law and/or whether the said act is void and thus incapable of producing any lawful effect. Where the Court is satisfied that the act is in violation of the law, constitutional or otherwise, the decision of the court will have the effect of nullifying the offending act; but direct formal annulment is not crucial to the notion of judicial review.

See Kaikobad, Kaiyan H., The International Court of Justice and Judicial Review: A Study of the Court's Powers with Respect to Judgments of the ILO and UN Administrative Tribunals, The Hague; London: Kluwer Law International, 2000, p. 11. Moreover Amr defined this concept as "a judicial body within a legal system of the community reviews the legality of the decisions and acts of the executive and legislative organs in the light of the existing rules of law and the provisions of the constitution that regulate their functions either directly or indirectly." See Amr, supra note 43, p. 290.

70 Rosenne, Shabtai, *The World Court: What It Is and How It Works*, Dordrecht, London: Martinus Nijhoff Publishers, 1995, p. 36; Malanczuk, Peter, "Reconsidering the Relationship Between the ICJ and the Security Council" in: Heere, Wybo p. (ed.), *International Law and the Hague's 750th Anniversary*, T.M.C Asser Press, 1999, p. 88.

and balances[71] and the ICJ is not a 'constitutional court' regardless of the fact that it has been described as the guardian of legality for the international community as a whole.[72] The absence of hierarchy among the six principal organs of the UN and the nature of the decisions adopted by the Court indicates that the Court lacks the power to annul the acts of the UN organs.[73]

In responding to those who claim that the ICJ may assume the power of judicial review, by analogy to the *Marbury v. Madison Case* in the US,[74] it must be said that the ICJ is not in the same position as a supreme court in a national constitutional structure.[75] In a word, the system of judicial review as understood in municipal law is, to some extent, difficult to apply at the international level.[76]

On the other hand, and while denying the possibility of applying the system of "judicial review" as known in domestic law to the UN system, one must acknowledge that it is difficult to have "any real democratization of the United Nations without raising *inter alia* the fundamental problem of controlling the acts of the political organs, above all of the kingpin, the Security Council."[77] In order to ensure the rule of law, UN decisions must be compatible with the law. Therefore, some sort of mechanism to assess legality must be evolved.

---

71 Reisman, Michael, "The Constitutional Crises in the United Nations", 87 *AJIL*, 1993, p. 95.

72 Sep. Op. of Judge Lachs, ICJ Rep., 1992, p. 138.

73 See Kaikobad Kaiyan who argues that the Court's judgments are binding only on the States which agree to put a dispute before the Court, therefore, these decisions cannot produce direct legal effects in terms of nullification of any act of an international organisation. On the other hand he continued to say that the same propositions apply to advisory opinions which are non-binding. See Kaikobad, *supra* note 69, pp. 45-46.

74 This case has introduced the system of "judicial review" into the American court. See Reisman, Michael, *supra* note 71, p. 92; Watson, *supra* note 68, pp. 1-45.

75 Brownlie, Ian, "The United Nations as a Form of Government" in: Fawcett, J. & Higgins, Rosalyn (eds.), *International Organization: Law in Movement, Essays in Honour of John McMahon*, Oxford University Press, 1974, p. 26; Malanczuk, *supra* note 71, p. 97.

76 In this sense Kaikobad Kaiyan argues that:

Any attempt to transpose the municipal notions of judicial review onto the plane of international law must take into account not only the fact that most international legal concepts, principles and institutions are different from national legal system. It is also important to bear in mind that the notion in municipal law is itself beset with so many variations in nature [and] scope.

Kaikobad defines 'judicial review' in terms of international law as:

[T]he power of an international tribunal to pass upon questions dealing with the validity of international institutions action and decisions in the light of various principles of law, but mainly those originating in the relevant constitutive instruments of international organizations.

See Kaikobad, *supra* note 69, p. 27.

77 Bedjaoui, *supra* note 13, p. 7.

6.2 'Judicial Review' Within the Coordination Context

Some writers refer to the possibility of utilising the ICJ to render advisory opinions on the political organs' interpretation of the Charter and on the validity of UN organs' resolutions.[78] They suggest that the advisory function might "provide an indirect path to a judicial supervision of the decisions of organs of the UN and other international organisations."[79] Judge Alvarez has also noted that the failure to use the device of the advisory opinion to determine the legality of UN organs' acts seems to be "short-sighted" in view of the importance of the advisory jurisdiction in developing the institutional law of the UN.[80] Despite Judge Alvarez's recognition of the potential importance of the use of advisory opinions to restrain the actions of UN organs, he maintained that the Court cannot effectively review Security Council decisions due to the non-binding nature of its advisory opinions.[81] However, some commentators argue that the determination by the Court through an advisory opinion that a particular decision of an organ was illegal, would undermine the legitimacy of that decision and weaken its claim for compliance.[82] To borrow the words of Schermers and Blokker, "[f]or all practical purposes, an advisory opinion holding a UN decision illegal will have the same effect as an annulment."[83]

In practice, as Section 6.3 will demonstrate the political organs have used the device of the advisory opinion to obtain an interpretation of the Charter several times. Nevertheless, it is unrealistic to expect any reference for an advisory opinion to be made by the organs when a legal argument is raised against one of their own decisions or proposed decisions. These organs are unlikely to encourage the

---

78 Elias has argued that "the International Court of Justice should, to the extent of its power of review, be able to say whether or not one of the principal organs has acted *ultra vires* in any given case, albeit by way of an advisory opinion only." See Elias, Taslim O., *New Horizons in International Law*, Dobbs Ferry, New York: Oceana Publications, 1979, p. 89.

79 Gros, A., "Concerning the Advisory Role of the International Court of Justice", in: Friedmann, Wolfgang, *et al.*, (eds.), *Transnational Law in Changing Society: Essays in Honour of Philip C. Jessup*, 1972, p. 324.

80 Alvarez, Jose E., "Judging the Security Council", 90 *AJIL*, 1996, p. 8.

81 Ibid, p. 5.

82 De Wet, Erika, *The Chapter VII Powers of the United Nations Security Council*, Oxford; Portland Oregon: Hart Publishing, 2004, p. 58; Schweigman, David, "*The Authority of the Security Council Under Chapter VII of the UN Charter: Legal Limits and the Role of the International Court of Justice*", The Hague; London; Boston: Kluwer Law International, 2002, p. 278.

83 Schermers, Henry & Blokker, Niels, *International Institutional Law*, The Hague; London; Boston: Martinus Nijhoff Publishers, 1995, p. 576. In fact the lack of powers of annulment by the Court ought not to be seen as necessarily weakening the notion of judicial review because this incapacity is not a crucial issue here.

practice of 'judicial review', even on a non-binding basis.[84] This might explain why some organs seem to be wary of the Court. In this regard, Rosenne argues that one of the considerations which has led the Security Council not to request advisory opinions are doubts concerning the effect of such a request upon a continued consideration of an issue by the Council.[85]

However, "judicial review" can still be used to set legal limits upon UN organs' decisions. Even though the Court cannot give an opinion on its own initiative and given the fact that organs may be hesitant to ask for an advisory opinion if the risk of embarrassment is great,[86] the Court, through the indirect use of its advisory function, might still be able to challenge the legality of UN organs' decisions. Thus one organ could properly ask for an interpretation of the decision of another organ by requesting an advisory opinion.

Judge Higgins foresaw this eventuality and speculated on the possibility that the General Assembly "if aggrieved at certain decisions of the Security Council, [could] ask for an Advisory Opinion on whether they were lawful." Higgins would leave it to the Court to decide whether it wished to exercise its discretion by answering the question put to it.[87] Similarly Judge Alvarez suggests that the General Assembly might conceivably request an advisory opinion on the congruency of a sanctions regime established by the Council with the corpus of existing human rights law, or that the WHO might request an opinion of the Court on the health impact of a particular sanctions regime, or that ECOSOC might seek an opinion on the economic effects.[88] Further one can imagine the General Assembly requesting an advisory opinion on the abuse of the veto power by Security Council Permanent Members. Such coordination among organs requesting opinions concerning the compatibility of certain acts with the law "might create a kind of control upon the acts of the GA and the SC, thereby helping to protect the institutional life of the organization."[89]

---

[84] Schachter, Oscar, "The United Nations Law", 88 *AJIL*, 1994, p. 8.

[85] Rosenne, *supra* note 54, p. 144. See also, Section 5 in Chapter Nine, *infra*. It is interesting to note that the Security Council has just once approached the Court for an advisory opinion. See the *Namibia* Case in Section 6.3 below.

[86] Alvarez, *supra* note 80, p. 8.

[87] Higgins, Rosalyn, "A comment on the current health of Advisory Opinions", in Lowe, Vaughan & Fitzmaurice, Malgosia (eds.), *Fifty Years of the International Court of Justice: Essays in Honour of Sir Robert Jennings*, Cambridge: Grotius Publications, 1996, p. 577.

[88] Alvarez, *supra* note 80, p. 9, note 49.

[89] Amr, *supra* note 43, p. 72. In accordance with Article 12 (1) of the Charter, the General Assembly is prohibited from dealing with any dispute or situation, that is currently, before the Security Council. As a consequence of this Article if a matter is on the Security Council's agenda, the General Assembly cannot discuss the matter, or request an advisory opinion from the ICJ. See Amr, ibid, p. 73.

Through its advisory opinions and by exercising its judicial function the Court could then pass on the validity of challenged acts. In this context Shaw argues that, "[w]here the Court considers that it flows from the proper exercise of its judicial function, the Court may assert the competence to examine thoroughly particular resolutions."[90] As argued previously, UN organs have a duty to respect the law and this duty "is capable of judicial determination and is part of the function of the Court."[91] Shaw conceives that this judicial determination could be achieved with care and respect for the other principal organs and in "spirit of co-operation and in the light of the subjection of all UN organs to the Charter."[92] Because the ICJ was established as the principal judicial organ within the UN, it has a judicial duty to achieve UN purposes. Moreover, Skubiszewski has noted that the contemporary perspective of the problem of "judicial review" might be achieved in a different perspective. Thus he proposed that:[93]

> *[T]o achieve this we need a more coherent system of dispute management and settlement. One element of building such a system would be a better definition of the place the Court would have in it, a place of less isolation and more links and co-ordination with other modes and institutions. The Court would here be conceived as constituting part of a process of settlement without detracting from, and complementing, the traditional adjudication as an autonomous means where one party wins and the other loses.*

In the final analysis, the need to assure the legality of the UN acts cannot be achieved without the active participation of its organs, member States and the Court itself. The Court as the principal judicial organ of the UN is in a position to carry out this task through its advisory opinions, and therefore Judge Bedjaoui suggests that it is for the Court "to develop its advisory role and to go beyond the mere interpretation of the Charter in order to broach questions of legality-control if it has the conviction that it is thereby assisting the organ in question and contributing to the proper functioning of the United Nations."[94] The Court within the framework of its advisory function "could give an opinion not only on interpretation of the Charter but also on any questions with bearing upon the assessment of the validity of the acts of the political organs. From that angle, the Court is on a par (so far as the *scope* of its advisory jurisdiction is concerned) with the tribunals of broad contentious jurisdiction created by the most highly integrated organizations."[95]

---

[90] Shaw, *supra* note 1, p. 257.

[91] Skubiszewski, *supra* note 64, p. 627.

[92] Shaw, *supra* note 1, p. 257.

[93] Skubiszewski, *supra* note 64, p. 629.

[94] Bedjaoui, *supra* note 13, p. 86.

[95] Ibid, p. 85. In the above text the author was referring to the system of judicial review in the European system.

Therefore, coordination is a prerequisite in order to use advisory jurisdiction as a route for controlling the acts of the political organs. Any request for an advisory opinion needs the required votes of the majority in the General Assembly and the non-use of the veto by the Permanent Security Council Members. Unless this pre condition is satisfied a political organ can never be brought before the Court for the interpretation of a Charter text shedding light on the validity of a proposed decision.[96] Of course, the Court as a principal judicial organ of the UN must continue to assist the UN organs and consequently "contribute to the proper functioning" of the various organs by providing "useful" answers to the questions put to it."[97]

In this connection, it is interesting to note that despite scholarly controversy, the Court's jurisprudence provide several examples of the use of "judicial review", and, perhaps, precedents upon which its expanded use could be justified.

6.3 The Advisory Function as a Route for 'Judicial Review': Some Case Studies

This Section demonstrates how in practice the Court through its advisory opinions has dealt with questions of compatibility with the UN Charter. In this sense one must distinguish between situations in which there is an explicit request to pass upon the validity of an act of an organ or specialised agency, and second, where there is no such request but the Court passes on the validity while executing its judicial function. In the first case, it is obvious that the source of the power for testing the validity is clear: a definite request by the concerned organ. Instances of such requests include the 1960 *Constitution of the Maritime Safety Committee of the Inter-Governmental Maritime Consultative Organisation* Case,[98] and the 1955 *Voting Procedure on Questions Relating to Reports and Petitions Concerning the Territory of South-West Africa* Case.[99]

As for the second situation, the Court's power to pronounce on the validity of an act of a UN organ emerges from the fact that nobody can place any limitations on the Court when it is deliberating and formulating its answer to admissible question. As Rao observed "[i]t thus appears quite conceivable to acknowledge that the exercise of the judicial function of the ICJ could some times result in

---

96 Bedjaoui, *supra* note 13, p. 81.

97 Ibid, p. 86.

98 Hereinafter cited as: "the *IMCO* Case", ICJ Rep., 1960, p. 150.

99 In this case the question posed was whether "Rule F" formulated by the Assembly in Resolution 844 (IX) with respect to the voting procedure relating to questions and petitions on South Africa, was consistent with the Court's earlier advisory opinion of the 1950 *International Status of South West Africa* Case where the Court had held that the degree of supervision effected by the General Assembly must not exceed that which was applied in the Mandate system under the League". The Court decision was that "Rule F" was consistent with its previous advisory opinion. ICJ Rep., 1955, p. 75.

judicial review."[100] Cases relating to this second situation might include the 1962 *Certain Expenses of the United Nations (Article17, Paragraph 2, of the Charter)* Case,[101] and the 1971 *Legal Consequences for States of the Continued Presence of South Africa in Namibia (South West Africa) Notwithstanding Security Council Resolution 276(1970)* Case.[102] One example from the first situation (IMCO) and two examples from the second situation will be discussed to shed light on the way the Court has dealt with the question of compatibility with the UN Charter or with a constituent instrument of a specialised agency.

6.3.1 The 1960 *IMCO* Case[103]

The Court here exercised the power of 'judicial review' over the acts of one of the Specialised Agencies (IMCO) now (IMO). This Case involved the interpretation of Article 28(9) of the IMCO Convention after the failure of the IMCO Assembly to elect Liberia and Panama to the Maritime Safety Committee.[104] This failure led to controversy over the interpretation of Article 28 of the Convention. Article 28(9) laid down the rules to be followed for electing members of the Committee. Under this article the Assembly had to elect the eight largest ship-owning nations. Liberia and Panama were among the first eight on the relevant list of registered tonnage of IMCO Members.[105] Therefore, the IMCO Assembly raised the question as to whether IMCO, by refusing to elect Liberia and Panama, had acted in accordance with the Convention.

The Court examined the meaning of the terms "elected" and "the largest ship-owning nations" and concluded that "ship–owning nations" refers to registered tonnage, so that the largest ship–owning nations are those which have the largest registered ship tonnage.[106] Therefore, the Court held that "the Maritime Safety

---

[100] Rao, Pemmaraju Sreenivasa, "The United Nations and International Peace and Security- An Indian Perspective" in: Tomuschat, Christian (ed.), *The United Nations at Age Fifty: A Legal Perspective*, Kluwer Law International, 1995, p. 179; Judge Morelli also argues that "[i]t is exclusively for the Court to decide, in the process of its reasoning, what are the questions which have to be solved in order to answer the question submitted to it." He also argued that the requesting organ cannot "place any limitations on the Court as regards the logical processes to be followed in answering it.... Any limitation of this kind would be unacceptable because it would prevent the Court from performing its task in a logically correct way." ICJ Rep., 1962, p. 217.

[101] Hereinafter cited as: "the *Expenses* Case", ICJ Rep., 1962, p. 151.

[102] Hereinafter cited as: "the *Namibia* Case", ICJ Rep., 1971, p. 16.

[103] ICJ Rep., 1960, p. 150. The question posed was "[i]s the Maritime Safety Committee of the Inter-Governmental Maritime Consultative Organization, which was elected on 15 January 1959, constituted in accordance with the Convention for the Establishment of the Organization? Ibid, p. 15.

[104] Ibid, p. 155.

[105] Liberia was third and Panama eighth on the list.

[106] ICJ Rep., 1960, p. 170.

Committee of the Inter-Governmental Maritime Consultative Organization, which was elected on 15 January 1959, was not constituted in accordance with the Convention for the Establishment of the Organization."[107]

Although the Court was unable directly to nullify the election itself, this Opinion led to a substantial revision of the Agency's constituent instrument and to its transformation from an advisory body to an organisation with executive powers.[108] It was further decided to constitute a new Maritime Safety Committee in accordance with Article 28 of the Convention as interpreted by the ICJ in its Opinion.

6.3.2 The 1962 *Certain Expenses of the UN* Case[109]

The central question in this case, discussed in greater detail in Chapter Six, was whether the expenditure as authorised by the General Assembly, in relation to UN peacekeeping operations in the Congo and in the Middle East, constituted "expenses of the organisation." This question was not directed to the validity of the General Assembly resolutions which had led to the establishment of the peacekeeping forces. This is evident from the General Assembly rejection of the French amendment to the resolution requesting an advisory opinion which had called for a ruling as to whether the resolutions authorising the expenditures were decided in conformity with the Charter.[110] Nevertheless, the Court was convinced that in order to answer the question put to it, it had to review the resolutions authorising the expenditures. The Court stated that:[111]

> *The rejection of the French amendment does not constitute a directive to the Court to exclude from its consideration the question whether certain expenditures were "decided on in conformity with the Charter, if the Court finds such consideration appropriate. It is not to be assumed that the General. Assembly would thus seek to fetter or hamper the Court in the discharge of its functions; the Court must have full liberty to consider all relevant data available to it in forming an opinion on a question posed to it for an advisory opinion.*

---

[107] ICJ Rep., 1960, p. 171.

[108] Rosenne, Shabtai, "The Perplexities of Modern International Law", 291 *RCADI*, 2001, p. 454, footnote 832. Lauterpacht, Elihu, "The Legal Effect of Illegal Acts of International Organizations" in: *Cambridge Essays in International Law. Essays in Honour of Lord McNair*, London: Stevens and Sons, 1965, pp. 100-103.

[109] ICJ Rep., 1962. For details about the fact of this case and its significant impact on the scope of the General Assembly's powers *vis-à-vis* the Security Council, see Chapter Six, *infra*.

[110] Judge Bedjaoui argues that even when the Court is called upon to examine only certain aspects of a problem, "it is not required to shut its eyes to any part of the relevant legal background." Bedjaoui, *supra* note 13, p. 86.

[111] ICJ Rep., 1962, p. 157.

The Court examined the resolutions which established the UN Emergency Force in the Middle East (UNEF) and concluded that they were valid.[112] However, the Court in this case endorsed " a presumption of validity" for decisions taken by the political organs whenever these decisions are appropriate for the fulfilment of the UN purposes and concluded that "when the Organization takes action which warrants the assertion that it was appropriate for the fulfilment of one of the stated purposes of the United Nations, the presumption is that such action is not *ultra vires* the Organization."[113]

6.3.3 The 1971 *Namibia* Case

As a consequence of the continuing presence of South Africa in South West Africa, and its maintenance a system of apartheid there, the General Assembly adopted Resolution No 2145 (XXI) of 27 October 1966 which declared that South Africa had violated the League of Nations Mandate. It therefore terminated the Mandate and declared that South Africa had no right to administer the territory.[114] Subsequently, the Security Council adopted several resolutions including Resolution 264 (1969) declaring that South West Africa's continued presence in Namibia was illegal and called upon South Africa to withdraw.[115] However, South Africa refused to comply and the Security Council, for the first time, requested an advisory opinion on the legal consequences of South Africa's continued presence in Namibia.[116]

South Africa objected, *inter alia*, that a series of Assembly and Council resolutions particularly General Assembly Resolution 2145 (XXI) and Security Council Resolutions 264 (1969) and 248 (1970) were invalid and had no legal effect on the Mandate of South West Africa. The Court after deciding its competence to hear the case considered the contention of France and South Africa that the General Assembly, when adopting resolution 2145 (XXI), had acted *ultra vires*. The Court stated that:[117]

> *Before considering this objection, it is necessary for the Court to examine the observations made and the contentions advanced as to whether the Court should go into this question. It was suggested that though the request was not directed to the question of the General Assembly resolution and of the related Security Council resolutions, this*

[112] Higgins noted that the Court, by reaching this decision in the *Expenses* Case, had confirmed the legality of peace- keeping operation in Middle East and in the Congo. See Higgins, Rosalyn, "Peace and Security Achievements and Failures", 6 *EJIL*, 1995, p. 448.

[113] ICJ Rep., p. 168.

[114] GA Res. No. 2145 (XXI) of October 27 1966. UN. GAOR, 21st session, supp No, 16.

[115] See SC Res. No. 264, 1969, UN, SCOR, 24th session.

[116] SC Res. No. 284, 1970, SCOR, 15th session, 1550th meeting.

[117] ICJ Rep, 1971, para. 88-89, p. 45.

did not preclude the Court from making such an enquiry. On the other hand it was contended that the Court was not authorized by the terms of the request, in the light of the discussions preceding it, to go into the validity of these resolutions. It was argued that the Court should not assume powers of judicial review of the action taken by the other principal organs of the United Nations without specific request to that effect, nor act as a Court of appeal from their decisions.

Undoubtedly, the Court does not possess powers of judicial review or appeal in respect of the decisions taken by the United Nations Organs concerned. The question of the validity or conformity with the Charter of General Assembly resolution 2145 (XXI) or of related Security Council resolutions does not form the subject of the request for advisory opinion. However, in the exercise of its judicial function and since objections have been advanced the Court, in the course of its reasoning, will consider these objections before determining any legal consequences arising from those resolutions.

A careful reading of the above long passage demonstrates that although the Court stated that it did not possess the power of judicial review, it nevertheless reviewed the validity of the Security Council Resolution and examined the relationship of the Security Council Resolution to the UN's purposes.

The Court also examined the validity of the General Assembly Resolution which terminated the Mandate in South West Africa. It concluded that the Assembly had the power to terminate the Mandate, and that it did not exceed its competence by declaring South Africa's presence illegal and consequently terminating the mandate.[118] The Court stated that:[119]

The resolution in question is therefore to be viewed as the exercise of the right to terminate a relationship in case of a deliberate and persistent violation of obligations which destroys the very object and purpose of that relationship.

The Court stated also that the General Assembly "lacking the necessary powers to ensure the withdrawal of South Africa from the Territory, it enlisted the co-operation of the Security Council by calling the latter's attention to the resolution, thus acting in accordance with Article 11, paragraph 2, of the Charter."[120] The

---

[118] ICJ Rep., 1971, para. 88-89, p. 45.

[119] Ibid, Para. 95, p. 47. The Court also concluded that it would not be correct to assume that because the General Assembly is, in principle, vested with recommendatory powers, it is debarred from adopting in special cases, within the framework of its competence, resolutions which make determinations or have operative design. See para. 105, p. 50.

[120] Ibid, para. 106, p. 51.

Court, further held that the Security Council Resolutions leading up to Resolution 276 (1970)[121] were valid as they were adopted in accordance with the purposes and principles of the Charter and in the exercise of the Council's responsibilities of maintaining peace and security.[122] Consequently the decisions bound all member States.[123]

It has been observed that despite the careful drafting of the Security Council's request to the Court in order to avoid testing the underlying issue of the validity of General Assembly Resolution 2145, the Court considered the validity of both the General Assembly and the Security Council Resolutions.[124]

Before ending the discussion about 'judicial review' and for the sake of completeness, one contentious case namely the Case Concerning Questions of Interpretation and Application of the 1971 Montreal Convention Arising from the Aerial Incident at Lockerbie,[125] will be singled out for a brief legal analysis to illustrate the relationship between one of the political organs and the Court.

6.3.4 The 1992 *Lockerbie* Case

In 1992 the Security Council adopted Resolution 731 requiring Libya to surrender two Libyan nationals charged with terrorism to the UK and the US and to pay appropriate compensation.[126] Libya claimed that the Security Council's resolution was *ultra vires* because it violated the fundamental principle of international law by which a State cannot be forced to extradite its own nationals. Libya also regarded the question of extradition as falling within the scope of the Montreal Con-

---

[121] This Resolution adopted on January 30, 1970 reaffirmed General Assembly Resolution 2145 (XXI) of October 1966, whereby the General Assembly had decided that the Mandate of South Africa was terminated and declared that all acts taken by the Government of South Africa on behalf of, or concerning Namibia after the termination of the Mandate were illegal and invalid. This resolution also recalled Security Council Resolution 269 (1960) which was adopted on 12 August 1969 and condemned South Africa for its refusal to comply with Resolution 264(1969) and called upon States to refrain from all dealings with South Africa in respect of Namibia.

[122] ICJ Rep, 1971, pp. 51–53. The Court stated: "the decisions made by the Security Council in paragraphs 2 and 5 of the resolution 276 (1970), as related to paragraph 3 of the resolution 264 (1969) and paragraph 5 of resolution 269 (1969), were adopted in conformity with the purposes and principles of the Charter and in accordance with its Articles 24 and 25." Ibid, para. 115, p. 53.

[123] Ibid, para. 116, p. 54.

[124] Butcher, Goler T., "The Consonance of U.S. Positions with the International Court's Advisory Opinions" in Damrosch Lori F. (ed.), *The International Court of Justice at a Crossroads*, Dobbs Ferry, New York: Transnational Publishers Inc., 1987, p. 436.

[125] Hereinafter cited as: "the *Lockerbie* Case."

[126] For the discussion of the *Lockerbie* Case, see Marcella, David, "Passport to Justice: Internationalizing the Political Question Doctrine for Application in the World Court", 40 *HILJ,* 1999, pp. 81-150.

vention for the Suppression of Unlawful Acts against the Safety of Civil Aviation of 23 September 1971 to which all three States were parties.[127]

On the basis of Article 14 of the Montreal Convention, Libya requested the ICJ to determine whether Libya was under a legal obligation to extradite two of its own nationals.[128] In addition, Libya brought an application before the ICJ asking the Court to indicate provisional measures against the UK and US under Article 41 of the ICJ Statute, which provides for such an order in circumstances where it is necessary to preserve the respective rights of the parties.

While the case was *sub judice*, the Security Council adopted Resolution 748 under Chapter VII of the Charter requiring Libya to extradite its two nationals, and providing that in the case of non-compliance, the Security Council would impose an arms embargo on Libya.[129] Bedjaoui suggested that the Council by adopting this resolution:[130]

> *[F]aced the Court with the highly invidious choice to "follow" the Council at the cost of resigning its role or to take the responsibility of entering into open conflict with the Council. Above all, it would mean disregarding the duty of United Nations organs to place their* functional co-operation *in the forefront of their concerns. It is a necessary extrapolation from the inter-state co-operation hymned by so many articles of the Charter that co-ordination should prevail within the Organization itself.*

The Court rejected the Libyan request for provisional measures and did not question the validity of the Council's Resolution.[131] In light of this outcome Akande argues that the Court assumed the validity of the resolution and proceeded accordingly.[132] In trying to understand why the Court was so hesitant to pronounce on

---

[127] Hereinafter cited as: "Montreal Convention", Reprinted in 10 International Legal Materials, 1971.

[128] Article 14 provides that: "Any dispute between two or more Contracting States concerning the interpretation or application of this Convention which cannot be settled through negotiation, shall, at the request of one of them, be submitted to arbitration. If within six months from the date of the request for arbitration the Parties are unable to agree on the organization of the arbitration, any one of those Parties may refer the dispute to the International Court of Justice by request in conformity with the Statute of the Court."

[129] See SC Res. 748, UN, SCOR, 47th Session, 3063rd mtg., 31 March 1992.

[130] Bedjaoui, *supra* note 13, p. 74.

[131] The Court by eleven votes to five, found that the circumstances of the case were not "such as to require the exercise of its power under Article 41 of the Statute to indicate provisional measures."

[131] ICJ Rep., 1992, p. 127.

[132] Akande, Dapo, "The International Court of Justice and the Security Council: Is There Room for Judicial Control of Decisions of the Political Organs?", 46 *ICLQ*, 1997, p. 341.

the Security Council Resolution, Rosenne concluded that the Court was careful "not to trespass on the competence of the Security Council, despite powerful urgings, both in the pleadings and in the internal deliberations of the Court, that it take[s] action which could be interpreted as "judicial control" of the decisions of the Security Council."[133] Some commentators suggest that the Court realised that "had it acted otherwise, had it indicated any measures (whether those requested by Libya or those of its own choice), it would have contradicted the Council."[134]

Indeed, one must acknowledge that due to a lack of complete separation of powers between the Security Council and the Court in the issue of settlement of disputes, the two organs have to work in harmony, not in competition, in order to avoid any divergence between the decisions of the two organs on the same issue. It is submitted here that the political organs and more specifically the Security Council, have to coordinate with the Court by doing several things: first, although nothing requires any UN organ to ask for an advisory opinion of the Court, it would be important if these organs approached the Court through the medium of an advisory opinion before taking a decision in a delicate and important matter.

For instance, in the *Lockerbie* Case the Security Council, before adopting resolution 731 of 21 January 1992, could have requested an advisory opinion on the proposed measures to be taken. Second, although the Security Council, by adopting both resolutions, was acting within the sphere of its competence, it would have been better if the Council had delayed its second Resolution until the Court had given its opinion. Finally, the Court's attitude in *Lockerbie* might be criticised because, by not examining the legality of the Security Council resolution, the Court placed its integrity and its role as a judicial organ in question.

7 Concluding Remarks

This Chapter has examined the institutional relationship between the ICJ and the UN and the effects of this relationship on the Court's advisory function. It has been shown through examining some of the relevant Court case-law that this relationship has been highly relevant to the attitude of the Court when giving advisory opinions.

As the remainder of this study will argue, the Court seems to adopt a liberal approach when considering requests for advisory opinions. In a word, the Court's assertion of the organisational interest underlying requests for an advisory opinion, the Court's practice in reformulating requests for an advisory opinion in order to give maximum assistance to a fellow organ and the Court's practice in giving effect to the UN organs' decisions are examples of the impact of the institutional setting on the Court's advisory function.

---

[133] Rosenne, *supra* note 70, p. 251.

[134] Skubiszewski, *supra* note 37, p. 617.

On the other hand, this 'organic relationship' between the Court and the UN has had less effect on the attitude of the political organs which have been largely cautious of developing the habit of approaching the Court whenever the need arises. The reasons for this caution are discussed in Chapters Seven and Nine. However, it should be clear that the Court's coordination with the UN organs, which is manifested by its liberal approach in dealing with requests for advisory opinions, did not affect the integrity of the Court as the following Chapter demonstrates.

CHAPTER FOUR

The Judicial Character of the ICJ's Advisory Function and the Problem of Consent

1 Introduction

The preceding Chapter discussed how the institutional link between the Court as the 'principal judicial organ of the United Nations' and the rest of the UN Organisation has influenced the Court's behaviour.[1] Because of this relationship the Court has reasoned that, as an organ of the UN, its answer to requests for advisory opinions "represents its participation in the activities of the Organization, and, in principle, should not be refused."[2] Consequently, only "compelling reasons" should prevent the Court from giving the opinion requested.[3]

Although the Court regards the rendering of advisory opinions as a kind of participation in UN activities, there are certain limits to this participation.[4] These limits flow from the fact that the Court, while acting in an advisory capacity, must still adhere to its judicial character. This principle was laid down by the PCIJ in the *Status of Eastern Carelia* Case where the Court held that "the Court, being a Court of Justice, cannot, even in giving advisory opinions, depart from the essen-

---

1 Nantwi has suggested that a logical consequence of the special relationship between the Court and the UN is that the Court "is *bound* to co-operate with the organs of the United Nations and to act in conformity with the provisions of the Charter as well as those of its Statute" as far as it is consistent with the Court's essentially judicial character. Nantwi, Emmanuel K., *The Enforcement of International Judicial Decisions and Arbitral Awards in Public International Law*, Leyden: A.W. Sijthoff, 2nd printing, 1966, p. 14. (Emphasis in original).

2 See the *Difference Relating to Immunity From Legal Process of A Special Rapporteur of the Commission on Human Rights* Case, ICJ Rep., 1999, p. 78; the *Interpretation of Peace Treaties, First Phase*, ICJ Rep., 1950, p. 71.

3 *The Legality of the Threat or Use of Nuclear Weapons* Case, ICJ Rep., 1996, para.14, p. 235; see also the *Applicability of Article VI, Section 22, of the Convention on the Privileges and Immunities of the United Nations* Case, ICJ Rep., 1989, para.37, pp. 190-191; the *Certain Expenses of the UN* Case, ICJ Rep., 1962, p. 155.

4 The *Interpretation of Peace Treaties* Case *(First Phase)*, ICJ Rep., 1950, p. 71.

tial rules guiding their activity as a Court."[5] This Chapter explores how the Court has reconciled its role as a principal organ of the UN with its duty to adhere to its judicial character.

2 The Court as an Organ of the UN and the Nature of Its Judicial Character

Pomerance claims that the Court's awareness of its duty to cooperate with other UN organs has led to the "overlooking and overcoming of difficulties in order to extend maximal assistance to fellow organs and agencies of the UN" when dealing with a request for an advisory opinion.[6] Consequently, Pomerance, basing her conclusions on some of the Court's case law, has stated that the Court has not embraced the philosophy of "judicial restraint" in its advisory opinions.[7] In the absence of restraint on the part of the Court, Pomerance suggests that the UN political organs themselves must exercise "political restraint" when requesting advisory opinions.[8]

---

5 Hereinafter cited as: "the *Eastern Carelia* Case", PCIJ, Ser.B, No.5, p. 29.

6 Pomerance claims that over the years many compelling reasons have been invoked to prevent the Court from giving advisory opinions such as (the political nature of the question and the absence of consent on the part of states principally concerned), however, none of those reasons have ever been found compelling. Pomerance, Michla, "The Advisory Role of the International Court of Justice and its 'Judicial' Character: Past and Future Prisms", in: Muller, A. S. & Raic, D. *et al.* (eds.), *The International Court of Justice: Its Future Role After Fifty Years,* The Hague; Boston; London: Martinus Nijhoff Publishers, 1997, p. 290 *ff.* For a discussion about this statement, namely, ' a duty to cooperate' see Section 5 in Chapter Three, *supra.*

7 Pomerance while auditing the Court's advisory practice concluded that:

[T]he Court has not prone to adopt a philosophy of 'judicial restraint'. As opposed to the US Supreme Court, which often asserts a 'political question doctrine' and, even when it does not, frequently exhibits a "political questions mentality", the ICJ has embraced a 'legal question' doctrine, and has habitually demonstrated a 'legal question mentality'. Difficulties which have stood in the way of compliance with requests have, ineluctably and consistently, been either overlooked or overcome…The absence of an ICJ philosophy of 'judicial restraint' has also been linked to the dearth of cases with which the Court has been seized. "It is because the [US] courts decide so many political questions that there are a few from which they abstain". But for the ICJ, such self-denial cannot be expected unless it were a "court as abstemious as a panel of panda bears.

See Pomerance, ibid, pp. 318-319.

8 Pomerance asked the political organs to protect the "judicial character" of the Court by abstaining from using the Court's advisory procedure as a backdoor to the Court's contentious jurisdiction. Therefore Pomerance remarks that "if the Court chooses, or feels compelled, to ignore or minimize the effect of the absence of consent by interested states, the same should not be true of the requesting organ, whose responsibility it should be to shield the Court from such inept requests." Ibid, pp. 320-321.

Amerasinghe notes that the principle that the Court must participate as the principal judicial organ in the work of the Organisation might sometimes conflict with its judicial character.[9] However, unlike Pomerance, he believes that while the Court has striven to satisfy the interests of the Organisation, it has nevertheless taken a "sagacious approach to interpreting and applying the principle that its own judicial character must be protected."[10]

Rather than rely on commentators and on theory, careful examination of the Court's jurisprudence is needed to determine if in fact the Court's role as a principal organ has in any way interfered with its judicial character as a court of justice. The Court throughout its existence has considered that, in principle, it should if possible comply with any advisory requests. According to Rosenne this seems to imply two presumptions.[11] One relates to the competence of the requesting organ,[12] and the other one relates to the subject matter of the request which should be legal in nature.[13]

The Court in more than fifty-five years of experience with the advisory function has only once concluded that a request for an advisory opinion was *ultra vires*, insofar as it did not lie within the competence of the requesting organ.[14] In no case has the Court decided that the subject matter of the request was not a legal question.[15]

2.1 The Court's Judicial Character and States' Consent

Under its Statute, the Court's competence in contentious cases is dependent primarily on the consent of States parties to the dispute. However, the Statute does not provide clear guidance on the need for consent by States when the exercise of advisory jurisdiction is requested. Consequently, there has always been disagreement over whether the ICJ can comply with requests for an advisory opinion that relate to a pending dispute between States or between a State and an international organisation without the consent of the concerned parties.[16]

---

9 Amerasinghe, Chittharanjan F., *Jurisdiction of International Tribunals*, The Hague; London: Kluwer Law International, 2003, p. 537.

10 Ibid.

11 Rosenne, Shabtai, *The Law and Practice of the International Court, 1920-1996,* The Hague; London; Martinus Nijhoff Publishers, 1997, p. 1028.

12 The request is *intra vires* the organ means out of its competence. See Section 3.1.1 of Chapter Two, *supra.*

13 See Chapter Two, *supra.*

14 See the discussion of the 1996 *Legality of the Use by a State of Nuclear Weapons in Armed Conflict* Case, in Section ii, Chapter Two, *supra.*

15 For details about the scope of the legal question, see Section 3.2 in Chapter Two, *supra.*

16 A general principle in international adjudication indicates that States are not subject to adjudication without their consent.

Rosenne has observed that most challenges to the Court in regard to its judicial character were based on the principle *audiatur et altera pars*,[17] so that where the request related to legal disputes between two States the Court could not give the opinion requested without the consent of the States parties to the dispute.[18] The following two Sections examine the work of publicists and the Court's views concerning consent as a precondition to rendering advisory opinion.

2.1.1 Publicists' View of Consent as a Precondition for Exercising Jurisdiction

Some scholars consider that States' consent may in some circumstances constitute a precondition to the exercise of the Court's advisory jurisdiction.[19] The States concerned may also argue that the Court should not give an advisory opinion against their opposition.[20] These views must be examined in light of the fact that the purpose of the advisory procedure is not to circumvent the rights of States to determine whether to submit their disputes to judicial settlement.[21] Consequently, the Court must respect the independence of States which retain sovereign control over whether to submit a dispute to which they are party to the Court.

In accordance with this view, the Court must be aware that it would be incompatible with the advisory procedure for an opinion to be used to determine the substantive outcome of a particular legal dispute between parties without their prior consent. Moreover, it has been suggested that an advisory opinion is "ill-suited" to the application of principles of law to particular factual situations without the participation by an interested State which could provide the Court with necessary or pertinent information.[22]

---

17 This principle means that one should not be condemned without being heard. See Fox, James, *Dictionary of International and Comparative Law*, Dobbs Ferry, New York: Oceana Publications, Inc. 2003, p. 26.

18 Rosenne, *supra* note 11, p. 1014.

19 Pomerance, *supra* note 6; Oda, Shigeru, "The International Court of Justice Viewed from the Bench (1976-1993)", 244 *RCADI*, 1993, p. 92; Hudson, Manley O., *International Tribunals: Past and Future*, Washington [D.C.]: Carnegie Endowment for International Peace and Brookings Institution, 1944, p. 69; The committee of jurists which prepared the PCIJ Statute was of the view that consent would be necessary for the exercise of the Courts advisory function. See Hambro, Edvard, "The Authority of Advisory Opinions of the International Court of Justice", 3 *ICLQ*, 1954, p. 11.

20 See the arguments by the US in its written statement in the *Legal Consequences of the Construction of a Wall in the Occupied Palestinian Territory* Case, available at: http://www.icj-cij.org/icjwww/idocket/imwp/imwpframe.htmpp. pp. 19-20, (accessed 25 October 2004).

21 US argument in the *Wall* Case, ibid.

22 See the written statements of the US in the *Wall* Case, *supra* note 20, pp. 19-20.

Nevertheless other commentators maintain that States' consent is not a precondition for the Court to give an advisory opinion.[23] For instance, Sir Hersch Lauterpacht argued that:[24]

> *There seems to be no decisive reason why the sovereignty of States should be protected from a procedure, to which they have consented in advance as Members of the United Nations, of ascertaining the law through a pronouncement which, notwithstanding its authority, is not binding upon them.*

Rosenne also suggests that the Court is entitled "to act independently of any formal expression of consent on the part of States individually."[25] Moreover, Conforti suggests that nothing prevents a question posed for an advisory opinion "from being the object of a dispute between States; nor is there anything to prevent, for instance, the General Assembly or the Security Council from asking the Court, even against the will of one or more of the parties, to indicate which is the correct legal solution of a given dispute submitted to them."[26] Conforti points out that his conclusion was drawn not only from Article 96 of the UN Charter, which talks vaguely of a legal question, but also from Articles 14 and 37 of the UN Charter, which entitle the General Assembly and the Security Council respectively "to recommend to the parties terms of settlement on the merits-not excluding legal terms."

In a more recent work, discussing the Court's 'discretionary power', Conforti has argued that the Court should once and for all state that the existence of a dispute does not limit in any way its competence to render an advisory opinion. In this regard Conforti has stated that the idea of discretionary power is puzzling:[27]

> *The textual argument on which it is based (the "may" in Article 65 of the Statute) is very weak and should yield to the spirit of the provision on the advisory function which testifies to the* obligatory co-operation of the Court *with the UN organs in the solution of legal questions. It is clear that the most delicate point of the whole matter is that of the connection between the advisory function and conten-*

23 Lauterpacht, Hersch, *The development of International Law by the International Court*, London: Stevens and Sons Ltd, 1958, pp. 357-358. This point of view is based on the fact that requesting an advisory opinion does not constitute litigation in the strict sense because there are no real parties before the Court.

24 Lauterpacht, ibid, p. 358.

25 Rosenne, *supra* note 11, p. 989.

26 Conforti, Benedetto, "Observations on the Advisory Function of the International Court of Justice" in: Cassese, Antonio (ed.), *UN Law/ Fundamental Rights: Two Topics in International Law*, Alphen aan den Rijn: Sijthoff and Noordhoff, 1979, p. 86.

27 Conforti, Benedetto, *The Law and Practice of the United Nations*, The Hague; London: Kluwer Law International, 2000, p. 270.

> *tious or binding jurisdiction. However, it is exactly on this point that the Court, once and for all, should say that the existence of a dispute does not limit* in any way *its competence to render an opinion, rather than quibbling as it has done up to now. Why should the Court be authorized to sacrifice, at its discretion, the advisory function to the contentious function, thereby sacrificing co-operation between the organs to respect for the desire of an individual State to avoid the opinion (even the non-binding opinion!) of the judicial organ? Such a sacrifice may have been justified at the time of the League of Nations and of the advisory function of the old Permanent Court it seems anachronistic today.*

An examination of the relevant case law demonstrates that the Court has placed great emphasis on its role as the principal judicial organ of the UN and therefore has rightly rejected arguments that it should decline to give advisory opinions simply because the request is related to pending disputes between States or between a State and an international organisation.

2.1.2 The Court's Case Law on Consent as a Precondition for Exercising Jurisdiction

The Court on several occasions has rejected arguments that it should decline to render an advisory opinion because the request was related to a dispute between States or between a State and an international organisation. The comments of the Court in the 1950 *Interpretation of Peace Treaties* Case, the 1951 *Reservations to the Convention of Genocide* Case, the 1975 *Western Sahara* Case, the 1989 *Applicability of Article VI, Section 22, of the Convention on the Privileges and Immunities of the United Nations* Case and, lastly, the 2004 *Legal Consequences of the Construction of a Wall in the Occupied Palestinian Territory* Case illustrate how it dealt with the problem of consent.[28]

In each of these cases the States concerned contended that the Court should decline to give an advisory opinion on the basis *inter alia* of the principle laid down in the *Eastern Carelia* Case.[29] Here the League Council requested an opinion from

---

28 Hereinafter cited as: "the *Wall* Case", available at: http://www.icj-cij.org/icjwww/idocket/imwp/imwpframe.htm (accessed 21 October 2004).

29 The *Eastern Carelia* Case arose out of a dispute between Finland, a member of the League, and the Soviet Union, a non-member of the League. Articles 12-16 of the Covenant laid down procedures for peaceful settlement of disputes between members only. According to these Articles, members that were parties to a dispute were required, in the absence of settlement by diplomatic means, to submit the matter to the League Council. According to Article 17 of the Covenant, the Council had the power to adopt resolutions regarding disputes only between member States of the League, unless a non-member State accepted the Council's intervention in the case. Finland alleged that the Soviet Union had failed to carry out its obligations under the peace treaty and therefore expressed

the Court, on a legal dispute between Finland which was a member of the League of Nations and the Soviet Union which was not yet a member of the League, despite the objection of Soviet Union. The PCIJ stated that: "no State can, without its consent, be compelled to submit its dispute with other States to adjudication."[30] However, in all these cases, the Court distinguished the *Eastern Carelia* Case from the case in question and decided to exercise its jurisdiction despite the objections of the States concerned. The Court in its most recent advisory opinion, the *Wall* Advisory Opinion, followed its previous findings and explained that only on one occasion did its predecessor, the PCIJ, take the view that it should not reply to a question put to it. The Court explained that such a refusal was due to:[31]

> *[T]he very particular circumstances of the case, among which were that the question directly concerned an already existing dispute, one of the States parties to which was neither a party to the Statute of the Permanent Court nor a Member of the League of Nations, objected to the proceedings, and refused to take part in any way" (*Legality of the Threat or Use of Nuclear Weapons, I.C.J. Reports 1996 (I)*, pp. 235-236, para. 14).*

The Court in all the above cases emphasised that lack of consent had no bearing on its jurisdiction to give an advisory opinion. The following two Sections examine the Court's reasoning for not requiring consent where the question relates to a dispute between States or between States and international organisations.

(i) The Court's Case Law on Consent in Disputes Pending Between Two or More States

In both the *Peace Treaties* and *Reservations* Cases it was argued that the General Assembly's decision to request an advisory opinion was *ultra vires*. In the *Peace Treaties* Case, which concerned the interpretation of the 1947 peace agreements with Bulgaria, Hungary, and Romania, these States argued that questions of human rights and fundamental freedoms were matters of domestic jurisdiction and

its desire that the Council consider[ed] the matter. On February 1923 the Soviet Union informed the Council its rejection of any invitation, claming that the Eastern Carelia was a domestic matter. Under these circumstances the Council requested an advisory opinion from the PCIJ regarding this matter since it involved a treaty interpretation. Russia denied the Court's competence to deal with the matter. The Court declined to answer the question put to it on the ground that "[a]nswering the question would be substantially equivalent to deciding the dispute between the parties." Since the question submitted to the Court concerning a pending dispute between two States (Russia and Finland), the consent of the two States was required by the Court in order to render its opinion. PCIJ, Ser. B, No. 5, 1923; pp. 27-29; Keith, Kenneth, *The Extent of the Advisory Jurisdiction of the International Court of Justice*, Leyden: A.W. Sijthoff, 1971, pp. 93-94.

[30] PCIJ, Ser. B, No. 5, 1923; pp. 27-29.

[31] See para. 44 of the *Wall* Case, *supra* note 28.

therefore not proper subjects for an advisory opinion.[32] The Court disagreed on the grounds that the object of the request was to obtain from the Court legal clarification on the applicability of the procedure for dispute settlement established by the peace treaties. The Court stated that:[33]

> *The object of the Request is much more limited. It is directed solely to obtaining from the Court certain clarifications of a legal nature regarding the applicability of the procedure for the settlement of disputes by the Commissions provided for in the express terms of Article 36 of the Treaty with Bulgaria, Article 40 of the Treaty with Hungary and Article 38 of the Treaty with Romania. The interpretation of the terms of a treaty for this purpose could not be considered as a question essentially within the domestic jurisdiction of a State. It is a question of international law which, by its very nature, lies within the competence of the Court.*

Although Article 2(7) of the UN Charter restricts the jurisdiction of the UN by preventing it from intervening "in matters which are essentially within the domestic jurisdiction of any State", in practice, Pogany has observed, this Article has been given a restrictive meaning, especially "where issues of human rights or self-determination are involved, United Nations organs are unlikely to construe the question as falling 'essentially within the domestic jurisdiction' of the state concerned."[34] Moreover, the Court reasoned in the *Peace Treaties* Case that its reply to the request was only of an advisory character and had no binding force. Therefore, no State, whether a member of the UN or not, could prevent the Court giving an advisory opinion which the UN needed for guidance on the course of action it should take.[35]

In the *Reservations* Case, the question referred to the Court, by the General Assembly, concerned the effects of reservations to the Genocide Convention, which did not expressly provide for reservations of any kind.[36] Here the Government of

---

[32] It has been argued before the Court that the request for an opinion was "interfering" in matters essentially within the domestic jurisdiction of a State. This argument had been also raised in the General Assembly but was rejected.

[33] ICJ Rep., 1950, pp. 70-71.

[34] Pogany, Istvan, *The Security Council and the Arab-Israeli Conflict*, Aldershot: Gower Publishing, 1984, p. 4.

[35] Ibid, p. 71.

[36] ICJ Rep., 1951, p. 16. While ratifying or acceding to the Genocide Convention of 1948, several States, including the Soviet Union, , made reservations to which other contracting parties objected. Therefore, the Secretary-General informed the reserving States that they could not become parties to the Convention unless they withdrew their reservations. The Secretary-General's view was contested by the reserving states, thus, the General Assembly decided to request an advisory opinion from the Court to end this uncertainty about the legal effect of reservations to multilateral conventions.

the Philippines contended in its written statement that the dispute between Australia and Philippines concerning the Convention had arisen as a result of the disagreement of the two governments regarding the effect of the Philippines' reservation to the Convention. According to the Philippines' view, the Court should decline to give an opinion as the question put to it directly related to a dispute actually pending between the Philippines and Australia.[37] It was also contended that the request constituted an inadmissible interference by the General Assembly and by non-contracting States since only States parties to the Convention were entitled to interpret it or to seek an interpretation.[38] In reply the Court stated that:[39]

> *[N]ot only did the General Assembly take the initiative in respect of the Genocide Convention, draw up its terms and open it for signature and accession by States, but that the express provisions of the Convention (Articles XI and XVI) associate the General Assembly with the life of the Convention; and finally, that the General Assembly actually associated itself with it by endeavoring to secure the adoption of the Convention by as great a number of States as possible.*

The Court in the *Reservations* Case specifically referred to the principle laid down in the *Peace Treaties* Case to the effect that the response of the Court to a request represents its participation in the work of the Organisation and therefore should not be refused. The Court held that:[40]

> *[T]he Court can confine itself to recalling the principles which it laid down in its Opinion of March 30th, 1950 (ICJ reports, 1950, p. 71). A reply to a request for an Opinion should not, in principle, be refused.*

The Court concluded that the General Assembly, which drafted and adopted the Convention, and the Secretary-General who is the depositor of the instruments of ratification and accession, had an interest in knowing the legal effect of the reservations to the Convention.[41]

---

37 ICJ pled., 1951, p. 296.

38 ICJ Rep., 1951, p. 19.

39 Ibid, pp. 19-20.

40 ICJ Rep., 1951, p. 19. The Court also stated that: "[a]t the same time, Article 68 of the Statute recognizes that the Court has the power to decide to what extent the circumstances of each case must lead it to apply to advisory proceedings the provisions of the Statute which apply in contentious cases".

41 The Court had observed that the question put to the Court was limited to the Convention by the terms of the General Assembly resolution. The same resolution had invited the ILC to study the general question of reservations to multilateral Conventions from point of view of codification and progressive development of the International Law. Therefore, the Court considered that its reply was necessary to promote the interests of the UN. ICJ Rep., 1951, p. 20.

In the *Western Sahara* Case,[42] the Court gave an advisory opinion regarding the legal status of the Western Sahara, an area which had been disputed by Spain, on the one hand, and by Morocco and Mauritania on the other. The request by the General Assembly was aimed at ascertaining the status of the territory and the legal ties between Morocco and Mauritania at the time of colonisation. Spain had objected to the request, claming the Court lacked jurisdiction without its consent. However, the Court, after referring to its holding in the *Peace Treaties* Case, stated:[43]

> *The Court, it is true, affirmed in this pronouncement that its competence to give an opinion did not depend on the consent of the interested States, even when the case concerned a legal question actually pending between them. However, the Court proceeded not merely to stress its judicial character and the permissive nature of Article 65, paragraph 1, of the Statute but to examine, specifically in relation to the opposition of some of the interested States, the question of the judicial propriety of giving the opinion. Moreover, the Court emphasized the circumstances differentiating the case then under consideration from the* Status of Eastern Carelia *case and explained the particular grounds which led it to conclude that there was no reason requiring the Court to refuse to reply to the request. Thus the Court recognized that lack of consent might constitute a ground for declining to give the opinion requested if, in the circumstances of a given case, considerations of judicial propriety should oblige the Court to refuse an opinion. In short, the consent of an interested State continues to be relevant, not for the Court's competence, but for the appreciation of the propriety of giving an opinion.*

The Court, after stating that "consideration of judicial propriety should oblige the Court to refuse an opinion" held that:[44]

> *In certain circumstances, therefore, the lack of consent of an interested State may render the giving of an advisory opinion incompatible with the Court's judicial character. An instance of this would be when the circumstances disclose that to give a reply would have the effect of circumventing the principle that a State is not obliged to allow its disputes to be submitted to judicial settlement without its consent. If such a situation should arise, the powers of the Court under the discretion given to it by Article 65, paragraph 1, of the Statute, would afford sufficient legal means to ensure respect for the fundamental principle of consent to jurisdiction.*

In applying this principle to the request, the Court found that a legal controversy did indeed exist, but one that had arisen during the proceedings of the General As-

---

[42] ICJ Rep., 1975, p. 12.

[43] Ibid, para. 32, pp. 24-25.

[44] ICJ Rep., 1975, para. 33, p. 25.

sembly and in relation to matters with which the General Assembly was dealing. Therefore, it had not arisen independently in bilateral relations, so the Court could properly exercise its advisory function.[45]

The Court, in the 2004 *Wall* Advisory Opinion rejected the argument advanced by Israel and some other States that the Court should decline to give an advisory opinion because Israel had not consented to the request. According to the Israeli argument, the subject matter of the question posed by the General Assembly "is an integral part of the wider Israeli-Palestinian dispute concerning questions of terrorism, security, borders, settlements, Jerusalem and other related matters." Israel had also emphasised that:[46]

> *[I]t has never consented to the settlement of this wider dispute by the Court or by any other means of compulsory adjudication; on the contrary, it contends that the parties repeatedly agreed that these issues are to be settled by negotiation, with the possibility of an agreement that recourse could be had to arbitration.*

In responding to Israel's argument the Court acknowledged that:[47]

> *Israel and Palestine have expressed radically divergent views on the legal consequences of Israel's construction of the wall, on which the Court has been asked to pronounce. However, as the Court has itself noted, "Differences of views ... on legal issues have existed in practically every advisory proceeding."*

The Court concluded that it did not consider that the subject matter of the General Assembly's request could be regarded as only a bilateral matter between Israel and Palestine because of "the powers and responsibilities of the United Nations in questions relating to international peace and security." The Court added that, in its view, "the construction of the wall must be deemed to be directly of concern to the United Nations."[48] The Court then emphasised that:[49]

---

[45] Ibid, para. 34, p. 25. The Court in this case concluded that the object of the General Assembly request has not been to bring before the Court, by way of request for advisory opinion, a dispute on legal controversy. Rather the object was to obtain from the Court an opinion to assist the General Assembly in the proper exercise of its functions concerning the decolonisation of the territory. See ICJ Rep., ibid, para. 41, p. 37.

[46] See para. 46 of the *Wall* Advisory Opinion, *supra* note 28.

[47] See para. 48 of the *Wall* Advisory Opinion, *supra* note 28. It is worth noting that the Court in the last part of the above quotation was referring to its findings in Namibia Case, ICJ Rep., 1971, para.34, p. 24.

[48] The Court stated that the responsibility of the UN in this matter has been described by the General Assembly as:

"[A] permanent responsibility towards the question of Palestine until the question is resolved in all its aspects in a satisfactory manner in accordance with international legitimacy." See para. 49.

[49] See para. 50 of the Court's Opinion.

> *The object of the request before the Court is to obtain from the Court an opinion which the General Assembly deems of assistance to it for the proper exercise of its functions. The opinion is requested on a question which is of particularly acute concern to the United Nations, and one which is located in a much broader frame of reference than a bilateral dispute. In the circumstances, the Court does not consider that to give an opinion would have the effect of circumventing the principle of consent to judicial settlement, and the Court accordingly cannot, in the exercise of its discretion, decline to give an opinion on that ground.*

The above case law demonstrates that, despite the Court's findings in the *Western Sahara* Case and others about considerations of judicial propriety, the Court down to the present has never invoked this principle in order to decline to give an advisory opinion when requested.

Lastly, it is important to note that not only did the Court decline to apply the *Eastern Carelia* principle where there was a legal question pending between two or more States,[50] but that it has also chosen not to apply the principle in disputes pending between a State and an international organisation. The *South West Africa* Cases, *The Applicability of Article VI, Section 22, of the Convention on the Privileges and Immunities of the United Nations* Case,[51] and the *Interpretation of the Agreement of 25 March 1951 between the WHO and Egypt* Case[52] are illustrative of this proposition.

(ii) The Court's Dicta on Consent in Disputes Pending Between a State and an International Organisation

In the *Legal Consequences for States of the Continued Presence of South Africa in Namibia (South West Africa) notwithstanding Security Council Resolution 276 (1970)* Case,[53] the Government of South Africa contended that the question referred to the Court related to a dispute between South Africa and other Members

[50] The Court's view has always been that an Opinion should be given when a competent organ desires to obtain guidance on its course of action while carrying its duties. Furthermore, under Article 7 of the Charter, because the Court is an organ of the United Nations, it has a duty to participate in the activities of the Organisation. The PCIJ, however, was not an organ of the League of Nations, and, indeed, the ICJ cannot depart from its duties as the principle judicial organ of the United Nations. See the discussion in Chapter Three, *supra*.

[51] Hereinafter cited as: "the *Mazilu* Case".

[52] Hereinafter cited as: "the *WHO/Egypt* Case".

[53] Hereinafter cited as: "the *Namibia* Case." For details about this Case see Section 6.3.3 in Chapter Three, *supra* and Section 6 in Chapter Six, *infra*.

of the UN. Therefore, the Court should refuse to give an opinion.[54] South Africa argued that even if the Court had competence to give the opinion requested, it should nevertheless refuse to do so as a matter of judicial propriety.[55] Also South Africa had requested for the appointment of a judge ad hoc based on Article 83 of the 1946 Rules, now Article 102 (2).[56] However, the Court had refused this application. In replying to the request, the Court stated:[57]

> *South Africa, as a Member of the United Nations, is bound by Article 96 of the Charter, which empowers the Security Council to request advisory opinions on any legal question. It has appeared before the Court, participated in both the written and oral proceedings and, while raising specific objections against the competence of the Court, has addressed itself to the merits of the question.*

The Court asserted that by replying to the request "it would not only 'remain faithful to the requirements of its judicial character'… but also discharge its functions as "the principal judicial organ of the United Nations."[58]

In the *Mazilu* Case, the Economic and Social Council concluded that a difference had arisen between the UN and the Government of Romania as to the applicability of Article VI, Section 22, of the Convention on the Privileges and Immunities of the UN in the case of Mr. Mazilu as a Special Rapporteur of the Sub-Commission on Prevention of Discrimination and Protection of Minorities.[59] Romania had made a reservation to Section 30 of the General Convention for the Settlement of Disputes between the UN and States Parties to the Convention which provides:

> *If a difference arises between the United Nations on the one hand and a Member on the other hand, a request shall be made for an advisory opinion on any legal question involved in accordance with Article 96 of the Charter and Article 65 of the Statute of the Court. The opinion given by the Court shall be accepted as decisive by the parties.*

---

[54] South Africa contested the validity of the Security Council Resolution 284. See Section 6.3.3 in Chapter Three, *supra*.

[55] ICJ Rep., 1971, para. 27, p. 23.

[56] This Article provided for the application of Article 31 of the Statute which relates to the appointment of judges *ad hoc* "if the advisory opinion is requested upon a legal question actually pending between two or more States." For details about South Africa's application for the judge *ad hoc*, see Section 3.1 in Chapter Five, *infra*.

[57] ICJ Rep., 1971, para. 31, pp. 23-24.

[58] Ibid, para 41, p. 27.

[59] ICJ Rep., 1989, p. 178.

Because of the reservation made by Romania to Section 30, Romania argued that the Court could not give an advisory opinion without its consent.[60] In reply the Court stated:[61]

> *The jurisdiction of the Court under Article 96 of the Charter and Article 65 of the Statute, to give advisory opinions on legal questions, enables United Nations entities to seek guidance from the Court in order to conduct their activities in accordance with the law. These opinions are advisory, not binding. As the opinions are intended for the guidance of the United Nations, the consent of States is not a condition precedent to the competence of the Court to give them.*

The Court had then to consider, in view of Romania's reservation to Article 30 and absent its consent to the request, whether giving an opinion would circumvent the principle that "a State is not obliged to allow its disputes to be submitted to judicial settlement without its consent."[62] The Court concluded that in the case under consideration a reply by the Court would have no such effect and that:[63]

> *[T]he Council, in its resolution requesting the opinion, did conclude that a difference had arisen between the United Nations and the Government of Romania as to the* applicability *of the Convention to Mr. Dumitru Mazilu. But this difference, and the question put to the Court in the light of it, are not to be confused with the dispute between the United Nations and Romania with respect to the* application *of the General Convention in the case of Mr. Mazilu.*
>
> *In the present case, the Court thus does not find any compelling reasons to refuse an advisory opinion.*

Judge Higgins argues that in this case, the Court sought to distinguish between the abstract applicability of the UN Convention on Privileges and Immunities of 1946

---

[60] Romania made the following reservation:

The Romanian People's Republic does not consider itself bound by the terms of section 30 of the Convention which provide for the compulsory jurisdiction of the International Court in differences arising out of the interpretation or application of the Convention; with respect to the competence of the International Court in such differences, the Romanian People's Republic takes the view that, for the purpose of the submission of any dispute whatsoever to the Court for a ruling, the consent of all the parties to the dispute is required in every individual case.

See ICJ Rep., 1989, p. 188.

[61] ICJ Rep., 1989, para. 31, pp. 188-189.

[62] This principle was laid down by the Court in its advisory opinion in the *Western Sahara* Case. See the above discussion.

[63] ICJ Rep., 1989, para. 38-9, p. 191.

and its actual application to the specific case. However, Higgins concluded that the Court has performed the former task.[64] Indeed, the distinction between "applicability" and "application" is subtle.[65]

In the *WHO/Egypt* Case, the Court had been requested by the WHO Assembly to render an advisory opinion about whether any transfer of the WHO Regional Office would be covered by Section 37 of the 1951 Agreement between the WHO and Egypt which provides that:[66]

> *The present Agreement may be revised at the request of either party. In this event the two parties shall consult each other concerning the modifications to be made in its provisions. If the negotiations do not result in an understanding within one year, the present Agreement may be denounced by either party giving two years notice.*

There were different views expressed in the World Health Assembly on the question whether transfer of the Regional Office could occur without regard to Section 37 mentioned above. In its meeting on 16 May 1980, the WHO Assembly's committee had before it a draft resolution submitted by 20 Arab States under which the Assembly would decide to transfer the Regional office to Jordan as soon as possible. On the other hand, the Committee also had before it another draft resolution submitted by the US under which the Assembly would decide "prior to taking any decision on removal of the Regional Office" to request an advisory opinion from the Court. This was the request submitted to the Court.[67] It is worth noting that 17 Arab States had addressed a letter to the Director-General of the Organisation informing him of their decision to "boycott" the Regional Office in Alexandria, and to deal with the Headquarters in Geneva instead.[68]

It was in these circumstances that the Assembly found it necessary to request an advisory opinion from the Court. What is of importance in this case is that the Court emphasised that "if it is to remain faithful to the requirements of its judicial character in the exercise of its advisory jurisdiction, it must ascertain what are the legal questions really in issue in questions formulated in a request."[69] Accordingly, the Court redrafted the legal question at issue and decided that the true legal question under consideration in the WHO Assembly was "[w]hat are the legal principles and rules applicable to the question under

---

[64] Higgins, Rosalyn, "A Comment on the Current Health of Advisory Opinions", in: Lowe, Vaughan and Fitzmaurice, Malgosia (eds.), *Fifty Years of the International Court of Justice: Essay in Honour of Sir Robert Jennings,* Cambridge: Grotius Publications, 1996, p. 571.

[65] See Rosenne, *supra* note 11, p. 1019; Amerasinghe, *supra* note 7, p. 534.

[66] ICJ Rep., 1980, para. 34, p. 88.

[67] ICJ Rep., 1980, para. 34, p. 88.

[68] Ibid.

[69] ICJ Rep., 1980, ibid.

what conditions and in accordance with what modalities a transfer of the Regional Office from Egypt may be effected?"[70]

The Court observed that regardless of the different views expressed concerning the relevance of the 1951 Agreement and the interpretation of Section 37, the Court had to examine certain legal principles and rules.[71] The Court decided that the mutual relationship between Egypt as the host State and the WHO Organisation was based upon a body of mutual obligations of co-operation and good faith. Therefore the situation arising in the event of any transfer was one which, by its nature, called for consultation, negotiation and co-operation between the Organisation and Egypt.[72] The Court considered a considerable number of host agreements of different kinds that had been concluded between States and international organisations containing various provisions regarding the revision, termination or denunciation of these agreements.[73] The Court explained after its review that those agreements confirmed the existence of mutual obligations which made it incumbent upon the parties to resolve the problems attendant upon a revision, termination or denunciation of a host agreement.[74]

On commenting upon the Courts findings, Thirlway argues that:[75]

> *[W]hile it is well recognized that the conclusion of similar treaties may amount to State practice constitutive of a customary rule, yet to deduce the existence of a custom from similar provisions in a number of treaties is always open to the objection that the existence of such treaties might, in many instances, equally well be taken to point to a conviction on the part of the States concerned that there was no customary rule to the effect suggested, since if such rule had existed, the treaty provisions might have been thought unnecessary.*

Thirlway continued to say that in the case of a dispute, as the WHO/Egypt Case clearly was, the treaty must be given effect and the customary rule can only be in-

---

70 The original questions were:

1. Are the negotiation and notice provisions of Section 37 of the Agreement of 25 March 1951 between the World Health Organization and Egypt applicable in the event that either party to the Agreement wishes to have the Regional Office transferred from the territory of Egypt?
2. If so, what would be the legal responsibilities of both the World Health Organization and Egypt, with regard to the Regional Office in Alexandria, during the two-year period between notice and termination of the Agreement?

See ICJ Rep., 1980, para. 1 and 35, p. 74 and pp. 88-89.

71 Ibid, para. 42, p. 92.

72 Ibid, para. 46, p. 94.

73 Ibid., para. 45, p. 94.

74 Ibid., para. 46, p. 94.

75 Thirlway, Hugh, "The Law and Procedure of The International Court of Justice, 1960-1989", 67 *BYIL*, 1996, p. 17.

voked to supplement the treaty but not to contradict it.[76] However, one could argue here that the choice of the law to be applied by the Court in accordance with Article 38 of the ICJ's Statute is germane to the judicial reasoning as will be shown in the next Chapter, and hence, should not be confined to a hierarchical structure. The Court, in the *WHO/Egypt* Case stated:[77]

> *[T]he Court must first ascertain the meaning and full implications of the question in the light of the actual framework of fact and law in which it falls for consideration. Otherwise its reply to the question may be incomplete and, in consequence, ineffectual and even misleading as to the pertinent legal rules actually governing the matter under consideration by the requesting Organization.*

In a Separate Opinion Judge Oda argued that it was necessary to redraft the question because the 1951 Agreement did not govern the transfer procedure. Moreover, Section 37 of the Agreement did not apply to such a transfer.[78] However, the Court as a judicial organ has the power to interpret any request for an advisory opinion to determine the object of the request before it. It has been rightly argued that if the Court is to fully exercise its duty as a Court of justice:[79]

> *[I]t cannot content itself with giving a formalistic or simplistic reply based on a narrow construction of the question as drafted. It is incumbent upon it to establish what is at issue and what is involved when an international organization is contemplating a certain course of action and seeking clarification of legal issues and the provision of guidelines based on legal principles and rules.*

The case law of the ICJ shows that the Court's general approach is to place a heavy emphasis on the "organisational interest" aspects of requests for advisory opinions and thus inclined the Court to uphold such requests.[80] The Court has also emphasised that consent of the States concerned is not necessary for exercising its advisory function.[81] Pomerance argues that the Court attributes greater weight to the form of the request than the substance because the latter might be of a quasi-contentious

---

76 Ibid.

77 ICJ Rep., 1980, para. 10, p. 76.

78 See Sep. Op. of Judge Oda, ICJ Rep., 1980, p. 131.

79 See Sep. Op. of Judge El-Erian, ICJ Rep., 1980, p. 167.

80 Sugihara, Takane, "The Advisory Function of the International Court of Justice", 17 *JAIL*, 1973, p. 4. ; Pomerance, Michla, "The Badinter Commission: The Use And Misuse of The International Court of Justice's Jurisprudence", 20 *Michigan JIL*, 1989, p. 45.

81 The PCIJ, in the Interpretation of the *Treaty of Lausanne* Case, stated that the absence of the consent of one of the States concerned was not a sufficient reason to prevent giving an advisory opinion on a question of procedure and the interpretation of the Covenant. PCIJ, Ser. B, No. 12, 1925, pp. 6-33.

character. She concluded that because of the status of the Court as the principal judicial organ of the UN and its desire to cooperate to the fullest extent with the political organs, the Court tends in practice to ignore the quasi-contentious elements involved in requests for advisory opinions in order to reply to the request.[82]

One could argue that the Court sees its advisory function as not dependent on a State's consent but as flowing from the general acceptance by member States of Article 96 of the UN Charter and consequently of Article 65 of the ICJ's Statute.[83] Nevertheless, the Court has sought to establish a balance between its role as a principal organ of the UN and as a judicial institution with a duty to administer justice. The case law shows that the Court has recognised only one circumstance which could lead the Court to refrain from giving the opinion requested. That was when the opinion requested would have the effect of circumventing the principle that "a State is not obliged to allow its disputes to be submitted to judicial settlement without its consent."[84]

On the other hand, one must note that although the Court repeatedly states that only compelling reasons should lead it to decline to give an opinion, it nevertheless has not identified these compelling reasons.[85] Rosenne has observed that despite the powerful trend manifested by the Court to reject all suggestions that it should exercise its discretion and decline to render a requested opinion, the Court has on the whole been careful to limit the apparent generality of its observations by relating them closely to the circumstances of each concrete case, including the asserted purposes for which the request was made.[86] In other words, the Court is mindful not to generalise its findings but, on the contrary, to restrict them to a particular case.

2.2 *Forum Prorogatum* in Advisory Proceedings

It would be pertinent to examine the possible relevance of the doctrine of *forum prorogatum* to advisory proceedings. This doctrine suggests that if there is no explicit consent to the Court's jurisdiction, the parties may nevertheless be deemed to have acquiesced to the jurisdiction of the Court through their subsequent acts, such as their participation in the proceedings.[87]

---

82 Pomerance, Michla, "The Admission of Judges Ad Hoc in Advisory Proceedings: Some Reflections in the Light of the Namibia Case", 67 *AJIL*, 1973, p. 454.

83 See the discussion regarding the Court's statement in the *Namibia* Case in Section II above.

84 See the above discussion about the *Western Sahara* Case.

85 However, the Court in the *ILO* Case stated that it must consider whether "its Statute and its judicial character" do or do not stand in the way of its participating in the procedure by complying with the request put for an advisory opinion. See *Judgments of the Administrative Tribunal of the International Labour Organization Upon Complaints Made Against the United Nations Educational, Scientific and Cultural Organization* Case, ICJ Rep., 1956, p. 85.

86 Rosenne, *supra* note 11, pp. 1027-1028.

87 See Fox, *supra* note 17, p. 121.

Judge Bedjaoui maintains that the Court has applied this doctrine in its advisory proceedings.[88] As an example he took the *Namibia* Case where the Court observed that South Africa had given its consent by participating in the proceedings and addressing the merits.[89] Contrary to this view, Yee argues that there is no place for this doctrine in advisory proceedings.[90] He bases his argument on the grounds that the absence of a concerned State's consent does not affect the Court's advisory jurisdiction as consent cannot enlarge or reduce the Court's jurisdiction. He concludes that *forum prorogatum* only figures in the Court's decision "as to whether it should *exercise discretion* to decline a request for an advisory opinion, either because of the Court's judicial character or because of its special status as a principal organ of the United Nations."[91]

In light of the above argument and in view of the Court's case law that when giving an advisory opinion the Court does not pronounce on the merits of the dispute, it seems safe to conclude that there is no need to rely on this doctrine to ascertain the consent of States. This conclusion is based on the Court's practice that a State's consent is not a requirement for the advisory jurisdiction except where giving an opinion might affect the judicial propriety of the exercise of its jurisdiction, as the Court emphasized in the *Western Sahara* Case.[92]

3 Judicial and Political Restraints and the Judicial Function

The Court must decline to render an advisory opinion whenever its independence and the integrity of its judicial function are at stake. In this connection, Bedjaoui suggests that no obligation could be imposed upon the Court to comply with a request for an advisory opinion "if it risks prejudicing the integrity of its judicial function."[93] Indeed, as Szasz has observed, any legal process is subject to misuse by the parties.[94] However, Szasz suggests that the ICJ can counter any threat of abuse by declining to render an opinion requested; calling for the views of a large

---

88 Bedjaoui, Mohammed, *"The Forum prorogatum Before the International Court of Justice: The Resources of an Institution or the Hidden Face of Consensualism"*, (speech before the Sixth Committee of the UNGA on November 4, 1996 as President of the ICJ. ICJ Year Book, 1996-97, No. 51, p. 216.

89 Bedjaoui, *supra* note 88, p. 232.

90 Yee, Sienho, "*Forum Prorogatum* and the Advisory Proceedings of the International Court", 95 *AJIL*, 2001, p. 381.

91 Ibid, p. 383, (emphasis in original).

92 ICJ Rep., 1975, Para. 21, p. 20.

93 Bedjaui, Mohammed, "Expediency in the Decisions of the International Court of Justice", 71 *BYIL*, 2000, p. 18.

94 Szasz, Paul C., "Enhancing the Advisory Competence of the World Court" in: Gross, Leo, (ed.), *The Future of the International Court of Justice*, Dobbs Ferry, New York: Oceana Publications, 1976, p. 521.

number of entities if it considers this desirable;[95] and rendering a deliberately narrow opinion closely and explicitly restricted to the terms of the submission. In fact, the Court alone can reconcile the problem of non-consent to the advisory proceedings with the essentially judicial character of the Court through its awareness of its role and its status within the Organisation and by exercising the discretion provided in Article 68 of its Statute.[96]

The Court when exercising its advisory function acts judicially and applies legal principles and rules, including Article 68 of the Statute. Judge Moore stated that:[97]

> *The Court has not thought it feasible to fill a dual role, acting at one moment as a judicial body rendering judgments on international differences, and at the next moment as a board of counselors giving private and* ex parte *advice on such matters. Indeed, an auditor or spectator would detect no difference between a proceeding for a judgment and a proceeding for a judgment and a proceeding for an advisory opinion. Moreover, the Court has in all its proceedings shown an appreciation of the fact that the very breath of its life is ... public confidence.*

As a result, in practice the Court has largely assimilated its advisory procedure to that followed in contentious proceedings with respect to publicity, the right of parties to present written and oral statements, and the right to admit *ad hoc* judges.[98] In other words, it recognises that the judicial function remains the same whether the proceedings are contentious or advisory.[99] The Court in *Northern Cameroon* Case stated that:[100]

> *Both Courts have had occasion to make pronouncements concerning requests for advisory opinions, which are equally applicable to the proper role of the Court in disposing of contested cases; in both situations, the Court is exercising a judicial function.*

It has been suggested that the judicial guarantees of the advisory opinion are fundamental requirements to the administration of justice, because there always re-

---

95 See Articles 66, 34 (2)- (3) of the ICJ Statute.

96 Gross, Leo, "The International Court of Justice and the United Nations", 120 *RCADI*, 1967, p. 419.

97 See collected Papers of John Bassett Moore, 1944, vol. 6, p. 104, cited in Pomerance, *supra* note 6, p. 277. See also Chapter Five, *infra*. In fact, no dual procedure for "dispute" and "non-dispute" cases was ever invoked, therefore, the procedure for all advisory opinions is a judicial procedure.

98 See Chapter Five, *infra*.

99 See Goodrich, Leland, "The Nature of the Advisory Opinions of the Permanent Court of International Justice", 32 *AJIL, p.* 756.

100 The *Northern Cameroons* Case, ICJ Rep., 1963, p. 30.

mains the possibility that a subsequent contentious case will bear on matters previously considered in advisory proceedings.[101]

Also, in practice the Court has shown independence while articulating its reasoning and the choice of the legal basis of its decision, relying on the principle of *jura novit curia.*[102] This was made amply clear in the *WHO/Egypt* Case where the Court reformulated the question in order to apply the legal rules that the Court believed appropriate. Indeed, as Abi Saab has stated, the Court is not restricted to the parties' arguments in support of their claims, provided that the Court is capable of rendering a complete answer to the subject matter of the dispute as defined by the parties in their submissions.[103] In this regard, the Court held in the *Northern Cameroons* Case that:[104]

> *There may thus be an incompatibility between the desires of an applicant, or, indeed, of both parties to a case, on the one hand, and on the other hand the duty of the Court to maintain its judicial character. The Court itself, and not the parties, must be the guardian of the Court's judicial integrity.*

The exercise of the advisory function is essentially a two-sided process involving the interplay between UN organs and the ICJ. Each must be mindful of the need for some degree of restraint. Thus, organs should request an opinion only if there is a genuine need for a legal answer which is clearly demonstrated in the question, and, consequently, an accurate formulation of the relevant point of law. The request has to be the product of careful drafting.[105] Most importantly, the question must be formulated in such a manner that the responding advisory opinion will provide the needed clarification to the requesting organ.[106]

If Pomerance is correct in her conclusion that the Court has no self imposed policy of "judicial restraint", then exercise of some sort of restraint by the political organs in their requests for advisory opinions becomes particularly important. The

---

[101] This was one of the principal arguments in Moore's Memorandum on Advisory Opinions submitted to the Court in its preliminary session. See PCIJ, Ser. D, No.2, p. 383.

[102] This maxim influences the manner in which the International Court handles questions of international law. As a consequence the Court is not restricted to the law presented by the parties, but is free to pursue its own research. See Fox, *supra* not 17, p. 180 ; Abi-Saab, Georges, "The International Court as a World Court" in Lowe, Vaughan & Fitzmaurice, Malagosia, (eds.), *Fifty years of the International Court of Justice: Essays in Honour of Sir Robert Jennings*, Grotius Publications, Cambridge University Press, 1996, p. 8.

[103] Abi Saab, ibid.

[104] The *Northern Cameroons* Case, ICJ Rep., 1963, p. 23.

[105] Rosenne, *supra* note 11, p. 355. Rosenne believes that the formulation of the request as a whole, and of the question in particular, carry the same importance in advisory cases as the formulation of questions in contentious cases.

[106] Ibid, p. 360.

way that the requesting organ drafts the request is of vital importance. Such drafting may lead to one or more of the following outcomes: turning down of the request by the Court;[107] the Court's answering the request with only a minimal contribution to the clarification of the point at issue;[108] a failure to address the real issue by the Court which consequently might lead the Court to redraft the question.[109] In fact, a satisfactory answer would require that the question be a legal question which is sufficiently specific and clear so that the Court is able to answer it by the application of judicial methods. For the Court's part it should decline to render an opinion if giving the requested opinion would jeopardise its judicial integrity. In this regard it has been suggested that requests which are "devoid of object or purpose" or "remote from reality" have to be regarded as compelling reasons for preventing the Court from rendering a requested opinion.[110]

In the final analysis, as argued in the previous Chapter, the request for and giving of an advisory opinion is a collective coordinated response involving more than one organ, or part of the Organisation. Restraint, therefore, should not rest exclusively with the Court. Restrain in formulating requests must be exercised by the requesting bodies which should not seek to use the Court for purposes other than guidance concerning applicable legal principles.

4 The Judicial Character of the Court and Its Effect on the Authority of Advisory Opinions

The extent to which advisory opinions have a binding effect has always been debated.[111] The Court's case law was always that the Court's reply to a request put

[107] The *Legality of the Use by a State of Nuclear Weapons in Armed Conflict* Case, ICJ Rep., 1996, p. 66.

[108] The *Legality of the Threat or Use of Nuclear Weapons* Case, ICJ Rep., 1996, p. 226. See the discussion in Chapter Six and Chapter Nine, *infra*.

[109] See Section 4.1 in Chapter Five, *infra* (relating to the *WHO/ Egypt* Case).

[110] See the written statement of the United Kingdom of Great Britain and Northern Ireland in the *Wall* advisory opinion available at: http://www.icj-cij.org/icjwww/idocket/imwp/imwpframe.htm (accessed 25 October 2004). See ICJ Rep., 1975, p. 37. See ICJ Rep., 1963, p. 33.

[111] The majority of international lawyers consider that advisory opinions of the ICJ are not binding. Hudson has pointed out that "[i]t is advisory. It is not in any sense a judgment under Article 60 of the Statute, nor is it a decision under Article 59". Hudson, Manley O., *The Permanent Court of International Justice, 1920-1942*, New York: The Macmillan Company, 1943, p. 511; Janis, Mark W., "The International Court" in: Janis, Mark W. (ed.), *International Courts for the Twenty-First Century*, Dordrecht; Boston; London: Martinus Nijhoff Publishers, 1992, p. 29. However, this point of view does not detract from the legal and moral authority of the Advisory Opinions. Hudson argued that: "they are advisory not legal advise in the ordinary sense, not views expressed by counsel for the guidance of client, but pronouncements as to the law applicable in given situation formulated after deliberation by the court." Hudson, Manley, "The Effect of Advisory Opinions of the World Court", 42 *AJIL*, 1948, p. 630.

for an advisory opinion "is only of an advisory character: as such, it has no binding force."[112] The opinions are not binding in the sense of *res judicata* and the doctrine of *stare decisis* is not applicable. In this regard, Nantwi suggestes that "the binding force of advisory opinions, since it does not stem from the principle of *res judicata*, belongs to a class of its own."[113] Advisory opinions are, nevertheless, authoritative as Thirlway rightly stated:[114]

> *The essence of an advisory opinion is that it is advisory, not determinative: it expresses the view of the Court as to the relevant international legal principles and rules, but does not oblige any State, nor even the body that asked for the opinion, to take or refrain from any action. The distinction, clear in theory, is less so in practice: if the Court advises, for example, that a certain obligation exists, the State upon which it is said to rest has not bound itself to accept the Court's finding, but it will be in a weak position if it seeks to argue that the considered opinion of the Court does not represent a correct view of the law.*

While recognising the non-binding nature of advisory opinions, they could be seen as binding under certain circumstances as so-called "compulsive opinions", which have been described as an attempt to overcome the procedural incapacity of the international organisations before the Court.[115] This system of "compulsive opinions" is based on the acceptance by the parties to an agreement of an obligation to request an advisory opinion in certain circumstances and to act in conformity with such an opinion.[116]

An example of this can be found in Article VIII, Section 30 of the Convention on the Privileges and Immunities of the UN which provides that if differences

---

Some other scholars consider the Court's opinion as having a legal effect upon the requesting organ. See Gros, A, "Concerning the Advisory Role of the International Court of Justice" in: Friedmann, Wolfgang, *et al.*, (eds.), *Transnational Law in a Changing Society. Essays in Honour of Philip C. Jessup*, New York: Columbia University Press, 1972, p. 315. Politis pointed out that "advisory opinions, being in reality no longer such, were accordingly equivalent in the eyes of the Council, of public opinion and of the interested parties to a judgment", cited in Hudson, 1943, p. 513; De Visscher, 26 *RCADI*, 1929, p. 23.

[112] ICJ Rep., 1950, p. 71. This statement has been affirmed in subsequent Cases see for instance ICJ Rep., 1956, p. 84.

[113] Nantwi, *supra* note 1, p. 74.

[114] Thirlway, Hugh, "The International Court of Justice" in: Evans, Malcolm D. (ed.), *International Law*, Oxford University Press, 2003, p. 582.

[115] Rosnne, *supra* note 11, p. 1056. It is known that the international organisations headed by the UN are not permitted to appear before the Court as parties to contentious proceedings, in accordance with Article 34 (1) of the Court's Statute, which provides that "only states may be parties in cases before the court."

[116] Rosenne, ibid.

arise out of the interpretation or application of the Convention an advisory opinion may be requested provided that such opinion given "shall be accepted as decisive by the parties."[117] Another example is Section 32 of the 1947 Convention of the Privileges and Immunities of the Specialised Agencies.[118] This procedure was also incorporated in section 21 of the 1947 Headquarters Agreement between the UN and the US regarding the headquarters of the UN.[119] More examples include Article XIII, Section 26 of the 1954 Agreement Relating to the Headquarters of the "Economic Commission for Asia and the Far East" between the UN and Thailand; Article 66(2) of the 1986 Vienna Convention on the Law of Treaties between States and International Organisations or between International Organisations.[120] Moreover, one might say that this system of advisory opinions might be used to resolve legal disputes within the framework of the internal affairs of the United Nations. Provisions for binding opinions are to be found in the Statutes of the ILO Tribunal, and previously in the UNAT.[121]

---

[117] ICJ Yearbook, 1946-47, p. 229.

[118] This Section provides that if a difference arises between one of the specialised agencies, on the one hand, and a member of that agency, on the other hand, a request shall be made for an advisory opinion on any legal question involved in accordance with Article 96 of the Charter and Article 65 of the Statute and the opinion given by the Court shall be accepted as decisive by the parties.

[119] Article VIII, Section 21, of the Headquarters Agreement addresses the eventuality of a dispute between the United Nations and the United States concerning the interpretation or application of the agreement. Paragraph (a) of Section 21 provides that in such an eventuality, and once the various modes of settlement failed, the dispute shall be referred for final decision to a tribunal of three arbitrators to be named in a specified way. Moreover paragraph (b) states:

The Secretary-General or the United States may ask the General Assembly to request of the International Court of Justice an advisory opinion on any legal question arising in the course of such proceedings. Pending the receipt of the opinion of the Court, an interim decision of the arbitral tribunal shall be observed by both Parties. Thereafter, the arbitral tribunal shall render a final decision, having regard to the opinion of the Court.

See "Treaties and Other International Agreements of the United States of America, 1776-1949", Department of State Publication 8761, Volume 12, 1974, p. 964.

[120] For a comprehensive study about these agreements see Ago, Roberto, "Binding Advisory Opinions of the International Court of Justice", 85 *AJIL*, 1991, p. 441.

[121] According to Article XII of the Statute of the ILOT, the question of the validity of the decision given by the tribunal shall be submitted by the governing body, to the ICJ for an advisory opinion. The opinion given by the Court shall be binding. In the case of the UNAT, the abolished Article 11 called for the right of member States, the Secretary-General or a person aggrieved by the tribunal's judgments to request the General Assembly to seek an advisory opinion of the International Court of Justice. Article 11 was abolished by the General Assembly Resolution 50/54 on 11 December 1995. This resolution provides: "[n]oting that the procedure provided for under article 11 of the Statute of the Administrative Tribunal of the United Nations has not proved to be a constructive or useful element in the adjudication of staff disputes within the organization, and noting also the view of the Secretary-General to that effect, decides ....a) Delete article 11."

The Court has remarked that "[t]he special feature of this procedure is that advisory proceedings take the place of contentious proceedings which would not be possible under the Statute of the Court", according to which only States may be parties before it.[122] Moreover, the Court has held that such clauses in international agreements are in no wise:[123]

> *[A]ffects the way in which the Court functions; that continues to be determined by its Statute and its Rules. Nor does it affect the reasoning by which the Court forms its Opinion or the content of the Opinion itself. Accordingly, the fact that the Opinion of the Court is accepted as binding provides no reason why the Request for an Opinion should not be complied with.*

Kaikobad argues that even if advisory opinions are not judgements by definition, they are nevertheless "in terms of essential quality, not far removed from the latter. That they are not judgements in the proper sense of the term has nothing to do with the intrinsic elements of the decisions themselves, but with the nature of the Court's advisory jurisdiction as a whole. It is this fact which precludes advisory opinions from descending to mere legal advice given as an institution either collectively or individually by members of the International Court."[124]

The authority of the Court does not depend upon the binding or non-binding nature of its opinions or its judgements. Rather, it is derived from the extent to which it fulfils conscientiously and persuasively its obligations to provide the necessary legal guidance to enable the requesting organs to carry out the objectives of the Organisation. Consequently, the opinion will be authoritative once it has served its purpose of providing guidance for the requesting organ and can be used for future action in the specified field.[125] Rosenne argues that advisory opinions have sometimes contributed to preventing the particular issue from resurfacing on the diplomatic level.[126] Hambro has summarised factors relating to the authoritativeness of advisory opinions:[127]

> *The Opinions of the Court can really be useful only if the question submitted for opinion is a legal question not charged with political tension, if the question is important enough to warrant the seising of the principal judicial organ of the United Nations, if it is sufficiently*

[122] ICJ Rep., 1956, p. 85.

[123] ICJ Rep., 1956, p. 84.

[124] Kaikobad, Kaiyan H., *The International Court of Justice and Judicial Review: A Study of the Court's Powers with Respect to Judgments of the ILO and UN Administrative Tribunals*, The Hague; London: Kluwer Law International, 2000, p. 56.

[125] Rosenne, *supra* note 11, p. 1055.

[126] Rosenne, Shabtai, "On the Non-use of the Advisory Competence of the International Court of Justice", 39 *BYIL*, 1963, p. 38.

[127] Hambro, *supra* note 19 , pp. 21-22.

> *well framed to provide a good basis for the work of the Court, if the Opinion carries conviction on account of its intrinsic value and if the Court is not divided and the majority Opinion is not undermined by the dissenting judges. And if all these conditions are fulfilled, it does not matter much if the Opinion is characterized as 'binding' or not.*

It should also be emphasised here that the reasoning of the Court in the advisory cases plays a considerable role in the authoritativeness of its opinions. Whether a case is contentious or advisory the Court's decision represents "the Court's legal conclusion concerning the situation which is being dealt with, and its weight is the same in both cases: there are no two ways of declaring law."[128] Indeed, Hambro has observed that advisory opinions of the Court even more than judgments in contentious cases will be judged on their merits as well as upon the degree of consensus among the Court's judges:[129]

> *A judgment of the Court, even if it is not perfect and even if there reasoning can be criticised, can serve a useful purpose because it will put an end to a dispute between two or more States. An Advisory Opinion, on the other hand, does not serve this purpose.* It stands or falls with the legal arguments that can be deduced from the reasoning of the majority *and it is very much to be feared that a Court seriously split on any legal question submitted to it for an Advisory Opinion will not contribute anything useful to the solution of that question.*

5 Concluding Remarks

An examination of the Court's advisory opinions demonstrates that it has been careful not to overlook difficulties and not to sacrifice its judicial character for the sake of assisting the requesting organ. In fact, the Court's jurisprudence recognises one important circumstance where the lack of an interested State's consent may render the giving of an opinion incompatible with the Court's judicial character, that is, when the circumstances disclose that to give an opinion would have the effect of circumventing the principle that "a State is not obliged to allow its dispute to be submitted to judicial settlement without its consent." If such a situation arose, the Court's discretion "would afford sufficient legal means to ensure respect for the fundamental principle of consent to jurisdiction."[130]

---

[128] Gros, A., "Concerning the Advisory Role of the International Court of Justice" in: Friedmann, Wolfgang, *et al.*, (eds.), "*Transnational Law in a Changing Society. Essays in Honour of Philip C. Jessup*", 1972, p. 315. It could also be argued that Article 38 of the Court's Statute which provides that judicial decisions are sources of law does not distinguish between advisory and contentious cases.

[129] Hambro, *supra* note 19, p. 21. (Emphasis added).

[130] ICJ Rep., 1989, para. 33, p. 191.

Finally it could be argued that the success of the advisory procedure depends on the interplay between both the Court and the UN. Each side must be aware of the need for restraint. The genuine need for legal advice can be the only motive for requesting an advisory opinion, but the Court must always be mindful of the need to protect its judicial character and not to sacrifice its independence in order to satisfy the interest of the requesting organ. The following Chapter will demonstrate that the Court, when exercising its advisory function, acts judicially by applying largely the same procedures that are used in contentious cases. The judicial function remains the same whether proceedings are contentious or advisory.

CHAPTER FIVE

Procedural Aspects of the Advisory Function of the ICJ[1]

1 Introduction

The task of this Chapter is to stress the judicial character of the advisory function by shedding light on the Court's procedure in exercise of its advisory jurisdiction. A true gauge of the quality of the law administered by a court of law is its procedure, as the quality of the law administered by the Court is reflected, at least in part, in the procedures employed.

A legal system cannot resolve disputes by means of substantive law alone. Thus, a body of procedural law is required to govern the modalities by which questions are referred to and handled by courts or tribunals.[2] However, this does not imply that procedure can remedy any defects in the substantive law, but rather that both go hand in hand. Some scholars suggest that procedure "is often one of the keys to success in litigation."[3] Others consider that procedure is, by definition, "no more than a way of getting somewhere; and in the sphere of international

---

1 The terms "procedure" and "proceedings" are used interchangeably in the English version of the Statute of the ICJ, contrary to the French version. See Hudson, Manley O., *The Permanent Court of International Justice, 1920-1942*, New York: The Macmillan Company, 1943, p. 547.

According to Oxford Dictionary "proceeding" means: the action of going on with something already begun, while the term "procedure" means: a system of proceedings. See The Oxford English Dictionary: Being A Corrected Re-Issue with an Introduction, Supplement, and Bibliography of a New English Dictionary on Historical Principles, vol. VIII, Poy-Ry, Oxford, 1961, pp. 1406-1407. This definition seems to fit with what Hudson has suggested that the term "procedure" is used as a global term, hence it is used as the title for Chapter III of the Statute and in various provisions such as: "the rules for regulating the Court's procedure." In the Anglo-American, and most other legal systems, the term "procedural" indicates the machinery as distinct from the principles. See Wehle, Louis B., "The U.N. By-Passes the International Court as the Council's Advisor, a Study in Contrived Frustration", (1949-50), 98 *UPLR*, p. 309.

2 O'Connell, Mary E. (ed.), *International Disputes Settlement*, Aldershot: Ashgate, 2003, p. xxvi.

3 Shaw, Malcolm N., "The International Court of Justice: A Practical Perspective", 46 *ICLQ*, 1997, p. 854.

judicial action, the destination (the decision) is usually of more interest to jurists than the anfractuosities of the route (the procedural incidents)."[4] Whatever the purpose of procedural rules, however, they must be applied fairly and evenly in keeping with a Court's judicial character.

This Chapter examines the ICJ's procedure in advisory cases, including the source of the procedural rules, the use of *ad hoc* judges and the issues of impartiality and independence. Then the Chapter addresses three additional issues: first, the procedures to be followed by the organs requesting advisory opinions; second, the implications of the assimilation of the Court's procedure in advisory proceedings to its procedure in contentious proceedings whenever appropriate, and, finally the process of decision making, which includes the choice of law to be applied by the Court in accordance with Article 38 (1) of the Court's Statute, and rules governing the deliberations of the Court and the reading of the opinion.

2 Sources of the Procedural Rules Governing Advisory Proceedings

Under Article 30 of its Statute, the Court has the general power to make rules 'for carrying out its functions', including rules of procedure. Certain procedures to be observed with respect to the advisory function are then set out in Articles 65 (2), and 66 of the Court's Statute.[5] These Articles are supplemented by Articles 102-109

---

4 Thirlway, Hugh, "Procedural Law and the International Court of Justice" in: Lowe, Vaughan & Fitzmaurice, Malgosia (eds.), *Fifty Years of the International Court of Justice: Essays in Honour of Sir Robert Jennings*, Grotius Publications, Cambridge University Press, 1996, p. 389.

5 Article 65(2) provides:

"Questions upon which the advisory opinion of the Court is asked shall be laid before the Court by means of a written request containing an exact statement of the question upon which an opinion is required, and accompanied by all documents likely to throw light upon the question."

Article 66 provides:

(1) "The Registrar shall forthwith give notice of the request for an advisory opinion to all States entitled to appear before the Court."

(2) "The Registrar shall also, by means of a special and direct communication, notify any State entitled to appear before the Court or international organization considered by the Court, or, should it not be sitting, by the President, as likely to be able to furnish information on the question, that the Court will be prepared to receive, within a time-limit to be fixed by the President, written statements, or to hear, at a public sitting to be held for the purpose, oral statements relating to the question."

(3) "Should any such State entitled to appear before the Court have failed to receive the special communication referred to in paragraph 2 of this Article, such State may express a desire to submit a written statement or to be heard; and the Court will decide."

of the Rules of the Court made pursuant to Article 30 of the Statute.[6] The resolution concerning the internal judicial practice of the Court, adopted by the Court in 1976 indicates that its provisions should apply "whether the proceedings before the Court are Contentious or Advisory."[7]

3 The Composition of the Court when Exercising Its Advisory Function

The ICJ is composed of fifteen judges of different nationalities,[8] elected by the General Assembly and the Security Council "from among persons of high moral character, who possess the qualifications required in their respective countries for appointment to the highest judicial offices, or are jurisconsults of recognized competence in international law."[9] While the Court may sit in chambers in certain contentious proceedings, pursuant to Article 26 of the Court's Statute, there is no corresponding arrangement provided for advisory opinions and, in accordance with Article 25 of the Court's Statute, "[t]he full Court shall sit except when it is expressly provided otherwise." Therefore, according to Rosenne, advisory opinions should be given by the full court and not by a chamber.[10] In practice most advisory cases before the Court are heard and decided by the full Court unless a judge *ad hoc* is appointed, or if one or more members of the bench do not take part in a particular case. These two exceptions are discussed below.

---

(4) "States and organizations having presented written or oral statements or both shall be permitted to comment on the statements made by other States or organizations in the form, to the extent, and within the time limits which the Court or, should it not be sitting, the President, shall decide in each particular case. Accordingly, the Registrar shall in due time communicate any such written statement to States and organizations having submitted similar statements."

6 For the full texts of these Articles, see appendix 1 appended to this book. Article 30(1) provides that: "The Court shall frame rules for carrying out its functions. In particular, it shall lay down rules of procedure." Rosenne observes that the Rules of Court "constitute the Court's generalized and practical interpretation of the Statute put in the form of a regulatory text" and "the Rules are an international example of delegated or subordinate lawmaking." Rosenne, *The Law and Practice of the International Court, 1920-1996*, The Hague; London: Martinus Nijhoff Publishers, 1997, p. 1073.

7 See Article 10 of the Resolution available at: http://www.icjcij.org/icjwww/ibasicdocuments/ibasictext/ibasicotherdocuments.html, (accessed 18 November 2004).

8 Article 9 of the ICJ's Statute provides that "[a]t every election, the electors shall bear in mind not only the person to be elected should individually possess the qualifications required, but also that in the body as a whole the representation of the main forms of civilization and of the principal legal systems of the world should be assured."

9 See Article 2 of the ICJ's Statute.

10 Rosenne, *supra* note 6, p. 1722. Rosenne argues that it is doubtful whether it would be appropriate to form an *ad hoc* chamber in advisory proceedings even if the request related to a question pending between two or more States.

3.1 National Judges and Judges *Ad hoc* in Advisory Cases[11]

The appointment of a judge *ad hoc* was initially used for contentious cases where there was no judge of the nationality of one or both of the parties on the bench. In such a case each party may nominate a judge *ad hoc* of its own nationality under Article 31 of the Court's Statute.[12]

Although the Statute did not provide for the use of *ad hoc* judges in advisory opinions, Article102 (3) of the Rules of the Court, that were adopted subsequently, declares that if an advisory opinion is requested in connection with a legal question actually pending between two or more States, the provisions regarding judges *ad hoc* shall apply.[13]

The procedure for the appointment and use of judges *ad hoc* has been criticised. The basic complaint is that this procedure is the antithesis of the principle which calls for the composition of the Court to remain detached from the influence of the parties. The *ad hoc* procedure, in one way or another, it is argued, introduces the principles of international arbitration into the sphere of international adjudication.[14]

---

[11] It has been shown in Chapter One that the PCIJ in 1927 amended Article 71 of its Rules to provide for the application of Article 31 of the Statute to "a question relating to an existing dispute between two or more States or members of the League of Nations."

[12] Article 31 provides:

1. *Judges of the nationality of each of the parties shall retain their right to sit in the case before the Court.*
2. *If the Court includes upon the Bench a judge of the nationality of one of the parties, any other party may choose a person to sit as a judge.*
3. *If the Court includes upon the Bench no judge of the nationality of the parties, each of these parties may proceed to choose a judge as provided in paragraph 2 of this Article.*

If several parties have the same interest in the case, they are considered as one party only in accordance with Article 31(5) of the Statute. Any doubt on this point shall be settled by the decision of the Court. In this regard, Article 36 of the Rules states:

1. *If the Court finds that two or more parties are in the same interest, and therefore are to be reckoned as one party only, and that there is no Member of the Court of the nationality of any one of those parties upon the Bench, the Court shall fix a time-limit within which they may jointly choose a judge ad hoc.*
2. *Should any party amongst those found by the Court to be in the same interest allege the existence of a separate interest of its own, or put forward any other objection, the matter shall be decided by the Court, if necessary after hearing the parties.*

In the *South West Africa* Case, the two States, Ethiopia and Liberia, were allowed to appoint one judge jointly. See ICJ Rep., 1966, p. 6.

[13] Article 102(3) provides if an "advisory opinion is requested upon a legal question actually pending between two or more States, Article 31 of the Statute shall apply." Article 68 of the Statute conveys clearly the discretion of the Court to assimilate a request for an advisory opinion to the Court's contentious procedure.

[14] See Oellers-Frahm, Karin, "International Court of Justice", in: Bernhardt, R. (ed.), *Encyclopedia of Public International Law*, North-Holland: Elsevier, 1995, vol. 2, p. 1088.

It is also feared that judges *ad hoc* might act as advocates for the States that chose them.[15]

One might suppose that if appointing a judge *ad hoc* is meant to constitute an opportunity for continuation of a State's pleadings during the deliberation phase, the concept would clash with Article17 of the Court's Statute, since the judge *ad hoc* would be advocating the interests of the State that nominated him.[16] It has been suggested that a judge *ad hoc* has a twofold purpose: first, he is expected to supply local knowledge and to explain the appointing State's point of view, thus promoting the States' confidence in the process.[17] Second, Judge Elihu Lauterpacht maintains that a judge *ad hoc* seeks to re-state the arguments of the party that has appointed him, making sure that they are appreciated, though not necessarily accepted during this collegial consideration.[18] Rosenne notes that, in practice, with very few exceptions, most judges *ad hoc* have voted against the majority in favour of the States that appointed them.[19]

The propriety of the use of judges ad hoc in advisory proceedings arose for the first time in the1971 Legal Consequences for States of the Continued Presence of South Africa in Namibia (South West Africa), notwithstanding Security Council Resolution 276 (1970) Case.[20] Here South Africa had submitted that the question on which the Court was asked to advise, should be regarded as 'a legal question actually pending between two or more States within the meaning of Article 83 of the Rules of Court, and that the South African Government was therefore entitled to choose a judge ad hoc in the terms of Article 31, paragraph 2, of the Statute.[21]

The Court, once it had heard South Africa's arguments, decided by its order of 29 January 1971[22] to reject South Africa's interpretation even though South Africa had insisted that it was an "absolute logical priority."[23] The Court's finding was based on its view that there was no legal dispute pending between two or more States. The Court, after taking into consideration the circumstances in which the request had been submitted and the absence of a dispute, concluded that South

---

15 Judge Oda questions the fears that a judge *ad hoc* is liable to be an advocate for the State which proposed him. See Oda, Shigeru, "The International Court of Justice Viewed From the Bench (1976-1993)", 244, *RCADI*, 1993, p. 115.

16 For the full text of Article 17 see Section 3.2 below.

17 Report of the Informal Inter-Allied Committee, Section 4, para 39 *AJIL*, 39 supp., 1945, p. 11.

18 Sep. Op. of Judge Elihu Lauterpacht, *Application of the Genocide Convention* Case, ICJ Rep., 1993, para.6, p. 409.

19 For further details see Rosenne, Shabtai, *The World Court: What It Is and How It Works*, Dordrecht, London: Martinus Nijhoff Publishers, 1995, p. 74.

20 Hereinafter cited as: "the *Namibia* Case", ICJ Rep., 1971, p. 16.

21 ICJ Rep., 1971, para 35, p. 25.

22 Ibid, p. 13.

23 Ibid, para. 36, p. 25.

Africa was not entitled under Article 83 [now Article 102(2)] of the 1946 Rules of the Court to appoint a judge *ad hoc*.[24]

The Court's decision was criticised by a dissenting minority judges who stated that even if there were no legal dispute actually pending, the Court should have exercised the discretion conferred on it by Article 68 of the Statute.[25] Judge Onyeama, who agreed with the majority of the Court that there was no legal question pending between South Africa and any other State, nevertheless stated that, "in view of the wide discretion vested in the Court by Article 68 of the Statute of the Court, the inapplicability of Article 83 of the Rules would not, in my view, conclude the matter."[26]

Four years later, the judge *ad hoc* question arose again in the 1975 *Western Sahara* Case.[27] Here Morocco and Mauritania alleged that there was "a legal question actually pending" between each of those Sates and Spain.[28] Therefore they requested the appointment of two judges *ad hoc* to sit on the bench. The Court by its order of 22 May 1975 decided that:[29]

> *[W]hen resolution 3292 (XXIX) was adopted, there appeared to be a legal dispute between Morocco and Spain regarding the Territory of Western Sahara; that the questions contained in the request for an opinion may be considered to be connected with that dispute; and that, in consequence, for purposes of application of Article 89 of the [1972] Rules of the Court, the advisory opinion requested in that resolution appears to be one "upon a legal question actually pending between two or more states.*

The Court accordingly concluded that "Morocco is entitled under Articles 31 and 68 of the Statute of the Court and Article 89 of the Rules of the Court to choose a person to sit as judge *ad hoc* in the present proceedings."[30] Concerning Mauritania, the Court found that:[31]

---

24 Ibid, para. 35, p. 24.

25 See Sep. Op. of Judge Petrén who argued that there was a legal question pending which justified the appointment of judge *ad hoc*. ICJ Rep., 1971, pp. 129-130.

26 Sep. Op of Judge Onyeama, ibid, p. 139. However, the Court decided that "[i]n the present case the Court, having regard to the Rules of Court adopted under Article 30 of the Statute, came to the conclusion that it was unable to exercise discretion in this respect." See ICJ Rep., 1971, para. 39, p. 27.

27 ICJ Rep., 1975, p. 6.

28 The Court in this case included on its bench a judge of Spanish nationality (Judge De Castro).

29 ICJ Rep., 1975, pp. 7-8.

30 Ibid.

31 ICJ Rep., 1975, p. 8.

> *[T]here appeared to be no legal dispute between Mauritania and Spain regarding the Territory of Western Sahara" and consequently concluded that the conditions for the application of Article 31 and 68 of the Court's Statute and Article 89 of the Court's Rules were not satisfied.*

Lastly, it is interesting to note that although the issue was not raised in the *Legal Consequences of the Construction of a Wall in the Occupied Palestinian Territory* Case,[32] had the appointment of a judge *ad hoc* been requested, the Court would have been confronted with an unprecedented and awkward situation. Palestine, which may be characterised as a party to the dispute, is not recognised as a State for the purposes of the Court's Statute, or under general International Law. However, it is a member of the league of Arab States and is thus treated as a State by League members. Judge Awada asked hypothetically what would happen if Israel sought to appoint a judge *ad hoc* while Palestine could not.[33]

3.2 Impartiality and Independence of Judges

Article 20 of the Court's Statute provides that "[e]very member of the Court shall, before taking up his duties, make a solemn declaration in open court that he will exercise his powers impartially and conscientiously."[34] From a legal standpoint 'impartiality' has been defined as:[35]

> *An aspect of equality, a quality generally accepted as desirable in judges and administrators of law, connoting determination to deal equally with both or all parties to a dispute, and not to favour any, but to apply the law equally and fairly to all. Partiality of an arbitrator would justify setting his award aside.*

To guarantee impartiality the ICJ Statute lays down some particular requirements. Article 2 provides that "[t]he Court shall be composed of a body of independent judges." This is reinforced in Article 16 (1) which prohibits any member of the Court from exercising any political or administrative function or indeed any other occupation of a professional nature. A judge on the bench of the Court is in a full-time occupation and his duties take priority over any other activities.[36]

Parties are, however, not prohibited from challenging the participation of one or more members of the bench. Challenges may be based on a conflict of interest,

---

32 Hereinafter cited as: "the *Wall* Case", available at: http://www.icjcij.org/icjwww/idocket/imwp/imwpframe.htm, (accessed 21 October 2004).

33 Sep. Op. of Judge Hisashi Owada, para. 19. Available at: http://www.icjcij.org/icjwww/idocket/imwp/imwpframe.htm (accessed 25 October 2004).

34 Article 17(2) and 24 of the Statute corroborate the requirement of impartiality.

35 Walker, David, *Oxford Companion to Law*, Oxford: Clarendon Press, 1980, p. 601.

36 Rosenne, *supra* note 19, p. 70.

previous statements or the advocacy of a position on an issue before the Court. Articles 17 and 24 of the Court's Statute are considered as safeguards for judicial independence. Article 17 provides:

1. *No member of the Court may act as agent, counsel, or advocate in any case.*
2. *No member may participate in the decision of any case in which he has previously taken part as agent, counsel, or advocate for one of the parties, or as a member of a national or international court, or of a commission of inquiry, or in any other capacity.*
3. *Any doubt on this point shall be settled by the decision of the Court.*

Moreover, Article 24 provides:

1. *If, for some special reason, a member of the Court considers that he should not take part in the decision of a particular case, he shall so inform the President.*
2. *If the President considers that for some special reason one of the members of the Court should not sit in a particular case, he shall give him notice accordingly.*
3. *If in any such case the member of the Court and the President disagree, the matter shall be settled by the decision of the Court.*

In light of paragraph 1 of Article 24, French Judge Basdevant did not participate in the *Effect of Awards of Compensation Made by the United Nations Administrative Tribunal* Advisory Opinion[37] because his daughter was president of that Tribunal.[38] Later, in the *Application for Review of Judgment No.158 of the United Nations Administrative Tribunal* Case,[39] Judges Petrén and Pinto informed the President that they had participated in the development of the jurisprudence of the Tribunal referred to in the case and they therefore asked to be excluded from sitting on the case.[40]

Articles 17 and 24, referred to above, are intended to ensure the independence and impartiality of judges. A court of law must be impartial or else it will not be considered a true court of law and will therefore lose legitimacy. A corollary to impartiality is the principle of equality. This means parties should be given equal chances to present their cases. This principle will be undermined by a judge who has already made up his mind about the case through his previous involvement

---

37 Hereinafter cited as: "the *Effect of Awards* Case", ICJ Rep., 1954, p. 47.

38 ICJ Pled., 1954, p. 281.

39 Hereinafter cited as: "the *Review of Judgment No 158 of UNAT* Case", ICJ Rep., 1973, p. 166.

40 ICJ Pled., 1973, p. 179. See also: http://www.icjcij.org/icjwww/idecisions/isummaries/irjsummary730712.htm (accessed 25 October 2004).

with it in one way or another.[41] The application of the provisions pertaining to judicial independence is an internal matter for the Court, which is governed by Article 34 of the Rules.[42] Consequently, in line with the principle of judicial independence, only the Court itself is entitled, through use of its discretion, to determine the disqualification of any judge.

The first challenge to judges in advisory proceedings occurred in the *Namibia* Case.[43] Here South Africa objected to the participation of three judges, namely, Zafrulla Khan, Padilla Nervo, and Morozov. South Africa's objections were based "on statements made or other participation by the Members concerned, in their former capacity as representatives of their Governments, in the United Nations organs which were dealing with matters concerning South West Africa."[44] The Court by its three orders on 26 January 1971 rejected the South African challenges.[45] In each case, the Court found that:[46]

> *[T]he participation of the Member concerned in his former capacity as representative of his Government, to which objection was taken in the South African Government's written statement, did not attract the application of Article 17, paragraph 2, of the Statute of the Court.*

Pursuant to Article 34(2) of the Rules of Court, the Government of Israel in the *Wall* Case asked the Court to exclude Judge Elaraby, one of the two Arab Judges

---

41 Jennings, Robert Y., "The Role of the International Court of Justice", 68 *BYIL*, 1997, p. 43.

42 Article 34 (1) provides: [i]n case of any doubt arising as to the application of Article 17, paragraph 2, of the Statute or in a case of a disagreement as to the application of Article 24 of the Statute, the President shall inform the Members of the Court, with whom the decision lies. See also Rosenne, *supra* note 6, p. 1102.

43 ICJ Rep., 1971, p. 16.

44 Ibid, para 9, p. 18.

45 Ibid, p. 4, 7 and 10.

46 Ibid, para 9, p. 18. The Court concluded that there was no reason to depart from the decision made earlier in the *South West Africa* cases with reference to Judge Padilla Nervo. As far as the other two judges were concerned, the Court found that the U.N activities to which South Africa referred did not justify a different conclusion from those raised in the application which the Court had rejected in 1965. Ibid, para. 9, p. 19. The Court's decision regarding Judge Morozov was controversial. Judge Petrén was not persuaded by the Court's finding that the previous activities of a judge as a representative of his country at the UN did not contravene Article 17(2) and argued that "if a person has formulated or defended the text of resolutions upon the validity of which the Court has to decide, he may not take part in the case as a judge, whether the matter be contentious or advisory." See Sep. Op. of Judge Petrén, ICJ Rep., 1971, p. 130; Similarly, Judge Gros noted that "[o]rder No. 3 of 26th January 1971 marked a change in practice, and that the Court has discarded the criterion of active participation." Diss. Op. of Judge Gros, ICJ Rep., 1971, p. 324.

in the Bench, from sitting in the case.[47] Israel argued that its request was due to the previous participation of Judge Elaraby in the Tenth Emergency Special Session of the General Assembly from which the advisory opinion request has originated. Moreover, Israel contended that Judge Elaraby has participated as principal legal adviser to the Egyptian Delegation to the Camp David Middle East Peace Conference of 1978. The Court rejected Israel's arguments and noted that the activities of Judge Elaraby were performed in his capacity of a diplomatic representative of his country, most of them many years before the question of the construction of the wall arose. Therefore, the Court held that "Judge Elaraby "could not be regarded as having "previously taken part" in the case in any capacity."[48]

Lastly, it is worth mentioning that the procedural rules do not cover situations where the disqualification of several judges leaves the Court with less than the required quorum[49] Hypothetically, Thirlway speculates how the Court would deal with the disqualification of seven judges, a theoretical issue not covered by the rules of procedure.[50]

4 The Process of Requesting an Advisory Opinion

It is important to shed light on the procedures to be followed by requesting organ and by the Court in advisory cases. These procedures, as mentioned previously, are codified in the Court's Statute and in the Rules of the Court adopted by virtue of Article 30 of the Court's Statute.

4.1 Initiating the Request

A formal request for an advisory opinion is necessary to initiate advisory proceedings.[51] This means that the Court cannot give an opinion on its own motion, i.e. *proprio motu*. The request may take the form of a resolution adopted by the requesting organ to seek the Court's opinion on a legal question. In some cases the requesting organs turn to special internal committees for legal advice to assist

[47] A letter of 31 December 2003, and a confidential letter of 15 January 2004 which both addressed to the President.

[48] Order of 30 January 2004, available at: http://www.icj-cij.org/icjwww/idocket/imwp/imwpframe.htm (accessed 25 November 2004) See also para. 8 of the *Wall* Case, *supra* note 32.

[49] The term "disqualification" means: "[a]ny fact which has the legal effect of making a person previously qualified or entitled to do something no longer qualified or entitled to do so". See Walker, *supra* note 35, p. 364.

[50] Thirlway, Hugh, "The Law and Procedure of the International Court of Justice, 1960-1989", 72 *BYIL*, 2001, p. 45.

[51] Pasqalucci, Jo M., *The Practice and Procedure of the Inter-American Court of Human Rights*, Cambridge: Cambridge University Press, 2003, p. 71.

them in formulating the request.[52] The request is then submitted to the Court in a letter from the Secretary-General containing the text of the question for which an opinion is requested.[53] This request should contain an exact statement of the question which means that the question should be formulated in a clear way to avoid any ambiguity.[54]

The fact that the question submitted to the Court has been formulated by the requesting organ after debating its content and not directly by the requesting parties generally has the effect of making the Court less strict in interpreting the question. Rosenne argues that the Court deals with the question leniently, through exercising its interpretation power, in order to accommodate any drafting inadequacies.[55]

In practice, there has even been some fundamental reformulation by the Court of a number of requests. For instance, the Court in the 1980 *Interpretation of the Agreement of 25 March 1951 between the WHO and Egypt* Case,[56] decided that the request should be reformulated. The Court asserted that rules do not operate in a vacuum but must relate to facts and the context of a wider framework of legal rules. If it is to remain faithful to the requirements of its judicial character, the Court "must first ascertain the meaning and full implications of the question in the light of the actual framework of fact and law in which it falls for consideration."[57]

The Court also reformulated the request in the *Application for Review of Judgment No.273 of the United Nations Administrative Tribunal Case.*[58] In spite of a series of irregularities in drafting the question, the Court used its power to reformulate the question submitted by the Committee on Application for Review of Administrative Tribunal judgements rather than rejected it. The Court found that

[52] For the General Assembly, in an Annex to its Rules of procedure, previous advice is recommended by the Sixth Committee. Other organs and agencies have special legal committees. See Eyffinger, Arthur, *The International Court of Justice, 1946-1996*, The Hague; London: Kluwer Law International, 1999, p. 148.

[53] Article 104 of the Rules provides that: [a]ll requests for advisory opinions shall be transmitted to the Court either by the Secretary General of the United Nations or, as the case may be, the chief administrative officer of the body authorized to make the request. The documents referred to in Article 65, paragraph 2, of the Statute shall be transmitted to the Court at the same time as the request or as soon as possible thereafter, in the number of copies required by the Court."

[54] For the full text of Article 65(2) of the Statute, see Section 2 above.

[55] Rosenne, *supra* note 6, p. 357; Weissberg, Guenter, "The Role of the International Court of Justice in the United Nations System: the First Quarter Century" in: Gross, Leo, *The Future of the International Court of Justice*, Dobbs Ferry, New York: Oceana Publications, 1976, p. 136.

[56] Hereinafter cited as "the *WHO/Egypt* Case", ICJ Rep., 1980, p. 73. For details about this case see Section II of Chapter Four, *supra*.

[57] ICJ Rep., 1980, Para.10, p. 76.

[58] Hereinafter cited as: "the *Review of Judgment No. 273* Case", ICJ Rep., 1982, p. 325.

the question was, "on the face of it, at once infelicitously expressed and vague."[59] However, it decided that:[60]

> *While it would have been a compelling reason, making it inappropriate for the Court to entertain a request, that its judicial role would be endangered or disregarded, that is not so in the present case, and the Court thus does not find that considerations of judicial restraint should prevent it from rendering the advisory opinion requested.*

Thirlway, while criticising the Court's finding, observed that the Court had had in this case to balance the requirements of its judicial character, which would point to a refusal to appear to endorse the thoroughly flawed quasi-judicial procedure underlying the request with its role as the UN's principal judicial organ "which would point to co-operation in the review procedure" and give it the opportunity to call the Committee to order for its slovenly procedure. A refusal of the request, however, "would leave in suspense a very serious allegation against the Administrative Tribunal, that it had in effect challenged the authority of the General Assembly."[61] Therefore, the Court had to reformulate the question in order to give a legal opinion which would assist a subsidiary UN body.

However, whenever the Court undertakes such a reformulation process it is still limited by the basic elements of the question. Thus, the PCIJ in *the Interpretation of the Greco-Turkish Agreement of 1 December 1926 (Final Protocol)* Case stated that:[62]

> *[I]t is essential that it should determine what this question is and formulate an exact statement of it, in order more particularly to avoid dealing with points of law upon which it was not the intention of the Council or the Commission to obtain its opinion.*

Moreover, Article 65(2) of the Statute and Article104 of the Rules require that the written request be "accompanied by all documents likely to throw light upon the question." In fact, this requirement has not been interpreted literally in practice and the Court's jurisprudence suggests that requisite documents did not always accompany the request but followed later. Keith believes that although a delay in submitting documents may be regarded as a breach of the letter of Article 65(2) there is no breach of the spirit of the provision.[63]

---

59 Ibid, para. 46, p. 348.

60 ICJ Rep., 1982, para. 45, p. 347.

61 Thirlway, Hugh, "The Law and Procedure of the International Court of Justice", 71 *BYIL*, 2000, pp. 133-134.

62 PCIJ, Ser. B, No.16, 1928, p. 14.

63 Keith, Kenneth, *The Extent of the Advisory Jurisdiction of the International Court of Justice*, Leyden: A.W. Sijthoff, 1971, p. 49. In the *WHO/Egypt* Case, the Court noted that the dossier which was received in the Registry on 11 June 1980 was not accompanied by written statements, a synopsis of the case and an index of documents. In response to requests by the President, the WHO supplied the Court with a number of additional documents. ICJ Rep., 1980, para 5, p. 75.

4.2 Participation in Advisory Proceedings

As soon as a request is filed with the Court, The Court's Registrar, in accordance with Article 66 (2) of the Court's Statute, send to any States and international organisations that are likely to be able to furnish information on the question a ' special and direct communication' notifying them that the Court is ready to receive their written statements within a certain time-limit.[64]

In accordance with Article 66(3) of the Statute, the Court has discretion to allow written or oral statements to be made by States which were not so notified, although they were entitled to appear before the Court.[65] The purpose of this provision is to encourage States and international organisations to assist the Court by submitting relevant information. Table 1 below shows the number of participating States in the oral and written proceedings in advisory cases.

Table 1. The Number of Participating States in the Oral and Written Proceedings in Advisory Cases

Case Name	**States' Participation**	
	Written Phase	**Oral Phase**
Conditions of Admission of a State to Membership in the United Nations (Article 4 of the Charter), ICJ Reports, 1948, p. 57	14	6
Reparation for Injuries Suffered in the Service of the United Nations, ICJ Reports, 1949, p. 174	5	3
Competence of the General. Assembly for the Admission of a State to the United Nations, ICJ Reports, 1950, p. 4	9	1
Interpretation of Peace Treaties with Bulgaria, Hungary and Romania, ICJ Reports, 1950, First Phase, p. 65	11	3
Interpretation of Peace Treaties with Bulgaria, Hungary and Romania, ICJ Reports, 1950, Second Phase, p. 221	1	3
International Status of South-West Africa, ICJ Reports, 1950, p. 128	5	3
Reservations to the Convention on the Prevention and Punishment of the Crime of Genocide, ICJ Reports 1951, p. 15	16	4
Effects of Awards of Compensation made by the United Nations Administrative Tribunal, ICJ Reports 1954, p. 47	15	6
Voting Procedure on Questions Relating to Reports and Petitions Concerning the Territory of South-West Africa, ICJ Reports 1955, p. 67	6	-

64 For the full text of Article 66(2) of the Court's Statute, see *supra* note 5. This Article distinguishes between States and international organisations.

65 For the full text of Article 66(3) of the Court's Statute, see *supra* note 5.

Table 1 (continued)

Case Name	States' Participation	
	Written Phase	**Oral Phase**
Judgments of the Administrative Tribunal of the International Labour Organisation Upon Complaints Made Against the United Nations Educational, Scientific and Cultural Organisation, ICJ Reports 1956, p. 77	5	-
Admissibility of Hearings of Petitioners by the Committee on South West Africa, ICJ Reports 1956, p. 23	2	1
Constitution of the Maritime Safety Committee of the Inter-Governmental Maritime Consultative Organization, ICJ Reports 1960, ICJ Reports 1960, p. 150	13	7
Certain Expenses of the United Nations (Article 17, Paragraph 2, of the Charter), ICJ Reports 1962, p. 151	23	9
Legal Consequences for States of the Continued Presence of South Africa in Namibia (South West Africa) Notwithstanding Security Council Resolution 276 (1970), ICJ Reports 1971, p. 16	12	10
Application for Review of Judgment No. 158 of the United Nations Administrative Tribunal, ICJ Reports 1973, p. 166	1	-
Western Sahara, ICJ Reports 1975, p. 12	12	5
Interpretation of the Agreement of 25 March 1951 Between the WHO and Egypt, ICJ Reports 1980, p. 73	9	5
Application for Review of Judgment No. 273 of the United Nations Administrative Tribunal, ICJ Reports 1982, p. 325	3	-
Application for Review of Judgment No. 333 of the United Nations Administrative Tribunal, ICJ Reports 1987, p. 18	5	-
Applicability of the Obligation to Arbitrate Under Section 21 of the United Nations Headquarters Agreement of 26 June 1947, ICJ Reports 1988, p. 12	3	1
Applicability of Article VI, Section 22, of the Convention on the Privileges and Immunities of the United Nations, ICJ Reports 1989, p. 177	5	2
Legality of the Use BY a State of Nuclear Weapons in Armed Conflict, ICJ Reports 1996, p. 66	35	20
Legality of the Threat or Use of Nuclear Weapons, ICJ Reports 1996, p. 226	28	22
Difference Relating to Immunity From Legal Process of a Special Rapporteur of the Commission on Human Rights, ICJ Reports 1999, p. 62	5	4
Legal Consequences of the Construction of a Wall in the Occupied Palestinian Territory. Available at: http://www.icj-cij.org/icjwww/idocket/imwp/imwpframe.htm	44	12

4.3 The Role of the Secretary General in Advisory Proceedings

Article 104 of the1978 Rules of the Court requires that the Secretary-General or the chief administrative officer of the authorised requesting organisation shall forward all requests for advisory opinions to the Court. The Secretary-General or his representatives must be available to answer the Court's questions concerning a request.[66] However, the Secretary-General frequently comments on the subject matter of the question, either orally or in writing, or in both forms.[67]

The range of issues in such comments have included detailed statements of "observations" on the legal problem;[68] historical analyses;[69] surveys of all summaries of the discussions, arguments and debates relating to the question that have arisen in the UN;[70] and explanatory notes.[71] Rosenne has observed that the Secretary- General has not offered his own substantive opinions when the request related to controversial issues where the requests were made after a "bitterly divisive vote",[72] except when the request had related to, or had an effect on, the Secretary General's performance or his functions.[73]

---

[66] For example in the *Namibia* Case the Secretary-General had addressed himself to the question of whether action taken under Article 24 of the UN Charter could bind members under Article 25, which he answered in the affirmative. See Higgins, Rosalyn, "The Advisory Opinion on Namibia: Which UN Resolutions are Binding under Article 25 of the Charter", 21 *ICLQ*, 1972, p. 286.

[67] Bowett, D.W, *The Law of International Institutions*, London, Stevens and Sons, 1982, p. 281.

[68] In the *South West Africa* (Status) Case, the role of the Secretary-General took the form of a long and reasoned statement of the legal issues involved in the case, emphasizing the conflict of views between the majority of the General Assembly and the Union of South Africa. Rosenne, Shabtai "The Secretary-General of the United Nations and the Advisory Procedure of the International Court of Justice" in: Wellens, Karel, (ed.), *International Law: Theory and Practice Essays in Honour of Eric Suy*, The Hague; Boston; London: Martinus Nijhoff Publishers, 1998, pp. 709-710.

[69] See for instance, the *Peace Treaties* Case and the *Competence of the* General Assembly Case. In these cases the Secretary-General refrained from giving any indication of his legal views and confined himself to historical analysis. Rosenne, *supra* note 6, p. 1749.

[70] Like the Secretary-General's representative oral statement in the *Admissions* Case. See Rosenne *supra* note 68, p. 709.

[71] In the *South West Africa* (Voting) Opinion, two written statements were filed containing an incomplete survey of the discussion that took place since 1950 additional notes related to the voting rules in the League Council and UN General Assembly were included. See Rosenne, *supra* note 68, pp. 709-710.

[72] Like the WHO and General Assembly requests on the *Legality of Threat or Use of Nuclear Weapons* Opinions. Rosenne, *supra* note 68, p. 708.

[73] Like the *Peace Treaties* Case concerning functions which concerned peace treaties "sought to impose on the Secretary-General as appointing authority for treaty commissions", Rosenne, ibid, p. 708.

The statements of the Secretary-General, or those of his representatives, are expected to provide a neutral point of view or to reflect the specific interests of the UN in the outcome of the proceedings.[74] The Secretary-General's statements, however, seem to be influential. Regarding the *Admissions* Case, Rosenne has noted that the Court's opinion and the individual opinions appended to it suggest that the Secretary-General's statement played a significant role in the Court's deliberations.[75] Moreover, in the *United Nations Administrative Tribunal* Case, thc Secretary-General's statement had a decisive influence on the Court.[76]

Lastly, in the *Wall* Case, the Court relied largely on the Secretary-General's reports from 14 April 2002 to 20 November 2003, which described the works constructed by Israel in the Occupied Territory. For developments subsequent to the publication of that report the Court referred to complementary information contained in the UN's written statement which was intended by the Secretary-General to supplement his report.[77]

4.4 Written and Oral Proceedings

As in contentious cases, advisory proceedings are generally divided into written and oral phases so that the Court may be in full possession of the facts before it renders an opinion.[78] While there are no specific provisions regulating written and oral stages in advisory proceedings, the Rules for contentious cases concerning written or oral proceedings, as well as internal procedures, apply *mutatis mutandis*.[79] The Court also has discretion to apply Article 43(1) of the Statute, which relates to contentious proceedings, to advisory proceedings as well.[80]

Written proceedings consist of communications to the Court and to the parties in the form of memorials and counter-memorials, and if necessary, replies, in addition to all supporting papers and documents.[81] The Court may invite States and organisations to file written statements within a time-limit, usually of two months.[82]

---

74 Rosenne, ibid.

75 In this case the representative of the Secretary-General surveyed the treatment of admission problems in the Security Council and the debates in the General Assembly which led to the request and appended to his oral statement two memoranda consisting of guides to the relevant records of the San Francisco Conference. See Rosenne, *supra* note 6, p. 1749; Rosenne, *supra* note 68, p. 709.

76 In this Case, the Secretary-General submitted a detailed written statement which dealt with the functions and powers of the Administrative Tribunal itself which was of a great importance to the Court. Rossene, ibid, p. 713.

77 See paras. 79-80 of the Court's Opinion, *supra* note 32.

78 See http://www.icj-cij.org/icjwww/igeneralinformation/ibbook/Bbookframepage.htm. (accessed 25 October 2004).

79 Oda, *supra* note 15, p. 119.

80 Article 43 divides procedures into written and oral.

81 See Article 43(2) of the Statute.

82 The time limit might be extended on the request of any State or organisation.

In the *Namibia* Case and in the *Legality of the Use by a State of Nuclear Weapons in Armed Conflict Case* the time limit for written statements was extended. The function of pleadings, whether written or oral, is to clarify the core issues which the Court's decision must address.

As stated previously, by virtue of Article 66(2) of the Court's Statute, the Registrar must by means of a special, direct communication notify any State or international organisation entitled to appear before the Court and likely to be able to furnish information on the submitted question, of the readiness of the Court to receive within a fixed time limit written statements or to hear oral statements. As a corollary to this, States and international organisations having presented written or oral statements or both are permitted within fixed time limits to comment on statements made by other States or international organisations.[83]

The oral stage takes place after the closure of the written proceedings, and in advisory cases time limits are shorter than in contentious cases. The parties are represented by agents who may call upon the assistance of counsel or advocates. Rosenne maintained that these agents, in advisory cases, are technically known as representatives as the Court tends to reserve the designation "agent" to States' representatives in contentious or quasi-contentious cases, although there is no consistency in such usage.[84] As a general rule, oral proceedings in advisory cases do not take more than a few sittings. However, in the *Namibia* Case, the Court held 24 sittings; in the *Western Sahara* Case 27 sittings and in the *Legality of the Use by a State of Nuclear Weapons* Case the Court held 13 sittings.[85]

Oral proceedings are important to any court of law as they guarantee the principle of publicity. This stage is, in fact, a continuation of the written stage and gives parties the opportunity to argue their positions in the presence of the bench and of the opposing party, which has the right to reply. This is quite different from a system, which relies only upon written statements argued at a distance on paper.[86] Nevertheless, in some advisory cases the Court has dispensed with oral proceedings, without undermining its judicial character, where it was satisfied that it had sufficient information to enable it to decide the question before it.

This situation has most typically arisen where the Court has been authorised to review the judgments of Administrative Tribunals established to settle disputes between international organisations and their staff over the terms of their contracts of appointment.[87] For example, the ICJ was empowered under Article 11 (1) of the

---

[83] See Article 66(4) of the ICJ's Statute.

[84] Rosenne, *supra* note 6, p. 1736.

[85] Available at: http://www.icj-cij.org/icjwww/igeneralinformation/ibbook/Bbookframepage.htm (accessed 25 October 2004).

[86] Jennings, *supra* note 41, p. 14.

[87] These Tribunals were established within the framework of the UN to decide disputes between international organisations and their officials regarding staff contracts of employment and conditions of appointment.

UNAT Statute[88] and it is still empowered under Article 12 of the ILOAT Statute[89] to review the judgements of these administrative tribunals, if requested to do so, through binding advisory opinions. However, because individuals, namely staff members, are not entitled to appear before the Court, they cannot participate in oral proceedings. The absence of equality between the parties before the Court was advanced as a reason for challenging requests for advisory opinions. In order to carry out its advisory function and still comply with its obligation to hear all parties equally, the Court developed the practice, in such cases, of refusing to hold any oral hearings at all. The Staff's views were, instead, to be transmitted to the Court by the requesting organ in written form. In other words, the Court in these cases refused to hold oral hearings as a means of providing equality.

The 1956 Judgments of the Administrative Tribunal of the International Labour Organisation Upon Complaints Made Against the United Nations Educational Scientific and Cultural Organization[90] illustrates the way in which the Court dealt with this type of cases. Here the problem of lack of equality was raised in the context of an ILOAT judgment handed down in favour of the four UNESCO officials.[91] Subsequently, the UNESCO Executive Board challenged these judgments. The Court observed that there was inequality between UNESCO and its officials as Article 12 only permits the concerned organisation or specialised agency to apply for a request to the Court. No equal right was vested in favour of staff members of the organisation.[92] Similarly, Article 66 (2) of the Court's Statute provides that only States and international organisations have access to the Court in advisory

---

[88] For the full text of the previous Article 11 and the General Assembly's resolution No. 50/54 1995 which deleted Article 11, see appendix 2 appended to this book. The Administrative Tribunal of the UN has jurisdiction in respect of the UN and IMO. Under Article 11 (1) of the UNAT, the Committee on Application for Review of Administrative Tribunal Judgments was authorized until this system was abolished altogether in 1995.

[89] For the full text of Article XII, see appendix 2 appended to this book. The Administrative Tribunal of the ILO has jurisdiction in respect of the ILO; the WHO and UNESCO; Under Article XII of the ILOAT, the request for an advisory opinion may be initiated either by governing body of the ILO or its Executive Board.

[90] Advisory opinion of 23 October 1956.

[91] The background of this Case was that four staff members obtained fixed-term appointments with UNESCO. These appointments, subsequently renewed, were due to expire on 31 December 1954. The failure by the Director General of UNESCO to renew the fixed term contracts forced the employees to complain to the UNESCO Appeals Board. The Board decided that the contracts had to be renewed. Despite the Board decision, the Director General maintained his decision not to renew the contracts for the employees concerned. Therefore, a complaint was referred to ILOAT, which in its judgment of April 26th, 1955 declared itself competent and decided on the merits of the case.

[92] Judge Klaestad noted that Article 12, which introduced a review procedure, had failed to observe the primary principle of equality of justice and impartiality of procedure. See his Sep. Op. in ICJ Rep., 1956, p. 111.

cases. Therefore, only UNESCO and not its staff members enjoy the right to make written and oral presentations.

The Court's view was that its judicial character requires that both parties may be affected by the Court's proceedings and that they should therefore be in an equal position to submit their own views and arguments to the Court.[93] Therefore, to meet the obstacles raised by Article 66(2), the Court allowed staff members to submit their views through UNESCO as an intermediary and thus to dispense with oral proceedings.[94] In this way, the Court was "satisfied that the adequate information has been made available to it" and held that "the principle of equality of the parties follows from the requirements of good administration of justice."[95]

In the 1973 *Application for Review of Judgment No. 158 of the United Nations Administrative Tribunal* Case, the Court reviewed a UNAT judgment with respect to the application of a UN's staff member who had objected to a decision rendered by the Tribunal in his case.[96] This opinion was requested by the Committee on Application for Review of Administrative Tribunal Judgments established by Article 11(4) of the Statute.[97]

The Court found that any absence of equality between staff members and the Secretary- General inherent in the terms of Article 66 of the Court's Statute could be cured by the adoption of appropriate procedures to ensure equality in the particular proceedings.[98] The Court also observed that when written statements have been submitted to the Court in advisory proceedings, under Article 66(2) of the Statute, the further proceedings in the case and, in particular, the holding of oral proceedings, lies within the discretion of the Court:[99]

---

[93] ICJ Rep., 1956, p. 86.

[94] The Court's decision to dispense with the oral phase was subject to criticism. Judge Khan claimed that such a decision deprived the court of a means of obtaining valuable assistance in the discharging of its judicial function. See Sep. Op. of Judge Muhammed Khan, ICJ Rep., 1956, p. 114.

[95] ICJ Rep., 1956, p. 86.

[96] Mr. Fasla, an official of the UN Development Program (UNDP), made a fixed-term contract which was due to expire on 31 December 1969. Due to the non-renewal of his contract, Mr. Fasla complained to the Joint Appeals Board and to UNAT. The Tribunal ruled against Mr. Fasla. However, Mr. Fasla objected to the decision and asked the Committee on Applications for Review of Administrative Tribunal Judgments to request an advisory opinion of the Court.

[97] This Committee is authorised by Article 96 (2) of the UN Charter to request an advisory opinion of the Court. The Committee is composed of the Member States "the representatives of which have served on the General Committee of the most recent regular session of the General Assembly." See paragraph (4) of Article 11 of the UNAT Statute.

[98] ICJ Rep., 1973, p. 180.

[99] Ibid, para. 36, p. 181.

> *In exercising that discretion, the Court will have regard both to the provisions of its Statute and to the requirements of its judicial character. But it does not appear to the Court that there is any general principle of law which requires that in review proceedings the interested parties should necessarily have an opportunity to submit oral statements of their case to the review tribunal. General principles of law and the judicial character of the Court do require that, even in advisory proceedings, the interested parties should each have an opportunity, and on the basis of equality, to submit all the elements relevant to the questions which have been referred to the review tribunal. But that condition is fulfilled by the submission of written statements.*

In this case, the procedural safeguards afforded to the staff member were more secure than in the previous case, the 1956 *UNESCO* Case, because Article 11(2) of the UNAT Statute expressly provides that when the Committee requests an advisory opinion the Secretary- General shall transmit to the Court the views of the staff members concerned. The Court noted that under this Article there was a "right guaranteed by the Statute" with regard to the transmission of views of staff member and thus:[100]

> *[T]he equality of a staff member in the written procedure before the Court is not dependent on the will or favour of the Organization, but is made a matter of right guaranteed by the Statute of the Administrative Tribunal.*

Therefore, pursuant to the above Article, the Secretary-General transmitted the statements of the staff member, Mr. Fasla, to the Court, which thereafter dispensed with oral statements. The Court asserted that dispensing with oral proceedings was a matter of discretion for the Court, and therefore "if the Court is satisfied that adequate information has been made available to it, the fact that no public hearings have been held is not a bar to the Court's complying with the request for an opinion."[101]

This conclusion was reiterated by the Court in subsequent cases, such as the 1982 *Application for Review of Judgment No. 273 of the United Nations Administrative Tribunal* Case.[102] Here the Court as in its previous cases received a staff

[100] ICJ Rep., 1973, para. 35, p. 180.

[101] Ibid, para. 36, p. 181. The Court found that the UNAT had not failed to exercise jurisdiction vested in it as claimed by Mr. Fasla in his application to the review committee, and that the Administrative Tribunal had not committed a fundamental error in procedure which had occasioned a failure of justice as contended in the application to the Committee.

[102] Advisory Opinion of 20 July 1982. In this Case the US had applied to the Committee for Review of Administrative Tribunal Judgments to request an advisory opinion of the

member's submission through an intermediary, namely the Secretary-General, and reiterated its findings in the1973 *Review of Judgment No 158 of UNAT* Case. The Court noted that the decision "to do without oral proceedings, while for the Court it amounts to depriving itself of a very useful procedure, appears to be a sacrifice which is justified by concern thereby to ensure actual equality."[103]

Finally, the same procedure was adopted in the *Application for Review of Judgment No.333 of the United Nations Administrative Tribunal* Case.[104] The Court stated that the submissions of Mr. Yakimetz were transmitted to it by the Secretary -General and that it had no intention of holding any public sitting for the purpose of hearing oral statements.[105]

The cases discussed indicate that the Court considers maintaining equality between parties to be central part of its judicial function.

5 The Legal Bases Relied Upon by the Court for Decision-Making

Rosenne suggests that the law to be applied by the Court ultimately governs how the Court reaches its decision and, indeed, provides the reason for the decision.[106] Shaw also argues that the authoritativeness of a Court's decision in any particular case "relates to the very nature and content of the decision itself."[107] This is because the legal arguments that underpin the decision of the Court must be sound.[108] Against this background this Section examines the sources of the applicable law and the Court's jurisprudence in advisory cases when dealing with these sources.

Court in accordance with Article 11 (1) of the UNAT Statute. The background of this case was that Mr. Mortished, entered the service of the International Civil Aviation Organization (ICAO) in 1949. In 1958 he was transferred to New York, and in 1967 to the UN office at Geneva. Attaining the age of 60 he retired on 30 April 1980. The question was about the eligibility for repatriation grants of retiring UN employees. This request was the first request to arise from the Committee's consideration of an application by a Member State. Mortished had argued that allowing a third party (US) to object to judgments constituted an intervention by an entity not a party to the original proceedings. However, the Court rejected this challenge on the ground that UN members even if they are not party to the UNAT still have an interest sufficient to initiate the review procedure. The Court also decided to dispense with oral proceedings in this case to ensure equality between the parties.

[103] ICJ Rep., 1982, p. 339.

[104] Advisory opinion of 27 May 1987.

[105] ICJ Rep., 1987, p. 20.

[106] Rosenne, *supra* note 6, p. 1070.

[107] Shaw, *supra* note 3, p. 847.

[108] Ibid, p. 848.

5.1 Sources of the Applicable Law

Contrary to international arbitration where the parties generally have the right to choose the law which they wish to apply, the ICJ is presumed to be applying existing and recognised rules or principles of International Law. This dictates that its decisions must be clearly derived from recognised sources of law.[109] Shaw defines "sources" of law as the "provisions operating within the legal system on a technical level, and such ultimate sources as reason or morality are excluded, as are more functional sources such as libraries and journals."[110]

Article 38(1) of the ICJ Statute provides:

1. *The Court, whose function is to decide in accordance with international law such disputes as are submitted to it, shall apply:*
   (a) *international conventions, whether general or particular, establishing rules expressly recognized by the contesting states;*
   (b) international custom, as evidence of a general practice accepted as law;
   (c) the general principles of law recognized by civilized nations;
   (d) subject to the provisions of Article 59, judicial decisions and the teachings of the most highly qualified publicists of the various nations, as subsidiary means for the determination of rules of law.
2. *This provision shall not prejudice the power of the Court to decide a case* ex aequo et bono, *if the parties agree thereto.*

The sources of law applied by the Court have been divided by some scholars into two parts: law creating processes, which include international conventions, custom and general principles of law, and law-determining agencies which include judicial decisions and academic writings of publicists.[111] Other scholars divide these sources into constitutional and subsidiary sources. According to them treaties, custom and general principles of law form what are considered as constitutional sources, while judicial decisions and the writings of the most highly qualified publicists form a subsidiary means for the determination of rules of law.[112] A distinction has also been made between formal and material sources.[113] Formal sources, it is suggested, are "those legal procedures and methods for the creation of rules of general application which are legally binding on the addressees", while material

---

[109] Jennings, *supra* note 41, p. 43.

[110] Shaw, Malcolm N., *International Law*, Cambridge: Cambridge University Press, 5th edition, 2003, p. 66.

[111] Schwarzenberger, Georg, *International Law*, London: Stevens and Sons, vol. 1, pp. 26-27.

[112] Waldock, Humphrey, "General Course on Public International Law", 106 *RCADI*, 1962, Chapter 6, "Subsidiary and Derivative Sources of International Law", p. 88.

[113] Brownlie, Ian, *Principles of Public International Law*, Oxford: Oxford University Press, 2003, p. 5.

sources "provide evidence of the existence of rules which, when proved, have the status of legally binding rules of general application."[114]

The following Section examines the practice of the Court when applying Article 38(1) of the Statute in advisory opinions.[115]

5.1.1 International Conventions

International conventions or treaties are express agreements which reflect the principle of freedom of contract in International Law. Hence, treaties are a form of substitute legislation undertaken by States and they create binding obligations for parties.[116] Article 38 of the ICJ Statute does not distinguish between types of treaties. Despite that, some publicists distinguish two types of treaties, i.e. law making and contractual treaties.[117] While the first are said to be universal and to have a general purpose, the second are between two or a small number of States.[118]

In practice, the Court has intensively relied on the UN Charter as a law making treaty when rendering advisory opinions. For instance the Court in the *International Status of South West Africa* Case[119] relied on several Articles of the UN Charter to conclude that a supervisory function should be exercised by the UN's General Assembly over south Africa's conduct in South West Africa.[120] In the *Admission of a State to the United Nations (Charter, Article 4),* Case the Court based itself on Article 4(2) of the Charter to conclude that the General Assembly does not have the power to admit a State to membership in the absence of a recommendation of the Security Council.[121] In the *United Nations Administrative Tribunal* Case, the Court basing its decision on Articles 7, 22, and 101(1) of the Charter, concluded that "the power to establish a tribunal to do justice between the Organization and the staff members may be exercised by the General Assembly."[122]

---

[114] Ibid.

[115] Jennings noted that although Article 38(1) seems to be applied just to contentious cases since it refers to "dispute", in practice the same sources have been applied in advisory cases. See Jennings, Robert Y., "General Course on Principles of International Law", 121 *RCADI*, 1967, Chapter 1 "The Sources of the Law", p. 330.

[116] Shaw, *supra* note 110, p. 89; Bobbitt, Philip, "Public International Law" in: Patterson, Dennis (ed.), *A Companion to Philosophy of Law and Legal Theory*, Blakwell Publishing, 2nd reprint, 2003, p. 101.

[117] Shaw, *supra* note 110, p. 88.

[118] Ibid.

[119] ICJ Rep., 1950, p. 128.

[120] The Court has relied on Articles 10, 75, 77, 79, 80 and 85. See ICJ Rep., 1950, pp. 133-142.

[121] ICJ Rep., 1948, p. 9.

[122] ICJ Rep., 1954, p. 58.

In the *Certain Expenses of the United Nations (*Article *17, paragraph 2, of the Charter*) Case[123] the Court relied on several Articles of the Charter to conclude that the responsibility conferred on the Security Council to maintain international peace and security is a "primary" responsibility and not exclusive.[124] Later, in the *Western Sahara* Case, the Court invoked Article 1(2) of the Charter which refers to one of the purposes of the UN as "to develop friendly relations among nations based on respect for the principle of equal rights and self-determination of peoples." It further relied on Articles 55 and 56 of the Charter, whose provisions have direct the particular relevance for non-self governing territories, to conclude that "... the subsequent development of international law in regard to non-self- governing territories, as enshrined in the Charter of the United Nations made the principle of self-determination applicable to all of them."[125]

More generally, some commentators claim that the Court through its advisory opinions has had an important influence on the law of treaties because it has developed and applied the teleological approach to the interpretation of the constituent instruments of international organisations.[126]

5.1.2 International Custom

Article 38 refers to international custom as evidence of a general practice accepted as law and is more usually referred to as customary international law. Schwarzenberger suggests that the word order of the Article should be reversed since general practice accepted as law is the test by which international custom is ascertained.[127]

Customary international law is considered to be the most responsive source to the changing needs of the international community.[128] This is contradicted by some writers who say that custom cannot any longer be of major significance as a source of law because International Law is developing at a much more rapid pace than before, mainly through the conclusion of treaties, due to the complex issues that international law has to confront.[129] However, this view ignores the existence

---

123 Hereinafter cited as: "the *Expenses* Case", ICJ Rep., 1962, p. 151.

124 Ibid, pp. 157-164.

125 ICJ Rep., 1975, para. 54, p. 31.

126 Mendelson, Maurice "The International Court of Justice and the sources of international law" in: Lowe, Vaughan & Fitzmaurice, Malgosia (eds.), *Fifty years of the International Court of Justice: Essays in Honour of Sir Robert Jennings*, Grotius Publications, Cambridge University Press, 1996, p. 65. See the findings of the Court in the *Reparations* Case, ICJ Rep., 1949, p. 174.; the *International Status of South West Africa* Case, ICJ Rep., 1950, p. 128; the *Expenses* Case, ICJ Rep., 1962, p. 151 and the *Namibia* Case, ICJ Rep., 1971, p. 16.

127 Schwarzenberger, *supra* note 111, p. 39.

128 Higgins, Rosalyn, *The Development of International Law through the Political Organs of the United Nations*, Oxford University Press, 1963, p. 1; Shaw, *supra* note 110, p. 69.

129 Friedmann, Wolfgang, *The Changing Structure of International Law*, New York, 1964, pp. 121-123, cited in Shaw, *supra* note 110, p. 69.

of "instant" customary law, which may create rules without any need for an extended period of time.

In the *Namibia* Case, the Court had to rule on a South African objection to the validity of the resolution requesting the opinion because the resolution had been adopted by the Security Council with the voluntary abstention of two Permanent Members. However, the Court nevertheless recognised the validity of the resolution and asserted that the practice of voluntary abstention has been "generally accepted by Members of the United Nations and evidences a general practice of that Organization."[130] It was claimed that the Court, by adopting this principle, established that customary law could be created not only by States but also by international organisations, although this cannot be deduced from Article 38 of the Statute.[131] However, it has been rightly observed that international organisations may, in fact, be instrumental in the creation of customary law. For example, the Advisory Opinion of the ICJ, in the *Reparations* Case, declaring that the UN possessed international personality, was based partly on the actual practice of the UN and it led to the recognition of a new customary norm.[132]

5.1.3 General Principles of Law

It is true that Article 38(1)(C) refers to general principles of law as recognised by civilised nations, and does not expressly distinguish between national and international law. Still, some writers have considered that "general principles of law" can refer to general principles of international law as well as to general principles of municipal law.[133] In other words, this term is sufficiently broad to embrace both. As noted by Sir Hersch Lauterpacht, this source is an "ultimate safeguard against the possibility of *non liquet.*"[134]

The way that the Court has applied the concept of general principles of law has been reflected in several advisory opinions, two of which are mentioned here. In the *Reservations to the Convention on Genocide* Case,[135] the Court pointed out that it was a generally recognised principle that a multilateral treaty is the result of an agreement freely concluded, and this principle is linked to the notion of the in-

---

130 ICJ Rep., 1971, p. 22.

131 Aréchaga, Eduardo, "International Law in the Past Third of a Century", Chapter One "Custom as a Source of International Law", 159 *RCADI*, 1978, p. 29.

132 Shaw, *supra* note 110, p. 79.

133 Akehurst, Michael, "The Hierarchy of the Sources of International Law", 47 *BYIL*, 1974-5, p. 278.

134 Lauterpacht, Hersch, *The Development of International Law by The International Court*, London: Stevens and Sons, 1958, p. 166; The same meaning was conveyed by Hudson, *supra* note 1, p. 611; See also Rosenne, Shabtai, "The Perplexities of Modern International Law", 291 *RCADI*, 2001, p. 64.

135 Hereinafter cited as: "the *Reservations* Case", ICJ Rep., 1951, p. 15.

tegrity of the treaty.[136] The Court has also referred to the existence of a general principle of law which states that "[i]t is well established that in its treaty relations a State cannot be bound without its consent" in order to justify its statement that "no reservation can be effective against any State without its agreement thereto."[137] Moreover, in its advisory opinion on the *Judgments of the Administrative Tribunal of the ILO* Case, the Court relied upon the principle of efficiency to conclude that the General Assembly has the power to establish a tribunal. The Court found that:[138]

> *[T]he power to establish a tribunal, to do justice as between the Organization and the staff members, was essential to insure the efficient working of the Secretariat, and to give effect to the paramount consideration of securing the highest standard of efficiency, competence and integrity.*

5.1.4 Judicial Decisions[139] and the Teachings of the Most Highly Qualified Publicists

Article 38(1)(d) of the Statute of the ICJ refers to judicial decisions and the teachings of the most highly qualified publicists "as subsidiary means for the determination of rules of law." Schwarzenberger regarded these as 'law-determining agencies' rather than as sources of international law. It was suggested that this term was used because findings of other courts are evidentiary sources which may assist the Court in determining the existence of a conventional or of a customary rule or of a general principle of law.[140] However, the Court alone can determine which rules of law are acceptable to it as rules of international law.[141]

Courts, whether national or international, are not empowered to make new laws, at least in theory. However, they possess the power and creativity to adapt rules to new situations and needs and, even more, to develop law to such an extent that they might be regarded as having changing it.[142]

---

136 ICJ Rep., 1951, p. 21.

137 ICJ Rep., 1951, p. 21.

138 ICJ Rep., 1956, p. 57.

139 The term "judicial decisions" includes judgments, advisory opinions and orders of the ICJ and of other standing and *ad hoc* courts and awards of international arbitral tribunals. See Rosenne, *supra* note 134, p. 66.

140 Waldock, *supra* note 112, p. 88.

141 Waldock, *supra* note 112, p. 92.

142 Jennings, Robert Y., "The Judiciary, International and National, and the Development of International Law", 45 *ICLQ*, 1996, p. 3.

Although the Court does not observe a doctrine of precedent, it nevertheless strives to maintain judicial consistency.[143] Sir Hersch Lauterpacht explained that the Court follows its own decisions at least in practice:[144]

> *[B]ecause such decisions are a repository of legal experience to which it is convenient to adhere; because they embody what the Court has considered in the past to be good law; because respect for decisions given in the past makes for certainty and stability ... ; and ... because judges are naturally reluctant, in the absence of compelling reasons to the contrary, to admit that they were previously in the wrong ... reliance on precedent is not only in keeping with the ever-present requirement of certainty in the administration of justice, but with the necessity of avoiding the appearance of any excess of judicial discretion.*

The ICJ, when referring to previous decisions, has not differentiated between contentious and advisory cases. In fact, there is great value in advisory opinions as precedents, although in theory the Court's opinions are not supposed to constitute binding precedents for later cases. However, judges of the ICJ do refer to previous opinions in order to support their arguments in later cases. Indeed, it is hard to find any judgment or advisory opinion which does not refer to some previous Court's decision. For example, the Court in its advisory opinion in the *Legality of the Use by a State of Nuclear Weapons in Armed Conflict* Case, quoted from its previous opinion in the *Western Sahara* Case in order to define what the legal question was.[145]

However, the Court has rarely referred to the decisions of other international tribunals. Mendelson has suggested more than one reason for this reticence. The most important of these is the reason given by the Court in the *Barcelona Traction* Case (Second Phase) where it stated that decisions of other international tribunals may be conditioned by the terms of the instruments establishing them.[146]

Rosenne suggests that the teaching of publicists is a subsidiary source for two reasons: first, teachings are not considered positive law and therefore do not stand on the same footing as judicial decisions; second, they are not the product, directly or indirectly, of the authority of States.[147] However, the Court in some rare instances has referred in general terms to "writers."[148] It is noted that such refer-

[143] Brownlie, *supra* note 113, p. 21.

[144] Lauterpacht, *supra* note 134, p. 14.

[145] ICJ Rep., 1996, p. 73 Quoted from the *Western Sahara* Case; ICJ Rep., 1975, p. 18.

[146] ICJ Rep., 1970, para 63, p. 40. For some other possible reasons see Mendelson, *supra* note 126, p. 83.

[147] Rosenne, *supra* note 134, p. 75. Rosenne also suggests that there is no authoritative way of establishing who is "most highly qualified" in any nation.

[148] See the *Nottebohm* Case, ICJ Rep. 1955, p. 22; see also Rosenne, ibid, p. 75. *In Land, Island and Maritime Frontier Dispute Judgment* Case, the Court has cited Oppenheim, Hersch Lauterpacht and Gidel, which is considered to be a new departure in the view of Mendelson. See Mendelson, *supra* note 126, p. 84.

ences are more likely to appear in the separate and dissenting opinions of judges and in the pleadings of parties. In any event, both the PCIJ and ICJ have displayed reticence in citing publicists' names in support of any principle law.[149]

In addition to the sources of law enumerated in Article 38(1), the Court may also look to Article 38(2) which allows it to decide a case *ex aequo et bono* if the parties agree. This is not the same as "equity" in the English sense. Indeed, "equity" employed as a general concept in the judicial function is imperative and represents a constituent part of the integrity of the Court and the fairness of its decisions in all cases. It is related to reasonableness and good faith in the application of a rule of law and was basically introduced to moderate the harshness of the strict application of rules of law.

Brownlie sees equity as comprising considerations of fairness, reasonableness and policy in the sensible application of settled rules of law. He considers equity to be an important factor in the process of making a decision, even though it is not listed as a source of law.[150] He also maintains that the "power of decision *ex aequo et bono* involves elements of compromise and conciliation whereas equity in the English sense is applied as a part of the normal judicial function."[151]

The Court in the Application for Revision and Interpretation of the Judgment of 24 February 1982 in the case concerning the Continental Shelf (Tunisia/ Libyan Arab Jamahiriya Case[152] distinguished between equity and the notion of ex aequo et bono by stating that:[153]

> *Equity as a legal concept is a direct emanation of the idea of justice. The Court whose task is by definition to administer justice is bound to apply it. ... Application of equitable principles is to be distinguished from a decision* ex aequo et bono

As far as advisory opinions are concerned, the power given to the parties by Article 38(2) has remained nominal only.[154] In the *Judgments of the Administrative*

---

149 Rosenne, *supra* note 6, p. 1615. An example of such a reference is to be found in the dissenting opinion of Judge Levi Carneiro in the *Effect of Awards* Case. Judge Carneiro quoted the writings of two leading French publicists, Laferriére and Louis Renault. This reference was to support his opinion in rejection of the views of the Court which treated the Administrative Tribunal as a judicial body. In this regard, he stated that:

'Administrative Tribunals'- whatever may be the binding force of their decision- are not, and never have been, regarded in France as judicial organs: they are administrative organs.

See ICJ Rep., 1954, p. 93.

150 Brownlie, *supra* note 113, p. 25.

151 Ibid, p. 26.

152 ICJ Rep., 1985, p. 192.

153 ICJ Rep., 1985, para. 45, p. 39.

154 Jenks, Clarence, *The Prospects of International Adjudication*, London: Steven and Sons, 1964, p. 320.

Tribunal of the ILO Case, it was alleged that the judgments of the ILO Administrative Tribunal were flawed because the Tribunal had exceeded its jurisdiction by not awarding compensation in accordance with legal rules, but based on the notion of *ex aequo et bono*. The Court rejected the allegation and held that:[155]

> *It does not appear from the context of the judgment that the Tribunal thereby intended to depart from principles of Law ... the Tribunal fixed what the Court, in other circumstances, has described as the true measure of compensation and the reasonable figure of such compensation.*

Although in advisory opinions there are no 'parties' in the strict sense, concerned parties can, if they so wish, include within the request submitted to the Court by the requesting organ an agreement to allow a determination *ex aequo et bono*.

5.1.5 Resolutions of the General Assembly as a Supplementary Source of International Law?[156]

Regardless of the controversy over the legal nature of the General Assembly's resolutions, these resolutions are, generally, in the nature of recommendations. In general, they are non-binding,[157] and are not included in Article 38(1) of the Statute which outlines the sources of law to be applied by the Court. However, General Assembly resolutions can contribute to the creation of customary international law or assist in the interpretation of treaties, notably the UN Charter.

Schachter considers that resolutions are declarative of international law and therefore may play a role in the formation of customary international law.[158] He argues that the intent of the States to express a rule of law in a declaratory resolution is an important factor in weighing the legal effect of the resolutions.[159] Aréchaga also maintains that resolutions in the form of declarations may constitute a process of formulating principles and rules that might contribute to the develop-

155 ICJ Rep., 1956, p. 100.

156 While this Section deals exclusively with the General Assembly resolutions, it is to be noted that the Court has also cited the resolutions of the Security Council in the *Expenses* Case. ICJ Rep. 1962 and in the *Nuclear Weapons* Case where the Court took note of Resolution 984 of 1955. See ICJ., Rep, 1996, p. 225. For further discussion about the impact of the Security Council decisions on the ICJ see Greenwood, Christopher, "The Impact of Decisions and Resolutions of the Security Council on the International Court of Justice" in: Heere, Wybo P, *International Law And the Hague's 750th Anniversary*, The Hague: T.M.C Asser Press, 1999, p. 83.

157 An exception to this rule is that certain resolutions of the Assembly are binding upon the UN organs and member States. See Article 17 of the UN Charter.

158 Schachter, Oscar, "International Law in Theory and Practice", Chapter VI, "Resolutions and political texts", 178 *RCADI*, 1982, p. 117.

159 Ibid.

ment of International Law.[160] On this view, which remains controversial, "such declarations may constitute a source of rules of international law similar to the consensus reached in conferences for the codification and progressive development of international law."[161]

Thirlway suggests that some of the General Assembly's resolutions are "convenient material sources of law, inasmuch as they state, with apparent authority, propositions of general law, and are often assented to by a very large majority of the Members, and thus of the States of the world."[162] Lastly, Shaw maintains that "the way states vote in the General Assembly and the explanations given upon such occasions constitute evidence of state practice and state understanding as to the law."[163]

Contrary to the above views, Judge Schwebel argues that UN resolutions are only recommendations and before they can be treated as law they must be supported by actual State practice.[164] This is necessary, in Schwebel's view, because UN member States may vote on resolutions to please other members rather than with the intention of creating legal obligations.[165]

At any rate the salient question is to what extent, if any, does the Court through its advisory opinions apply General Assembly resolutions? In practice, the General Assembly has adopted numerous resolutions which have had great impact on International Law and which have been cited frequently in the Court's decisions. A notable example is Resolution 1514(XV), the Declaration on the Granting of Independence to Colonial Countries and People. This Resolution, which related to decolonisation has had a great effect. For example, the Court in the *Namibia* Case has relied on it as important evidence of customary law. Moreover the Court has characterised this Resolution as a "[a] further important stage in this development", and went on to say that "... the Court must take into consideration the changes which have occurred in the supervening half-century, and its interpretation cannot remain unaffected by the subsequent development of law through the Charter of the United Nations and by way of *customary law*."[166]

---

[160] Aréchaga, *supra* note 131, p. 31.

[161] Aréchaga, ibid.

[162] Thirlway, Hugh, "The Sources of International Law" in: Evans, Malcolm D., (ed.), *International Law*, Oxford University Press, 2003, p. 141. Thirlway has suggested some examples of General Assembly resolutions which constitute material sources of law including the Declaration on Principles of International Law Concerning Friendly Relations and Cooperation among States in Accordance with the Charter of the United Nations, General Assembly Res. 2625 (XXV).

[163] Shaw, *supra* note 110, pp. 108-109.

[164] Schwebel, Stephen M., "The Effect of Resolutions of the United Nations General Assembly on Customary Law", *Proceedings of American Society of International Law*, 1979, pp. 301-304.

[165] Ibid, pp. 301-304.

[166] ICJ Rep., 1971, p. 31. (Emphasis added).

Again, in the *Western Sahara* Case, the Court indicated that Resolution 1514(XV) had become a rule of positive customary law through the subsequent actions of States. The Court observed that "General Assembly resolution 1514(XV) provided the basis for the process of decolonisation which has resulted since 1960 in the creation of many States which are today Members of the United Nations."[167]

Most recently, in the *Wall* Case, the Court relied on General Assembly Resolution 2625 (XXV) of 1970 as expressing two principles of customary international law relevant to its decision, that is, the illegality of the acquisition of territory resulting from the threat or use of force, and the right of people in non-self governing territories to self -determination.[168]

5.2 Deliberation by the Court and the Giving of Advisory Opinions

Deliberations of the Court are conducted in *camera* and remain confidential.[169] In accordance with Article 54(3) of the Court's Statute "the deliberations of the Court shall take place in private and remain secret." Indeed, the majority decisions of the Court are 'collegiate' ones based on the judges' serious deliberations and exchanges of views and thoughts.[170] These procedures and formalities may result in a decision which cannot be accurately predicted. The Court's opinion is given after deliberation by the Court and indicates the number and identity of the judges constituting the majority.

Advisory opinions are delivered in open Court, just as in contentious proceedings, in accordance with Article 67 of the Statute. Article 107 of the Rules requires that advisory opinions shall contain the date of delivery, the names of judges participating, a summary of the proceedings, a statement of the facts, the reasoning on points of law, the reply to the question put to the Court, the number and names of the judges constituting the majority and a statement as to which language text is authoritative. Any judge is entitled to attach a separate or dissenting opinion.[171] This means that the secrecy of the deliberation does not extend to preventing an individual judge from making his view's known.[172]

Under Article 108 of the Rules the Registrar must inform the Secretary-General of the UN, and, where appropriate, the chief administrative officer of the body which requested the opinion, as to the date on which the opinion will be delivered.

---

167 ICJ Rep., 1975, para. 57, p. 32.

168 See para 87of the *Wall* Opinion, *supra* note 32.

169 Oda, *supra* note 15 , p. 119.

170 Jennings, *supra* note 41, p. 47.

171 Article 85 of the Court's Rules.

172 Thirlway, Hugh, "Procedures of International Courts and Tribunals", in: Bernhardt, R. (ed.), *Encyclopedia of Public International Law*, Amsterdam: Elsevier Science B.V., Vol. 3, 1997, p. 1130.

Then, under Article 109 of the Rules one original copy of the opinion duly signed and sealed is placed in the archives of the Court, and another sent to the secretariat of the requesting organisation. Finally, the opinion is printed in two official languages of the Court in the official reports of judgements, advisory opinions and orders.

6 Concluding Remarks

The ICJ under Article 30 of its Statute has the power to set its own procedural rules. The procedures followed by the Court in considering advisory requests generally mirror the procedures observed in contentious proceedings. The Court's decisions examined above illustrate that in some cases where a problem of equality between the parties to the advisory case has arisen, the Court's view has been that its judicial character requires that both parties which may be affected by the Court's opinion must be able to submit their views to the Court on an equal footing. Therefore, in such cases the Court dispensed with the oral phase.

In fact, what a requesting organ seeks when approaching the Court in its advisory capacity is an authoritative statement of law based on well-established reasons and informed by International Law. This desire will in turn require that the requesting organ should lodge an exact and clear statement of the question. The Court, on the other hand, is expected to act justly. Therefore, the independence and impartiality of the judges, and equality between parties, are not to be compromised. The next Chapter will continue by demonstrating the effect of the Court's judicial character on the development of International Law through its advisory proceedings.

CHAPTER SIX

The Contribution of Advisory Opinions to the Development of the Law of International Institutions and to Public International Law

1 Introduction

The ICJ as the principal judicial organ of the UN, through its contentious and advisory procedures, has played a major role in the development of the law of international institutions and of International Law in general. Some commentators have even suggested that the ICJ's greatest utility lies in its capacity for developing or clarifying rules of International Law rather than in contributing to the pacific settlement of disputes.[1]

The task of this Chapter is to acknowledge that the real measure of the role of the ICJ's advisory function cannot be determined exclusively in terms of the number of advisory opinions handed down. Of more importance is the Court's contribution to providing authoritative statements of law, thus aiding the development of International Law in a wide variety of areas. This Chapter argues that the Court's advisory opinions, in addition to providing guidance to the requesting organs for the solution of international legal problems and questions, have also contributed to the growth and development of International Law.

The term "development" is employed here to refer to instances where the Court has, arguably, established new rules, as well as to instances where the Court has clarified existing rules. However, while establishing new norms and clarifying older ones, the Court has still been mindful of the evolving nature of International Law, particularly as it relates to the law of international organisations, the law of treaties, human rights law, humanitarian law and international environmental law as will be articulated in the discussion below.

---

1 Lissitzyn, Oliver J., *The International Court of Justice: Its Role in the Maintenance of International Peace and Security*, New York: Carnegie Endowment for International Peace, 1951, p. 18 ; Lauterpacht, Hersch, *The Development of International Law by the International Court*, London: Stevens and Sons, 1958, pp. 4-5; Janis, Mark W., "The International Court" in: Janis, Mark W. (ed.), *International Courts For the Twenty-First Century*, Dordrecht; Boston; London: Martinus Nijhoff Publishers, 1992, pp. 29-30.

2 Advisory Opinions and the Development of the Law of the United Nations

The ICJ's advisory opinions have contributed to the development of the law of the UN by developing new rules in three areas: first, the concept of the international legal personality of international organisations, second, the implied powers of international organisations, and third "succession" as between international organisations.[2]

2.1 The International Legal Personality of the United Nations

The doctrine that international organisations may possess a measure of international personality largely owes its origins to the reasoning of the ICJ in the 1949 *Reparation for Injuries Suffered in the Service of the United Nations* Case.[3] Prior to this milestone opinion, it had been widely assumed since the nineteenth century that only States could be subjects of International Law.[4] However, in the *Reparations* Case, the Court asserted that international personality is not restricted to States and that a degree of personality can also be possessed by international organisations like the UN. Consequently, legal personality is now considered to be an important feature of international organisations.[5]

The origin of the General Assembly's request for the *Reparations* Advisory Opinion was the assassination of the UN mediator in Palestine in a sector of Jerusalem then under the *de facto* control of the Israeli armed forces. The question submitted to the Court was:[6]

> *In the event of an agent of the United Nations in the performance of his duties suffering injury in circumstances involving the responsibility of a State, has the United Nations, as an Organization, the capacity*

---

[2] Whether the Court ought to apply the law as it exists or whether it can be creative in applying the law, is a debated subject. See Jennings, Robert Y., "The Role of the International Court of Justice", 68 *BYIL*, 1997, p. 41; Fitzmaurice, Gerald, "Judicial Innovation-Its Uses and its Perils- As exemplified in some of the Work of the International Court of Justice During Lord McNair's Period of Office" in *Cambridge Essays in International Law: Essays in honour of Lord McNair*, London: Stevens and Sons, 1965, p. 25; Weeramantry, Christopher G, "The Function of the International Court of Justice In the Development of International Law", 10 *LJIL*, 1997, pp. 309-340.

[3] Hereinafter cited as: "the *Reparations Case*", ICJ Rep., 1949, p. 174.

[4] Bederman, David J., "The Souls of International Organizations: Legal Personality and the Lighthouse at Cape Spartel", 36 *VJIL*, 1996, p. 367. Prior to the *Reparations* case there was controversy over whether international organizations can be regarded as possessing legal personality. For more details see Jenks, Wilfred, "The Legal Personality of International Organizations", *BYIL*, 1943, p. 267.

[5] Sands, Philippe & Klein, Pierre, *Bowett's Law of International Institutions*, London: Sweet and Maxwell, 2001, p. 469.

[6] ICJ Rep., 1949, pp. 176-177.

> *to bring an international claim against the responsible* de jure *or* de facto *government with a view to obtaining the reparation due in respect of the damage caused (a) to the United Nations, (b) to the victim or to persons entitled through him?*

The approach adopted by the Court to this question was to ask "whether the Charter has given the Organization such a position that it possesses, in regard to its Members, rights which it is entitled to ask them to respect."[7] The Court then related this question to whether the Organisation possessed international personality. Because the actual terms of the Charter did not provide an answer,[8] the Court had to consider what characteristics the drafters of the Charter had intended to give to the Organisation. It stated that despite the fact that the term "international legal personality" had sometimes given rise to controversy, it could be used in this case to mean that "if the Organization is recognized as having the personality, it is an entity capable of availing itself of obligations incumbent upon its Members."[9]

The Court concluded that the UN possesses an international personality because of the purposes and principles laid down in the UN Charter.[10] The Court then proceeded to enumerate the various functions entrusted to the UN and concluded that international personality distinct from that of its members is indispensable if the UN is to carry out its functions and duties. The Court stated that:[11]

> *[T]he Organization was intended to exercise and enjoy, and is in fact exercising and enjoying, functions and rights which can only be explained on the basis of the possession of a large measure of international personality and the capacity to operate upon an international plan. It is at present the supreme type of international organization, and it could not carry out the intentions of its founders if it was devoid of international personality. It must be acknowledged that its Members, by entrusting certain functions to it, with the attendant duties and responsibilities, have clothed it with the competence required to enable those functions to be effectively discharged.*

---

7 Ibid, p. 178.

8 The preparatory work of the UN Charter made it clear that the lack of provision to regulate the international legal personality of the Organization was intentional. Only Article 104 provides for the legal capacity of the organization "in the territory of each of its member states." However, it has been argued that even if the Charter had regulated the question under consideration, Israel was not, at that time, a member of the organization. See Klabbers, Jan, *An Introduction to International Institutional Law*, Cambridge: Cambridge University Press, 2002, p. 52.

9 ICJ Rep., 1949, p. 178.

10 See Article 1 of the UN Charter.

11 ICJ Rep., 1949, p. 179.

The Court in reaching the above conclusion relied on several factors such as the privileges and immunities enjoyed by the UN in the member States' territory and the capacity of the UN to conclude treaties.[12] The Court pointed out that the Organisation "occupies a position in certain respects in detachment from its Members."[13] Still, the Organisation for its part is under certain duties towards its members, for instance "to remind them, if need be, of certain obligations."[14]

It is interesting to note that the Court had to decide the question of whether the legal personality of the UN is subjective, in the sense that only member States are bound to recognise this personality, or whether this personality is objective, thus even non-member States have to recognise the UN's international personality. This question was important because Israel was not at that time a UN member. The Court held that:[15]

> *[F]ifty States, representing the vast majority of the members of the international community, had the power, in conformity with international law, to bring into being an entity possessing objective international personality, and not merely personality recognized by them alone, together with capacity to bring international claims.*

Lastly, some commentators observed that although the Court affirmed that the UN has the capacity to bring international claims, it did, however, fall short of identifying the precise source of its legal personality.[16] Nevertheless, the Advisory Opinion in the *Reparations* Case has put an end to all controversies over whether international organisations can have legal personality, provided they satisfy certain recognised criteria, and thereby contributed to the establishment and the crystallisation of the concept of the international personality of international organisations.

---

12 Sands, Philippe & Klein, Pierre, *supra* note 5, pp. 471-472.

13 ICJ Rep., 1949, p. 179.

14 Ibid.

15 Ibid, p. 185.

16 There are two schools of thought on how to determine whether or not an organisation possesses international personality in the absence of an express treaty provision. The first school, employing the inductive method, asserts that legal personality relies on the existence of certain rights and duties conferred upon the organization in order to derive from these rights and duties a general international personality. That is to say that the international personality can only be established by the will of member States which confers personality on the organization. The second school, the objective method, asserts that international personality is not derived from the will of member States, but can be acquired once the organization, which exists as a matter of law, carries out the purposes and requirements of its establishment. See Rama-Montaldo, Manuel, "International Legal Personality and Implied Powers of International Organizations", 44 *BYIL*, 1970, p. 112.

2.2 The Doctrine of Implied Powers

The advisory opinion in the *Reparations* Case has been considered to be "the initial legal and theoretical foundation for implied powers of international organizations."[17] Having found that the UN possesses international personality, the Court proceeded to inquire whether such personality includes the capacity to bring an international claim for damage caused to the UN. The Court stated that "the rights and duties of an entity such as the Organization must depend upon its purposes and functions as specified or implied in its constituent documents and developed in practice." The Court concluded that "the Members have endowed the Organization with capacity to bring international claims when necessitated by the discharge of its functions."[18]

Having found that the Charter did not explicitly confer on the UN the capacity to bring an international claim,[19] the Court proceeded to enquire whether the provisions of the Charter concerning the functions of the Organisation implied such a capacity. The Court concluded that:[20]

> *Under international law, the Organization must be deemed to have those powers which, though not expressly provided in the Charter, are conferred upon it by necessary implication as being essential to the performance of its duties.*

On this basis the Court found that the UN's need to ensure that its agents were able to perform their missions required that the Organisation should be able to protect them. The Court concluded that:[21]

---

17 Makarczyk, Jerzy, "The International Court of Justice on the Implied Powers of International Organizations" in: Makarczyk, Jerzy (ed.), *Essays in International Law in Honour of Judge Manfred Lachs*, The Hague; Boston: Martinus Nijhoff Publishers, 1984, p. 506.

18 ICJ Rep., 1949, p. 180.

19 Article 34 (1) of the ICJ Statute provides that "only states may be parties in cases before the Court". This provision undoubtedly imposes a limitation on international organisations to be parties before the Court in contentious proceedings.

20 ICJ Rep., 1949, p. 182. The Court relied on the experience of the PCIJ where this principle had been applied to the ILO in its advisory opinion No. 13 of July 1926. See ICJ Rep., ibid, p. 183.

21 ICJ Rep., 1949, p. 184. The Court's application of the principle of implied powers did not escape criticism. Judge Hackworth, in his dissenting opinion, stated that: "[p]owers not expressed cannot freely be implied. Implied powers flow from a grant of expressed powers, and are limited to those that are "necessary" to the exercise of powers expressly granted". See Diss. Op. of Judge Hackworth, ibid, p. 198. Contrary to this view, Judge Alvarez in his Separate Opinion maintained that the powers of international organisations are not limited to what is expressed in their constitution, but include all powers which are necessary to enable an organisation to develop in accordance with contemporary international life. See Sep. Op. of Judge Alvarez, ICJ Rep., 1949, p. 190.

> *Upon examination of the character of the functions entrusted to the Organization and of the nature of the missions of its agents, it becomes clear that the capacity of the Organization to exercise a measure of functional protection of its agents arises by necessary intendment out of the Charter.*

Consequently "[i]t cannot be doubted that the Organization has the capacity to bring an international claim against one of its Members which has caused injury to it by a breach of its international obligations towards it."[22]

The ICJ applied the principle of implied powers which it developed in the *Reparations* Case in various subsequent cases, such as the 1950 *International Status of South West Africa* Case[23] and in the 1954 *Effect of Awards of Compensation made by the UN Administrative Tribunal* Case.[24] Sir Hersch Lauterpacht rightly observed in 1958 that the contribution of the Court, in the *Reparations* Case, to international law was of double significance. The Opinion expressly affirmed the international personality of the UN as well as the principle of implied powers which provides additional rules for the interpretation of the constitutions of international organisations.[25]

---

22 ICJ Rep., 1949, p. 180. Klabbers notes that the Court has failed to refer to the specific source of the right of international organisation to bring claims. See Klabbers, *supra* note 8, p. 47.

23 In the *South West Africa Status* Case, in the absence of express provisions in the Charter empowering the General Assembly to exercise supervisory functions over mandated territories which were not placed under trusteeship, the Court stated that the General Assembly "is legally qualified to exercise the supervisory functions previously exercised by the League of Nations with regard to the administration of the Territory." ICJ Rep., 1950, p. 137.

24 In this Case the question was whether or not the General Assembly had the right to refuse to give effect to an award of compensation made by the Tribunal. In considering the arguments advanced before the Court by States which contended that the General Assembly may refuse to give effect to a Tribunal's award because the General Assembly had no power to establish a judicial organ with a 'legal power' to render judgments binding upon the General Assembly, the Court noted that there was no express provision regulating the establishment of a judicial body by political organs. Nonetheless, the Court concluded the General Assembly had the power to establish tribunals to do justice as between the Organisation and the staff members. The Court held that "[i]t would, in the opinion of the Court, hardly be consistent with the expressed aim of the Charter to promote freedom and justice for individuals ...that it should afford no judicial or arbitral remedy to its own staff for the settlement of any disputes which may arise between it and them". ICJ Rep., 1954, p. 57.

25 Lauterpacht, *supra* note 1, p. 181.

2.3 Succession of International Organisations

An organisation's existence may come to an end by a variety of means. A question then may arise as to the extent to which a successor organisation inherits the rights and obligations of its predecessor. A succession of international persons "occurs when one or more international persons takes the place of another international person, in consequence of certain changes in the latter's condition."[26] Few difficulties will be encountered if the replacement of one institution by another is regulated in treaties that specify whether the rights and duties of the predecessor devolve upon the successor, or whether they lapse. However, the situation may be quite difficult and complicated in the absence of such provisions in the constitution of an organisation.[27]

The Court had an occasion in its advisory opinion in the *International Status of South West Africa* Case[28] to deal with a new situation in International Law.[29] It is well known that South West Africa had been a German overseas possession, and that, following the First World War, it was placed under a League of Nations Mandate, i.e. an international regime provided for by Article 22 of the League Covenant. The idea behind the mandates system was to provide an effective administration for former colonies the peoples of which were considered to be unready, as yet, for independence.[30] Under the mandates system, the Union of South Africa was given a mandate over South West Africa with the object of promoting the well-being and development of the inhabitants. However, the League was dissolved on 18 April 1946 by the unanimous decision of the League Assembly.[31] Unfortunately, the dis-

---

26 Jennings, Sir Robert & Watts, Sir Arthur, *Oppenheim's International Law*, London: Longman, 1996, vol. 1, 9th edition, p. 208.

27 In some instances the organisation may be dissolved by the decision of its highest representative body. See Amerasinghe, Chittharanjan F., "Dissolution and Succession", in: Dupuy, René-Jean (ed.) *A Handbook On International Organizations*, Dordrecht; Boston; London: Martinus Nijhoff, 2nd edition, 1998, p. 367; Schermers, Henry & Blokker, Niels, *International Institutional Law: Unity Within Diversity*, The Hague; London: M. Nijhoff, 1955, p. 1015.

28 Hereinafter cited as: "*the South West Africa Status Case*", ICJ Rep., 1950, p. 128.

29 Traditional international law concerned itself with the subject of succession between States. However, there were no authoritative views on succession as between international organizations. See in general: Chiu, Hungdah "Succession in International Organizations", 14 *ICLQ*, 1965, p. 119; See also Diss. Op. of Judge Alvarez, ICJ Rep., 1950, p. 181.

30 The mandate system was created in order to give effect to two principles of paramount importance: the principle of non-annexation and the principle that the well-being and development of the peoples of such territories should form "a sacred trust of civilization". ICJ Rep., 1950, p. 131. On the hypocrisy in the operation of the mandates system, especially in the Middle East, see e.g. Pogany, Istvan, *The Arab League and Peacekeeping in the Lebanon*, Aldershot: Gower, 1987.

31 The League was ineffective in stopping the military aggression that led to World War II. It ceased its work during the war and dissolved on April 18, 1946. The United Nations assumed its assets and carries on much of its work. See: http://www.library.northwestern.edu/govpub/collections/league/background.html#introduction (accessed 24 October 2004).

solution resolution did not deal with the status of the mandated territories, nor did the UN Charter provide that former mandated territories should automatically come under the UN trusteeship system.

A serious problem thus arose when the Union of South Africa contended that the Mandate had lapsed with the dissolution of the League, along with the machinery for its supervision, which included an obligation to submit annual reports on the territory and its development under the Mandate.[32] Therefore, the General Assembly requested an advisory opinion about the status of the Mandate for South West Africa and the obligations of the Union under the Mandate.[33]

The Union argued, *inter alia*, before the Court that the mandate had terminated with the dissolution of the League,[34] that there was no legal *nexus* between the League and the UN because each of these organisations was a creation of a different treaty.[35] Consequently, South Africa submitted that the UN had no supervisory jurisdiction over the territory, and that therefore the Union was under no obligation to submit annual reports on its Mandate to the General Assembly.[36]

The Court held that the dissolution of the League and its supervisory machinery had not brought about the lapse of the Mandate and, therefore, the Mandatory power was still under an obligation to give an account to the UN for its administration of the Territory. The Court reasoned, *inter alia*, that Article 80(1) of the UN Charter preserved the rights of States and peoples and the terms of existing international instruments until the territories in question were placed under the trusteeship system.[37] The Court noted that the object of the Mandate was the well-being of the inhabitants of the territory and of humanity in general, and the authority of South Africa to administer the territory was based on the Mandate. Therefore,

---

[32] It is of interest to note that Article 18 of the UN Charter requires a two-thirds majority for the adoption of resolutions on important questions by the General Assembly.

[33] The question was: "[d]oes the Union of South Africa continue to have international obligations under the Mandate for South-West Africa and, if so, what are those obligations?" See GA Res. 338 (IV) of 6 December 1949; ICJ Rep., 1950, p. 131.

[34] ICJ Rep., 1950, p. 132; Lauterpacht, *supra* note 1, p. 278.

[35] ICJ Pled., 1950, p. 75.

[36] In 1946 and 1947 the Union submitted annual reports to the UN. But a year later the Union contended that it was under no obligation to submit any report and the previous annual report was submitted voluntarily and not in any way as a precedent and a commitment to further action. See Amr, Mohamed S., *The Role of the International Court of Justice as the Principal Judicial Organ of the United Nations*, The Hague: Kluwer Law International, 2003, p. 132; ICJ Rep., 1950, p. 135.

[37] Article 80 provides "[e]xcept as may be agreed upon in individual trusteeship agreements, made under Articles 77, 79, and 81, placing each territory under the trusteeship system, and until such agreements have been concluded, nothing in this Chapter shall be construed in or of itself to alter in any manner the rights whatsoever of any states or any peoples or the terms of existing international instruments to which Members of the United Nations may respectively be parties."

"[t]o retain the rights derived from the Mandate and to deny the obligations thereunder could not be justified."[38]

Having determined that the obligations of South Africa continued beyond the League's dissolution, the Court next decided that the General Assembly was competent to exercise the League's supervisory function and to receive and examine reports.[39] The Court adopted the view that this competence of the General Assembly derived from Article 10 of the Charter which authorises the General Assembly to discuss any question and any matters within the scope of the Charter.[40]

Although the Court did not state that there was an 'automatic succession' from the League to the UN it found that, in essence, there had been passed on to the UN certain supervisory functions of the League regarding the mandated territories. However, Judge McNair in his Dissenting Opinion stated that there were no legal grounds to justify the Court's decision to replace the Council of the League with the UN for the purposes of the administrative supervision of the Mandate. In McNair's view this decision was "a piece of judicial legislation" as the Charter contained no provisions for succession .[41] He argued that if the succession of the UN to the administrative functions of the League in regard to the Mandates had been intended, it would have been expressly vested in the UN in wording similar to Article 37 of the Statute of the ICJ regarding the jurisdiction of the PCIJ:[42]

> *Whenever a treaty or convention in force provides for reference of a matter to a tribunal to have been instituted by the League of Nations, or to the Permanent Court of International Justice, the matter shall, as between the parties to the present Statute, be referred to the International Court of Justice.*

One can conclude from the Court's findings that in the case of the League and the UN there was a functional continuity between predecessor and successor. In this regard, Sir Hersch Lauterpacht in his Separate Opinion in the *Admissibility of*

[38] ICJ Rep., 1950, p. 133.

[39] The Court noted that the degree of supervision to be exercised by the General Assembly should not exceed that which applied under the mandates system and should conform as far as possible to the procedure followed in this respect by the League's Council.

[40] The Court concluded that the General Assembly "is legally qualified to exercise the supervisory functions previously exercised by the League of Nations with regard to the administration of the Territory, and that the Union of South Africa is under an obligation to submit to supervision and control of the General Assembly and to render annual reports to it." ICJ Rep., 1950, p. 137.

[41] Sep. Op. of Judge McNair, ICJ Rep., 1950, pp. 161-162.

[42] For the reasoning of Judge McNair dissenting from the Court's findings see ICJ Rep., ibid, pp. 159-162. McNair's view was shared by Judge Read who concluded that, in the absence of any express provision in the Charter, no implications or inference should be drawn from the nature of the League and the UN and that "[s]uch a succession could not be implied, either in fact or in law". See Sep. op. of Judge Read, ICJ Rep., 1950, pp. 172-173.

Hearings of Petitioners by the Committee on South West Africa Case stated "[i]t will be noted that the supervision by the United Nations of the mandate for South West Africa constitutes the most important example of succession in international organization."[43]

3 The Contribution of ICJ Advisory Opinions to the Rules Governing the Interpretation of Treaties

Interpretation, in general, has been defined as "the art or process of discovering and expounding the intended signification of the language used, that is, the meaning which the authors of the law designed it to convey to others."[44] Indeed, interpretation is often required even where terms of provisions and words seem clear.[45]

Although various techniques of interpretation were already recognised in International Law, their present development owes much to the ICJ, primarily cases in which the Court has interpreted the UN Charter and agreements between the UN and its specialised agencies *vis-à-vis* member States.

3.1 The Interpretive Function of the ICJ

The issue of the ICJ's power to interpret the UN Charter was raised at the San Francisco Conference, where Belgium submitted a proposal to give the Court the exclusive right to interpret the Charter. However, this proposal was defeated and another approach to interpretation adopted. It was stated:[46]

> *In the course of the operations from day to day of the various organs of the Organization, it is inevitable that each organ will interpret such parts of the Charter as are applicable to its particular functions. This process is inherent in the functioning of any body which operates under an instrument defining its functions and powers. It will be manifested in the functioning of such a body as the General Assembly, the Security Council, or the International Court of Justice. Accordingly, it is not necessary to include in the Charter a provision either authorizing or approving the normal operation of this principle ... If two Member States are at variance concerning the correct interpretation of the Charter, they are of course free to submit the dispute to the International Court of Justice as in the case of any other treaty. Similarly, it would always be open to the*

---

[43] Hereinafter cited as "the *South West Africa (Admissibility)* Case", ICJ Rep., 1956, p. 48.

[44] Garner, Bryan (ed. in Chief), "Black's Law Dictionary", 7th edition, p. 824.

[45] Fitzmaurice argued that the conclusion that the meaning of the text is clear is in itself a process of interpretation. See, Fitzmaurice, Gerald G., *The Law and Procedure of the International Court of Justice*, Grotius Publications Limited, 1986, p. 46.

[46] See UNCIO, 13, p. 709.

> *General Assembly and to the Security Council, in appropriate circumstances, to ask the International Court of Justice for an advisory opinion concerning the meaning of a provision of the Charter.*

Although the ICJ does not have an exclusive right to interpret the Charter, it may nevertheless do so.[47] Indeed, the Court has not hesitated to do so since its inception and it regards the interpretative function as falling within the normal exercise of its judicial function.[48] The Court throughout its jurisprudence has exercised its interpretative function not only of Charter's provisions,[49] but also of treaties other than the Charter,[50] of agreements between the UN and its specialised agencies *vis-à-vis* their member States,[51] and of some of its previous advisory opinions.[52]

---

[47] The General Assembly in its second session, during its discussion of the "[n]eed for greater use by the United Nations and its organs of the International Court of Justice", considered the issue of whether the UN organs may refer questions on constitutional interpretations of the Charter. Subsequently, under General Assembly Resolution No.171 it was recommended that points of law relating to the interpretation of the Charter or the constitutions of the special agencies "should be referred to the Court for an advisory opinion." See GA Res. No. 171 (11), 1947. This Resolution has encouraged other UN organs and specialised agencies to refer to the Court any question pertaining to Charter interpretation.

[48] Rosenne, Shabtai, *The Law and Practice of The International Court, 1920-1996*, The Hague; London: Martinus Nijhoff Publishers, vol. 1, 1997, p. 79; the *Admissions* Case, ICJ Rep., 1948, p. 61.

[49] The Court exercised an interpretative function in a number of cases, *inter alia*, the 1948 *Admission of a State to the United Nations (Charter,* Article *4)* Case, ICJ Rep., p. *61; the 1950 Competence of the General Assembly regarding admission to the United Nations* Case, ICJ Rep., p. 6*; the 1949 Reparation for injuries suffered in the service of the United Nations* Case where the Court interpreted the Charter so as to recognise the legal personality of the UN. For further details about the international personality of international organisations, see discussion above*; the 1962 Expenses* Case *where* the Court affirmed the General Assembly's power in respect of the "expenses of the organisation", and in respect of the maintenance of international peace and security. For further details about this Case, see the discussion below. Lastly in the *2004 Legal Consequences of the Construction of a Wall in the Occupied Palestinian Territory* Case the Court interpreted the Charter and several international conventions to determine the illegality of the Wall built by Israel in the West Bank and Occupied Territories.

[50] The Court has had an opportunity to interpret treaties other than the UN Charter on various occasions: the 1950 *Interpretation of Peace treaties* Case and the 1951 *Reservations to the Convention on Genocide* Case.

[51] Examples of such agreements are headquarters agreements and host agreements which regulate the diplomatic privileges and immunities of the organisations and their employees. See Muller, Sam A., *International Organizations and their Host States: Aspect of their Legal Relationship*, The Hague; Boston: Kluwer Law International, 1995, p. 17.

[52] The Court in the 1955 *South West Africa Voting Procedure* Case and in the 1956 *Admissibility of Hearings by the Committee on South West Africa* Case was asked to interpret its advisory opinion in the 1950 *International Status of South West Africa* Case. For details about these three Advisory Opinions, see Section 5 in Chapter Eight, *infra.*

3.2 The Special Legal Position of the UN Charter

The objective legal personality attributed to the UN by the Court has, in the view of some scholars, made the UN different from most other international organisations[53] and the Charter also has certain features, which distinguishes it from other treaties.[54] In the *Certain Expenses of the United Nations (*Article.*17, paragraph 2, of the Charter*) Case[55] the Court recognised the Charter's special characteristics and held that:[56]

> *On the previous occasions when the Court has had to interpret the Charter of the United Nations, it has followed the principles and rules applicable in general to the interpretation of treaties, since it has recognized that the Charter is a multilateral treaty, albeit a treaty having certain special characteristics.*

The UN Charter, therefore, is not only the multilateral treaty which established the organisation and outlined the rights and obligations of those States signing it, it is also the constitution of the UN, laying down its functions and limitations.[57] The Charter, in fact, has been characterised as a constitution for the world community[58] containing both "constitutional[59]" and "contractual[60]"characteristics.

According to Article 5 of the Vienna Convention of the Law of Treaties (VCLT), the instrument applies to any treaty concluded between States. A logical consequence of this is that Articles 31 to 33 of the Convention apply to the inter-

---

53 Simma, Bruno, *et al.,* (eds.), *The Charter of the United Nations: A Commentary*, Oxford University Press, 2nd edition, 2002, p. 16. See also the discussion above.

54 See Amr, *supra note* 36, p. 122.

55 Hereinafter cited as "the *Expenses* Case". ICJ Rep., 1962, p. 151.

56 ICJ Rep., 1962, p. 157.

57 Shaw, Malcolm N., *International Law*, Cambridge: Cambridge University Press, 5th edition, 2003, p. 1083.

58 Simma, *supra* note 53, p. 16; Conforti, Benedetto, *The Law and Practice of the United Nations*, The Hague; London: Kluwer Law International, 2000, p. 10.

59 The Charter has constitutional elements since it authorises the UN to make decisions binding upon the member States and to exercise jurisdiction over their territories. See, Amr, *supra* note 36, p. 123. Moreover, the so called "objective legal personality" attributed to the UN by the ICJ in the *Reparations* Case constitutes evidence that the Charter is more than an ordinary treaty as this objective personality contradicts the general principle that treaties have no effect on third parties. For details about the objective personality of the UN, see the above discussion.

60 An example of this is the conclusion and termination of the treaty, and the provisions in Chapter 9 on human rights and Chapters 11 and 12 dealing with the position of non-self-governing, mandated and trust territories. See Lauterpact, Elihu, "The Development of the Law of International Organization by the Decisions of International Tribunals", 152 *RCADI*, 1976, p. 416; Rosenne, Shabtai, *Developments in the law of Treaties: 1945-1986,* Cambridge: Cambridge University Press, 1989, p. 224.

pretation of the Charter. Nevertheless, techniques relating to treaty interpretation may not be fully adequate or applicable to the interpretation of a constitution.[61] Sir Robert Jennings and Sir Arthur Watts maintain that a treaty of a 'constitutional' character "should be subject to somewhat different rules of interpretation so as to allow for the intrinsically evolutionary nature of a constitution."[62]

The present study does not claim that the methods of interpretation adopted by the Court, in its advisory opinions, are totally different from the ordinary rules of treaty interpretation. Rather, it is suggested here that the development of general techniques of interpretation owes much to their application by the Court which has developed a system of constitutional interpretation. As Simma and others claim, the ICJ has emphasised the "functional interpretation" principle by calling attention to the purposes of the Organisation.

(i) The Principle of Natural and Ordinary Meaning of the Words in Their Context

This principle is considered the main principle of interpretation in the VCLT, which in Article 31(1) provides that a treaty shall be interpreted "in good faith in accordance with the ordinary meaning to be given to the terms of the treaty in their context and in the light of its object and purpose." The natural and ordinary meaning of the treaty can be determined by looking at the context in which it is used. The Court in the *Constitution of the Maritime Safety Committee of the Inter-Governmental Maritime Consultative Organization* Case, while interpreting the term 'elected', emphasised the importance of the context and held that:[63]

> *The meaning of the word 'elected' in the Article cannot be determined in isolation by recourse to its usual or common meaning and attaching that meaning to the word where used in the Article. The word obtains its meaning from the context in which it is used. If the context requires a meaning which connotes a wide choice, it must be construed accordingly, just as it must be given a restrictive meaning if the context in which it is used so requires.*

The Court then held that:[64]

> *The words of Article 28(a) must be read in their natural and ordinary meaning, in the sense which they would normally have in their context. It is only if, when this is done, the words of the Article are ambiguous in any way that resort needs to be had to other methods of construction.*

---

[61] Lauterpacht, Elihu, *supra* note 60, p. 416.

[62] Jennings & Watts, *supra* note 26, p. 1268.

[63] Hereinafter cited as "the *IMCO* Case", ICJ Rep., 1960, p. 158.

[64] Ibid, p. 159.

In the Competence of the General Assembly Regarding Admission to the United Nations Case the Court found that:[65]

> *[T]he first duty of a tribunal which is called upon to interpret and apply the provisions of a treaty, is to endeavour to give effect to them in their natural and ordinary meaning in the context in which they occur. If the relevant words in their natural and ordinary meaning make sense in their context, that is an end of the matter. If, on the other hand, the words in their natural and ordinary meaning are ambiguous or lead to an unreasonable result, then, and then only, must the Court, by resort to other methods of interpretation, seek to ascertain what the parties really did mean when they used these words.*

(ii) Functional or Teleological Interpretation Principle

According to Article 31(1) of the VCLT a treaty shall be interpreted, in part, by reference to its object and purpose. The main objective of this functional or teleological method of interpretation is to give full effect to a treaty and to avoid any interpretation that runs counter to the purpose served by the treaty.[66] Shaw notes that this approach centralises the role of the judge, since he will be called upon to define the object and purpose of the treaty and this may lead to judicial law-making.[67]

The Court applied the teleological approach in the *Reparations* Case when it held that the UN Organisation could not carry out its functions unless it was regarded as having an international legal personality.[68] In its advisory opinion on the *International Status of South West Africa*,[69] the Court held that the Mandate conferred by the League of Nations over South West Africa was, *inter alia*, instituted for the benefit of the inhabitants of the territory, and that it was an international institution with an international aim. The Court then interpreted Article 80 (1) of the UN Charter in the light of the objectives and purposes of the mandates system which was created to give effect to two principles,[70] non-annexation of overseas territories ceded by the defeated powers in the peace settlement after World War One, and the well being and development of the peoples inhabiting the mandated

---

65 ICJ Rep., 1950, p. 8.

66 Schwarzenberger, Georg, *International Law*, London: Stevens and Sons, vol. 1, p. 518.

67 Shaw, *supra* note 57, p. 839.

68 ICJ Rep., 1949, p. 179.

69 ICJ Rep., 1950, p. 128.

70 See ICJ Rep., 1950, pp. 131-133. Article 80(1) of the UN Charter provides: "[e]xcept as may be agreed upon in individual trusteeship agreements, made under Articles 77, 79, and 81, placing each territory under the trusteeship system, and until such agreements have been concluded, nothing in this Chapter shall be construed in or of itself to alter in any manner the rights whatsoever of any states or any peoples or the terms of existing international instruments to which Members of the United Nations may respectively be parties." ICJ Rep., 1950, pp. 131-133.

territories. The interests of the latter, who were judged to be unready, as yet, to stand by themselves, were said to form "a sacred trust of civilization."[71]

The Court relied on the objects of the mandate treaty between the League and the Union of South Africa and held that the 'necessity' for supervision continued and, therefore, the obligation to submit to supervision could not disappear "merely" because the supervisory organ had vanished, particularly when the UN had "another international organ performing similar, though not identical, supervisory functions."[72] In light of this interpretation, the Court concluded that:[73]

> *[T]he General Assembly of the United Nations is legally qualified to exercise the supervisory functions previously exercised by the League of Nations with regard to the administration of the Territory, and that the Union of South Africa is under an obligation to submit to supervision and control of the General Assembly and to render annual reports to it.*

(iii) The Use of Travaux Préparatoires *as Supplementary Means of Interpretation*[74]

Article 32 of the VCLT stipulates that recourse may be had to "supplementary means of interpretation" in certain circumstances:

> *Recourse may be had to supplementary means of interpretation, including the preparatory work of the treaty and the circumstances of its conclusion, in order to confirm the meaning resulting from the application of article 31, or to determine the meaning when the interpretation according to article 31:*
>
> *(a) leaves the meaning ambiguous or obscure; or*
>
> *(b) leads to a result which is manifestly absurd or unreasonable.*

---

[71] Judge McNair in his Separate Opinion analysed the "sacred trust" by stating that:

Nearly every legal system possess some institution whereby the property (and sometimes the persons) of those who are not sui juris, such as a minor or a lunatic, can be entrusted to some responsible person such as a trustee or tuteur or curateur. The Anglo-American trust serves this purpose, and another purpose even more closely akin to the Mandates System, namely, the vesting of property in trustees, and its management by them in order that the public or some class of the public may derive benefit or that some public purpose may be served. The trust has frequently been used to protect the weak and the dependent.

See Sep. Op. of Judge McNair, ICJ Rep., 1950, p. 149.

[72] ICJ Rep., 1950, p. 136.

[73] Ibid, p. 137.

[74] The term "*travaux préparatoires*" is a French term which means "preparatory work" and may include materials used in preparing the ultimate form of an agreement or statute, and especially of an international treaty; such materials constitute a legislative history. See Garner, Bryan, *supra* note 44, p. 1505.

Thus, The Court may refer to the preparatory work when there is a lack of clarity in the text and persisting ambiguity, or where a literal interpretation would lead to a result that is 'unreasonable'. In the *Admissions* Case, the request for an opinion arose in the context of a deadlock over the criteria to be applied to the admission of States to the UN and which reflected the bipolar division of the world into Eastern and Western blocs. Following the establishment of the UN, a number of States applied for admission. However, their applications were rejected by the Security Council because of vetoes by one or more permanent members of the Council. The General Assembly referred to the Court the question whether a member of the UN must make its consent to admission of another State to the UN dependent on conditions not expressly stated in Article 4(1) of the Charter.[75] The Court considered that:[76]

> *[T]he text [of the Charter] is sufficiently clear; consequently it [the Court] does not feel that it should deviate from the consistent practice of the Permanent Court of International Justice, according to which there is no occasion to resort to preparatory work if the text of a convention is sufficiently clear in itself.*

Therefore, the Court declared that the conditions laid down in the Charter for the admission of States were exhaustive and that, if they were fulfilled by a State which was a candidate, the Security Council ought to make a recommendation which would enable the General Assembly to decide upon the admission. The Court reaffirmed its view in the *Competence of the General Assembly* Case and held that it had no difficulty in ascertaining the natural and ordinary meaning of the words in question. Therefore, it was not permissible to resort to the *travaux préparatoires.*[77]

On the other hand, the Court has relied on the *travaux préparatoires* in subsequent cases such as the *IMCO* Case, which involved interpretation of Article 28(a) of the Convention establishing the Organisation.[78] According to Article 28 (a) the

---

[75] Article 4 provides:

(1) "Membership in the United Nations is open to all other peace-loving states which accept the obligations contained in the present Charter and, in the judgment of the Organization, are able and willing to carry out these obligations.

(2) "The admission of any such state to membership in the United Nations will be effected by a decision of the General Assembly upon the recommendation of the Security Council."

[76] ICJ Rep., 1947-48, p. 63. The minority judges referred to the preparatory work for the purpose of showing that members were free to refer to any kind of consideration in determining whether or not a State should be admitted. See Joint Opinion of Judges Basdevant, Winiarski, McNair and Read, ibid, pp. 87-90.

[77] ICJ Rep., 1950, p. 8.

[78] The question referred to the Court was: "[i]s the Maritime Safety Committee of the Inter-Governmental Maritime Consultative Organization, which was elected on 15 January 1959, constituted in accordance with the Convention for the Establishment of the Organization?"

IMCO Committee, consists of 14 members elected by the Assembly from members of the organisation having an important interest in maritime safety, "of which not less than eight shall be the largest ship-owning nations."

On 15 January 1959, the IMCO Assembly failed to elect Liberia and Panama to the Committee, although those two States were among the eight members of the Organisation who possessed the largest registered tonnage. Subsequently, the Assembly decided to ask the Court whether the Maritime Safety Committee was constituted in accordance with the Convention for the establishment of the Organisation. The Court decided that the preparatory work of the Convention establishing IMCO confirmed that the underlying principle of Article 28(a) was that the largest ship owning nations should constitute the majority at the Committee.[79] Consequently the Court replied to the requested question in the negative.

Most recently, in the *Legal Consequences of the Construction of a Wall in the Occupied Palestinian Territory* Case,[80] the Court, in order to determine the scope of application of the Fourth Geneva Convention, resorted to the intentions of the drafters of both the Convention and of the Hague Regulations of 1907 to conclude that the Geneva Convention was applicable to Israel regardless of the status of the occupied territories.[81] The Court noted that, according to the first paragraph of Article 2 of the Fourth Geneva Convention, that Convention is applicable when two conditions are fulfilled: that there exists an armed conflict (whether or not a state of war has been recognised); and that the conflict has arisen between two contracting parties. If those two conditions are satisfied, the Convention applies, in particular in any territory occupied in the course of the conflict by one of the contracting parties.[82] The Court stated that:[83]

> *The object of the second paragraph of Article 2 is not to restrict the scope of application of the Convention, as defined by the first paragraph, by excluding therefrom territories not falling under the sovereignty of one of the contracting parties. It is directed simply to making it clear that, even if occupation effected during the conflict met no armed resistance, the Convention is still applicable.*

The Court then held that the above interpretation:[84]

---

79 ICJ Rep., 1960, pp. 161-164.

80 Hereinafter cited as: "the *Wall* Case", See http://www.icj-cij.org/icjwww/idocket/imwp/imwpframe.htm (accessed 21 October 2004).

81 Israel had objected that the Fourth Geneva Convention is not applicable *de jure* within those territories because Article 2 (2) applies only in the case of occupation of territories falling under the sovereignty of a High Contracting Party involved in an armed conflict. Israel explained that while Jordan was admittedly a party to the Convention in 1967, the territories occupied by Israel during that conflict had not previously been under Jordanian sovereignty. See Para. 94 of the *Wall* Opinion.

82 See para. 95 of the *Wall* Advisory Opinion, *supra* note 80.

83 Ibid.

84 Ibid.

> *[R]eflects the intention of the drafters of the Fourth Geneva Convention to protect civilians who find themselves, in whatever way, in the hands of the occupying Power. Whilst the drafters of the Hague Regulations of 1907 were as much concerned with protecting the rights of a State whose territory is occupied, as with protecting the inhabitants of that territory, the drafters of the Fourth Geneva Convention sought to guarantee the protection of civilians in time of war, regardless of the status of the occupied territories, as is shown by Article 47 of the Convention.*

The Court explained that, according to the Convention's *travaux préparatoires*, the drafters of the second paragraph of Article 2:[85]

> *[H]ad no intention, when they inserted that paragraph into the Convention, of restricting the latter's scope of application. They were merely seeking to provide for cases of occupation without combat, such as the occupation of Bohemia and Moravia by Germany in 1939.*

In sum, the Court has not been hesitant to resort to the preparatory work whenever it considered it to be essential to determine or to confirm the meaning of words obtained by the application of other principles.[86]

(iv) Subsequent Practice as a Guide to Interpretation

Article 31(3)(b) of the Vienna Convention permits reference, by the interpreting organ, to any subsequent practice in the application of a treaty. In the *Wall* Case, in order to examine the significance of Article 12(1) of the UN Charter, the Court referred to UN practice.[87] The Court held that:[88]

---

[85] Ibid.

[86] Judge Alvarez, as a general rule, did not favour using the *préparatoires* work method. He stated in the *Competence of the General Assembly* Case that: "[i]t is therefore necessary, when interpreting treaties-in particular, the Charter of the United Nations-to look ahead, that is to have regard to the new conditions, and not to look back, or have recourse to *travaux préparatoires*. A treaty or a text that has once been established acquires a life of its own. Consequently, in interpreting it we must have regard to the exigencies of contemporary life, rather than to the intentions of those who framed it." ICJ Rep., 1950, p. 18.

[87] Article 12 (1) of the Charter provides: "[w]hile the Security Council is exercising in respect of any dispute or situation the functions assigned to it in the present Charter, the General Assembly shall not make any recommendation with regard to that dispute or situation unless the Security Council so requests."

[88] See para. 27 of the *Wall* Opinion. See *supra* note 80. It is interesting to know that the Court in the *Expenses* Case said that initially the General Assembly cannot deal with a matter while it is on the Council's agenda, but provided the General Assembly did not propose measures that could amount to 'action', it could deal with matters affecting international peace and security and even establish peacekeeping operations. See discussion below.

As regards the practice of the United Nations, both the General Assembly and the Security Council initially interpreted and applied Article 12 to the effect that the Assembly could not make a recommendation on a question concerning the maintenance of international peace and security while the matter remained on the Council's agenda.

In the *Competence of the General Assembly* Case, the Court found that UN organs have consistently interpreted the text of Article 4 of the UN Charter to mean that the General Assembly could decide to admit a State to UN membership only on the basis of a recommendation of the Security Council.[89] The Court thus confirmed the consistent application by UN organs of the natural and ordinary meaning principle to Article 4 of the Charter.

Once again, in the *Expenses* Case, the Court referred to the practice of the Organisation in order to interpret the word "budget" in Article 17(2) of the Charter as encompassing both the administrative and operational budgets of the UN. The Court held that "the practice of the Organization is entirely consistent with the plain meaning of the text."[90]

From the above cases it is clear that the ICJ through its advisory opinions has had occasions to develop and consolidate jurisprudence in the area of treaty interpretation and to confirm the various recognised techniques of treaty interpretation.

4 The Contribution of Advisory Opinions to the Interpretation and Application of Agreements Between the UN, Its Agencies and Member States

This Section illustrates how the Court's advisory opinions have provided guidance regarding the interpretation and application of conventions between the UN and/or its agencies on the one hand, and the member States on the other.

4.1 The Court's Interpretation of the Convention on the Privileges and Immunities of the UN

International organisations, in the pursuit of their objectives, need protection from undue interference by States.[91] Therefore, they are often granted privileges and immunities as a matter of "functional necessity"[92] which enable them to "function properly without undue interference in their affairs by States and thus ensure the

89 ICJ Rep., 1950, p. 9.

90 The *Expenses* Case, ICJ Rep., 1962, p. 160.

91 Schermers & Blokker, *supra* note 27, p. 235.

92 Ibid.

independent discharge of the tasks entrusted to them."[93] Article105 of the UN Charter regulates the immunities given to the UN within the sovereign territory of Member States and provides:[94]

(1) The Organization shall enjoy in the territory of each of its members such privileges and immunities as are necessary for the fulfillment of its purposes.

(2) Representative of the members of the United Nations and officials of the Organization shall similarly enjoy such privileges and immunities as are necessary for the independent exercise of their functions in connection with the Organization.

The UN Charter is supplemented by the General Convention on the Privileges and Immunities of the UN which regulates these privileges and immunities in Article VI Section (22).[95] The Court has constantly in its advisory opinions ruled that this protective measure provides privileges and immunities for experts while on mission for the UN even if they are not permanent UN officials or employees. In the 1989 *Applicability of Article VI, Section 22, of the Convention on the Privileges and Immunities of the United Nations Case,*[96] a dispute arose between the ECOSOC and Romania over the applicability of the Convention on the Privileges and Immunities to Mr. Mazilu, a Romanian national and Special Rapporteur of the Sub-Committee on the Prevention of Discrimination and Protection of Minorities.

The background of this case is that the Sub-Commission had asked Mazilu to prepare a report on human rights and youth analysing the efforts and measures for securing the implementation and enjoyment by youth of human rights, particularly, the right to life, education and work.[97] However, no report had been received from Mr Mazilu. Romania informed the UN that Mr. Mazilu had been taken into

---

93 Scobbie, Iain, "International Organizations and International Relations", in Dupuy, R, (ed.) *A Handbook On International Organizations,* 2nd edition, Dordrecht; Boston; London: Martinus Nijhoff Publishers, 1998, p. 833.

94 Simma, *supra* note 53, p. 1315. Although the General Convention supplements Article 105 and regulates the privileges and immunities enjoyed by the UN, it has been suggested that Article 105 is a self-executing Article and needs no further international agreement to confer functional immunity on the UN. Therefore, even members which did not accede to the General Convention of 1946 must provide identical immunities. Simma, ibid, p. 1316.

95 This Section provides that:

Experts (other than officials coming within the scope of Article V) performing missions for the United Nations shall be accorded such privileges and immunities as are necessary for the independent exercise of their functions during the period of their missions, including the time spent on journeys in connection with their missions. Cited in the ICJ Rep., 1989, p. 192.

96 Hereinafter cited as: "the *Mazilu* Case", ICJ Rep., 1989, p. 177.

97 ICJ Rep., 1989, p. 180.

hospital, and he had not yet begun to draw up the report entrusted to him. Mazilu claimed that the Romanian Ministry of Foreign Affairs requested him not to submit the report, and that the Romanian authorities were refusing him a travel permit. Romania, for its part, claimed that due to Mazilu's illness he had "applied personally for disability retirement because of this condition, submitting the appropriate medical certificate." The Romanian Government also argued that the case of Mazilu was an internal matter between a citizen and his government and that any intervention of the UN Secretariat would be considered as interference in Romania's internal affairs. Therefore, Romania argued that "the problem of the application of the General Convention does not arise in this case."[98]

Under these circumstances, ECOSOC requested an advisory opinion of the Court on the applicability of Article VI, Section 22 of the General Convention to Mazilu. The Court found that the treaty did not itself define "experts on mission", and that the relevant Section does not refer to the nature, duration or place of such missions. Nevertheless, using a functional interpretation of the Convention, the Court stated:[99]

> *The purpose of Section 22 is nevertheless evident, namely, to enable the United Nations to entrust missions to persons who do not have the status of an official of the Organization, and to guarantee them "such privileges and immunities as are necessary for the independent exercise of their functions". The experts thus appointed or elected may or may not be remunerated, may or may not have a contract, may be given a task requiring work over a lengthy period or a short time. The essence of the matter lies not in their administrative position but in the nature of their mission.*

The Court, therefore found that Section 22 also applies to experts who are not permanent officials of the UN and unanimously ruled that:[100]

> *The privileges and immunities of Articles V and VI are conferred with a view to ensuring the independence of international officials and experts in the interests of the Organization. This independence must be respected by all States including the State of nationality and the State of residence.*

Some commentators have noted that this case demonstrates the potentially important role of judicial organs "in preventing states from abusing their sovereignty, and enabling international organizations to perform their functions."[101]

---

98 ICJ Rep., 1989, para. 24, p. 185.

99 Ibid, para. 47, p. 194.

100 Ibid, para. 51, p. 195.

101 Schermers & Blokker, *supra* note 27, p. 266.

The Court again ruled on Article VI of Section 22 of the General Convention in the1999 *Differences Relating to Immunity from Legal Process of a Special Rapporteur of the Commission On Human Rights* Case.[102] Here the Court concluded that Article VI, Section 22 of the General Convention applied to Mr. Cumaraswamy, a Special Rapporteur of the Commission on Human Rights who had been entrusted with a mission by the UN and was therefore an expert within the terms of the Section. The Case arose because Mr. Cumaraswamy had given an interview to *International Commercial Litigation*, a magazine published in the UK and Northern Ireland but circulated in Malaysia. Two commercial companies in Malaysia claimed that an article published on the basis of that interview contained defamatory words that had 'brought them into public scandal, odium and contempt.' Therefore, the companies sued Mr. Cumaraswamy in the Malaysian Courts.

The issue was whether words used by Mr. Cumaraswamy during an interview could be regarded as words spoken in the course of the performance his mission, which would mean that he would be entitled to immunity. The UN's Legal Counsel, acting on behalf of the UN Secretary-General, said that the interview was conducted in Mr. Cumaraswamy's official capacity as Special Rapporteur on the Independence of Judges and Lawyers. Accordingly, he requested the Malaysian authorities to advise the Malaysian courts of Mr. Cumaraswamy's immunity from legal process. However, Counsel's request was rejected and the competent judge of the Malaysian High Court concluded that she was "unable to hold that the Defendant is absolutely protected by the immunity he claims." Therefore, the Legal Counsel considered that there was a dispute between Malaysia and the UN and referred to Section 30 of the 1946 Convention which provides that all differences arising out of the interpretation or application of the Convention shall be referred to the ICJ. Under these circumstances ECOSOC requested an advisory opinion on the applicability of Article VI, Section 22 of the General Convention to Mr. Cumaraswamy.

In response the Court referred to its previous findings in the *Mazilu* Case, where it concluded that the purpose of Section 22 was to enable the UN to entrust missions to persons who do not have the status of an official of the Organisation and that it guarantees them the privileges and immunities necessary to execute their function. Therefore, on the basis of *Mazilu* Case and after examining Article105 of the UN Charter, the Court concluded that Mr. Cumaraswamy must also be regarded as an 'expert on mission' within the meaning of Article VI of the General Convention and that he therefore enjoyed immunity.[103] The Court acknowledged also that the Secretary-General, as "the chief administrative officer of the Organization, has the authority and the responsibility to exercise the necessary

[102] Hereinafter cited as: "the *Immunity from Legal Process Case*", ICJ Rep., 1999, p. 62.

[103] ICJ Rep., 1999, pp. 83-84.

protection where required."[104] The Court considered that when a national court confronted the issue of immunity of a UN agent:[105]

> *[T]hey should immediately be notified of any finding by the Secretary-General concerning the immunity. That finding, and its documentary expression, creates a presumption which can only be set aside for the most compelling reasons and is thus to be given the greatest weight by national courts.*

It has been suggested that the Court's finding did not go so far as to state that the Secretary-General has the final word on the issue of immunity which leaves room for the possibility of a rebuttal.[106] However, the Court did conclude that the Government of Malaysia had an obligation to inform its courts of the Secretary-General's position and an obligation to deal with the question of immunity from legal process as a preliminary issue to be decided in *limini litis.*[107]

4.2 The Court's Interpretation of the Headquarters Agreement Between the UN and the US

The request for an advisory opinion on the *Applicability of the Obligation to Arbitrate Under Section 21 of the United Nations Headquarters Agreement of 26 June1947,*[108] arose out of an existing dispute between the UN and the US regarding the application of the Agreement. The background to the request was the US closure of the New York Office of the Palestine Liberation Organisation (PLO) under a law "to make unlawful the establishment or maintenance within the United States of an office of the Palestine Liberation Organization."[109]

The Secretary-General pointed out to the General Assembly that the members of the PLO Mission were invitees of the UN and therefore covered by Sections 11, 12 and 13 of the Agreement.[110] The General Assembly then voted to request an advisory opinion about the applicability of Section 21 of the Agreement which

---

[104] Ibid, para. 50, p. 84.

[105] Ibid, para. 61, p. 87.

[106] Klabbers, *supra* note 8, p. 161.

[107] ICJ Rep., 1999, pp. 89-90.

[108] ICJ Rep., 1988, p. 9.

[109] ICJ Rep., 1988, para. 9, p. 15. The US had taken a number of measures against the PLO in New York. The Secretary General had regarded these measures as contrary to the Headquarters Agreement. The US did not dispute this point and stated that the measures were taken "irrespective of any obligations the United States may have under the Agreement." para. 49, p. 32.

[110] Para. 21, p. 21.

provided for arbitration of disputes.[111] In its subsequent opinion, the Court concluded that "the United States is bound to respect the obligation to have recourse to arbitration under section 21of the Headquarters Agreement."[112] It also concluded that the provisions of a treaty prevail over the domestic law of a State party to that treaty, thereby affirming "the fundamental principle of international law that international law prevails over domestic law."[113]

5 The Contribution of Advisory Opinions to the Clarification of the Functions and Powers of UN Political Organs

This Section focuses exclusively on the use of the advisory function to provide guidance for UN political organs, specifically the General Assembly and the Security Council, on difficult or contested legal issues concerning their powers, jurisdiction or functions. While Charter provisions variously categorise the powers and functions of the General Assembly and of the Security Council as exclusive,[114] concurrent,[115] or joint,[116] in practice many problems have arisen out of the allocation of these powers and functions as set out in the Charter.

This is primarily because, at the San Francisco Conference, the participating States left it to the discretion of each organ to interpret and apply the Charter provisions within its own field of competence.[117] The Court's advisory opinions have

---

[111] Section 21, paragraph (a) provides:

Any dispute between the United Nations and the United States concerning the interpretation or application of this agreement or of any supplemental agreement, which is not settled by negotiation or other agreed mode of settlement, shall be referred for final decision to a tribunal of three arbitrators, one to be named by the Secretary General, one to be named by the Secretary of State of the United States, and the third to be chosen by the two, or, if they should fail to agree upon a third, then by the President of the International Court of Justice.

Cited in ICJ Rep., 1988, p. 14.

[112] ICJ Rep., 1988, para. 57, p. 34. The Court has reached its Opinion unanimously.

[113] Ibid.

[114] See Vallat, F. A., "The General Assembly and the Security Council of the United Nations", 29, *BYIL*, 1952, p. 70; El-Rashidy, Ahmad, *The Advisory Jurisdiction of the International Court of Justice* , Cairo: Alhaia Al-Masria Al- Amaa Lelketab, 1992 [in Arabic], pp. 341-510 ; Amr, *supra* note 36, pp. 137-143. The exclusive powers of the General Assembly are set out in many articles of the United Nations Charter, e.g. Article 11, 13(1) and 17. The exclusive powers of the Security Council are contained in Articles 40, 41 and 42 of the UN Charter.

[115] The UN Charter entrusted both the General Assembly and the Security Council with the responsibility to achieve the main objectives of the UN.

[116] Articles 4, 5, and 6 of the UN Charter.

[117] Vallat, *supra* note 114, p. 67.

helped clarify the distribution of the powers and functions of the political organs as shown in the following sections.

5.1 Concurrent and Exclusive Functions of the General Assembly and of the Security Council

In practice, problems have arisen as a result of the overlapping activities of the two political organs, the Security Council and the General Assembly. The ICJ's opinions regarding the exclusive and concurrent functions of these organs have been helpful in indicating the spheres of responsibility of the Council and of the Assembly.

5.1.1 Peace-Keeping Operations: Concurrent Roles of the General Assembly and of the Security Council

The term "peace-keeping" does not appear in the UN Charter. However, since the establishment of the first United Nations Emergency Force (UNEF) by the General Assembly in 1956, the term and the institution of peace-keeping have been frequently used.[118] The object of peace-keeping has been found to be consistent with the aims of the UN Charter which are to 'maintain international peace and security'.[119] However, the lack of any express provisions in the Charter on peace-keeping has led to controversy over the scope of the powers of the various organs that have been involved in peace-keeping.[120]

---

[118] Suy, Eric "Peace-Keeping Operations" in: Dupuy, R. (ed.), *A Handbook on International Organizations*, Dordrecht; Boston; London: Martinus Nijhoff Publishers, 1989, p. 53; Gray, Christine, "The Use of Force and the International Legal Order" in: Evans, Malcolm D., (ed.), *International Law*, Oxford University Press, 2003, p. 611; Zemanek, Karl, "Peace Keeping or Peace Making" in: Blokker, Niels & Muller, Sam (eds.), *Towards More Effective Supervision by International Organizations: Essays in Honour of Henry G. Schermers*, Martinus Nijhoff Publishers, vol. 1, 1994, p. 32.

[119] Article 1(1) of the UN Charter.

[120] The Security Council, the General Assembly and the Secretary General are the main organs involved in peace-keeping. See Suy, *supra* note 118, p. 545. In accordance with Article 24(1) of the Charter the Security Council has the primary responsibility on issues of maintaining international peace and security and enjoys, under Chapters VI, and VII, a wide range of powers to maintain peace and security including the right to establish peacekeeping forces. In accordance with Chapter VI, the Security Council has the right to investigate any dispute or situation which might lead to international friction or give rise to a dispute in order to determine whether the continuance of the dispute is likely to endanger the maintenance of international peace and security. If the situation or dispute is one which may endanger the maintenance of international peace and security, the Security Council also has the right to decide whether to act under Article 36 or merely to make recommendations for an appropriate settlement, and call upon the parties to settle their disputes by peaceful means in accordance with Article 33(1). The General

In the late 1940s, because of the paralysis of the Security Council as a result of the Cold War, the need for General Assembly involvement in maintaining peace and security had increased.[121] However, some States objected on the grounds that the Assembly was assuming powers which properly belong to the Security Council alone. The Court had to confront this issue in the *Expenses* Case which arose out of the refusal of some member States, most notably the Soviet Union and France, to pay their shares of the costs of the UN Emergency Forces (UNEF) and of the UN force in the Congo (ONUC).[122]

The objecting States maintained that peace-keeping operations fell within the exclusive competence of the Security Council. Therefore, the General Assembly requested an advisory opinion as to whether certain expenditures authorised by it to finance peace keeping operations in the Congo and the Middle East, in some of which the Assembly has been significantly involved, constituted "expenses of the Organization" within the meaning of Article 17(2) of the Charter. To determine the issue the Court had first to examine the powers of the General Assembly and the Security Council with respect to establishing peace keeping operations and the maintenance of international peace and security. It was argued before the Court that peace-keeping lies within the exclusive competence of the Security Council and, therefore, that the General Assembly had no role to play in such matters.[123]

Assembly also has a considerable role to play in peace-keeping. Article 10 of the UN Charter gives the General Assembly wide competence to discuss any matter within the scope of the Charter. Therefore, it would seem to be perfectly acceptable for the General Assembly to deal with issues of peace and security provided it does not encroach on the exclusive powers of the Security Council. Article 11(1) of the UN Charter also empowers the General Assembly to deal with any situation which might threaten the peace or be considered as an act of aggression.

[121] Pogany, Istvan, *The Security Council and the Arab-Israeli Conflict*, Aldershot: Grower, 1984, p. 76. Due to the failure of the Security Council, during the Cold War era, to exercise its responsibility in maintaining peace and security because of the vetoes cast by some of its permanent members, the General Assembly on 3 November 1950 adopted the Uniting for Peace Resolution to enhance its role in maintaining international peace and security. See GA Res. 377(V). Pogany has emphasised that this resolution was "consistent with the provisions of the Charter, and did not involve a *de facto* amendment of the constitution of the United Nations". Pogany, ibid. In contrast to this view Shaw is of the opinion that Article 11 of the UN Charter, which states that any question regarding international peace and security issue has to be referred to the Security Council, appeared to cast some doubts upon the validity of the provisions in the Uniting for Peace Resolution. See Shaw, *Supra* note 57, p. 1152.

[122] The Soviet Union declined to pay its share to either UNEF or to the ONUC while France declined to contribute to the latter. The UNEF was established by the General Assembly in 1956. See Res. 1000 (ES-1) of 5 November 1956 and 1001 (ES) of 7 November 1956. The ONUC was established by the Security Council in 1960. See Res. 143 of 14 July 1960; Res. 145 of 22 July 1960 and lastly Res. 146 of 9 August 1960.

[123] ICJ Rep., 1962, p. 162.

The Court, in reply, examined Articles 11(2), 14, and 24 of the Charter, and found that Article 24(1) provides: "[i]n order to ensure prompt and effective action by the United Nations, its Members confer on the Security Council primary responsibility for the maintenance of international peace and security ..." However, the Court also noted that the Charter's provisions[124] made it clear that the General Assembly is "also to be concerned with international peace and security." Thus, the Court concluded that the powers of the Security Council with regard to maintaining peace and security are primary but not exclusive, and that:[125]

> *[T]he functions and powers conferred by the Charter on the General Assembly are not confined to discussion, considerations, the initiation of studies and the making of recommendations; they are not merely hortatory.*

The Court recognised that the General Assembly, by virtue of Article 14 of the UN Charter, could:[126]

> *[R]ecommend measures for the peaceful adjustment of any situation, regardless of origin, which it deems likely to impair the general welfare or friendly relations among nations, including situations resulting from a violation of the provisions of the present Charter setting forth the purposes and principles of the United Nations.*

Moreover, Article 11(2) of the Charter confirms the General Assembly's competence to discuss any questions relating to the maintenance of international peace and security, as well as its recommendatory powers with regard to such questions. However, Article 11(2) sets limits on the Assembly's competence where it provides that "[a]ny such question on which action is necessary shall be referred to the Security Council by the General Assembly either before or after discussion."

The Court interpreted the term "action" in Article 11(2) to mean "coercive or enforcement action" which would be solely within the province of the Security Council. However, the term did not refer to recommendations which the Security Council might make, as for instance under Article 38, because the General Assembly under

---

[124] Article 11(2) refers to the duty of the General Assembly to refer any question relating to international peace and security on which action is necessary to the Council. See also Article 14 of the UN Charter which provides: "the General Assembly may recommend measures for the peaceful adjustment of any situation, regardless of origin, which it deems likely to impair the general welfare or friendly relations among nations, including situations resulting from a violation of the provisions of the present Charter setting forth the Purposes and Principles of the United Nations."

[125] ICJ Rep., 1962, p. 163.

[126] ICJ Rep., 1962, p. 163.

Article 11 also has a comparable power.[127] Consequently, the Court found that the establishment by the General Assembly of UNEF in the Middle East was not contrary to Article11 (2) of the UN Charter since no enforcement action was involved.[128] Despite the inability of the Security Council to fulfil its primary responsibility for maintaining international peace and security, particularly during the Cold War era, Pogany has pointed out, with reference to the Suez crisis of 1956, that:[129]

> *[T]he UN system had shown itself to be sufficiently supple to respond to this situation. The resolve of the General Assembly to discharge its responsibility under the Uniting for Peace Resolution ... made a significant contribution to the restoration of peace in the Middle-East.*

5.1.2 The Exclusive Competence of the Security Council to Take Coercive Action

The Security Council under Chapter VII of the UN Charter and more specifically by virtue of Articles 41 and 42 may adopt or authorise enforcement action in the event of any threat to the peace, breach of the peace or act of aggression within the meaning of article 39. In the *Expenses* Case, the Court confirmed the exclusive competence of the Security Council regarding coercive action to maintain international peace and security and stated that:[130]

> *[I]t is the Security Council which is given a power to impose an explicit obligation of compliance if for example it issues an order or command to an aggressor under Chapter VII. It is only the Security Council which can require enforcement by coercive action against an aggressor.*

The Soviet Union had argued that:[131]

> *[T]he analysis of the relevant provisions of the Charter leaves no doubt that while Article 17 lays down a general rule, Article 43 contains a particular rule, a* lex specialis, *which relates to expenditures for certain actions for the purpose of maintaining international peace and security. Such actions may be undertaken in pursuance of a decision of the Security Council.*

---

[127] ICJ Rep., 1962, p. 165.

[128] Shaw, *supra* note 57, p. 1153, footnote 345.

[129] Pogany, *supra* note 121, p. 78.

[130] ICJ Rep., 1962, p. 163. It is clear that the Court has based its arguments on the provisions in Chapter VII, more specifically Articles 39, 41, 42, and 24 of the UN Charter.

[131] ICJ Pled., 1961, p. 404.

Responding to this argument the Court held that the General Assembly's establishment of UNEF and the far-reaching activities of ONUC[132] were not enforcement action as understood by Chapter VII of the Charter and that therefore Article 43 could not have applicability to this case.[133] The Court further emphasised that even if Article 43 were applicable the Court did not accept any limited interpretation of the Article because that would impede the efficiency of the Council. The Court stated:[134]

> *The Court cannot accept so limited a view of the powers of the Security Council under the Charter. It cannot be said that the Charter has left the Security Council impotent in the face of an emergency situation when agreements under Article 43 have not been concluded.*

As some commentators have observed the failure to conclude agreements in accordance with Article 43 was a consequence of the Cold War and of the resulting inability to achieve consensus among the Security Council's permanent members.[135] Because the Security Council could rarely obtain agreement among its permanent Members, peace- keeping authorised by the General Assembly became an important means for dealing with conflicts during the Cold War period.[136]

5.1.3 The Exclusive Competence of the General Assembly over the UN's Budget

According to Article 17(1) of the Charter, the General Assembly enjoys exclusive power over the UN's budget.[137] Although this exclusivity was not disputed in the *Expenses* Case, the extent of the Assembly's authority in this regard has been questioned. It was argued by some States that the costs of peace-keeping operations

---

[132] In the case of ONUC, the Secretary-General assumed broader powers with respect to the direction of the operation than might otherwise have been the case. The main issue in regard to ONUC was the role of the Secretary-General and the departure of ONUC from conventional peacekeeping to a more coercive function. See e.g. Gray, Christine, *International Law and the Use of Force*, Oxford University Press, 2000, pp. 151-152.

[133] Article 43(1) provides that: "All Members of the United Nations, in order to contribute to the maintenance of international peace and security, undertake to make available to the Security Council, on its call and in accordance with a special agreement or agreements, armed forces, assistance, and facilities, including rights of passage, necessary for the purpose of maintaining international peace and security."

[134] ICJ Rep., 1962, p. 167.

[135] Pogany, *supra* note 121, p. 13.

[136] Katayanagi, Mari, *Human Rights Functions of United Nations Peace-Keeping Operations*, Ph.D. thesis, University of Warwick 2000, p. 20.

[137] Article 17 provides (1) "[t]he General Assembly shall consider and approve the budget of the Organization". (2) "[t]he expenses of the Organization shall be borne by the Members as apportioned by the General Assembly."

were not the 'expenses of the Organisation' within the meaning of Article 17(2) to be borne by Members as apportioned by the General Assembly. The Security Council, in the view of the Soviet Union, was the only organ empowered to finance these operations.[138]

It was also argued that "budget" as used in Article 17(1), applied only to the "administrative budget" and, therefore, that expenses related to operations for the maintenance of international peace and security were not 'expenses of the Organisation' within the meaning of Article 17(2), and could not be described as administrative expenses.[139] The Court however, stated that the term "expenses" in Article 17(2) could not be limited to the normal administrative budget of the Organisation.[140] The Court observed that the Charter distinguishes between the words in Article 17(1), "[t]he General Assembly shall consider and approve the budget of the Organization" and paragraph 3 of the same Article which provides that the General Assembly "shall examine the administrative budgets of such specialized agencies." The Court concluded that:[141]

> *If it had been intended that paragraph 1 should be limited to the administrative budget of the United Nations Organization itself, the word "administrative" would have been inserted in paragraph 1 as it was in paragraph 3.*

The Court's approach to determining whether the actual expenditures authorised constituted 'expenses of the Organisation' was to test whether such expenditures were incurred to achieve one of the UN purposes. The Court stated that it:[142]

> *[A]grees that such expenditures must be tested by their relationship to the purposes of the United Nations in the sense that if an expenditure were made for a purpose which is not one of the purposes of the United Nations, it would not be considered an 'expenses of the Organization.*

The Court also found that:[143]

> *[W]hen the Organization takes action which warrants the assertion that it was appropriate for the fulfilment of one of the stated purposes of the United Nations, the presumption is that such action is not* ultra vires *the Organization.*

---

[138] The Opinion of the Soviet Union.

[139] ICJ Pled., 1961, p. 273.

[140] ICJ Rep., 1962, p. 159.

[141] Ibid.

[142] Ibid, p. 167.

[143] Ibid, p. 168.

6 The Joint Competence of the Political Organs[144]

The Court had occasion in its advisory opinion in the *Competence of the General Assembly* to rule on the problem of the joint competence of the two political organs. When the Court's opinion in the *Admissions* Case did not lead to a settlement of the problem of admissions to the UN and in order to avoid a veto in the Security Council, members of the General Assembly proposed that the word 'recommendation' in Article 4(2) of the Charter should be interpreted as not necessarily signifying a favourable recommendation by the Security Council and sought the opinion of the Court on this matter. The question posed by the General Assembly was the following:[145]

> *Can the admission of a State to membership in the United Nations, pursuant to Article 4, paragraph 2, of the Charter, be effected by a decision of the General Assembly when the Security Council has made no recommendation for admission by reason of the candidate failing to obtain the requisite majority or of the negative vote of a permanent Member upon a resolution so to recommend?*

The Court examined Article 4(2) of the Charter, which provides that the "admission of any such State to membership in the United Nations will be effected by a decision of the General Assembly upon the recommendation of the Security Council." The Court found that the Charter requires two steps to admit a new member, firstly a "recommendation" by the Security Council and secondly a decision by the General Assembly. It concluded:[146]

> *The Court has no doubt as to the meaning of this text. It requires two things to effect admission: a "recommendation" of the Security Council and a "decision" of the General Assembly. It is in the nature of things that the recommendation should come before the decision. The word "recommendation", and the word "upon" preceding it, imply the idea that the recommendation is the foundation of the decision to admit, and that the latter rests upon the recommendation. Both these acts are indispensable to form the judgment of the Organization to which the previous paragraph of Article 4 refers. The text under consideration means that the General Assembly can only decide to admit upon the recommendation of the Security Council; it determines the respective roles of the two organs whose combined action is required before admission can be effected: in other words, the rec-*

---

[144] The joint functions of the two political organs include: the admission of new Members in accordance with Article 4 of the Charter, the suspension or expulsion from the Organization and the appointment of the Secretary-General. Decisions on these issues are to be taken by the General Assembly upon recommendation of the Security Council.

[145] ICJ Rep., 1950, p. 5.

[146] ICJ Rep., 1950, pp. 7-8.

> *ommendation of the Security Council is the condition precedent to the decision of the Assembly by which the admission is effected.*

In another paragraph the Court highlighted the relationship between the General Assembly and the Security Council and held that:[147]

> *The General Assembly and the Security Council are both principal organs of the United Nations. The Charter does not place the Security Council in a subordinate position. Article 24 confers upon it "primary responsibility for the maintenance of international peace and security", and the Charter grants it for this purpose certain powers of decision. Under Articles 4, 5 and 6, the Security Council cooperates with the General Assembly in matters of admission to membership, of suspension from the exercise of the rights and privileges of membership, and of expulsion from the Organization. It has power, without the concurrence of the General Assembly, to reinstate the Member which was the object of the suspension, in its rights and privileges.*

The Court's Opinion helped to clarify the respective functions of the two political organs and to preserve the integrity and the autonomy of each. Although some UN member States were hoping the Court would grant the General Assembly wider powers *vis-à-vis* the Security Council in order to improve the effectiveness of the Organisation in the Cold War period, the Court adhered to the intentions of the founders as expressed in the Charter. Rosenne has rightly concluded that any other approach in its findings upon the issue of the relationship between the two political organs "would have had the most far-reaching consequences, not excluding the complete disintegration of the Organization."[148]

7 The Contribution of Advisory Opinions to the Development of International Human Rights Law

A number of the Court's advisory opinions have made a profound contribution to the evolution of human rights norms and of the consequent responsibilities of States. This Section deals with the principal advisory opinions which have influenced the International Law of human rights, although the interpretation of human rights standards has also been evidenced in various contentious decisions.[149]

---

[147] ICJ Rep., 1950, pp. 8-9.

[148] Rosenne, Shabtai, "The Contribution of the International Court of Justice to the United Nations", *Indian Journal of International Law*, 1995, p. 73.

[149] See for instance *Corfu Channel* Case, ICJ Rep., 1949, p. 22; *Asylum* Case, ICJ Rep., 1950, p. 284; *Barcelona Traction* Case, ICJ Rep., 1970, p. 32. For the contribution of those opinions and others to human rights law, see Schwebel, Stephen, "Human Rights in the World Court" in: *Justice in International Law: Selected Writings of Stephen M. Schwebel, Judge of the International Court of Justice*, Cambridge University Press, 1994, pp. 159-168.

In *the Reservations to the Genocide Convention* Case, the General Assembly requested the ICJ to give an advisory opinion regarding the circumstances under which States can make reservations to the Convention and whether a State that makes a reservation could be still regarded as being a party to the Convention if some, but not all, of the parties objected to the reservation.[150] The Court noted that the Genocide Convention was adopted for humanitarian and civilising purposes and that the contracting States should have a common interest in the accomplishment of those high purposes which are the *raison d'etre* of the Convention. The Court held that:[151]

> *The origins of the Convention show that it was the intention of the United Nations to condemn and punish genocide as "a crime under international law" involving a denial of the right of existence of entire human group, a denial which shocks conscience of mankind and results in great losses to humanity, and which is contrary to moral law and to the spirit and aims of the United Nations (Resolution 96 (1) of the General Assembly, December 11th, 1946). The first consequence arising from this conception is that the principles underlying the Convention are principles which are recognized by civilized nations as binding on States, even without any conventional obligation. A second consequence is the universal character of both of the condemnation of genocide and of the cooperation required "in order to liberate mankind from such an odious scourge" (Preamble to the Convention).*

The Court, in this Case, introduced the object and purpose of a treaty as the criterion to assess the admissibility of reservations to the Convention and stated that:[152]

> *It is inconceivable that the contracting parties readily contemplated that an objection to a minor reservation should produce such a result. But even less could the contracting parties have intended to sacrifice the very object of the Convention in favour of a vain desire to secure as many participants as possible. The object and purpose of the Convention thus limit both the freedom of making reservations and that of objecting to them. It follows that it is the compatibility of a reservation with the object and purpose of the Convention that must furnish the criterion for the attitude of a State in making the reservation on accession as well as for the appraisal by a State in objecting to the reservation. Such is the rule of conduct which must guide every State in the appraisal which it must take, individually and from its own standpoint, of the admissibility of any reservation.*

[150] ICJ Rep., 1951, p. 16.

[151] ICJ Rep., 1951, p. 23.

[152] ICJ Rep., 1951, p. 24.

Judge Schwebel noted that the Court's finding in this case was important in two ways: first, it limited the use of reservations to international conventions with humanitarian objects; second, it stated that the obligation not to commit genocide was binding on all States as customary law. Therefore, he concluded that "the Court's references to the 'universality' of the obligation and its 'inderogability' were the ingredients for the conceptualization of *jus cogens.*"[153]

In its 1971 advisory opinion on the Legal Consequences for States of the Continued Presence of South Africa in Namibia (South West Africa), notwithstanding Security Council Resolution 276 (1970), the Court set out various fundamental principles of international human rights law,[154] including the right of people to self-determination and decolonisation.

In particular, the Court observed that:[155]

> *Under the Charter of the United Nations, the former Mandatory had pledged itself to observe and respect, in a territory having an international status, human rights and fundamental freedoms for all without distinction as to race. To establish instead, and to enforce, distinctions, exclusions, restrictions and limitations exclusively based on grounds of race, colour, descent or national or ethnic origin which constitute a denial of fundamental human rights is a flagrant violation of the purposes and principles of the Charter.*

---

[153] Schwebel, Stephen M., "The Contribution of the International Court of Justice to the Development of International Law" in: Heere, Wybo p. (ed.), *International Law And The Hague's 750th Anniversary*, The Hague: T.M.C. Asser Press, 1999, p. 411; Zemanek, K., "Some Unresolved Questions Concerning Reservations in the Vienna Convention in the Law of Treaties" in: Makarczyk, J. (ed.), *Essays in International Law in Honour of Judge Manfred Lachs*, The Hague; Boston; Lancaster: Martinus Nijhoff Publishers, 1984, pp. 325-326.

[154] Hereinafter cited as: "the *Namibia* Case." The 1971 Case was referred to the Court by the Security Council after General Assembly Resolution 2145 (XXI), of 27th October 1966 had revoked the mandate of South Africa over Namibia. The General Assembly, "convinced that the administration of the mandated territories by South Africa has been conducted in a manner contrary to the Mandate, the Charter of the U.N and the Universal Declaration of Human Rights", stated that "South Africa has failed to fulfil its obligations in respect of the administration of the Mandated Territory and to insure the moral and material well-being and security of the indigenous inhabitants of South West Africa and has, in fact, disavowed the Mandate." Therefore, the General Assembly concluded, "South Africa has no other right to administer the territory." The Security Council for its part called upon South Africa to withdraw its administration from the territory of Namibia. In other words the Security Council adopted and applied the General Assembly's decisions. All the objections raised concerning the validity of the resolutions were rejected by the Court and, in effect, the Court found that these decisions were constitutionally valid and beyond any challenge. See Section 6.3.3 in Chapter Three, *infra*.

[155] ICJ Rep., 1971, para. 131, p. 57.

The Court found that South Africa's policy of apartheid constituted a flagrant violation of the Charter's purposes and principles. Moreover, as Schwelb has rightly pointed out, the Court did not intend to convey that only Article 1 (3) of the UN Charter had been violated. Rather, it was the court's view that there had been a violation of international human rights norms in general.[156] The Court declared that "the continued presence of South Africa in Namibia being illegal, South Africa is under obligation to withdraw its administration from Namibia immediately and thus put an end to its occupation of the Territory."[157] Moreover, the Court held that member States of the UN are:[158]

> *Under obligation to recognize the illegality and invalidity of South Africa's continued presence in Namibia. They are also under obligation to refrain from lending any support or any form of assistance to South Africa with reference to its occupation of Namibia.*

Lastly, the Court affirmed that the UN Charter had made the principle of self-determination applicable to all non self governing territories,[159] stating that "the subsequent development of international law in regard to non-self-governing territories, as enshrined in the Charter of the United Nations, made the principle of self-determination applicable to all of them.[160] Commenting upon this finding Crawford notes that:[161]

> *[T]he court adopted a mode of co-operation with the political organs, and in particular the General Assembly, that has characterised its work in this field since ... the court has treated the 'subsequent development of international law in regard to non-self governing territories' as in large part resulting from the application of Charter norms by the political organs, and in particular the General Assembly ... it has sought whenever possible to align 'the corpus* iuris gentium' *with the policies and practice of the Assembly.*

---

[156] Schwelb, Egon "The International Court of Justice and The Human Rights Clauses of the Charter", 66 *AJIL*, 1972, p. 348. Schwelb's conclusion was based on the Court's referring to the pledge of Member states which is contained in Article 56 of the Charter.

[157] ICJ Rep., 1971, p. 58.

[158] ICJ Rep., 1971, para. 119, p. 54.

[159] The principle of self determination is enshrined in Articles 1(2), 55, 56 of the UN Charter. The principle has been confirmed and elaborated by a number of General Assembly resolutions, most importantly resolutions 1514(XV) and 2626(XXV). The last of these was endorsed by the Court in the *Namibia* Case.

[160] ICJ Rep., 1971, para. 52, p. 31.

[161] Crawford, James, "The General Assembly, the International Court of Justice and Self-Determination" in: Lowe, Vaughan & Fitzmaurice, Malgosia (eds.), *Fifty Years of the International Court of Justice: Essays in Honour of Sir Robert Jennings*, Cambridge: Grotius Publications, Cambridge University Press, 1996, p. 591.

The issue of self-determination and decolonisation came before the Court again in the1975 *Western Sahara* Case. To help it resolve the conflicting claims, the General Assembly requested an advisory opinion on the following questions:[162]

1. *Was Western Sahara (Rio de Oro and Sakiet El Hamra) at the time of colonization by Spain a territory belonging to no one (terra nullius)? If the answer to the first question is in the negative,*
2. *What were the legal ties between this territory and the Kingdom of Morocco and the Mauritanian entity?*

Spain had unilaterally withdrawn from the Western Sahara territory after holding it as a colony. Morocco and Mauritania subsequently claimed title to Western Sahara while the indigenous peoples asserted their right to self-determination. In answering the questions put to it, the Court supported and analysed the right to self-determination in light of the Charter's provisions and the "subsequent development of international law in regard to non-self governing territories."[163] It has been suggested that the UN Charter, while mentioning the word self-determination, does not clearly establish it as a binding requirement.[164] Moreover, the Charter "neither supplies an answer to the question as to what constitutes a 'people' nor does it lay down the content of the principle."[165] Nevertheless, the Court regarded the principle of decolonisation as an essential part of the question submitted to it,[166] and noted that the General Assembly's Resolution 1514 (XV), which asserted that "all people have the right to self-determination", had provided the basis for decolonisation which had resulted since 1960 in the creation of many of the UN's member States.[167]

The Court asserted that the decolonisation process should be accelerated to respect the right of the population of Western Sahara "to determine their future political status by their own freely expressed will",[168] and that it should be carried

[162] ICJ Rep., 1975, p. 12.

[163] ICJ Rep., 1975, p. 31. Article 1(2) of the Charter, reinforced by Articles 55 and 56, refers to the development of friendly relations among States based on respect for the principles of equal rights and self-determination.

[164] See Tomuschat, Christian, "International Law: Ensuring the Survival of Mankind on the Eve of a New Century", 281 *RCADI*, 1999, p. 242.

[165] Thurer, Daniel, "Self Determination" in: Bernhardt, R. (ed.), *Encyclopedia of Public International Law*, 2000, vol. 4, p. 365. Tomuschat suggests that the word "people" means, in view of the historical context, people under colonial rule. See Tomuschat, *supra* note 164, p. 242.

[166] ICJ Rep., 1975, p. 30.

[167] The General Assembly resolution provides that "[a]ll peoples have the right to self-determination; by virtue of that right they freely determine their political status and freely pursue their economic, social and cultural development". See ICJ Rep., 1975, p. 32. The Court also had occasion to refer to this resolution in the 1971 *Namibia* Case. See ICJ Rep., 1971, p. 31.

[168] ICJ Rep., 1975, p. 36.

out in accordance with the "principle of self-determination through the free and genuine expression of the will of the peoples of the Territory."[169]

In the Court's opinion the ties which had existed between the claimants and the territory during the colonial period in the 1880s could not affect the application of Resolution 1514 (XV) and, in particular, could not affect the principle of self determination.[170] Finally, the Court examined the concept of *terra nullius* and found that territories already inhabited by tribes or peoples cannot be regarded as *terra nullius* and thus open to occupation and ownership by their discoverers.[171] The Court asserted that the population of Western Sahara had in no case ever been under the legitimate sovereignty of other States but were peoples who retained the right to self-determination. The Court's opinion was an important pronouncement on the principle of self-determination and has been held to be "a fair refutation of assertions minimising the relevance of self-determination."[172]

In the 1996 *Legality of the Threat or Use of Nuclear Weapons* Case, the question referred by the General Assembly for the Court's advisory opinion was whether the threat or use of nuclear weapons was in any circumstance permitted under International Law.[173] The General Assembly linked violation of human rights with the use of nuclear weapons by stating that nuclear war is "a violation of the foremost human right – the right to life."[174] More specifically, it was contended by some of the proponents of the illegality of nuclear weapons[175] that their use would violate the right to life guaranteed under Article 6 of the International Covenant on Civil and Political Rights.[176] However, other States argued that the International Covenant did not mention either war or weapons. Therefore, they maintained that the question before the Court related to the unlawful loss of life in armed hostilities, which is governed by the law applicable to armed conflict and not by the Covenant.[177]

---

169 Ibid, p. 68.

170 ICJ Rep., 1975, p. 68.

171 Ibid, para. 80, p. 39.

172 Shaw, Malcolm, "The Western Sahara Case", 49 *BYIL*, 1978, p. 153.

173 International law scholars had been debating the legality of the use of nuclear weapons long before the Court's decision. See Pogany, Istvan (ed.), *Nuclear Weapons and International Law*, Avebury: Gower Publishing, 1987; Dewar, John, *et al.*, (eds.), *Nuclear Weapons, the Peace Movement and the Law*, The Macmillan Press, 1986.

174 GA. Res. 38/75 of 15 December 1983.

175 See for example the Written Statements of Malaysia, Egypt and Indonesia. One of the rights that was enshrined in the Universal Declaration of Human Rights is the right to life. See Article 3 of the Declaration; see also the International Covenant on Civil and Political Rights. Article 6(1) which provides: "[e]very human being has the inherent right to life. This life shall be protected by law." see also Article 2 of the European Convention for the Protection of Human Rights and Fundamental Freedoms of 1950 and Article 4 of the American Convention of Human Rights of 1969 and certain other human rights instruments.

176 Article 6 (1) provides "Every human being has the inherent right to life. This right shall be protected by law. No one shall be arbitrarily deprived of his life."

177 See the written statements of US, Netherlands, UK, France and Russia.

The Court stated, however, that the International Covenant "does not cease in times of war, except by operation of Article 4 of the Covenant whereby certain provisions may be derogated from in a time of national emergency."[178] However, in examining what might constitute an arbitrary deprivation of life under Article 6 of the Covenant, the Court found that arbitrary deprivation must be determined by the applicable *lex specialis,* namely, the law applicable in armed conflict which is designed to regulate the conduct of hostilities.[179] The Court stated:[180]

> *[W]hether a particular loss of life, through the use of a certain weapon in warfare, is to be considered an arbitrary deprivation of life contrary to Article 6 of the Covenant, can only be decided by reference to the law applicable in armed conflict and not deduced from the terms of the Covenant itself.*

As far as genocide is concerned, it was argued before the Court that the prohibition contained in the Convention on the Prevention and Punishment of the Crime of Genocide of 9 December 1948 was a relevant rule of customary international law which the Court must apply. It was also contended before the Court that:[181]

> *[T]he number of deaths occasioned by the use of nuclear weapons would be enormous; that the victims could, in certain cases, include persons of a particular national, ethnic, racial or religious group; and that the intention to destroy such groups could be inferred from the fact that the user of nuclear weapon would have omitted to take account of the well-known effects of the use of such weapons.*

In response, the Court examined the definition of genocide in the Convention and concluded that its prohibition would be applicable only if recourse to nuclear weapons entailed the element of intent and was directed against one of the groups falling under Article II.[182] However, the Court could only arrive at such a conclusion after taking into account the specific circumstances of each case.[183]

---

[178] ICJ Rep., 1996, para. 25, p. 240.

[179] Ibid.

[180] Ibid.

[181] Ibid, para. 26, p. 240.

[182] Genocide has been defined in the Convention as "any of the following acts committed with intent to destroy, in whole or in part, a national, ethnical, racial or religious group, as such:

a) Killing members of group;
b) Causing serious bodily or mental harm to members of the group;
c) Deliberately inflicting on the group conditions of life calculated to bring about its physical destruction in whole or in part;
d) Imposing measures intended to prevent births within the group;
e) Forcibly transferring children of the group to another group."

[183] ICJ Rep., 1996, para. 26, p. 240.

Both the dissenting Judges in the Nuclear Weapons Case and various human rights scholars have criticised the Court's rather restrictive findings and have asserted that killing entire populations by nuclear weapons during armed conflict must definitely constitute the crime of genocide. Therefore, regardless of the circumstances, the use of nuclear weapons cannot be lawful.[184]

In 2004, the Court in the *Wall* Case was once again given the opportunity to rule on questions of human rights law. Here, the General Assembly by Resolution ES-10/14 sought the Court's opinion on the legal consequences arising from the construction by Israel, the Occupying Power, of a wall in the Occupied Palestinian Territories, including in and around East Jerusalem.

The Palestinian authority and other participants in the proceedings contended that the construction was, *inter alia*, an attempt to annex the territory contrary to International Law; and a violation of the legal principle prohibiting the acquisition of territory by the use of force. Moreover, the *de facto* annexation of land interferes with the territorial sovereignty and consequently with the right of the Palestinians to self determination. Israel, however, maintained that the wall's sole purpose was to enable it to effectively combat terrorist attacks launched from the West Bank, and that the barrier was a temporary measure.[185]

The Court, after unanimously establishing its jurisdiction, decided by 14 votes to 1 that Israel's building of the wall contravened International Law; that Israel was obliged to stop construction of the wall which should be dismantled immediately; and that Israel was obliged to make reparations for any damage caused. Finally, the Court stated that the General Assembly and Security Council could take further action to terminate the illegal situation resulting from the wall's construction in light of the Court's advisory opinion.[186]

In particular, The Court found that the act of building the wall violated a number of international humanitarian and human rights law provisions:[187]

> *[T]he construction of the wall and its associated régime impede the liberty of movement of the inhabitants of the Occupied Palestinian Territory (with the exception of Israeli citizens and those assimilated thereto) as guaranteed under Article 12, paragraph 1, of the*

---

[184] See the Diss. Op. of Judges Weeramantry and Korma, pp. 517, 577 respectively. See also Gowlland-Debbas, Vera, "The Right to Life and Genocide : The Court and An International Public Policy" in: Boisson De Chazournes, Laurence & Sands, Philippe (eds.), *International Law, the International Court of Justice and Nuclear Weapons*, Cambridge University Press, 1999, p. 333.

[185] Agora: ICJ Advisory Opinion on Construction of a Wall in the Occupied Palestinian Territory, *AJIL*, January, 2005. See Akram, Susan & Quigley, John, "A Reading of the International Court of Justice Advisory Opinion on the Legality of Israel's Wall in the Occupied Palestinian Territories" , available at: http://www.palestinecenter.org/cpap/pubs/update_on_wall_072004.pdf ,(accessed at 24 October 2004).

[186] See para. 163 of the *Wall* Opinion note 80, *supra*.

[187] See para. 134, ibid.

> *International Covenant on Civil and Political Rights. They also impede the exercise by the persons concerned of the right to work, to health, to education and to an adequate standard of living as proclaimed in the International Covenant on Economic, Social and Cultural Rights and in the United Nations Convention on the Rights of the Child. Lastly, the construction of the wall and its associated régime, by contributing to the demographic changes referred ... contravene Article 49, paragraph 6, of the Fourth Geneva Convention and the Security Council resolutions cited [cited above].*

In response to Israel's argument that the main purpose of constructing the wall was to enhance its security, the Court held that it was not convinced that:[188]

> *[T]he specific course Israel has chosen for the wall was necessary to attain its security objectives. The wall, along the route chosen, and its associated régime gravely infringe a number of rights of Palestinians residing in the territory occupied by Israel, and the infringements resulting from that route cannot be justified by military exigencies or by the requirements of national security or public order. The construction of such a wall accordingly constitutes breaches by Israel of various of its obligations under the applicable international humanitarian law and human rights instruments.*

Regarding the applicability of international human rights provisions to Israel in the Occupied Palestinian Territories, the Court held that the International Covenant on Civil and Political Rights (ICCPR), the International Covenant on Economic, Social and Cultural Rights (ICESCR) and the UN Convention on the Rights of Child, all of which were ratified by Israel were all applicable in the occupied Territory.[189] Although Israel argued that human rights law does not apply in times of armed conflict, the Court ruled that the protection offered by these human rights conventions did not cease in case of armed conflict.[190]

As to the right of Palestinian peoples to self determination, the Court pointed out that "the existence of a "Palestinian people" is no longer in issue."[191] The Court recalled its previous case law which emphasised that current development in "international law in regard to none self governing territories, as enshrined in the Charter of the United Nations, made the principle of self determination applicable to all [such territories]." The Court observed that beside UN Resolutions recognising the Palestinian people as a people, Israel's own agreements with the Palestinians showed that it recognised them as a people. The Court therefore found that Israel was legally obligated to respect the rights of the Palestinian people to self-

---

[188] See para. 137 of the *Wall* Opinion, *supra* note 80.

[189] See paras. 102-104, ibid.

[190] See para. 105, ibid.

[191] See para. 118, ibid.

determination. The Court found that "the construction of the wall and its associated régime create a "*fait accompli*" on the ground that could well become permanent, in which case, and notwithstanding the formal characterization of the wall by Israel, it would be tantamount to *de facto* annexation"[192] which "severely impedes the exercise by the Palestinian people of its right to self-determination, and is therefore a breach of Israel's obligation to respect that right."[193]

As regards Israeli settlements, the Court noted that Article 49(6) of the Fourth Geneva Convention provides that "[t]he Occupying Power shall not deport or transfer parts of its own civilian population into the territory it occupies." The Court noted that this provision "prohibits not only deportations or forced transfers of population such as those carried out during the Second World War, but also any measures taken by an occupying Power in order to organise or encourage transfers of parts of its own population into the occupied territory." The Court observed that since 1977 Israel had conducted a policy and developed practices involving the establishment of settlements in the Occupied Palestinian Territory contrary to the terms of Article 49 (6) of Fourth Geneva Convention. As a result, the Court concluded, "the Israeli settlements in the Occupied Territories (including East Jerusalem) have been established in breach of international law."[194]

Finally, the Court considered whether Israel could rely on a state of necessity which would preclude the wrongfulness of the construction of the wall. The Court stated that Israel could not rely on this excuse for its action because a state of necessity is a ground recognised by customary international law that "can only be invoked under certain strictly defined conditions which must be cumulatively satisfied." The Court noted that one of those conditions is that the act taken must be the only way for the State to protect an essential interest.

In the light of the material before it, the Court was not convinced that the construction of the wall along the route chosen was the only means to safeguard the interests of Israel against the peril which it had invoked as a justification for its actions.

The Court acknowledged that Israel has the right and the duty to respond to the numerous and deadly acts of violence directed against its civilian population in order to protect the life of its citizens, however, the measures taken must conform with International Law. In this regard the Court stated:[195]

> *The fact remains that Israel has to face numerous indiscriminate and deadly acts of violence against its civilian population. It has the right, and indeed the duty, to respond in order to protect the life of its citizens. The measures taken are bound nonetheless to remain in conformity with applicable international law.*

---

[192] See para. 121 of the *Wall* Opinion, *supra* note 80.

[193] See para. 122, ibid.

[194] See para. 120, ibid.

[195] See para. 141.

8 The Contribution of Advisory Opinions to the Development of International Humanitarian Law

In the *Legality of the Threat or Use of Nuclear Weapons* Case, the Court had to determine whether the use of nuclear weapons is illegal in light of international humanitarian law. Some States have contended that the principles and rules of international humanitarian law evolved prior to the invention of nuclear weapons and so were not relevant. Moreover, the Geneva conferences of 1949 and of 1974-1977 did not specifically address the problem of nuclear weapons.[196] The Court nevertheless concluded that the rules of humanitarian law were applicable to the threat or use of nuclear weapons, as the intrinsically humanitarian character of these laws applies to all forms of warfare and weapons.[197] To the credit of the Court, on this point the Court has reaffirmed the celebrated Martens' clause which is considered applicable to the whole of humanitarian law.[198] The Court, despite the outcome of the case, contributed to humanitarian law by asserting two basic principles: first, States must avoid civilian targets and, as a corollary to this, they must avoid using weapons that are incapable of distinguishing between military and civilian targets.[199] Second, States are forbidden to cause unnecessary suffering to combatants and therefore are prohibited from using weapons which would cause them needless suffering. In the words of the Court:[200]

> *The cardinal principles contained in the text constituting the fabric of humanitarian law are the following. The first is aimed at the protection of the civilian population and civilians objects and establishes the distinction between combatants and non-combatants; States must never make civilians the object of attack and must con-*

---

[196] ICJ Rep., 1996, para. 85, p. 259.

[197] ICJ Rep., 1996, para. 86, p. 259. The Court unanimously agreed that the threat or use of nuclear weapons is governed by "the international law applicable in armed conflict, particularly those of the principles and rules of international humanitarian law, as well as with specific obligations under treaties and other undertakings which expressly deal with nuclear weapons." See para. 105(2) D, p. 266.

[198] Dieter, Fleck, (ed.) *The Handbook of Humanitarian Law in Armed Conflicts*, Oxford University Press, 1995, p. 29. The Marten Clause provides: "Until a more complete code of the Laws of war has been issued, the High Contracting Parties deem it expedient to declare that, *in cases not included in the Regulations adopted by them*, the inhabitants and the belligerents remain under the protection and the rule of the principles of the law of nations, as they result from the usages established among civilized peoples, from the laws of humanity, and the dictates of the public conscience." The Marten clause was originally devised to cope with a disagreement between the parties to The Hague Peace Conference regarding the States resistance movement in occupied territory. See Fleck, ibid, p. 29.

[199] ICJ Rep., 1996, para. 92, p. 262.

[200] ICJ Rep., 1996, para. 78, p. 257.

> *sequently never use weapons that are incapable of distinguishing between civilian and military targets. According to the second principle, it is prohibited to cause unnecessary suffering to combatants: it is accordingly prohibited to use weapons causing them such harm or uselessly aggravating their suffering. In application of that second principle, States do not have unlimited freedom of choice of means in the weapons they use.*

While sections of the international community hoped that the Court would elaborate the concept of *jus cogens*,[201] the Court confined itself to stating:[202]

> *It has been maintained in these proceedings that these principles and rules of humanitarian law are part of* jus cogens *as defined in Article 53 of the Vienna Convention on the Law of Treaties of 23 May 1969. The question whether a norm is part of the* jus cogens *relates to the legal character of the norm. The request addressed to Court by the General Assembly raises the question of the applicability of the principles and rules of humanitarian law in cases of recourse to nuclear weapons and the consequences of that applicability for the legality of recourse to these weapons. But it does not raise the question of the character of the humanitarian law which would apply to the use of nuclear weapons. There is, therefore, no need for the Court to pronounce on this matter.*

This opinion is the first decision by any international tribunal that has clearly formulated limitations on nuclear weapons and declared that nuclear weapons are subject to the requirements of the UN Charter and of the International Law applicable in armed conflicts. The Court unanimously held that:[203]

---

201 Werksman, Jacob & Khalastchi, Ruth, "Nuclear Weapons and *Jus Cogens*: Peremptory Norms and Justice Pre-Empted", in: Boisson De Chazournes, Laurance & Sands, Philippe (eds.), *International Law, the International Court of Justice and Nuclear Weapons*, Cambridge University Press, 1999, p. 183. The authors argued that although the Court had failed to address the *jus cogens* status of international humanitarian law, by stating that "these fundamental rules are to be observed by all states ...... because they constitute intransgressible principles of international customary law" the Court had arrived at a similar conclusion. See ibid ; Debbas, *supra* note 184, p. 316.

202 ICJ Rep., 1996, para. 83, p. 258. It is worth mentioning that Judge Bedjaoui, President of the Court at the time of this Opinion, emphasised in his Declaration that he did not doubt that most of the principles of humanitarian law, specifically principles prohibiting the use of weapons with indiscriminate effect and proscribing the use of arms causing unnecessary suffering, constitute part of *jus cogens.* However, Bedjaoui maintained that the Court did not refer to the nature of these rules as the question addressed to the Court failed to cover this point. Declaration of Judge Bedjaoui, ICJ Rep., 1996, p. 273.

203 ICJ Rep., 1996, para. 105.2 (D), p. 266.

> *A threat or use of nuclear weapons should also be compatible with the requirements of the international law applicable in armed conflict, particularly those of the principles and rules of international and humanitarian law, as well as with specific obligations under treaties and other undertakings which expressly deal with the nuclear weapons.*

However, some observers believe that the rules and findings that led the Court to the above conclusion should, as a result, also have led it to conclude that any use of nuclear weapons is unlawful under International Law, in particular under the law applicable to armed conflicts. Unfortunately, contrary to its own findings, the final opinion of the Court was that:[204]

> *[I]n view of the current state of international law, and of the elements of fact at its disposal, the Court cannot conclude definitively whether the threat or use of nuclear weapons would be lawful or unlawful in an extreme circumstance of self-defence, in which the very survival of a State would be at stake.*

Shaw argues that the Court's weak conclusion should be seen "in the context of continuing efforts to ban all nuclear weapons testing, the increasing number of treaties prohibiting such weapons in specific geographical areas and the commitment given in 1995 by the five declared nuclear weapons states not to use such weapons against non-nuclear weapons states that are parties to the Nuclear Non-Proliferation Treaty."[205] One could also argue that the Court was simply reluctant to make new law in an area affecting the vital interests of certain States and that it sought to be politically pragmatic in its Opinion.

9 The Contribution of Advisory Opinions to the Development of International Environmental Law

The Court in the *Legality of the Threat or Use of Nuclear Weapons* Case addressed directly the issue of the environment and the right of future generations to health and to an adequate quality of life. It was argued before the Court that any use of nuclear weapons would be unlawful because of the constraints imposed by existing norms relating to the protection of the environment.[206] While the Court

---

[204] ICJ Rep., 1996, para. 105.2 (E), p. 266.

[205] Shaw, *supra* note 57, p 1067. See also SC Res. 984 (1995); Greenwood, Christopher, "The Law of War (International Humanitarian Law)" in: Evans, Malcolm D., *International Law*, Oxford University Press, 2003, p. 808.

[206] Reference was made to several existing treaties: Additional Protocol I of 1977, Geneva Conventions of 1949, Article 35(3) which prohibits the adoption of "methods or means of warfare which are intended, or may be expected, to cause widespread, long-term and severe damage to the natural environment" and Article 1 of the Convention of 18 May

rejected this argument, it nevertheless recognised that the "environment is under daily threat and that the use of nuclear weapons could constitute a catastrophe for the environment."[207] The Court emphasised also that the environment represents "the living space, the quality of life and the very health of human beings, including generations unborn."[208] Moreover, according to the Court, States are under a duty to protect the environment because:[209]

> *The existence of the general obligations of States to ensure that activities within their jurisdiction and control respect the environment of other States or of areas beyond national control is now part of the corpus of international law relating to the environment.*

The Court's approach reinforces Article 192 of the Law of the Sea Convention of 1982, which provides that "States have the obligation to protect and preserve the marine environment." Moreover, Article194 of the same convention provides that "States shall take all measures necessary to ensure that activities under their jurisdiction and control are so conducted as not to cause damage by pollution to other states and their environment."

The Court concluded that both provisions, taken together in Article 35 paragraph 3 and 55 of the Additional Protocol I of 1977 to the Geneva Convention of 1949, "embody a general obligation to protect the natural environment against widespread, long-term and severe environmental damage; the prohibition of methods and means of warfare which are intended, or may be expected, to cause such damage; and the prohibition of attacks against the natural environment by way of reprisals."[210]

Some scholars see this Opinion, despite its shortcomings, as an important step towards articulating general environmental obligations in international law.[211] For example, Philippe Sands argues that the Court's advisory opinion recognised for the first time the existence of norms of international environmental law as customary rules which are equally applicable in times of armed conflict.[212] He also maintains that the Court for the first time recognised a rule similar to that expressed in

---

of 1977 on the Prohibition of Military or Any Other Hostile Use of Environmental Modification Techniques, which prohibits the use of weapons which have "widespread, long-lasting or severe effects" on the environment. See ICJ Rep., 1996, para. 27, p. 241.

[207] Ibid, para. 29, p. 241.

[208] Ibid.

[209] Ibid, para. 29, p. 242.

[210] ICJ Rep., 1996, para. 31, p. 242.

[211] Weiss, Edith B., "Opening the Door to the Environment and to Future Generations" in: Boisson De Chazournes, Laurence & Sands, Philippe (eds.), *International Law, the International Court of Justice and Nuclear Weapons*, Cambridge University Press, 1999, p. 343.

[212] Sands, Philippe, *Principles of International Environmental Law*, Cambridge: Cambridge University Press, 2nd edition, 2003, p. 316.

Principle 21 of the UN Stockholm Declaration on the Human Environment of 1972, to the effect that States have a duty "to ensure that activities within their jurisdiction or control do not cause damage to the environment of other States or of areas beyond the limits of national jurisdiction."[213]

10 Concluding Remarks

This Chapter has argued that the true measure of the impact of the advisory function upon international legal norms cannot be determined solely by the number of opinions given by the Court but by the quality and persuasiveness of the Court's statements of law and of its reflections on the development of international law in a wide variety of areas. However, despite the significant contribution of advisory opinions to the development of International Law in various spheres, one can discern some reluctance on the part of many of *the* UN's member States to invoke the Court's advisory procedure. The reasons for this reluctance will be explored in the following Chapter.

[213] Ibid, p. 338.

CHAPTER SEVEN

The Attitude of United Nations Member States Towards the Use of the Advisory Procedure[1]

1 Introduction

While adjudication plays a significant role in most national systems, the situation is quite different in International Law. Adjudication is only one of many possible ways of dealing with international disputes.[2] Since its inception in 1945, the ICJ has handed down a total of 79 Judgements,[3] and 25 advisory opinions while the PCIJ rendered twenty nine judgements and twenty seven advisory opinions in only eighteen years of existence.[4]

As one commentator argues:[5]

---

[1] Attitude has been defined as "a mental state of readiness, organised through experience to behave in a characteristic way towards the object of the attitude." See Rollinson, Derek , *et al.*, *Organizational Behaviour and Analysis*, Addison Wesley Longman Limited, 1998, p. 740. Also attitude has been defined as a set of interrelated beliefs that are relatively enduring and produce behavioral consequences. See Davide Rhode and Harold Spaeth, *Supreme Court Decision Making*, San Francisco, W.H. Freeman and Company, 1976, p. 75.

[2] See Article 33 of the UN Charter.

[3] These cases concern *inter alia* land frontiers and maritime boundaries, territorial sovereignty, the non-use of force, non-interference in the internal affairs of States, diplomatic relations, hostage-taking, the right of asylum, nationality, guardianship, rights of passage and economic rights. Available at: http://www.icj-cij.org/icjwww/igeneralinformation/ icjgnnot.html (accessed 14 December 2004).

[4] It has been made clear in Chapter One that during the League era, requesting an opinion was confined to the Assembly and the Council, and was, usually initiated by a unanimously adopted resolution. In contrast to this, requesting an opinion in the UN era has been broadened: more organs and specialized agencies are now authorized to request advisory opinion of the Court, at the same time requests are initiated by a majority-adopted resolution.

[5] Rosenne, Shabtai, *The Law and Procedure of the International Court, 1920-1996*, The Hague; London: Martinus Nijhoff Publishers, vol. 1, 1997, p. 178, (emphasis added).

> *[T]he ability of the Court to perform its functions depends not so much on the institutional ties linking it with this or that organization or organ, or with this or that conception of the nature of its judicial task, as on the readiness of the States to make use of the Court. There is, in this respect, no real difference between a direct approach to the Court by States invoking the contentious jurisdiction, and an indirect approach by States invoking the advisory competence.* The decision whether and to what extent the Court shall be used always rests in the States, individually or collectively. That is not say, however, that how the Court views its tasks, and how States in organs of an international organization view its tasks, and how States in organs of the international organization view the possibility of organic co-operation, are not important, for all these factors will influence the policy decision. "

The attitude of States towards the advisory procedure cannot be assessed in isolation from their general attitude towards adjudication and the Court. The real test of States' attitude towards the Court and towards the judicial settlement of disputes as Rosenne wrote, is "to be found in their willingness in general to allow the law to occupy a prominent and constructive part in their international relations."[6]

The task of this Chapter is to discuss what States think and expect of the ICJ, and to identify several factors which may serve to influence States' decision as whether to use the Court. The Chapter also goes on to argue that despite the existence of several means for the resolution of legal disputes, and despite a few unfortunate decisions of the ICJ, judicial settlement should not be exceptional, particularly in a Court like the ICJ which has a significant body of jurisprudence.

2 Quantitative Significance

A survey of the requests made to the ICJ up to now reveals that of the twenty five advisory opinions rendered, fifteen were sought by the General Assembly and one by the Security Council in accordance with Article 96(1) of the Charter, which empowers those organs to request an opinion on "any legal question." Two opinions were requested by ECOSOC, and four by specialised agencies as follows: one by UNESCO, one by IMCO, and two by WHO. Moreover, the Court was asked for an advisory opinion by the Committee on Applications for Review of Administrative Tribunal Judgements.[7]

In the first decade of the Court's existence there were ten advisory opinions, nine of which were initiated by the General Assembly and one by UNESCO. During 1957-67, there was an obvious decline in requesting advisory opinions, as only

---

6 Rosenne, *supra* note 5, p. 180.

7 See Section 4.4 in Chapter Five, *supra*.

two were sought. Between 1967 and 1977, the low demand for advisory opinions persisted as only three advisory opinions were requested. During the following decade, 1977-87, a slight increase was achieved as five requests for advisory opinions were submitted to the Court. Since 1987 to the present, only five advisory opinions have been requested. During the years 1962, 1963-66, and 1968-69, the Court did not decide any new cases, neither contentious judgements nor advisory opinions.[8]

The above figures at least indicate that there has been an infrequent use of the advisory function. The reasons for this are many and complex, but largely have to do with the general attitude of States towards the Court. This largely negative attitude has its origins in the early years of the establishment of the ICJ as discussed in the following Section.

3 Historical Background, Preparatory Work and Attitudes

Key States have not been instrumental in promoting the role of the ICJ, most specifically the US which did not participate in the League of Nations due to concerns relating to the PCIJ as explained below. The US Government and the League of Nations in Geneva, during 1926 and 1929 were at an impasse over the American demand for a veto on the advisory jurisdiction of the PCIJ.[9] This demand stemmed mainly from two concerns: first, the US government feared that the advisory jurisdiction might develop into a form of compulsory jurisdiction, and second, the advisory opinion might be used to legitimise League policies, and thereby commit the US Government, as a potential member of the League, to such policies.[10]

While drafting Article 14 of the League Covenant, intensive discussions took place among the representatives of the US, Great Britain, and France which revealed basic divergences. President Wilson was in favour of resorting to "political adjustment" rather than "strict legal justice" as a method for resolving international disputes. At the same time, Cecil, Miller, and Hurst were for judicial resolution. Meanwhile Burgeois, the French Representative, was less committed to the idea of a new court of justice and preferred to rely on arbitration by enlarging the role of the Permanent Court of Arbitration.[11] The draft Covenant, of 14th February 1920, reflected these conflicting priorities.[12]

At San Francisco in 1945/46, the allied powers were cautious about the future role of the proposed new Court, the ICJ, evidenced by some lack of enthusiasm for

---

8 See Table I appended to Chapter Nine, *infra*; Gross, Leo, "Underutilization of the International Court of Justice", 27 *HILJ*, 1986, p. 573.

9 Dunne, Michael, *The United States and the World Court, 1920-1935*, London: Pinter, 1988, p. 4.

10 Ibid, p. 9.

11 Ibid, pp. 21-22.

12 Ibid. See discussion regarding drafting of the Covenant in Chapter One, *supra*.

proposals to authorise the Court to render advisory opinions.[13] However, in a major policy development, the US delegation at San Francisco initially accepted the principles of advisory and compulsory jurisdiction although with some limitations.[14] The reservations eventually made by certain States when accepting the Court's compulsory jurisdiction, most notably the US' Connally declaration of 14th August 1946,[15] and subsequent reservations of other States, evidenced a damaging lack of confidence in the Court.[16] Subsequently, in 1986, the US decided to terminate its acceptance of the Court's compulsory jurisdiction.[17]

One wonders whether the same conflicting priorities which emerged while drafting the Covenant and the Charter, which reflected a lack of confidence in international adjudication, have persisted to the present day. They clearly surfaced again at the very first, unpleasant, encounter of those States before the Court. Hence, France, since the *Nuclear Tests Case,* has essentially boycotted the Court.[18] Moreover, the US after the *Nicaragua* Case has shown some ambivalence towards the Court,[19] while the attitude of the Soviet Union (now Russia) was, almost one of mistrust of both International Law and the Court.[20] The Soviets considered po-

---

13 Mosler, Hermann & Rudolf Bernhardt, *Judicial Settlement of International Disputes, International Court of Justice, Other Courts and Tribunals, Arbitration and Conciliation: An International Symposium*, Berlin; Heidelberg; New York: Springer-Verlag, 1974, p. 197.

14 About the history of the US's participation in the compulsory jurisdiction system see Franck, Thomas, *Judging the World Court*, New York: Priority Press Publications, 1986.

15 The Connally Reservation excludes matters that fall within the domestic jurisdiction of the US from the Court's jurisdiction. However, this Reservation apparently permits the U S to determine for itself whether the dispute is a domestic one or not. See Franck, ibid, p. 22.

16 Gross, Leo, "The International Court of Justice: Consideration of Requirements for Enhancing its Role in the International Legal Order" in: Gross, Leo (ed.), *The Future of The International Court of Justice*, Dobbs Ferry, New York: Oceana Publications, vol. 1, 1976, p. 38.

17 The US terminated acceptance of the ICJ compulsory jurisdiction by its letter to the UN Secretary General in October, 7th, 1985. See U.S. Department of State, Bulletin, 86, 1986, p. 67.

18 Nuclear Tests Judgment, ICJ Rep., 1974, p. 253. Since then France seems to prefer arbitration. *The Continental Shelf* Case between France and the U.K, 1977; *La Bretugre* Case with Canada in 1989; The *Rainbow* Case in 1990 involving New Zealand and France have all been referred to *ad hoc* arbitration. See Bowett, Derek W., "The Court's Role in Relation to International Organizations", in: Lowe, Vaughan & Fitzmaurice, Malgosia, (eds.), *Fifty Years of the International Court of Justice: Essays in Honour of Sir Robert Jennings*, Cambridge: Grotius Publications, 1996, p. 182.

19 Military and Paramilitary Activities in and Against Nicaragua (Merits), ICJ Rep., 1986, p. 14. The U.S has withdrawn from the Proceedings Initiated by Nicaragua. See U.S Department of State, Bulletin, 85, March 1985, p. 46. However, the U.S still continues to appear before the Court on an *ad hoc* basis Like The *Aerial Incident* Case and the *Lockerbie* Case.

20 The Soviet Union (now Russia) has never seized the Court.

litical negotiations as the paramount and most appropriate method of settling international disputes peacefully, and relegated other peaceful methods to a secondary place.[21]

It is argued that any improvement in States' attitudes towards the judicial function should necessarily require a different approach on the part of the key States, and, most importantly, the US.[22] To borrow the words of Richard Bilder:[23]

> *If many states-particularly important ones-are willing to submit their disputes to impartial settlement and show respect for the International Court, this will be taken by the public as meaning that international law is in itself relevant and worthy of respect, and the public will believe in and support international law. If, on the other hand, important states show indifference or contempt for international adjudication and the Court, the public is likely to conclude that international law is meaningless-a joke-and withdraw its belief and support.*

4 The Role of Law and International Adjudication in International Affairs

Law is a social institution, that is an integrated process of shaping behavior and ideas which helps to restore, maintain and create social order.[24] De Visscher argued that a necessary condition for the success of law is peace.[25] However, as one commentator said, peace under law is an ideal.[26] Ferencz also maintained that there can be "no peace without justice."[27] Ferencz recalls that the first article of the UN Charter recognises that international security is linked to justice and law.[28] It is interesting to recall the remarks of Sir Gerald Fitzmaurice on this issue:[29]

---

21 Rosenne, Shabtai "On the Non-Use of the Advisory Competence of the International Court of Justice", 39 *BYIL*, 1963, p. 27.

22 Gross, Leo, *supra* note 16, p. 38.

23 Bilder, Richard B., "International Dispute Settlement and the Role of International Adjudication", in: Damrosch, Lori F. (ed.) *The International Court of Justice at A Crossroads*, Dobbs Ferry, New York: Transnational Publishers, Inc., 1987, p. 179.

24 Berman, Harold J. and Greiner, William R., *The Nature and Functions of Law*, Brooklyn: Foundation Press, 1966, p. 26.

25 De Visscher, Charles, "Reflections on the Present Prospects of International Adjudication", 50 *AJIL*, 1956, p. 474.

26 Joseph, Daly, "Is the International Court of Justice Worth the Effort", 20 *Akron Law Review*, 1987, p. 403.

27 Ferencz, Benjamin B., *Enforcing International Law: a Way to World Peace: A Documentary History and Analysis*, Oceana Publications, vol. 2, 1983, p. 489.

28 See Article 1 of the Charter.

29 Cited in: Jennings, Sir Robert Y., "The Role of the International Court of Justice", 68 *BYIL*, 1997, p. 40.

> *[J]ustice is very seldom achieved by directly aiming at it: rather it is a by-product of the application of legal rules and principles, a consequence of the general order, certainty and stability introduced into human and international relationships through the regular and systemic application of known legal rules and principles, even if these rules and principles are not always perfect and do not always achieve ideal results in every case.*

However, the function of maintaining peace and security and establishing social order in any society is not exclusive to law. International adjudication is only one among many possible methods of dispute settlement recognised by International Law, which also include negotiation, enquiry, mediation, conciliation, arbitration, and resort to regional agencies or arrangements, or to the UN itself. Weisberg notes that "States are more likely to prefer a process of negotiation, or the tactic of allowing the issues to linger in the hope that they may fade or that time may otherwise work to their advantage, than a system of adjudication. Such alternatives are chosen although the judicial method, more than any other procedure for resolving conflict, minimizes the inequality of the parties."[30] Nevertheless, judicial process may play an important part as one means of dispute settlement.

There are some intrinsic qualities pertaining to legal process:[31] First, the strength of the judicial process lies in the authoritativeness and impartiality of the Court's decisions. Second, the findings of a Court could represent judicial precedent, whereby a judicial decision on certain issues or rights will extend beyond the case in hand. Although there is no strict system of precedents in International Law, Shaw argues that the legal principles expounded by the ICJ may constitute "stepping stones to the development of further norms or the application of existing norms in other areas."[32] He also points out that the elucidation of legal principles by the Court in one case may prove useful in bilateral or multilateral negotiations in other situations.[33] Lastly, judicial settlement makes all parties to a dispute equal. Thus as Oduntan observes, "a Superpower state expects and gets no special concessions in relation to a weaker state before the international tribunal."[34]

---

30 Weisberg, Guenter, "The Role of the International Court of Justice in the United Nations System: the First Quarter Century" in: Gross, Leo (ed.), *The Future of the International Court of Justice*, Dobbs Ferry, New York: Oceana Publications, 1976, p. 185.

31 For advantages of international adjudication, see Bilder, Richard, *supra* note 23, pp. 163-166.

32 Shaw, Malcolm N., "The International Court of Justice: A Practical Perspective", 46 *ICLQ*, 1997, p. 833.

33 Ibid.

34 Oduntan, Gbenga, *The Law and Practice of the International Court of Justice (1945-1996): A Critique of the Contentious and Advisory Jurisdiction*, Enugu: Fourth Dimension, 1999, p. 215.

5 Assessment of Frequently Cited Reasons for the Reluctance to Use the Court

Despite the clear advantages of using legal processes to settle inter States differences, any decision to use the Court is largely dependent on States' willingness to allow law to play a constructive role in their international relations.[35] Scholars have identified several factors which may account for the reluctance of States to use the Court: the nature of the law which the Court applies, the risk of losing and the unpredictability of the decision outcome, fears of the Court's impartiality, lastly, the slowness of the procedure and the cost of litigation.

5.1 International Law Applied by the Court Is of Western Origins

Some commentators claim that States' perceptions of the law which the Court applies under Article 38 of its Statute is likely to have some influence on States' attitude towards judicial settlement.[36] Anand claims that this law does not always "correspond to the legitimate aspirations of many States, particularly those which had not participated in the formulation of the general or customary principles of international law.[37] Third World States sometimes contend that they are not bound by customary norms to which they did not consent and argue instead that UN resolutions are a new means for creating international legal norms.[38]

Richard Falk in his book "Reviving the World Court" also claims that the Court's Western judicial style and its narrow perspective have isolated it from the majority of other States. He asserts that:[39]

---

[35] Rosenne, *supra* note 5, p. 180; Couvreur, Philippe, "The Effectiveness of the International Court of Justice in the Peaceful Settlement of International Disputes", in: Muller, A.S & Raic, D. *et al.* (eds.) *The International Court of Justice: Its Future Role After Fifty Years*, The Hague; Boston; London: Martinus Nijhoff Publishers, 1997, p. 115; Bowett, Derek W., "Contemporary Developments in Legal Techniques in the Settlement of Disputes", 180 *RCADI*, 1983, p. 177.

[36] Merrills, John G., *International Dispute Settlement*, Cambridge: Cambridge University Press, 3rd edition, 1998, p. 148.

[37] The statement of Wolde Giorgis (Ethiopia), UN Doc. A/C.6/SR. 1277, 12 November 1971, p. 5, Cited in Anand, R.P, "Role of International Adjudication" in: Gross, Leo (ed.), *The Future of The International Court of Justice*, Dobbs Ferry, New York: Oceana Publications, vol. 1, 1976, p. 10.

[38] See Kelly, Patrick, "The Changing Process of International Law and the Role of the World Court", 11 *Michigan J. Int'l Law*, 1989, p. 152. For discussion about the General Assembly resolutions as source of international law, See Chapter Five, *supra.*

[39] Falk, Richard, *Reviving the World Court*, Charlottesville: University Press of Virginia, 1986, p. 180.

> *Western cultural hegemony in relation to the World Court has meant that this leading international judicial body operates overwhelmingly in relation to a seat of symbols and procedures associated with legal positivism (blended by some judges and on some occasions with a dose of natural law). This cultural hegemony is also evident in the general failure of Third World and non-Western members of the Court or other public officials to question the use of The Hague as the site for the World Court or to challenge, even symbolically, the retention of English and French as the Court's exclusive working languages.*

Falk concluded that the Court will not be revived until its judges "come to embody a spirit of cultural autonomy and pluralism that reflects the principal attitudes in the world system on the leading normative issues of the day, including a range of views about the lawmaking processes at work in international life"[40] In contrast Kieth Highet considerd 'cultural predisposition' as an important factor however, in his view, the appropriate legal response to the issue before the Court, is of most importance. For Highet, "this response will be formulated in accordance with policy needs, which may well be more acutely appreciated by judges who are sympathetic to the progressive development of international law."[41] It could be argued that regardless of the kind of law the Court applies, the reasoning behind the decision is of most important. As Sir Robert Jennings has argued, the reasoning as well as the reasons behind the Court's decision must be such as to bear and survive examination.[42]

The *Western Sahara* advisory opinion clearly underlines the cultural factor behind some of the arguments submitted by the participating States. In this case, after objections by Morocco and Mauritania to Spain's plan to hold a referendum in Western Sahara on decolonising the territory in which Spain had been the colonial power since 1884, General Assembly Resolution 3292 (XXIX) of 1974 requested the opinion of the Court on two questions:[43]

> *I Was Western Sahara (Rio de Oro and Sakiet el Hamra) at the time of colonization by Spain a territory belonging to no one (*terra nullius*)?*

If the answer to the first question is in the negative,

> *II What were the legal ties between this territory and the Kingdom of Morocco and the Mauritanian entity?*

40 Falk, Richard, ibid, p. 181.

41 Highet, Keith, "Reflections on Jurisprudence for the "Third World": The World Court, the "Big Case", and the Future", 27 *VJIL*, 1986-87, pp. 303-304.

42 Jennings, *supra* note 29, p. 44.

43 ICJ Rep., 1975, p. 14.

Both Morocco and Mauritania based their objection to the referendum on the alleged status of the territory at the time of its colonisation.[44] Hence Morocco claimed that the territory had been part of the Sherifan State,[45] while Mauritania claimed that it had been part of the "Mauritanian entity" or Bilad Shinguitti.[46]

Karen Knop points out that the basic legal concepts in the questions referred to the Court- *terra nullius*, legal ties and the notion of a legal entity- were concerned with the "degree of recognition to be given to patterns of identity [which] were based on European norms of political and social organization and on the relationship of European to non-European [societies]."[47] Karen observed that although the referred questions concerned non-European communities and the relationship that existed between them prior to European colonisation, the applicable international law was a colonial one, which worked against the recognition of non-Europeans and was insensitive to their claims.[48]

Addressing the concept of *terra nullius*, Mr. Bayona-Ba-Meya, representing Zaire, in his oral statement before the Court stated:[49]

> *It is clear that an aware Africa can no longer rally to the concept of* terra nullius *as elaborated by Western jurists ... Thus, the International Court of Justice must not contemplate and interpret the notion of* terra nullius *according to a Western conception and a Western authenticity, rather it must approach and adapt it so as to take account of African reality.*

---

44 In the proceedings before the Court, and in accordance with General Assembly Resolution 3292 (XXIX), paragraph 2: Spain (the territory's administering power) submitted a total of 8 volumes of "Information and Documents"; Morocco (as an interested party) submitted a large number of documents in support of "its written statement" and Mauritania (as an interested party) appended documentary annexes to its written statement. The United Nations Secretary-General transmitted a dossier of documents likely to throw light upon the question, Pursuant to Article 65 paragraph 2 of the Statute, and Article 88 of the Rules of the Court. Algeria and Zaire give their opinions. See ICJ Rep., 1975, p. 15.

45 Consequently there were religious links and political allegiance which was renewed by the Saharan caids (sheikhs) to every accessioned Sultan, who appointed them as evidenced by documents and imposed Koranic taxes. See Shaw, Malcolm, "The *Western Sahara* Case", 49 *BYIL*, 1978, p. 135.

46 ICJ Rep., 1975, pp. 65-67. Mauritania did not exist as a State during the critical period under consideration. In its claims Mauritania laid stress on the 'Mauritanian entity', or Bilad Shinguitti as a distinct entity inhabiting a certain area and possessing its own language, social structure and way of life. Therefore the question for it centered upon the unification of its people. See Shaw, ibid, p. 136.

47 Knop, Karen, *Diversity and Self-Determination in International Law*, Cambridge: Cambridge University Press, 2002, p. 117.

48 Ibid.

49 Oral Statement of Mr. Bayona-Ba-Meya (14 July 1975), Western Sahara, ICJ Pled., vol. IV, p. 439 at pp. 440- 445. Translated by Karen Knop, *supra* note 47, p. 120.

On the other hand Algeria argued that the *terra nullius* question should be addressed outside the nineteenth-century international law framework in order to avoid the Europocentric international law which regarded territories not belonging to "civilized" States as *terra nullius.*[50] Algeria demanded that the Court should acknowledge the existence of Arab-Islamic civilisation at the time in the region, with its own developed public law, hence Western Sahara was an integral part of Dar al-Islam (the Muslim civitas).[51] Spain for its part argued that the status of the territory at the time of colonisation and the *terra nullius* question must be determined in accordance with the application of international rule as the only legal framework governing relationships between independent States.[52]

On the question of legal ties, Spain argued against any cultural particularisation of international law, insisting that International Law is the general framework and common legal language without which States would be unable to reach true agreement.[53] Morocco, on the other hand, argued that the nineteenth-century structure could only be understood within the Islamic State model, and that the interpretation of the rules should be particularised in order to take account of the special structure of the Sherifan State.[54]

Castellino and Allen suggest that, in the absence of evidence that could be satisfactorily termed "documentary", when other arguments presented have their source in religion, tradition or culture and when the historical nature is bitterly contested by the parties and equally compelling, the Court is often "left badly exposed in terms of verifying the details of non-documentary evidence *per se.*"[55] The Court however emphasised that:[56]

> *The reference in those questions to a historical period cannot be understood to fetter or hamper the Court in the discharge of its judicial functions. That would not be consistent with the Court's judicial character; for in the exercise of its functions it is necessarily called upon to take into account existing rules of international law which are directly connected with the terms of the request and indispensable for the proper interpretation and understanding of its opinion.*

---

50 Oral Statement of Mohammed Bedjaoui, representing Algeria, (14 July 1975), Western Sahara, ICJ Pled., vol. IV, pp. 455-456. Translated from French by Karen Knop, *supra* note 47.

51 ICJ Rep., 1975, pp. 41-43; Shaw, *supra* note 45, p. 150.

52 Shaw, ibid, pp. 149-50.

53 Oral Statement of Fernando Arias-Salgado, representing Spain, (18 July 1975), Western Sahara, ICJ Pled., vol. V, p. 51 at p. 58. Translated by Karen Knop, p. 133.

54 ICJ Rep., 1975, p. 43.

55 Castellino, Joshua and Allen, Steve, *Title to Territory in International Law: A Temporal Analysis*, Ashgate, 2003, pp. 152-153.

56 ICJ Rep., 1975, para. 52, p. 30.

Although the Court applied International Law and not Islamic law to the question of legal ties, it still contextualized its analysis by taking into account the social and political structure of the Western Saharan population.[57] The Court concluded that: "the State practice of the relevant period indicates that the territory inhabited by tribes or peoples having social and political organization were not regarded as *terra nullius*."[58] This conclusion was not consonant with the nineteenth-century view that was common among jurists which denied any form of international legal personality for territorial entities that did not constitute States as recognised in Europe.[59]

Lastly, it is interesting to note Merrills' suggestion that "if judicial decisions are to be an "acceptable means of resolving disputes, the Court must recognise the diversity of its audience and frame its judgments in language which the bulk of the members of the international community can support and understand."[60]

5.2 The Court's Unpopular Judgments and Advisory Opinions

Any use of the judicial procedure depends upon States' expectations which are in turn usually influenced by the Court's previous decisions. Therefore, widespread acceptability of the Court's previous judgements may encourage more frequent resort to the Court, while the opposite is also right. Two cases discussed below have often been cited as discouraging resort to the Court.

5.2.1 The 1966 *South West Africa, Second Phase* Case[61]

In this case the two applicants, Ethiopia and Liberia, acting in the capacity of States which had been members of the League of Nations, put forward various allegations charging South Africa with violations of its obligations towards the inhabitants of the territory of South West Africa under the League of Nations mandate for South West Africa. The Applicants contended that South Africa was practising apartheid in the mandated territory, that it had failed to transmit petitions from the inhabitants of the territory to the UN and that it had attempted to modify the terms of the Mandate without the consent of the UN. The Court dismissed the applicants' request holding that "the Applicants cannot be considered to have established any legal right or interest appertaining to them in the subject-matter of the present claims, and that, accordingly, the Court must decline to give effect to them."[62]

---

57 Ibid, p. 42. See also Merrills, *supra* note 36, p. 149.

58 ICJ Rep., 1975, para. 80, p. 39.

59 Shaw, *supra* note 45, p. 133.

60 Merills, *supra* note 36, p. 149.

61 *South West Africa* Cases *(Ethiopia v. South Africa; Liberia v. South Africa) Second Phase* Case, ICJ Rep., 1966, p. 6.

62 ICJ Rep., 1966, p. 51.

The Court in this Case had to interpret the Mandate for South West Africa in order to determine whether the applicants had a legal right or interest in the matter. The Court recalled that the mandates system was instituted by Article 22 of the League Covenant. As a matter of interpretation, States had a legal interest in respect of certain provisions of the mandate which were characterised by the Court as the 'special interest' provisions.[63] The Court concluded, however, that the Applicants were not invoking interests protected by such provisions rather, the Applicants had referred to various provisions classified by the Court as 'conduct' provisions, in respect of which the only supervision was through the political organs of the League. Accordingly, the Court declared that:[64]

> *[I]n holding that the Applicants ... could only have had a legal right or interest in the 'special interests' provisions of the Mandate, the Court does not in any way do so merely because these relate to a material or tangible object. Nor, in holding that no legal right or interest exist for the Applicants, individually as States, in respect of the 'conduct' provisions, does the Court do so because any such right or interest would not have a material or tangible object. The Court simply holds that such rights or interests, in order to exist, must be clearly vested in those who claim them, by some text or instrument, or rule of law;-and that in the present case, none were ever vested in individual members of the League under any of the relevant instruments, or as a constituent part of the mandates system as a whole, or otherwise.*

In responding to arguments advanced before the Court that humanitarian considerations are sufficient in themselves to generate legal rights and obligations the Court stated that:[65]

> *It is a court of law, and can take account of moral principles only in so far as these are given a sufficient expression in legal form. Law exists, it is said, to serve a social need; but precisely for that reason it can do so only through and within the limits of its own discipline. Otherwise, it is not a legal service that would be rendered.*

Prott claims that the Court's decision in this case "created a crisis in the acceptance of the International Court."[66] With this finding the Court also appeared to have con-

---

[63] For examples those concerning freedom for missionaries who were nationals of members of the League to enter and reside in the territory for the purpose of prosecuting their calling. See ICJ Rep., 1966, p. 21. See also Brownlie Ian, *Principles of Public International Law*, 6th edition, Oxford University Press, 2003, p. 451.

[64] See ICJ Rep., 1966, pp. 32-33.

[65] Ibid, para. 49, p. 34.

[66] Prott, Lyndell V., *The Latent Power of Culture and the International Judge*, Abingdon, Oxon: Professional Books Ltd, 1979, p. 107.

tradicted its Judgement in the earlier phase of the Case, on 21 December 1962, in the *South West Africa Preliminary Objections* Case. In the earlier Case the Court found, by eight votes to seven, that the Mandate was a treaty that was still in force, and that the dispute between the parties was one envisaged in Article 7 of the Mandate i.e. a dispute that could not be settled by negotiation. Consequently, the Court found that it had "jurisdiction to adjudicate upon the merits of the dispute."[67]

Some commentators consider that the Court's strong positivist approach prevented it from following the new spirit of International Law, i.e. in harmony with the requirements of international life, in its 1966 judgment in the South West Africa Cases.[68] Thus, a majority of judges in this Case applied a narrow interpretation of the Mandate, refusing to adopt the teleological method in interpreting the legal question that had been referred to them.[69] For example, McWhinney considers the Court's decision in this Case as legally unnecessary and as politically disastrous.[70]

The impression that the Court's judgement left was that the Court was remote from the realities of international life. However, the Court subsequently realised the negative reaction towards its judgement. Consequently, it reviewed its role in relation to the UN policy-making institutions such as the General Assembly and the Security Council.[71]

Lastly, as Anand suggests, this unfortunate decision, should not jeopardise the Court's independence: "[i]n spite of all the criticism against the South West Africa case, there is no basis for any doubt about the independence of the Court as a whole … it is entirely wrong and rash to denounce a legal institution on the basis of a single case. In any case the Court seems to have regained confidence in the Namibia opinion."[72]

---

67 On 4 November 1960, Ethiopia and Liberia submitted to the Court separate applications against South Africa in accordance with Article 7 of the Mandate for South West Africa which subjected South Africa to the jurisdiction of the PCIJ whenever any dispute whatsoever arise between the Mandatory and another member of the League relating to the interpretation or application of the provisions of the Mandate and Article 37 of the Court's Statute, in addition to Article 80 (1) of the Charter. These applications concerned the continued existence of the League of Nations mandate for South Africa and the duties of South Africa as a mandatory power. South Africa filed four preliminary objections relating to the Court's jurisdiction. However, these objections were dismissed by a Court's judgment of 21 December 1962. For the details of this case, see Zacklin, Ralph, "The Problem of Namibia in International Law", 171 *RCADI*, 1981, p. 270.

68 Bodie, Thomas J., *Politics and the Emergence of an Activist International Court of Justice*, Westport, Connecticut; London: Praeger, 1995, pp. 62-63.

69 See the statement of the Court justifying the approach it took against teleological approach. ICJ Rep., 1966, para. 91, p. 48.

70 McWhinney, Edward, "Contemporary Conceptions of the Role of International Judicial Settlement", 22 *RCADI,* 1990, p. 37.

71 McWhinney, ibid; see also Rosenne, Shabtai, *The World Court: What It is and How It Works*, Dordrecht, London: Martinus Nijhoff Publishers, 1995, p. 175.

72 Anand, *supra* note 37, p. 16. For discussion about the Namibia advisory opinion see Chapters Three, Five and Six, *supra.*

5.2.2 The 1996 *Legality of the Use by a State of Nuclear Weapons in Armed Conflicts* Case

The effect and implication of the Court's refusal to give an opinion in *The Legality of the Use by a State of Nuclear Weapons in Armed Conflicts Case* is discussed extensively in Chapter Two. However, it is sufficient to note here that, as a refusal of the Court's to give an opinion to the World Health Organization, the Court set an unfortunate precedent for other international organisations that may require, through the Court's advisory function, an interpretation or a clarification of the provisions of their constitution, while executing their duties in evermore overlapping and sophisticated undertakings.[73]

5.3 The Risk of Losing and the Unpredictability of the Court's Decision

States, as a general rule, resist judicial settlement because they fear losing. Unsurprisingly, nations are rarely indifferent to losing even when disputes concern matters of minor importance.[74] Therefore, it is understandable that States are generally unwilling to resort to third party settlement.[75] In order to protect their essential interests, States are reluctant to lose control over any dispute resolution process. Thus Judge Bedjaoui argues that:[76]

> *Some States may perhaps tend to have misgivings about such judicial settlement on the grounds that, unlike a political settlement, it would be completely outside their control and hence, given the reputed rigidity of legal rules, always liable in the end to turn out less favourably to themselves.*

If a party intends to seek public support and legitimisation of its position, then it would be easier and safer to seek such legitimisation and endorsement from a political body such as the General Assembly.[77] However, Judge Bedjaoui's argues that there cannot be a "loser" when a dispute is:[78]

> *[S]ettled serenely and when peace prevails, it must be stressed that the Court- because of the nature of the law which it applies and the*

[73] For details about the ramifications of this Case see Section II in Chapter Two, *supra*.

[74] Rovine, Arthur, "The National Interest and The World Court", in: Gross, Leo, (ed.) *The Future of the International Court of Justice*, 1976, p. 317.

[75] Couvreur, *supra* note 35, p. 91. Lissitzyn, "International Law in a Divided World", 542 *International Conciliation*, 1963, p. 37; Ciobanu, Dan, "*Preliminary Objections Related to the Jurisdiction of the United Political Organs*", The Hague: Nijhoff, 1975, p. 9.

[76] UN Doc. A/49/PV.29, cited in Couvreur, *supra* note 35, p. 93.

[77] Bilder, *supra* note 23, p. 167.

[78] Bedjaoui, Mohammed, "The Contribution of the International Court of Justice Towards Keeping and Restoring Peace", in: *Conflict Resolution: New Approaches and Methods*, Paris: UNESCO Publishing, 2000, p. 19.

> *role which it plays- is sure never to apply the law blindly ... The Court itself has in fact explained on several occasions that it considers that its making legal judgments in no way excludes- quite the contrary- taking into account* infra legem *equity, meaning that form of equity that constitutes a method of interpreting the law and is one of its qualities.*

The issue of predictability constitutes an old dilemma associated with adjudication. Gross argues that if predictability means applying the law as the Court finds it, then the Court may suffer from disuse. However, if the Court strikes out in a new direction, it may be accused of unpredictability.[79] It can be criticised whichever way it turns. However, unpredictability may not be such a grave defect and should be treated as natural.

Sir Robert Jennings argues that:[80]

> *[I]n any case worth taking to the International Court of Justice, it will, after all its required formalities have been faithfully completed, produce a result which cannot accurately be foretold before this process has been carried out ... There would be little point in all this highly formalized ceremonial if the results were simply predictable. This makes the adjudication method one of great efficacy, particularly in disputes which have proved intractable by other methods.*

Some writers suggest that it might be difficult to predict the outcome of adjudication for two reasons: First, there may be no relevant rules of international law covering the issue to be adjudicated. Second, existing rules may be rather ambiguous or uncertain.[81] It is the role of the Court to clarify the law and find legal rules for unprecedented issues.

5.4 The Composition of the Court and the Impartiality of the Judges

The ICJ is composed of fifteen judges, elected to represent the major world civilisations regardless of their nationality.[82] The General Assembly and the Security Council, voting separately, elect the judges from a list of qualified persons drawn up by the national group of the Permanent Court of Arbitration (PCA), or by specially appointed national groups in the case of the UN Members not represented in the PCA.[83] The composition of the Court seems to be a source of concern to many commentators who distrust the Court. Some writers claim that the composition of the Court and the distribution of seats constitute a strong reason for avoiding the

---

79 Gross, *supra* note 16, p. 23.

80 Jennings, *supra* note 29, p. 47.

81 Bilder, *supra* note 23, p. 167.

82 Articles 2 and 3 of the Statute.

83 See Articles 4, 5 of the Court's Statute.

Court[84] because the composition, more often than not, is not representative of the different legal systems and of the evolving world situation.[85]

Third world countries have argued that their States have been under- represented on the Court, and consequently have suffered of judges from western States who, it is alleged, are biased against the newer, developing countries.[86] Prott argues that even third world judges are influenced by the west through their training in a particular system of law.[87] On the other hand, the US and some western States have asserted that there is "anti-western bias on the Court" and have complained of the "dominance of the Court by third world states."[88] The US after the *Nicaragua* Case in 1985 adopted a negative view towards the Court, believing that the Court was politically motivated rather than impartial.[89]

Despite the above assertions, it should be born in mind that when judges are elected "they are not supposed to represent the views and preferences of their electorate in the way required of legislators."[90] Nevertheless, there is a possibility that judges may reflect the legal and political opinions prevalent in their respective countries at least subconsciously. However, this is not a proof of a lack of independence in the strict sense of that term.[91]

Some writers have cited a mere two or three cases to support their claim that the judges' views vary from one case to another in accordance with their countries' interests.[92] However, an evaluation of the Court's or of the judges' impartiality cannot be determined on the basis of just a few cases. Any evaluation must be more comprehensive and must include both the advisory and contentious functions of the Court. It must also take into consideration relevant political considerations, such as the effects of the Cold War on the Court.[93] Hensley conducted an interesting study of the voting pattern of ICJ judges.[94] Although his study revealed some evidence of bloc voting by the judges, the patterns of such blocs were not closely

---

84 Mosler, *supra* note 13, pp. 278-79; Oduntan, *supra* note 34, pp. 216-224.

85 See statistical overview of the composition of the Court from 1946 until end of term for judges in 2003 in Oduntan, Ibid, pp. 218-221.

86 Hensley, Thomas, "Bloc Voting on the International Court of Justice", 22 *The Journal of Conflict Resolution*, 1978, p. 41.

87 Prott, *supra* note 66, pp. 224-226.

88 McWhinney, *supra* note 70, p. 137.

89 Tiefenbrun, S., "The Role of The World Court in Settling International Disputes: Recent Assessment", 20 *Loyola of Los Angeles Int'l & Comparative Law Journal*, 1997, p. 2.

90 Warner, Richard, "Argumentation" in: Gray, Christopher *The Philosophy of Law: An Encyclopedia* , New York; London: Garland Publishing, Inc, vol. I, 1999, p. 47.

91 A view expressed by M. Hambro cited in: Mosler, *supra* note 13, p. 57.

92 Oduntan, *supra* note 34, pp. 216-24.

93 The period between 1947-54 was marked by the confrontation between the USSR and the US. See Archer, Clive, *International Organizations*, London: Routledge, 1992, p. 31.

94 Hensley, Thomas, *supra* note 86, pp. 39-59.

related to the political alignments, common historical traditions, or common legal systems of the judges' countries. Instead, the analysis revealed that some judges from countries sharing similar political interests and cultural ties did not vote together to any significant extent.[95] Another study, conducted by Edith Weiss in 1987, reviewed the empirical studies of this issue and found that:[96]

> *[T]he record does not reveal significant alignments, either on a regional, political, or economic basis. There is a high degree of consensus among the judges on most decisions. The most that can be discerned is that some judges vote more frequently together during certain periods than do others, and that in rare instances, notably with the Soviet and Syrian judges, they have always voted the same way. But there have not been persistent voting alignments which have significantly affected the decisions of the Court.*

One could argue here that focusing on the question of the composition of the Court and the election of the judges does not help to explain the reluctance of States to use the Court, as such reluctance is hardly due to doubts about the judges' integrity and independence. Nevertheless, judicial partiality is not completely precluded, particularly when a pronouncement is made after a casting vote of the president, in accordance with Article 55(2) Statute.[97] Prott has suggested that such a decision is "somewhat less clearly regarded by the public as a decision of the Court."[98]

5.5 The Slowness of the Judicial Procedure and the Cost of Litigation

In 1996 the British Institute decided to investigate the assumption that the slowness of the Court's procedure was a possible reason for States reluctance to use the Court. The institute's 1996 report analysed over 21 opinions that the Court handed down between 1948 and 1990, and found that the average time taken from lodging the request to the rendering of the opinion was 254 days.[99]

---

95 Ibid, p. 52.

96 Weiss, Edith B., "Judicial Independence and Impartiality: A Preliminary Inquiry" in: Damrosch, L. (ed.), *The International Court of Justice at a Crossroad*, Dobbs Ferry, New York: Transnational Publishers Inc., 1987, p. 134; see also Posner, Eric & De Figueiredo, Miguel, "Is the International Court of Justice Politically Biased", available at: http://epstein.wustl.edu/research/courses.LAPSPosner.pdf (accessed 15 December 2004).

97 This happened twice in the history of ICJ. First, in the 1996 WHO request and secondly, with the 1966 South West Africa Judgment.

98 Prott, *supra* note 66, p. 60.

99 The report of the Study Group, "Efficiency of Procedures and working methods", 45 *ICLQ*, supp. 1996, p. S26. It is worth noting that one should take into consideration that a case like *Yakimetz Case* has taken 990 days ICJ Rep., 1987, p. 18.

Although slowness is a characteristic of the judicial process, the time taken to reach a decision is generally longer in contentious cases. Sir Robert Jennings defends the Court by stating that the Court "works remarkably quickly, and the time taken will be found in any event, I believe, to compare favourably with other superior courts of both domestic and international jurisdiction."[100] Judge Bedjaoui also claims that once the Court retires to deliberate in an advisory case the process quickens and, usually, the pronouncement of its decision is made within a few months or sometimes only a few weeks.[101] In the 1950 *Competence of the General Assembly Case*, the final opinion was handed down fifteen days after the end of public hearing. The advisory opinion on the *Applicability of the Obligation to Arbitrate under Section Twenty One of The U.N Headquarters Agreement of 26th June 1947*, although long and complex, it was given just eight days after the end of public hearings[102].

Article 103 of the Court's 1978 Rules, as amended in 2000, allows an accelerated procedure whenever the authorised requesting body informs the Court of the urgent need for a quick decision, or whenever the Court consider it desirable:[103]

> *When the body authorized by or in accordance with the Charter of the United Nations to request an advisory opinion informs the Court that its request necessitates an urgent answer, or the Court finds that an early answer would be desirable, the Court shall take all necessary steps to accelerate the procedure, and it shall convene as early as possible for the purpose of proceeding to a hearing and deliberation on the request.*

---

[100] See Speech by Sir Robert Jennings, President of the International Court of Justice, to the UN General Assembly, 88 *AJIL*, 1994, p. 423.

[101] Bedjaoui, *supra* note 78, p. 16.

[102] Report of the Study Group, *supra* note 99, p. S26. In this request the General Assembly asked, in resolution 42/229B of 2 March 1988, the Court to take "in mind the constraints of time". The total time for rendering the opinion was eight weeks.

[103] The Security Council's request for an advisory opinion concerning Namibia, Resolution 284 (1970) informed the Court of the need to receive an opinion at an early date. See ICJ Rep., 1971, p. 17. The General Assembly's request for the *Western Sahara* opinion, in resolution 3292(XXIX), asked the Court to give the opinion "at an early date", ICJ Rep., 1975, p 13. Also, in the *Headquarters Agreement* opinion, the General Assembly in resolution 42/229 B (1988), asked the Court to "bear in mind the constraint of time", ICJ Rep., 1988, p. 13. In its request for an opinion in the *Legality of the Threat or Use of Nuclear Weapons* opinion, the General Assembly requested the Court in resolution 49/75 K to render the opinion "urgently". ICJ Rep., 1996(I) p. 228. In the *WHO/Egypt* opinion, the Director-General of the WHO in his request letter stated that the request necessitated an urgent answer ICJ Rep., 1980, p. 68. Lastly in *the Legal Consequences of the Construction of a Wall in the Occupied Palestinian Territory* Case, the General Assembly had requested the Court to render urgently an advisory opinion on the legality of the wall built by Israel in the occupied territory.

Table 2. Case Duration

Case	**Date Request Filed**	**Date of Rendered Opinion**	**Duration in Days**
Conditions of Admission of a State to Membership in the United Nations (Article 4 of the Charter), ICJ Reports, 1948, p. 57.	29.11.1947	28.05.1948	182
Reparation for Injuries Suffered in the Service of the United Nations, ICJ Reports, 1949, p. 174.	07.12.1948	11.04.1949	126
Competence of the General. Assembly for the Admission of a State to the United Nations, ICJ Reports, 1950, p. 4.	28.11.1949	03.03.1950	95
Interpretation of Peace Treaties with Bulgaria, Hungary and Romania, ICJ Reports, 1950, First Phase, p. 65	03.11.1949	30.03.1950	149
Interpretation of Peace Treaties with Bulgaria, Hungary and Romania, ICJ Reports, 1950, Second Phase, p. 221	02.05.1950	18.07.1950	77
International Status of South-West Africa, ICJ Reports, 1950, p. 128	27.12.1949	11.07.1950	196
Reservations to the Convention on the Prevention and Punishment of the Crime of Genocide, ICJ Reports 1951, p. 15	20.11.1950	28.05.1951	188
Effects of Awards of Compensation made by the United Nations Administrative Tribunal, ICJ Reports 1954, p. 47	21.12.1953	13.07.1954	204
Voting Procedure on Questions Relating to Reports and Petitions Concerning the Territory of South-West Africa, ICJ Reports 1955, p. 67*)*	06.12.1954	07.06.1955	183
Judgments of the Administrative Tribunal of the International Labour Organisation Upon Complaints Made Against the United Nations Educational, Scientific and Cultural Organisation, ICJ Reports 1956, p. 77	02.12.1955	23.10.1956	308
Admissibility of Hearings of Petitioners by the Committee on South West Africa, ICJ Reports 1956, p. 23	22.12.1955	01.07.1956	192
Constitution of the Maritime Safety Committee of the Inter-Governmental Maritime Consultative Organization, ICJ Reports 1960, ICJ Reports 1960, p. 150	25.03.1959	08.06.1960	441
Certain Expenses of the United Nations (Article 17, Paragraph 2, of the Charter), ICJ Reports 1962, p. 151	27.12.1961	20.07.1962	205

Table 2 (continued)

Case	Date Request Filed	Date of Rendered Opinion	Duration in Days
Legal Consequences for States of the Continued Presence of South Africa in Namibia (South West Africa) Notwithstanding Security Council Resolution 276 (1970), ICJ Reports 1971, p. 16	10.08.1970	21.06.1971	317
Application for Review of Judgment No. 158 of the United Nations Administrative Tribunal, ICJ Reports 1973, p. 166	03.07.1972	12.07.1973	373
Western Sahara, ICJ Reports 1975, p. 12	21.12.1974	16.10.1975	299
Interpretation of the Agreement of 25 March 1951 Between the WHO and Egypt, ICJ Reports 1980, p. 73	28.05.1980	20.12.1980	206
Application for Review of Judgment No. 273 of the United Nations Administrative Tribunal, ICJ Reports 1982, p. 325	28.07.1981	20.07.1982	357
Application for Review of Judgment No. 333 of the United Nations Administrative Tribunal, ICJ Reports 1987, p. 18	10.09.1984	27.05.1987	988
Applicability of the Obligation to Arbitrate Under Section 21 of the United Nations Headquarters Agreement of 26 June 1947, ICJ Reports 1988, p. 12	07.03.1988	26.04.1988	50
Applicability of Article VI, Section 22, of the Convention on the Privileges and Immunities of the United Nations, ICJ Reports 1989, p. 177	13.06.1989	15.12.1989	185
Legality of the Use BY a State of Nuclear Weapons in Armed Conflict, ICJ Reports 1996, p. 66	03.09.1993	08.07.1996	1039
Legality of the Threat or Use of Nuclear Weapons, ICJ Reports 1996, p. 226	06.01.1995	08.07.1996	184
Difference Relating to Immunity From Legal Process of a Special Rapporteur of the Commission on Human Rights, ICJ Reports 1999, p. 62	10.08.1998	29.04.1999	261
Legal Consequences of the Construction of a Wall in the Occupied Palestinian Territory. Available at: http://www.icjcij.org/icjwww/idocket/imwp/imwpframe.htm	08.12.2003	09.07.2004	214

- The average time for rendering an advisory opinion is 281 days.
- The average time for rendering an advisory opinion exclusive of Administrative Tribunal cases is 239 days.
- It took 50 days to render the advisory opinion on the *Headquarters Agreement.* On the other hand it took 1039 days to render the *Legality of the Use by a State of Nuclear Weapons in Armed Conflict* Advisory Opinion.

The cost of litigation may be also cited as deterring States from using the Court. However, access to the Court, as a starting point is free for all Member States, although the litigants have to bear other costs including advocates fees. The Secretary-General in 1989 following General Assembly directive announced the establishment of a legal aid scheme to assist in the finance of cases brought by developing States.[104]

After reviewing the above reasons for the limited use of the ICJ, one might conclude that the principal reason for reticence seems to be States' unwillingness to subject their policies to judicial determination and thereby lose some control over the dispute. Although, the preference for non-judicial means to settle disputes is a common phenomenon, nevertheless depoliticising a dispute and referring it to the Court should become the normal not the exceptional method for resolving legal issues. Sir Robert Jennings has pointed out that the ICJ will be strong when resort to it on legal issues "is normal, habitual, routine, not exceptional."[105]

6 Concluding Remarks

States' negative attitude to judicial settlement is long-standing and is simply a consequence of their preference for methods of settlement over which they have some control. Judicial settlement is only one of several means for the resolution of legal disputes. Arbitration, mediation, negotiation, inquiry, submissions to political bodies like the General Assembly are also important. Moreover, it would be misleading to suggest that every legal question should be resolved by judicial means. Nevertheless, judicial settlement on the international plane should not be exceptional for the reasons examined in this Chapter, particularly when there exists a Court like the ICJ with a significant body of jurisprudence.

The Court is the chief interpreter of International Law and the UN's supreme judicial organ of the UN. The Court may be imperfect, but, as one commentator has asked "what other such institution do we possess?" Thomas Franck has also stated that:[106]

> *The World Court is neither the only court we could imagine nor the only court operating between states. But no other court has its historic legacy, extensive jurisprudence, or broad base of participating states.*

---

[104] Amr, Mohamed S., *The Role of the International Court of Justice as the Principal Judicial Organ of the United Nations*, The Hague: Kluwer Law International, 2003, p. 395.

[105] Jennings, Sir Robert Y., "The Proper Work and Purposes of The International Court of Justice", in: Muller, A.S. & Raic, D. *et al.*, *The International Court Of Justice Its Future Role After Fifty Years*, The Hague; Boston; London: Martinus Nijhoff Publishers, 1997, p. 42.

[106] Franck, Thomas, *supra* note 14, p. 76.

[illegible]

CHAPTER EIGHT

The Reception of Advisory Opinions

1 Introduction

This Chapter examines the reactions of the requesting organs when they receive the opinions they solicited. The extent of compliance by any State concerned with a given opinion will generally not be examined here. This is because the issue of implementation does not affect the authority of the Court's opinions, and in any case the question of implementation is outside the scope of this study.

The present Chapter also seeks to emphasise that the primary motive for most advisory opinions rendered so far has been for clarification of the law and guidance for future action, rather than judicial legitimisation of decisions already taken. When the law is clear, there is a greater chance of compliance.[1] This is evidenced by the fact that no advisory opinion has ever been disregarded by any requesting body.

2 The Possibility of Non-compliance and Its Effect on the Court's Discretion to Render Advisory Opinions

Some commentators suggest that the Court should avoid giving advisory opinions if there is a likelihood that its opinion will be ignored.[2] According to this view, if the Court finds that its opinion is likely to be dismissed by those States who objected to requesting an opinion at the outset, and if its opinion would contribute little to the solution of disputes, the Court should decline to give an opinion.[3] Contrary to

---

1 Keith, Kenneth, *The Extent of the Advisory Jurisdiction of the International Court of Justice*, Leyden: A.W. Sijthoff, 1971, p. 42.

2 Pomerance, Michla, "The Advisory Role of the International Court of Justice and its 'Judicial' Character: Past and Future Prisms, in: Muller, A.S & Raic, D. *et al.* (eds.), *The International Court of Justice: Its Future Role After Fifty Years*, The Hague; Boston; London: Martinus Nijhoff Publishers, 1997, p. 318; Bowett, Derek W., "The Court's role in relation to international organizations" in: Lowe, Vaughan and Fitzmaurice, Malgosia (eds.), *Fifty Years of the International Court of Justice: Essays in honour of Sir Robert Jennings*, Cambridge: Grotius Publications, 1996, p. 186.

3 Bowett, ibid.

this point of view, Shaw rightly argues that the possibility of non-compliance is no reason for not exercising jurisdiction because the Court:[4]

> *[I]s not in a position to assess the chances of successful implementation and in any event the very act of clarifying the law in the relevant circumstances itself constitutes a form of implementation.*

As for the Court's view of the possibility of non-compliance by the requesting organ with the Court's advisory opinion, the Court's findings in the *Western Sahara* Case is illustrative:[5]

> *In any event, to what extent or degree its opinion will have an impact on the action of the General Assembly is not for the Court to decide. The function of the Court is to give an opinion based on law, once it has come to the conclusion that the questions put to it are relevant and have a practical and contemporary effect and, consequently, are not devoid of object or purpose.*

It could be argued that it is a commonplace that compliance can never be guaranteed, not even in judgments in contentious cases. It is left to the receiving organ in the case of an advisory opinion to determine the effect and mechanisms for implementing the opinion.

Although the Charter does not include any express provision which allows UN organs to review the legal findings in the Court's decision, Tanzi claims that an interpretation of the functions and powers vested in the UN's political organs may suggest that such a process of review is possible.[6] However, the general view expressed by member States and publicists is that advisory opinions should be accepted by the Assembly without discussion of the Court's findings and reasoning. As the United States Representative commented on the advisory opinion in the *Certain Expenses of the United Nations (Article17, paragraph 2, of the Charter)* Case[7]:

> *[M]y Government sees no need for this Assembly to pass upon, or even go into, the reasoning of the Court ... The draft resolution [accepting the advisory opinion] anticipates the General Assembly per-*

4 Shaw, Malcolm N., "The Security Council and the International Court of Justice: Judicial Drift and Judicial Function", in: Muller, A.S.; Raic, D. *et al.* (eds.), *The International Court of Justice: Its Future Role After Fifty Years*, The Hague; Boston; London: Martinus Nijhoff Publishers, 1997, p. 248-249.

5 ICJ Rep., 1975, para. 73, p. 37.

6 According to Tanzi, The Security Council, under Article 94(2), Chapters VI and VII of the UN Charter, and the General Assembly, under Article 10 and Chapter VI of the Charter can discuss and make recommendations on the merits of a question decided upon by the Court in a way which might be at variance with the Court's decision. See Tanzi, Attila "Problems of Enforcement of Decisions of the International Court of Justice and the Law of the United Nations", 6 *EJIL*, 1995, pp. 542-43.

7 Hereinafter cited as: "the *Expenses* Case", ICJ Rep., 1962, p. 151.

> *forming a function which is proper to it. The General Assembly is not a Court. It is not a judicial organ of the United Nations, and still less it is `the principal judicial organ of the United Nations', as Article 92 of the Charter describes the International Court of Justice. It is not the function of this Assembly ... to act as a Court to review the International Court of Justice. To do so would depart from the Charter's clear intention. When the Court's opinion is asked, establishment and interpretation of the law, in the design of the Charter, is the function of the Court; action to implement the law is, as the case may be, the function of other organs of the United Nations.*[8]

While the possibility exists that UN organs may reject the requested opinion when the majority of members in the organ concerned agree on the inappropriateness, from a political viewpoint, of upholding the Court's decision, nevertheless, concerns over non-compliance should not discourage the rendering, or indeed, requesting of an advisory opinion.

3 Guidance as the Primary Motive for Requesting Advisory Opinions

Most advisory opinions requested so far have been initiated by the General Assembly and the rest by various other organs and specialised agencies of the UN.[9] The reception of advisory opinions by the requesting organs provides ample evidence that the requests were motivated by the need for guidance in the UN's work. There has been no case where the requesting organ has refused to comply with the opinion requested, and most importantly the requesting organ has always acted in accordance with this judicial advice.[10] Even more, the requesting organs sometimes state expressly in the preambles of the resolutions requesting an advisory opinion that they need the opinion in order to determine their position in light of the Court's findings.

In the Legal Consequences for States of the Continued Presence of South Africa in Namibia (South West Africa) notwithstanding Security Council Resolution 267(1970) Case[11], the Security Council indicated that:[12]

---

8 U.S. Del to UNGA, Press Release No.4112, 1962, p. 3.

9 See Chapter Seven, *supra*.

10 Amr, Mohamed, *The Role of the International Court of Justice as the Principal Judicial Organ of the United Nations*, The Hague: Kluwer Law International, 2003, p. 116; Pomerance, Michla, *The Advisory Function of the International Court in the League and U.N. eras*. Baltimore; London: john Hopkins University Press, 1973, p. 341.

11 Hereinafter cited as "the *Namibia* Case", ICJ Rep., 1971, p. 16.

12 ICJ Rep., 1971, p. 24.

> *[A]n advisory opinion from the International Court of Justice would be useful for the Security Council in its further consideration of the question of Namibia and in furtherance of the objectives the Council is seeking.*

In the *Western Sahara* Case, the General Assembly stated that it was asking the Court for an opinion so that it could be in a position to decide “on the policy to be followed in order to accelerate the decolonization process in the territory ... in the best possible conditions, in the light of the advisory opinion.”[13] The object of the General Assembly's request in this Case was also stressed in the preamble of its resolution 3292 (XXIX), when it stated that “it is highly desirable that the General Assembly, in order to continue the discussion of this question ..., should receive an advisory opinion on some important legal aspects of the problem.”[14]

Failure to perform or act in accordance with the requested advice does not attract sanctions or consequences similar in nature to those allowed by Article 94(2) of the Charter for failure to perform obligations arising from judgments.[15] However, some writers have observed that the status of the Court within the UN indicates that its advisory opinions must be respected, as repeated non-compliance with the rendered opinions by the requesting organs would affect negatively the advisory function and the status of the Court.[16]

In general terms, one can conclude that some advisory opinions have been complied with by both the requesting organ and the concerned States. Others were implemented by the requesting organ but not by the concerned States. However, it should not be forgotten that the effects of advisory opinions are not confined just to the ‘parties’ in a specific case. Advisory opinions rendered by the Court affect the understanding and interpretation of International Law for all the international community rather than for the particular ‘parties’ to an individual opinion. To borrow the words of Judge De Castro:[17]

> *[T]he effect of an advisory opinion is not confined to the parties as though it were a matter of a judgment; the opinion is authoritative* erga omnes, *and is not restricted to the States or organizations that make written or oral statements or submit information or documents to the Court.*

---

13 ICJ Rep., 1975, para. 40, p. 27.

14 Ibid.

15 Article 94(2) provides: “[i]f any party to a case fails to perform the obligations incumbent upon it under a judgment rendered by the Court, the other party may have recourse to the Security Council, which may, if it deems necessary, make recommendations or decide upon measures to be taken to give effect to the judgment”.

16 Amr, *supra* note 10, p. 38.

17 Sep. Op. of Judge De Castro, ICJ Rep., 1975, p. 138.

4 The Interests Which Are Served by Compliance with Rendered Advisory Opinions

In considering the issue of compliance, one should take into account the conditions existing in the pre-request stage. As Pomerance suggests, the post opinion stage will "serve merely to seal and confirm that fate [the opinion's fate]."[18]

In situations where no serious clashes of interest are present among UN member States at the pre request stage, advisory opinions provide legal guidance and sometimes lead to actual action. Indeed, compliance with the opinion in such a case leads to the initially desired end and serves the interests of each and every party involved in the situation, as well as the interests of the international community as a whole.[19] This category of opinions might include the *Reparation for Injuries Suffered in the Service of the United Nations* Case,[20] *Reservations to the Convention on Genocide* Case,[21] the *Effect of Awards of Compliance made by the United Nations Administrative Tribunal* Case[22] and the *Constitution of the Maritime Safety Committee of the Inter Governmental Maritime Consultative Organization* Case.[23]

On the other hand, where clashes of interest already existed at the pre request stage, compliance by States who are involved is not guaranteed because they are likely to act in their own self-interest. Nevertheless, such opinions have clarified legal points and principles which are ultimately beneficial to the entire international community. This second category of opinions might include the *Admission of a State to the United Nations (Charter, Article 4)* Case,[24] the *Interpretation of Peace Treaties* Case,[25] the *South West Africa* Cases,[26] the *Expenses* Case, the *Legality of the Threat or Use of Nuclear Weapons* Case[27] and lastly the *Legal Consequences of the Construction of a Wall in the Occupied Palestinian Territory* Case.[28]

---

[18] Pomerance, *supra* note 10, p. 330. See the tables appended to Chapter Nine, *infra* to see the size of the majority by which the requests were adopted.

[19] Ullmann, E., *The Emergence of Norms*, Oxford: Clarendon Press, 1977, pp. 101-106.

[20] Hereinafter cited as: "the *Reparations* Case", ICJ Rep., 1949, p. 174.

[21] Hereinafter cited as: "the *Reservations* Case", ICJ Rep., 1951, p. 15.

[22] Hereinafter cited as: "the *Effect of Awards* Case", ICJ Rep., 1954, p. 47.

[23] Hereinafter cited as: "the *IMCO* Case", ICJ Rep., 1960, p. 150.

[24] Hereinafter cited as: "the *Admission* Case", ICJ Rep., 1948, p. 57.

[25] Hereinafter cited as: "the *Peace Treaties* Case", ICJ Rep., 1950, p. 65.

[26] These cases include the 1950 *International Status of South West Africa Case*, the 1955 *South-West-Africa Voting Procedure Case*, the 1956 *Admissibility of Hearings of Petitioners by the Committee on South West Africa* Case and Lastly the 1971 *Namibia* Case.

[27] Hereinafter cited as: "the *Nuclear Weapons* Case", ICJ Rep., 1996, p. 226.

[28] Hereinafter cited as: "the *Wall* Case", Available at: http://www.icj-cij.org/icjwww/idocket/imwp/imwpframe.htm.(Accessed 21 October 2004).

5 Review of Actions Taken by Requesting Organs upon a Rendered Advisory Opinions

The actions taken by the requesting organs upon rendered advisory opinions will not be examined in chronological order. Instead, these cases will be examined in terms of the two categories explained in the preceding Section, beginning with the first category, where there was no serious clash of States' interests at the pre request stage. Thus, in the 1949 *Reparations* Case, the Court concluded that the UN is an international organisation with capacity to bring claims against States to obtain reparations for damages caused to the UN. The General Assembly acted upon the Court's finding and its Resolution of 1 December 1949 authorised the Secretary General:[29]

> *[T]o bring an international claim against the Government of a State, Member or non-member of the United Nations, alleged to be responsible, with a view to obtaining reparation due in respect of the damage caused to the United Nations and in respect of the damage caused to the victim of persons entitled through him and, if necessary, to submit to arbitration, under appropriate procedures, such claims as cannot be settled by negotiation.*

In response to the Secretary General's request, the Government of Israel paid the full amount of the claim presented by the UN. This opinion was considered by Rosenne as "a watershed in the development of the law of international organizations."[30] No State has since challenged the capacity of the UN to bring claims.[31]

The opinion in the 1960 *IMCO* Case was requested unanimously by the member States of IMCO's Assembly. As a result, the IMCO Committee was reconstituted in accordance with Article 28 of the IMCO Convention as interpreted by the Court in its opinion, and eventually the name of the Organisation was changed to the IMO.[32] In this case the Court had, for the first time, considered the action taken by the requesting organ to be unconstitutional.[33]

In the 1954 *Effects of Awards* Case, where the opinion was to be binding under Article XII of the International Labour Organisation's Statute, the Court concluded that the General Assembly did not have the right to refuse to give effect to an award made by the Administrative Tribunal.[34] The General Assembly then

[29] See GA Res. 365 (IV), 1 December 1949.

[30] Rosenne, Shabtai, *The Law and Practice of the International Court, 1920-1996*, The Hague; London: Martinus Nijhoff Publishers, 1997, p. 313.

[31] Non-compliance by Egypt, Jordan to meet similar claims was not because of their rejection of the court's findings in the *Reparations* Case, see Pomerance, *supra* note 10, p. 364.

[32] See IMCO Res. A. II/Res. 21, of 6 April 1961.

[33] See Section 6.3.1 in Chapter Three, *supra*.

[34] ICJ Rep., 1954, p. 62.

approved the Court's opinion unanimously and authorised the establishment of a Special Indemnity fund for the payment to staff members of compensation awards made by the Tribunal.[35] UNESCO's Executive Board took note of the Court's opinion, and the awards were paid.

In the 1951 *Reservations* Case, the General Assembly had requested an opinion about the effect of reservations to multilateral conventions. The General Assembly had noted the advisory opinion and called upon the Secretary General to "conform his practice to the advisory opinion of the Court."[36] The Assembly also asked the Secretary General "in respect of future conventions concluded under the auspices of the United Nations of which he is the depository" to continue to accept "the deposit of documents containing reservations or objections, without passing upon the legal effect of such documents." It also called upon the interested States to implement the opinion. However, the General Assembly, despite acceptance of the opinion, has limited its effect by confining its application to the Genocide Convention.

One can place the *South West Africa* cases, the *Peace Treaties, the Admissions, the Nuclear weapons, and the Wall* Cases in the second category because there was evident disagreement at the pre-request stage among the UN's member States. These advisory opinions, although not implemented by the States directly concerned, establish legal points and principles which serve the collective interests of the international community.[37]

In the 1948 *Admissions* Case, the Court concluded that the conditions laid down in Article 4(1) for the admission of States were exhaustive, and that if these conditions were met by an applicant State a member could not make its affirmative vote for the applicant's admission subject to the additional condition that other States must be admitted to Membership at the same time.[38] Following the rendering of this opinion, The General Assembly recommended that:[39]

> *[E]ach member of the Security Council and of the General Assembly, in exercising its vote on the admission of new members, should act in accordance with the foregoing opinion of the International Court of Justice.*

This recommendation had no effect on the Soviet Union's stance, however, so the General Assembly requested another advisory opinion, in1949, as to whether the General Assembly had the power to admit new Members to the UN in the absence

35 Res 888 (IX) on 17 December 1954. In this resolution the General Assembly decided to take note of the Court's opinion.

36 GA Res. 598 (VI), of 12 January 1952.

37 For the contribution of these opinions to International Law, see Chapter Six, *supra*.

38 ICJ Rep., 1948, p. 65.

39 Res. 197 A III of December 8, 1948. This resolution was followed by subsequent resolutions. See Res. 197(III) in which the General Assembly asked the Security Council to reconsider certain pending applications.

of a recommendation from the Security Council.[40] This request was another attempt by the General Assembly to overcome the deadlock in the Security Council regarding admitting new States. The Court's reply was in the negative.

This opinion was the only advisory opinion which was not followed by a resolution of the General Assembly. However, in its Resolution No. 620 (VII), 21 December 1952, the General Assembly recalled that the Court, at the request of the General Assembly, had on two occasions given advisory opinions on the problem of admission of new members and that The General Assembly had authorised a special committee to study the problem of admission in light of the Court's opinion. Subsequently, on 23 October 1953, the General Assembly adopted Resolution 718 (VIII) to establish a Committee of Good Offices to find a way to facilitate the admission of new members. Finally, the deadlock over the problem of admissions was resolved by the so-called "package deal" after the General Assembly Resolution 995 (X), of December 1955 admitted sixteen countries to the UN.[41]

Following the two phases of the *Peace Treaties* Case, the General Assembly noted the Court's opinion and condemned the "willful refusal" of Bulgaria, Hungary and Romania to carry out their obligations under the peace treaties.[42] The States concerned, however, did not accept the Court's opinion. Rosenne argues that the decision of the General Assembly to admit those States, in these circumstances, cannot "be regarded as an encouragement for the employment of the Court as part of the United Nations procedure."[43]

The Court has given four advisory opinions related to the problem of South West Africa. In the 1950 opinion, the Court responded to a request to answer several questions regarding the status of South West Africa. The most important finding by the Court was that the Mandate remained in force after the dissolution of the League.[44] Therefore the South African government continued to have international obligations such as the submitting of reports and transmitting petitions to the UN which would exercise the supervisory functions formerly carried out by the League.[45]

By its resolution of December, 13, 1950, the General Assembly accepted the Court's opinion and urged the Government of South Africa to give effect to the opinion, including the obligations concerning the transmission of reports on the administration of the territory and of petitions from its inhabitants.[46] Pomerance

---

[40] See the *Competence of the General Assembly regarding Admission of a State to the United Nations* Case, ICJ Rep., 1950, p. 4.

[41] See http://untreaty.un.org/cod/repertory/art4/english/rep_suppl_vol1-art4_e.pdf (accessed 1 January 2005).

[42] GA Res. 385(V), 3 November 1950.

[43] Rosenne, Shabtai, "On the Non-Use of the Advisory Competence of the International Court of Justice", 39 *BYIL*, 1963, p. 42.

[44] The Court was unanimous on this point.

[45] ICJ Rep., 1950, pp. 143-144.

[46] GA Res. 449 A (V), of 13 December 1950, UNYB, 1950, p. 821.

argues that this Resolution was a product of efforts to reconcile two different perceptions of the opinion.[47] This resolution also established an *ad hoc* committee to confer with the Government of South Africa concerning the procedural measures needed for the implementation of the Court's opinion, and to examine the reports on the administration of the territory.[48]

South Africa refused to cooperate with the committee or to submit annual reports, so that the committee was unable to discharge its functions.[49] Because of South Africa's non-cooperation, the General Assembly in 1953 established a South West Africa Committee to implement the substantive and procedural conclusions of the 1950 opinion.[50] The Committee was also to "prepare for the consideration of the General. Assembly, a procedure for the examination of reports and petitions which should conform as far as possible to the procedure followed in this respect by the Assembly, the Council and the Permanent Mandates commission of the League of Nations."[51]

In the 1950 Opinion the Court had indicated that the degree of supervision should follow closely the procedures utilised by the League, and, so the General Assembly requested the committee to assimilate the functions assigned to it "as far as possible" to the procedures of the mandate system. A problem arose because in the UN a two-thirds majority on important questions is required, while in the League unanimity was required and the mandatory was entitled, in accordance with Article 4(5) of the League Covenant, to participate and vote in the Council on matters affecting the mandatory interest.[52] It might therefore be argued that, as the Mandatory power had a right of veto in the League Council on questions concerning its own Mandate, it presumably could also exercise a veto in the UN.

Having failed to resolve this problem the General Assembly decided to ask for an advisory opinion to clarify whether under its less strict voting rules it could exercise a greater degree of supervision over the Mandate than the League Council, and whether the use of voting Rule F would be consistent with the

---

47 The US sponsored a proposal to the effect that the UN had to negotiate with South Africa to implement the opinion. On the other hand more radical States maintained that negotiation with South Africa would be fruitless and harmful, therefore they sponsored a proposal to the effect that the Assembly should implement the opinion by establishing an organ to examine reports and petitions. See Pomerance, *supra* note 10, p. 344, footnote, 75.

48 Ibid.

49 This Committee was reconstituted by Res. 570 A (VI) of 21 January 1952 as a needed step to implement the Court's Opinion.

50 GA Res. 749 A (VIII), of 28 November, 1953. This Committee resembled the Permanent Mandates Commission of the League. See UNYB, 1953, p. 546.

51 GA Res. 749A (VIII), para. 12 (d).

52 The League Council in accordance with Article 5 of the Covenant, could only take decisions by a unanimous vote.

1950 opinion.[53] In its 1955 advisory opinion the Court unanimously found that use of Rule F was consistent with the 1950 advisory opinion, and so the General Assembly would apply its own voting procedure.[54]

On reception of this opinion, South Africa's representative maintained that he would not accept the 1955 opinion as it was merely an interpretation of the 1950 opinion which his Government did not accept either.[55] Nevertheless, the General Assembly adopted Resolution 934 (X), of 3 December 1955, accepting and endorsing the opinion.

The General Assembly had to turn to the Court for clarification again when South Africa refused to submit annual reports on its administration of the territory to the General Assembly and withheld the petitions of the inhabitants.[56] The South West Africa Committee sought the General Assembly's approval to hear oral petitioners directly in order to carry out its supervisory function. The Assembly then asked for an advisory opinion as to whether the Committee could be authorised by the General Assembly to grant oral hearings to petitioners who had previously submitted written statements to the Committee.[57]

The Court found that it would be inconsistent with the 1950 opinion if the Committee did not to allow oral hearings by petitioners, provided this was necessary for the maintenance of effective international supervision of the territory.[58] This opinion like the ones that had preceded was not implemented due to South

---

53 "The General Assembly, on 11 October 1954, adopted a special Rule F on voting procedure to be followed by the Assembly in taking decisions on questions relating to reports and petitions concerning the Territory of South West Africa. According to this Rule, such decisions were to be regarded as important questions within the meaning of Article 18, paragraph 2, of the United Nations Charter and would therefore require a two-thirds majority of Members of the United Nations present and voting". Available at: http://www.icj-cij.org/icjwww/igeneralinformation/ibbook/Bbook8-2.05-8.htm (accessed 1 January 2005); see also GA Res. 904 (IX), of 23 November 1954. See UNYB, 1954, p. 330.

54 The opinion indicated that the General Assembly should not exceed levels of supervision that had applied under the Mandate and "should conform as far as possible to the procedure followed in this respect by the Council of the League of Nations." ICJ Rep., 1955, p. 67.

55 South Africa's repeated argument was that UN supervision had exceeded the level prescribed by the Court in its opinion, i.e. that "the degree of supervision to be exercised by the General Assembly should not therefore exceed that which applied under the Mandates system, and should conform as far as possible to the procedure followed in this respect by the Council of the League of Nations". ICJ Rep., 1950, p. 138. Therefore, South Africa maintained that the General Assembly's supervision functions over the territory were illegal.

56 GA Res. 942 (X) of 3 December, 1955. See UNYB, 1955, p. 272.

57 Admissibility of Hearings of Petitioners by the Committee of South West Africa, ICJ Rep., 1956, pp. 25-26.

58 ICJ Rep., 1956, p. 32.

African non-cooperation. The General Assembly, however, maintained its consistent stance by accepting and respecting the Court's opinion.[59]

South Africa's non-cooperation continued so that none of the three advisory opinions nor any of the General Assembly resolutions on South West Africa were ever implemented. Therefore, the Assembly made another attempt to implement the opinions, this was by requesting the Committee on South Africa to study the question of what legal action was open to the UN organs, UN members, or former League members acting individually or jointly to ensure that the Union fulfilled the obligations assumed by it under the Mandate.[60]

The Committee's report contemplated the possibility of approaching the Court either for a new advisory opinion or to invoke its contentious procedure.[61] Two years later, the Assembly drew the attention of member States to the conclusions of the Committee in favour of possible contentious proceedings against South Africa.[62] Subsequently, in 1960, two African States, Ethiopia and Liberia, both former members of the League and parties to the League Covenant, began contentious proceedings[63] based on the 1950 opinion on *the Status of South West Africa*.[64] In this new case the Court found, by eight votes to seven, that the Mandate was a treaty still in force, and that the dispute between the parties was one envisaged in Article 7 of the Mandate which could not be settled by negotiation. Consequently, the Court found that it had the jurisdiction to adjudicate upon the merits.[65]

Following the Court's decision in 1966 rejecting the same applicants' claim,[66] the General Assembly by Resolution 2145 (XXI) of 28 October 1966 terminated the Mandate and decided that "henceforth South West Africa comes under the

---

[59] The General Assembly accepted the opinion by its Resolution 1047 (XI) of 23 January 1957.

[60] GA Res. 1060 (XI) of 26 February 1957.

[61] GAOR, supp. 12A A/3625.

[62] Res. 1361 (XIV), of 17 November 1959.

[63] The General Assembly by its Resolution 1565 (XV) of 18 December 1960, praised the decision of the two African States to initiate contentious proceedings and declared that this decision was for the sake of the whole international community. The vote taken on this Resolution was 86 to 0 with 6 abstentions.

[64] Two applications, one submitted by Ethiopia and the other by Liberia, were instituted against South Africa relating to "the continued existence of the Mandate for South West Africa and the duties and performance of the Union, as Mandatory, thereunder." ICJ Rep., 1962, p. 321.

[65] For the details of this case, see Zacklin, Ralph, "The Problem of Namibia in International Law", 171 *RCADI*, 1981, p. 270; See Chapter Seven, *supra*.

[66] On 18 July 1966 the Court found that "the Applicants cannot be considered to have established any legal right or interest appertaining to them in the subject-matter of the present claims, and that, accordingly, the Court must decline to give effect to them." ICJ Rep., 1966, p. 51. See Section 5.2.1 in Chapter Seven, *supra*.

direct responsibility of the United Nations."[67] To implement this Resolution the Assembly established the UN Council for Namibia to administer the Territory.[68] South Africa nevertheless maintained its previous stance of non-cooperation and continued to occupy the territory. Therefore, the General Assembly sought the Security Council's assistance to implement its decision.[69] The Security Council adopted Resolution 264 (1969) in which it recognised that the Assembly had terminated the Mandate and that "the continued presence of South Africa in Namibia is illegal" and called upon South Africa to withdraw from the territory immediately.[70] The Security Council then, for the first time, requested an advisory opinion.[71]

It has been suggested that the motivation behind this request was that the Security Council wished to be seen to be taking a position over South West Africa consistent with that of the General Assembly, which had requested three advisory opinions without obtaining any change in South Africa's position.[72] Also, one commentator suggests that both political organs sought a judicial confirmation of the earlier advisory opinions.[73] The case moreover, has been seen as an opportunity for the Court to rehabilitate itself after the 1966 decision by clarifying the legal consequences of the illegal presence of South Africa in Namibia.[74] The Court held by 13 votes to 2 that the continued presence of South Africa in Namibia was illegal, and South Africa had to end its occupation of the Territory. On receiving this opinion, the Security Council adopted Resolution 301 of 20 October 1971 in which it noted with appreciation the Court's opinion, agreed with the Court's findings and called upon all States to comply with the Court's decision.

In the *Expenses* Case, the General Assembly had asked the Court whether the expenditures incurred in respect of the peace operations constituted "expenses of the organisation" within the meaning of Article 17(2) of the Charter.[75] The Court examined the issues and answered the question in the affirmative.[76] The Assembly

---

67 Res. 2145 (XXI), 28 October 1966.

68 GA Res. 2248 (S-V), 19 May 1967.

69 The Security Council adopted Resolution 245 of 25 January 1968 which took note of GA Res. 2145.

70 SC Res. 264 of 20 March 1969.

71 Res. 284 (1970), *Legal Consequences for States of the Continued Presence of South Africa in Namibia (South West Africa) notwithstanding Security Council Resolution 276 (1970)* Case. For more details about this Opinion see Section 6.3.3 in Chapter Three, *supra*.

72 See the General Assembly requests for Advisory Opinions in 1950; 1955 and 1956.

73 Zacklin, *supra* note 65, p. 291.

74 Ibid.

75 GA Res. 1731 (XVI), 20 December 1961.

76 ICJ Rep., 1962, pp. 179-180.

accepted the opinion in its Resolution number 1854 A (XVII), of 19 December 1962 to the effect that the costs of peace-keeping operations were expenses which could be apportioned by the Assembly among the Members. This opinion did not resolve the problem, which was highly political, so the General Assembly was forced to adopt a number of resolutions for dealing with the financial crisis of the organisation.[77]

Following the advisory opinion in the *Nuclear Weapons* Case, the General Assembly expressed its appreciation to the Court for responding to the request, took note of the opinion, called upon all States to fulfil their obligations in concluding negotiations leading to nuclear disarmament and included in the provisional agenda of the 52nd Session the following item: "Follow-up to the advisory opinion of the International Court of Justice on the Legality of the Threat or Use of Nuclear Weapons."[78]

Following the last advisory opinion, the *Wall* Case, the General Assembly in its Tenth special emergency session held on 20 July 2004, by 150 votes to 6 with 10 abstentions adopted Resolution ES-10/18 in which it accepted the advisory opinion rendered by the Court on 9 July 2004 calling for Israel and all UN member States to comply with the legal obligations embodied in the Court's opinion.[79]

The General Assembly also requested the UN Secretary General to set up a register of damages caused to all natural or legal persons resulting from Israel's construction of the wall in the occupied Palestinian Territory. The General Assembly also reaffirmed the right and duty of all States to take action in accordance with international law to counter deadly acts of violence against the civilian populations. Last, the Assembly reserved the right to reconvene to consider further action in the case of non-compliance, which could include non-binding sanctions.

[77] See Para. 28 of GA Res. 1875 (S- IV), 27 June 1963 which recommended that economically developed countries "make voluntary contributions in addition to their assessments under this resolution in order to finance authorized expenditure in excess of the total amount assessed under the present resolution". Most importantly, the General Assembly Resolution. 1877 of 27 June 1963 expressed that "Member States which are in arrears and object on political or juridical grounds to paying their assessments on these accounts nevertheless will, without prejudice to their respective positions, make a special effort towards solving the financial difficulties of the United Nations by making those payments." Available at: http://untreaty.un.org/cod/repertory/art17/english/rep_supp3_vol1-art17_2_e.pdf (accessed 1 January 2005).

[78] Available at: http://www.mint.gov.my/policy/nuc_disarm/unga56_24S.htm (accessed 1 January 2005).

[79] See Press Release /GA/10248. Available at: http://www.un.org/News/Press/docs/2004/ga10248.doc.htm (accessed 1 January 2005).

6 Concluding Remarks

This Chapter has emphasised that the requesting organs have always coordinated with the Court upon the receipt of an advisory opinion by accepting, adopting or taking note of the opinion and acting in accordance with it. Indeed, in no case have the requesting organs acted contrary to any given opinion, although the real implementations of the opinions, in some cases, have been hampered by States who have failed to act in accordance with the requesting organ's recommendations which had been made after the receipt of the Court's certain opinions.

Kaikobad notes that the positive attitude of the UN and its specialised agencies towards the Court's opinions is due to two factors: first, it is not in the interest of the organ, nor it is consistent with its authority and standing, to seek an advisory opinion and then disregard the terms thereof if the reply it receives is regarded as somehow unsatisfactory, second, the Court's deliberations are definitive, even if not dispositive, statements on the law by the principal judicial organ of the UN. Consequently they cannot be dismissed as non-authoritative. Moreover, a rejection of an advisory opinion would undermine the authority and prestige of the Court, which would not be in the interest of any UN organ.[80]

Given the lack of enforceability of the advisory opinion due to its non-binding nature, coordination of UN member States in receiving and acting upon the Court's decision seems vital.

---

80 Kaikobad, Kaiyan H., *The International Court of Justice and Judicial Review: a Study of the Court's Powers with Respect to Judgments of the ILO and UN Administrative Tribunals*, The Hague; London: Kluwer Law International, 2000, pp. 57-58.

CONCLUSION

The Advisory Function of the ICJ: Concerns, Limitations and Future Role

1 Introduction

As noted in Chapter One, the ICJ's advisory function has had a controversial history. The controversy centres on whether the mere giving of advice, even in a solemn form such as by means of an advisory opinion, is compatible with the true function of a court of law.[1] In this regard, one may refer to the comments of Judge Hudson concerning the necessity of the Court keeping within the limits which characterise judicial action, "more particularly when exercising its advisory jurisdiction, and not to act as an "academy of jurists", but as responsible "magistrature."[2] One could argue that both the PCIJ and the ICJ have treated their advisory function as judicial and have acted as a responsible "magistrature."[3]

As discussed in Chapter Three, changes in the institutional setting of the ICJ have largely turned the Court into a different kind of institution from its predecessor. These changes have made the Court particularly responsive to the needs of the UN Organisation, although the Court is not subordinate to any external authority in the exercise of its judicial function.[4] The present study has argued that the status of the Court within the UN has not affected in any way the essential character of the Court as a judicial organ and, therefore, the issue of the compatibility of the advisory jurisdiction with the true function of a court of law is no longer an issue. The quality of the advisory function is now too firmly established as judicial. The cases to date broadly demonstrate that advisory opinions have furthered the goals of the UN.[5] However, a review of these cases raises certain questions such as the following: what are the complexities of the institutional connection between the

---

1 See the discussion in Chapter One, *supra*; see also Hudson, Manley O, *The Permanent Court of International Justice*, 1920-1942, New York: The Macmillan Company, 1943, pp. 510-511; See also, Diss. Op. of Judge Fitzmurice, ICJ Rep., 1971, p. 302.

2 Hudson, *supra* note 1, p. 511.

3 For the experience of the PCIJ see Hudson, ibid. For the experience of the ICJ, see Chapter Four, *supra*.

4 Rosenne, Shabtai, *The Law and Practice of the International Court, 1920-1996*, The Hague; London: Martinus Nijhoff Publishers, 1997, p. 139.

5 See Chapter Six, *supra*.

Court and the UN Organisation? Has the advisory function fulfilled its intended purposes? Has its contribution to the UN and International Law been significant? What obstacles does the Court still face in exercising its advisory jurisdiction? What will the future role of the advisory jurisdiction be?

This concluding Chapter will recall, though not exhaustively, some of the principal issues examined in this study. The Chapter will discuss some of the concerns that have been raised about the advisory jurisdiction and its limitations, while also considering the future role of the advisory procedure. Finally, the Chapter will suggest certain ways to improve the Court's advisory function.

2 The Complexities of the Institutional Connection Between the Court and the United Nations

The Court's role as the principal judicial organ of the UN has been the subject of considerable scholarly comment. Gross has observed that the Court was created to function both as "an organ of the United Nations and as an organ of international law, to render advisory opinions in the former capacity and judgments in the latter",[6] while Judge Schwebel suggests that the organic connection between the Court and the Organisation highlights the fact that problems of interpretation are to be "solved on the basis that the Court exists and functions in line with the general existence and functioning of the UN."[7] It has also been argued that one of the implications of this organic relationship is that, in general, legal principles that apply to the Organisation also apply to the Court.[8]

In practice, the Court, within the limits of its competence, has participated at the highest level in the activities of the UN. Only once in the long history of the Court's advisory procedure has it failed to assist an agency of the UN when asked to do so.[9] Legally speaking, the Court seems to adopt a liberal approach when dealing with requests for advisory opinions. This liberal approach may be inferred from the Court's assumption of an 'organisational interest' underlying requests for advisory opinions,[10] the Court's repeated assertion that the consent of concerned

---

6 Gross, Leo, "The International Court of Justice and the United Nations", 120 *RCADI*, 1967, p. 320.

7 Schwebel, Stephen M., *Justice in International Law: Selected Writings of Stephen M. Schwebel*, Cambridge: Grotius Publications, 1994, p. 16, note 4.

8 For instance, respect for the domestic jurisdiction of a State, in accordance with Article 2(7) of the UN Charter, is considered to be one of the key principles of the UN. It restricts the competence and authority of all UN organs including the Court. See Amr, Mohamed, *The Role of the International Court of Justice as a Principal Judicial Organ of the United Nations,* The Hague: Kluwer Law International, 2003, p. 30.

9 See the WHO request in *the Legality of the Use by a State of Nuclear Weapons in Armed Conflict* Case. For details see Section II in Chapter Two, *supra.*

10 See discussion in Chapter Four, *supra.*

States is not necessary to enable the Court to give an advisory opinion,[11] the Court's consistent insistence that it has the power to render an advisory opinion on any legal question,[12] and the Court's practice in reformulating questions for advisory opinions in order to afford maximum assistance to the requesting organ while still preserving its judicial character.[13] Lastly, the Court has given maximum effect to UN organs' decisions if these decisions promote the goals of the UN.[14]

On the other hand, the institutional link between the Court and the other UN principal organs, along with the liberal approach which the Court applies in advisory opinions, have led some scholars to view requests for advisory opinions as akin to "client-lawyer" consultation.[15] One could argue that the term "client-lawyer" could imply the notion that the ICJ is like a law firm and, therefore, that the advisory opinion rendered is mere advice from an ordinary lawyer to a client. This expression could also imply that the Court may be ready to sacrifice its judicial character for the sake of assisting UN organs and of reaching whatever conclusions the organs want the Court to provide. Also, the expression underestimates the uniqueness of the ICJ as one of the UN's principal organs and most importantly as its "principal judicial organ." Viewing the relationship as that of "client-lawyer" would possibly change the Court from a judicial body, which should ultimately seek to achieve justice, into a legitimising entity for the political organs regardless of the validity of the organs' acts.

Fortunately, as argued in Chapter Five, it is doubtful that the status of the Court as 'a principal organ' of the UN has changed in any way the essential character of the Court as a judicial body. Rosenne has pointed out that:[16]

> *The functional detachment of the Court from the United Nations is maintained not only by material aspects such as its different location, the independence of its Members and staff and the complete absence of control over its activities by any other principal organ, but also by more metaphysical elements such as its own historical evolution and the tradition to which it is heir, the degree of impartial and learned scrutiny and criticism to which its activities are permanently subjected in the professional literature of the law, and the cherished place which the Court has earned for itself in the world of law.*

---

[11] See Chapter Four, *supra.*

[12] See Section 3.2 in Chapter Two, *supra.*

[13] See Section 4.1 in Chapter Five, *supra.*

[14] See the Court's finding in the *Expenses* Case. For further details see Section 3.1.1 in Chapter Two, *supra.*

[15] Pomerance, Michla, *The Advisory Function of the International Court in the League and U.N Eras*, Baltimore; London: John Hopkins University Press, 1973. pp. 292-296.

[16] Rosenne, *supra* note 4, p. 170.

Once the Court is requested to give an advisory opinion, as a court of law it must analyse all issues related to the facts and apply to them the appropriate law in a reasoned opinion with maximum neutrality, regardless of the desires of its fellow organs. Sir Robert Jennings has rightly pointed out that the "only authority a court has is to apply the law to a case submitted to it and to come to a decision accordingly."[17] The fact remains that the Court is a court of justice, not of ethics, morals or of political expediency.[18] It would be, in fact, detrimental to the Court's prestige to refrain from issuing a strong opinion in favour of a weaker one in order to satisfy overtures from the political organs. The Court's case law demonstrates that its institutional link with the UN and its liberal approach in handling advisory opinions has not affected its authority as a judicial organ. The Court, indeed, has taken a cautious approach to maintain its integrity and its judicial character.[19] Moreover, in the interests of consistency and fairness, the procedures applied by the Court in its advisory capacity have been largely assimilated to those applied in contentious procedures.[20]

3 The Usefulness of the Advisory Opinion to the United Nations Organisation

The advisory function was primarily designed to assist UN organs in the discharge of their functions and to guide their future course of action by affording authoritative opinions based on law. Consequently, an advisory opinion is expected to provide a concrete formulation of the law applicable to a situation facing the Organisation. Judge Bedjaoui maintains that the Court's advisory opinions make "a considerable contribution, not only to the smooth running of international organizations, but also to the advancement of law and legal discipline."[21] He further remarked that:[22]

> *[W]e must not lose sight of the fact that a relevant legal question, asked of the Court at the right moment, can, either by the reply it receives or simply in itself, prove to be an effective instrument for preventive diplomacy or make a substantial contribution to the solution of a dispute that has already arisen. There is no doubt that*

---

17 Jennings, Sir Robert Y., "Judicial Reasoning at an International Court", Universität Des Saarlandes, 1991, p. 2.

18 Rosenne, *supra* note 4, p. 172.

19 See Chapter Four, *supra.*

20 See Chapter Five, *supra.*

21 Bedjaoui, Mohammed, "The Contribution of the International Court of Justice Towards Keeping and Restoring Peace" in *Conflict Resolution: new approaches and methods*, UNESCO Publishing,, 2000, pp. 12-13.

22 Ibid, p. 13.

> *there are many ways in which the advisory procedure, used in the absence of any immediate conflict, constitutes a privileged means for the Court to prevent and defuse tensions by stating the law.*

To be sure advisory opinions are non-binding. However, one could argue that their authority does not depend upon their binding or non-binding nature, but rather on their ability to facilitate the work of the UN. In fact, as examined in Chapter Six, the contribution of the advisory opinions has been of a considerable importance for both the UN and International Law.[23] Moreover, the value of the contribution and the authoritativeness of the Court's opinions are not diminished by the non-compliance of some States concerned with the requested opinion.[24]

The experience of the Court over the past 55 years shows that the advisory opinions have been requested in six general areas:[25]

- First, most advisory opinions rendered during the early years of the Court dealt with the interpretation of the Charter, the interpretation of the constitutional instruments of the specialised agencies, procedural matters in connection with the work of international organisations, and legal questions arising out of the activities of the international organisations. Examples listed in table 1 below are: the *Admissions* Case (no.1); the *Reparation* Case (no.2); the *Competence of the General Assembly* Case (no.4); the *Effect of Awards of Compensation* Case (no.7); the *Voting Procedure* Case (no.8); the *Admissibility of Hearing of Petitioners* Case (no.9); the *IMCO* Case (no.24); and the *Expenses* Case (no.10).
- Second, Unlike the PCIJ, which dealt mostly with inter-State disputes in its advisory opinions,[26] the ICJ has dealt with inter-State disputes in only a few advisory opinions, namely: the *Interpretation of Peace Treaties* Case (no.3); and the *Western Sahara* Case (no.11) and the *Legal Consequences of the Construction of a Wall in the Occupied Palestinian Territory* Case (no.14). The Court has also dealt in advisory opinions with disputes between States and international organisations: *the International Status of South West Africa* Case (no.5), was between South Africa and the U.N; the *Namibia* Case (no.15), between South Africa and the U.N; *the WHO Regional Headquarters Agreement* Case (no.22) between the WHO and the Government of Egypt; the *United Nations Headquarters Agreement* Case (no.12) between the UN and the U.S; finally, the *United Nations Privileges and Immunities* Case (no.16) between the UN and the Romania.

---

23 See Chapter Six, *supra*.

24 See Chapter Eight, *supra*.

25 See Oda, Shigeru, "The International Court of Justice Viewed From the Bench (1976-1993)", 244 *RCADI*, 1993, pp. 90-92.

26 21 out of 27 advisory opinions given by the PCIJ were related to legal disputes.

- Third, Advisory opinions have also been used to review the judgements of the United Nations Administrative Tribunals. This procedure has been dispensed with as of 11 December 1995.[27] At any rate these cases included: the *Application for Review of Judgment No. 158 of the UNAT* Case (no.18); the *Application for Review of Judgment No. 273 of the UNAT* Case (no.19) and the *Application for Review of Judgment No. 158 of the UNAT* Case (no.20).
- Fourth, advisory opinions have also been used to seek clarification of earlier opinions. For example the 1955 *South-West-Africa Voting Procedure* Case (no. 8), and the 1956 *Admissibility of Hearings of Petitioners by the Committee on South West Africa* Case (no. 9) both sought clarification of *the 1950 International Status of South West Africa* Advisory Opinion (no.5).[28]
- Fifth, in certain unprecedented situations where the law has not been fully developed the Court has indicated the direction in which, in its view, International Law needs to be evolved by States as in the *Legality of Threat or Use of Nuclear Weapons* Case (no.13). In his declaration, in that case, President Bedjaoui expressed the hope that:[29]

  > *[T]he international community will give the Court credit for having carried out its mission-even if its reply may seem unsatisfactory- and will endeavour as quickly as possible to correct the imperfections of an international law which is ultimately no more than the creation of the States themselves. The Court will at least have had the merit of pointing out these imperfections and calling upon international society to correct them.*

Lastly, through its advisory opinions the Court has participated in UN activities by, for example, evaluating the lawfulness of the UN organs' decisions. As examined in Chapter Three, certain advisory opinions have engaged in this judicial evaluation. The case law of the Court, which has been examined throughout this study, demonstrates that the Court has justified its existence as one of the principal organs of the UN, and affirmed that its advisory function is not secondary in importance to its contentious jurisdiction.

However, the fact that only 25 advisory opinions have been rendered so far suggests a limited use of the function. Section 4 below examines some of the limitations of the advisory procedure system which may account for the relatively small number of cases. A clear evidence of such limitations on the successful use of the advisory procedure is suggested by situations which would have been appropriate for an opinion, but which failed to come before the Court.[30] The tables below containing details of the voting on requests for advisory opinions.

---

27 See Section 4.4 in Chapter Five, *supra*.

28 For details about these Cases see Section 5 in Chapter Eight, *supra*.

29 Declaration of President Bedjaoui, ICJ Rep., 1996, p. 269.

30 Space limitations do not permit the discussion of these cases, however, for an excellent study of all cases which failed to come before the Court see, Pomerance, *supra* note 15, pp. 221-276.

Table 3. Voting on Request for Advisory Opinion

No.	Requesting Organ	Resolution No.	Voting Pattern	Case Name
1	General Assembly	113 B (II) of 17 Nov. 1947	40 to 8 with 2 abstentions	Conditions of Admission of a State to Membership in the United Nations
2		258 (III) of 3 Dec. 1948	Unanimous	Reparation for Injuries Suffered in the Service of the United Nations
3		294 (IV) of 22 Oct. 1949	47 to 5 with 7 abstentions	Interpretation of Peace Treaties with Bulgaria, Hungary and Romania
4		296 J (IV) of 22 Nov. 1949	49 to 9 with 6 abstentions	Competence of the General Assembly for the Admission of a State to the United Nations
5		338 (IV) of 6 Dec. 1949	40 to 7 with 4 abstentions	International Status of South West Africa
6		478 (V) of 16 Nov. 1950	47 to 5 with 5 abstentions	Reservations to the Convention on the Prevention of the Crime of Genocide
7		785 A (VIII) of 9 Dec. 1953	41 to 6 with 13 abstentions	Effects of Awards of Compensation Made by the United Nations Administrative Tribunal
8		904 (IX) of 23 Nov. 1954	25 to 11 with 21 abstentions	Voting Procedure on Questions Relating to Reports and Petitions Concerning the Territory of South West Africa
9		942 (X) of 3 Dec. 1955	32 to 5 with 19 abstentions	Admissibility of Hearings of Petitioners by the Committee on South West Africa
10		1731 (XVI) of 20 Dec. 1961	52 to 11 with 32 abstentions	Certain Expenses of the United Nations (Article 17, paragraph. 2 of the Charter)
11		3292 (XXIX) of 13 Dec. 1974	87 to 0 with 43 abstentions	Western Sahara
12		42/229 B, of 2 March 1988	143 to 0	Applicability of the Obligation to Arbitrate Under Section 21 Of the United Nations Head Quarters Agreement of 26 June 1947
13	General Assembly	49/75 K of 15 Dec. 1994	78 to 43 with 38 abstentions	Legality of the Threat or Use of Nuclear Weapons

Table 3 (continued)

No.	Requesting Organ	Resolution No.	Voting Pattern	Case Name
14	General Assembly	Es-10/14 of 8 December 2003	90 to 8 with 74 abstentions	the *Legal Consequences of the Construction of a Wall in the Occupied Palestinian Territory*
15	Security Council	284 of 29 July 1970	12 to 0 with 3 abstentions	Legal Consequences for States of the Continued Presence of South Africa in Namibia (South West Africa) Notwithstanding Security Council Resolution 276 (1970)
16	Economic & Social Council	1989/75 of 24 May 1989	24 to 8 with 19 abstentions	Applicability of Article VI, Section 22 of the Convention on the Privileges and Immunities of the United Nations
17	Economic & Social Council	1998/297 of 5 August 1998		Difference Relating to Immunity From Legal Process of a Special Rapporteur of the Commission on Human Rights
18	Committee on Applications for Review of Administrative Tribunal Judgments	Decision of the Committee on Application for Review of United Nations Administrative Tribunal Judgments of 20 June 1972		Application for Review of Judgment No. 158 of the United Nations Administrative Tribunal
19	Committee on Applications for Review of Administrative Tribunal Judgments	Decision of the Committee on Application for Review of United Nations Administrative Tribunal Judgments of 13 July 1981		Application for Review of Judgment No. 273 of the United Nations Administrative Tribunal

Table 3 (continued)

No.	Requesting Organ	Resolution No.	Voting Pattern	Case Name
20	Committee on Applications for Review of Administrative Tribunal Judgments	Decision of the Committee on Application for Review of United Nations Administrative Tribunal Judgments of 23 August 1984		Application for Review of Judgment No. 333 of the United Nations Administrative Tribunal
21	United Nations Education and Scientific Organization (UNESCO)	UNSCO Executive Board Resolution of 25 Nov. 1955	12 to 5 with 4 abstentions	Judgments of the Administrative Tribunal of the ILO Upon Complaints Made Against UNESCO
22	World Health Organization (WHO)	WHO Resolution No. WHA 33.16 of 1980	53 to 43 with 20 abstentions	Interpretation of the Agreement of 25 March 1951 Between WHO and Egypt
23	World Health Organization (WHO	WHO Resolution No. WHA 46.40 of 14 May 1993	73 to 40 with 10 abstentions and 41 absentees	Legality of the Use by a State of Nuclear Weapons in Armed Conflict
15	Security Council	284 of 29 July 1970	12 to 0 with 3 abstentions	Legal Consequences for States of the Continued Presence of South Africa in Namibia (South West Africa) Notwithstanding Security Council Resolution 276 (1970)

Table 4. List of cases which did not come before the Court*

Requesting Organ	Voting Pattern	Case Name
General Assembly	21 to 31 with 2 abstentions	The Treatment of Indians in South Africa, 1946
General Assembly	Proposals of Arab States were rejected in 2 votes: 18 to 25 with 8 abstentions; and 20 to 21 with 13 abstentions	The Palestine Question (1947) in connection with the competence of the General Assembly to recommend the partition of Palestine
General Assembly	21 to 21 with 4 abstentions	The Palestine Question, 1948. In connection with the international status of Palestine after termination of the mandate
General Assembly	9 to 13 with 12 abstentions	The Violation by the Soviet Union of Fundamental Human Rights, in Connection with the Refusal to Grant Certain Exit Visas, 1948
General Assembly	13 to 26 with 19 abstentions	The Palestine Refugees, 1952
General Assembly	15 to 31 with 13 abstentions	The Compatibility with the Statute of The Court of The Amendments in The Statute of The United Nations Administrative Tribunal; introduced after the UNAT advisory opinion of 1954 (1955)
Security Council	4 to 1 with 6 abstentions	The Indonesian Question 1946-1947
Security Council	6 to 1 with 4 abstentions	The Palestine Question 1948 in connection with the international status of Palestine after the termination of the mandate
Security Council	0 to 0 with 0 (weird)	The Complaint of Armed Invasion of Taiwan (Formosa), 1950
Security Council	2 to 7 with 1 abstention	The Question of Cuba, 1962

* Cases, which were not put to vote and cases, which were withdrawn are not shown in this table

4 Reasons for the Limited Recourse to Advisory Opinions

Impediments restricting recourse to advisory opinions should be considered in the light of States' attitudes towards International Law and adjudication, which were extensively analysed in Chapter Seven. One cannot but notice that the UN organs, especially the political organs, are wary of developing a habit of approaching the Court for advisory opinions for various reasons which will be discussed shortly.

4.1 Voting Procedure and Lack of Coordination

The political organs may encounter great difficulties achieving the necessary number of votes to support a request for an advisory opinion.[31] Security Council permanent members may veto a request for an advisory opinion. Similarly, in the General Assembly States, by using the right of abstention or voting negatively, may also impede the successful invocation of the advisory function. Each political organ is constituted of individual State members who, in fact, represent their States' interests, although the total sum of those members are supposed to act in the name of the Organisation. Thus, voting is affected by both *ad hoc* coalitions and independent decision-making by States. The point which should be highlighted here is that the decision to request an advisory opinion is not immune from clashes of will and opinions. Such clashes, depending on their severity, can block entirely a resolution to request an opinion or water down its scope.

There are no express provisions in the UN Charter, in the ICJ's Statute or in the Rules of the Court regarding the majority required to pass a resolution to submit a question to the Court for an advisory opinion. Therefore, the voting procedure must be determined in accordance with the general rules governing voting by the concerned organ.[32] For example, voting in the General Assembly is regulated under Article 18 of the Charter, which distinguishes between the number of votes required on "important questions" as compared with votes on "other questions."[33] As far as the Security Council is concerned, Article 27 of the Charter provides that on all but procedural matters, decisions must be taken by an affirmative vote of

[31] Rosenne, Shabtai, *The World Court: What It Is and How It Works*, Dordrecht, London: Martinus Nijhoff Publishers, 1995, p. 255.

[32] Amr, *supra* note 8, p. 75.

[33] Article 18 provides: "[d]ecisions of the General. Assembly on important questions shall be made by a two-thirds majority of the members present and voting."

Although this Article specifies certain questions as included in the category of 'important' questions, it does not, however, include requests for an advisory opinion as such. It is important to note that Rule 86 of the General Assembly's rules of procedure, defines the term "members present and voting" which appear in paras. 2,3 of Article 18 of the Charter to mean members casting an affirmative or negative vote and so excludes those that abstain or are absent from the vote. The practice of the General Assembly has supported and applied this rule. See UN Doc. A/520/Rev. 15.

nine members, including the concurring votes of the permanent members.[34] The question which is often raised in the General Assembly is how to decide if a decision to request an advisory opinion falls within the category of "important questions" or within the category of "other questions." General Assembly practice does not provide a clear answer. Many General Assembly resolutions requesting advisory opinions were adopted by a two-thirds majority,[35] yet the resolution requesting an opinion on *the Legality of the Threat or Use of Nuclear Weapons* Case was adopted by a simple majority as the above table shows.[36] A similar problem could arise if the Security Council must decide whether the decision to request an advisory opinion is a procedural[37] or non-procedural matter.[38] However, Security Council practice is unclear since that organ has only once approached the Court for an advisory opinion.[39]

Since classifications such as "important", "other questions", "procedural" and "non-procedural" are not clearly defined and remain somewhat vague, some writers suggest that the voting procedure in the General Assembly on the resolution to request an opinion "should be regulated solely by para.3 of Article 18 as a non-important question which requires a simple majority."[40] A similar proposal on Security Council voting procedures suggests considering a request for an opinion as a "procedural matter" so that a negative vote by a Permanent Member could not block a request and thus would allow a wider participation for the Court in the activities of the Organisation.[41]

---

34 Article 27 provides:

1. *Each member of the Security Council shall have one vote.*
2. *Decisions of the Security Council on procedural matters shall be made by an affirmative vote of nine members*
3. *Decisions of the Security Council on all other matters shall be made by an affirmative vote of nine members including the concurring votes of the permanent members; provided that, in decisions under Chapter VI, and under paragraph 3 of Article 52, a party to a dispute shall abstain from voting.*

35 Rosenne, *supra* note 4, p. 301.

36 See also Amr, *supra* note 8, p. 77.

37 This requires an affirmative vote of nine of the fifteen members.

38 On which the veto is applicable.

39 The Security Council request for an advisory opinion on Namibia in 1971 was adopted with the abstention of two permanent members (The Soviet Union and the UK). In this case the Court rejected the argument advanced by the Government of South Africa that the resolution by which the advisory opinion has been requested was invalid due to the abstention of the two permanent members, noting the practice of "voluntary abstention by a permanent member as not constituting a bar to the adoption of the resolutions", ICJ Rep., 1971, para. 22, p. 22.

40 Amr, *supra* note 8, p. 77.

41 Ibid.

With respect to this proposal, it is difficult to envisage that a request for an advisory opinion would be treated by the Security Council as a procedural matter. If the matter were contested, a permanent member could use the veto to block a procedural vote.

4.2 The Autonomy of the Political Organs

Autonomy refers to the "degree of power and control an organization has over its environment, and reflects [its] ability to make decisions."[42] It is to be expected that the UN organs could view requesting advisory opinions as potential threats to their autonomy. Judge Bedjaoui has argued that the political organs, and especially the Security Council, could view consulting the Court as incompatible with their autonomy to determine their own powers.[43] The political organs must also consider that consulting the Court could make them subordinate to an outside organ.[44] This is because of doubts concerning the effect of such a request upon the continued ability of the organ to deal with the matter in question.

Judge Bedjaoui has observed that the Security Council has refrained over a long time from referring to the legal basis of its competence by "omitting any express reference to the chapter and article of the Charter on which its action was founded."[45] This practice may be explained by the Council's fear that the Court, in addressing some sensitive or controversial issues might limit the ways and means available to the political organs for their solution. The Court also might question the propriety of the procedure or the legality of the act of the political organs, and, in effect, subject them to a type of "judicial review."[46]

4.3 Limited Interdependence Between the UN Organs

The UN Charter did not empower any specific organ to interpret the Charter authoritatively.[47] Therefore the General Assembly and the Security Council can decide on any legal question within their spheres of competence. The political organs sometimes have been particularly jealous regarding their rights to be the sole judges of their own competence.[48] Judge Bedjaoui has pointed out that certain delegations in the Security Council, especially those from the former Soviet Union and the Eastern

---

42 Rogers, David; Whetten, David (et al), *Interorganizational Coordination: Theory, Research, and Implementation*, Ames: Iowa State University, 1982, p. 88.

43 Bedjaoui, Mohammed, *The New World Order and the Security Council: Testing the Legality of its Acts*, Dordrecht; Boston: Martinus Nijhoff Publishers, 1994, p. 19.

44 Ibid.

45 Ibid, p. 21.

46 See Section 6 in Chapter Three, *supra*.

47 See Section 3.1 in Chapter Six, *supra*.

48 Pomerance, *supra* note 15, p. 270.

Bloc, have often insisted upon the political nature of the Council's competence and its immunity from legal censure, especially by an organ such as the Court.[49]

Commentators have observed that in practice the political organs, acting in a quasi-judicial role, can decide what is legal or illegal by means of their resolutions.[50] The Security Council can even consider establishing tribunals if deemed necessary to decide questions before it.[51] According to this view, there is only limited need to refer to the Court's advisory function. Pomerance has rightly observed that the UN organs have been wary of the Court because they "feared any crystallization and consequent restriction of their absolute freedom to set their own precedents, on a pragmatic basis."[52] However, the fact remains as stated by Judge Higgins that "[a]ll institutional structures like to be masters of their own procedures. The longer they are in existence the less they are likely to want advice on their practices from the Court."[53]

4.4 The Effect of the "Cold War"

Due to the Cold War many proposals for requesting advisory opinions from the Court were not adopted because of the continued refusal of the Eastern Bloc to support them. In fact, the political environment in which the UN functioned in those years made political resolutions preferable to judicial resolutions.[54] One Commentator remarked that:[55]

---

49 Bedjaoui, supra note 43, p. 20.

50 Take for instance: the Security Council Resolution 687(1991) relating to Iraq's invasion of Kuwait; the Security Council & the General Assembly references to the illegality of changes in the status of territory including the South African administration in Namibia; the retention of territory occupied by Israel in 1967; and the status of northern Cyprus occupied by Turkey in 1974. See Brownlie, Ian, "International Law at the Fiftieth Anniversary of the United Nations", Chapter XV "The Role of the Security Council and the Rule of Law", 255 *RCADI*, 1995, pp. 211-212.

51 A finding made under Article 39 of the Charter, read in conjunction with Article 41 of the Charter, which states that "[t]he Security Council may decide what measures not involving the use of armed force are to be employed to give effect to its decisions", would lead to the conclusion that the Security Council can create tribunals. See Reisman, W. M., "*The Supervisory Jurisdiction of the International Court of Justice: International Arbitration and International Adjudication*", 258 *RCADI*, 1996, p. 122.

52 Pomerance, *supra* note 15, p. 272.

53 Higgins, Rosalyn, "A comment on the current health of Advisory Opinions", in Lowe, Vaughan and Fitzmaurice, Malgosia, (eds.), *Fifty Years of the International Court of Justice: Essays in honour of Sir Robert Jennings*, Cambridge: Grotius Publications, 1996, p. 576.

54 De Wet, Erika, *The Chapter VII Powers of the United Nations Security Council*, Oxford and Portland Oregon: Hart Publishing 2004, p. 49.

55 Greig, D.W, "The Advisory Jurisdiction of the International Court and the Settlement of Disputes between States", 15 *ICLQ*, 1966, pp. 139-140.

> *Once the actual text of the Charter had become the focal point of a universal conflict between two formidable power* blocs *it would be naïve to believe that a strictly legal interpretation of the disputed text would serve to relive tension.*

Consequently, it has been suggested that the effect of the Cold War was obvious in "the use-or misuse by the General Assembly of the advisory competence of the Court, especially in the early years of the United Nations."[56] The former Soviet Union almost always opposed any recourse to the Court and generally tried to keep controversies within the Security Council where it could exercise its veto.

5 Suggestions for Improving the Advisory Function

This study has avoided commenting at length on the standard suggestions to improve the advisory function by expanding the circle of organs authorised to request advisory opinions. These suggestions commonly place great emphasis on giving States,[57] international organisations,[58] national courts[59] and the Secretary General[60] the right to request advisory opinions and have already attracted extensive scholarly attention.

---

[56] Rosenne, Shabtai, "The Cold War and the International Court of Justice: A Review Essay of Stephen M. Schwebel's Justice in International Law", 34 *VJIL*, 1995, p. 671.

[57] Mosler, Hermann & Rudolf Bernhardt (eds.), *Judicial Settlements of International Disputes International Court of Justice, Other Courts and Tribunals, Arbitration and Conciliation: An International Symposium*, Berlin; Heidelberg; New York: Springer-Verlag, 1974. p. 259.

[58] Sztucki, Jerzy, "International Organizations as Parties to Contentious Proceedings before the International Court of Justice" in: Muller, A.S & Raic D. *et al.* (eds.), *The International Court of Justice: Its Future Role After Fifty Years*, The Hague; Boston; London: Martinus Nijhoff Publishers, 1997, pp. 141-168; Szasz, Paul C, "Granting International Organizations *Ius Standi* in the International Court of Justice", ibid, pp. 169-189; Seidl-Hohenveldern, Ignaz, "Access of International Organizations to the International Court of Justice", ibid, pp. 189-204.

[59] Schwebel, Stephen M., "Preliminary Rulings by the International Court of Justice at the Instance of National Courts", 28 *VJIL*, 1988, p. 495; Rosenne, Shabtai, "Preliminary Rulings by the International Court of Justice at the Instance of National Courts: A Reply", 29 *VJIL*, 1989, p. 40; Gross, Leo, "The International Court of Justice: Consideration of Requirement for Enhancing it Role in the International Legal Order" in: Gross, (ed.), *The Future of the International Court of Justice*, 1976, pp. 28-29; McLaughlin, William, "Allowing Federal Courts Access to International Court of Justice Advisory Opinion: Critique and Proposal", 6 *Hastings International and Comparative Law Review*, 1983, pp. 745-772.

[60] Schwebel, Stephen M, "Authorizing the Secretary-General of the United Nations to Request Advisory Opinion", 78 *AJIL*, 1984, p. 4, Amr; *supra* note 8, pp. 57-64; Bedjaoui, *supra* note 43, pp. 78-79.

However, as many scholars have pointed out, it is doubtful that such an expansion of the organs authorised to request opinions from the Court would enhance the Court's advisory jurisdiction.[61] In fact, a great deal is said about expansion while little is said about coordination and how it can be important.

On the other hand, a suggestion has been made for introducing a system of "advisory arbitration"[62] by the ICJ in order to effectively increase the scope of Court's advisory jurisdiction.[63] Despite the value of this suggestion, it could be argued that the advisory function was designed primarily to assist the UN organs with their work and not to settle disputes between States, especially if such disputes are not of interest to the work of the Organisation itself. The strength of the Court's advisory function has been in playing an "organisational role" through rendering advice on difficulties facing the UN. Therefore, any new quasi-contentious function could be better addressed by means of the Court's contentious jurisdiction.

Moreover, given the fact that the Court's primary mission is to contribute to the purposes of the UN, Richard Falk has proposed that the Court should act as an "academy of jurists" to make it more responsive to the "prevailing normative sensitivities of the General Assembly."[64] However, this proposal has several flaws. First, the Court cannot respond to the prevailing "sensitivities" of the General Assembly unless these are placed in issue before it.[65] Second, Falk's view means that the Court should act as a political not a judicial body, a role which the Court avoids. It is a court of law, not of political expediency. Indeed, the Court can contribute and it is, in fact, contributing to the purposes of the UN without being an "academy of jurists." It accomplishes this by carrying out its role as the principal judicial organ of the UN and by its participation within its competence in the activities of the UN. However, the UN and its member States should coordinate more effectively with the Court to give it more chances to participate in the achievement of UN principles and purposes. As Sir Robert Jennings has pointed out, the ICJ will be strong when resort to it on legal issues "is normal, habitual, routine, not exceptional."[66]

---

61 Pomerance, *supra* note 15, pp. 376-38. Keith, Kenneth, *The Extent of the Advisory Jurisdiction of the International Court of Justice*, Leyden: A.W. Sijthoff, 1971, p. 242.

62 So called "advisory arbitration" was practiced during the PCIJ era. This method is basically determined by the concerned States who agree in advance to be bound by the Court's rendered opinion.

63 Sugihara, Takane, "The Advisory Function of the International Court of Justice", 17 *JAIL*, 1973, pp. 23-50.

64 Falk, Richard, *Reviving the World Court*, Charlottesville: University Press of Virginia, 1986, pp. 182- 191.

65 Scobbie, Iain, *Legal Reasoning and The Judicial Function in the International Court*, Ph.D. Thesis, Cambridge University, 1991, p. 25.

66 Jennings, Sir Robert Y., "The Proper Work and Purposes of the International Court of Justice", in: Muller, A. S.; Raic, D.; and Thuránszky, J.M. (eds.), *The International Court Of Justice: Its Future Role After Fifty Years*, The Hague; Boston; London: Martinus Nijhoff Publishers, 1997, p. 42.

Lastly, some scholars have suggested establishing specialised chambers to deal with advisory opinions similar to those constituted for contentious proceedings in accordance with Articles 26-29 of the Statute.[67] Such suggestions seem to misconceive the nature and role of the advisory function: First, establishing chambers would place the emphasis on the interests of the concerned States rather than on the interest of the Organisation itself. Second, the parties to an advisory opinion are, in some sense, the whole international community. This is underlined by the wide range of States, international organisations and parties to agreements directly affected by opinions which take part in proceedings before the Court. Lastly, one must remember that at the inception of the ICJ's advisory jurisdiction, it was decided that the advisory opinion would be rendered by all the judges sitting together.[68]

6 Towards the Future

The standard diagnoses of the advisory function have criticised it for its inability to resolve disputes, even if it succeeds in providing a substantial legal opinion. These diagnoses have led some scholars to suggest that when a request is adopted by a majority rather than unanimously, the Court ought not to give an opinion.[69] One could argue that such suggestions, which might be inspired by the past disappointing experiences with some advisory opinions, tend to over generalise without employing adequate perspective.[70] Moreover, critics often misconceive the real role of the advisory function, which is "designed primarily to assist the Security Council and the General Assembly in the discharge of their duties of conciliating and reporting upon disputes submitted to them by affording them an authoritative legal opinion upon points of law."[71]

Other scholars praise the legal statements of the Court as authoritative statements of law contributing to the development of the Organisation, but at the same time criticise the opinions as ineffective because they were not implemented due to an opposing minority in the requesting organ.[72] The reasons behind these divergent views and how scholars can reconcile their appraisals of the function should be objects of concern.

---

67 Amr, *supra* note 8, p. 381.

68 See Chapter One, *supra.*

69 Greig, D.W., "The Advisory Jurisdiction of the International Court of Justice and the Settlement of Disputes between States", 15 *ICLQ*, 1966, pp. 325-368.

70 Advisory opinions that did not succeed in settling the related disputes include the *Admissions* cases, *Peace Treaties* case, *Expenses* case and *South West Africa* cases.

71 Singh Nagendra , *Recent Trends in the Development of International Law and organization promoting Inter-State Co-Operation and World Peace*, S. Chand and Co., 1969, p. 179.

72 Rosenne, *supra* note 4, pp. 1059-1060 ; Rosenne, Shabtai, "The Contribution of the International Court of Justice to the United Nations", 35 *IJIL,* 1995, pp. 67-76.

The problem is with our perspectives and expectations of the function. These two issues are strongly related, as a proper perspective on the role of the function will put the expectations in their proper place. Even where an opinion of the Court has been unable to solve a particular problem, the advisory opinion should not be considered useless or marginal. The opinions of the Court in the *Admissions, Expenses, Namibia*, and *Western Sahara* cases were unable to settle the disputes that had prompted referrals to the Court, but the opinions provided international society and decision makers with very valuable and insightful dicta on various international legal issues.[73]

What we need, then, is to change our perception of the advisory function. The role of the function is to clarify the law: "to remove ambiguities and to provide guidance for future behavior of the parties."[74] From this perspective it can be said without exaggeration that the advisory function has played an important role in assisting the UN. In this regard, it is worth saying that what was expected from the advisory function at San Francisco has been more than achieved, particularly where the function has led to new contribution to International Law.[75] This phenomenon has been referred to by Sir Hersch Lauterpacht as "a heterogeny of aims" where "[i]nstitutions set up for the achievement of definite purposes grow to fulfil tasks not wholly identical with those which were in the minds of their authors at the time of their creation."[76]

Since San Francisco the advisory function has proved a successful instrument for providing authoritative legal opinions to aid the UN and its organs in carrying out the objectives of the Organisation. Nevertheless the exercise of the function may still be improved. To enhance the usefulness of the function every actor in the process should carry out its own duties, restraints and responsibilities towards the Organisation.

The UN organs must place their complete faith in the Court's advisory function as an ultimate means for deciding important legal questions despite the availability of other channels to resolve legal problems. However, the organs should not turn to the Court for an opinion unless there is organisational interest for doing so. The Court, as the principal judicial organ of the UN, must also "participate at the highest level in the attainment of the Organisation's purposes, acting in consultation

73 See Chapter Six, *supra*.

74 Sohn, Louis B., "Peaceful Settlement of Disputes" in: Janis, Mark (ed.), *International Courts for the Twenty-First Century*, Dordrecht; Boston; London: Martinus Nijhoff Publishers, 1992, p. 5.

75 In contrast to this view Scobbie argues that the claim that international courts have an extensive role to play in the development of international law is a "central myth". Scobbie, *supra* note 65, p. 1.

76 Lauterpacht, Hersch, *The Development of International Law by the International Court*, London: Stevens and Sons, 1958, pp. 4-5.

and close collaboration with the other principal organs.[77] This participation can be carried out only with due deference to the autonomy of each UN organ.[78]

The commitment towards achieving the purposes of the Charter should be the ultimate joint goal for all organs. What is needed in this context, however, is coordination. If this will be difficult to obtain, it is also difficult to believe that the advisory function can be made more effective without coordination. The successes of the functional relationship between the Court and the political organs of the UN depends largely upon their coordination to achieve their shared tasks.

It is submitted, therefore, that international organisations should make full use of the advisory function, taking into consideration the safeguards of the advisory function recommended at San Francisco.[79] The advisory function can only operate effectively when its 'clients' are prepared to coordinate with it. Such coordination involving UN member States and the political organs would give the Court a chance to meet the demands of the international community by clarifying important legal issues.

It has been suggested that it would greatly help the international legal order if the Court, for instance, had the chance to clarify the concept of *jus cogens.*[80] It could be argued that the Court in the *Legality of the Threat or Use of Nuclear Weapons* case had this chance but failed to take it by not addressing the status of the rules of humanitarian law under consideration. However, the Court cannot be wholly blamed because the question addressed to it had failed to include this point.[81] The Court is not a legislative body, and the scope of an opinion is limited and determined by the content of the request. This example shows how coordination between the actors is necessary. The requesting organ must be sure that the request is the product of careful drafting,[82] and formulated in a manner which will provide an opinion which would yield the needed clarification for the requesting organ.[83] The Court for its part has to adopt a liberal interpretation of the request in order to offer maximum assistance to a fellow organ.

---

77 Couvreur, Philippe, "The Effectiveness of the International Court of Justice in the Peaceful Settlement of International Disputes" in: Muller, A. S.; Raic, D.; and Thuránszky, J.M. (eds.), *The International Court of Justice*: *Its Future Role After Fifty Years*, The Hague; Boston; London: Martinus Nijhoff Publishers, 1997, p. 84.

78 Ibid.

79 See Chapter One, *supra.*

80 Gowlland-Debbas, Vera, "Judicial Insights into Fundamental Values and Interests of the International Community" in: Muller, A. S.; Raic, D.; Thuránszky J. M. (eds.), *The International Court of Justice*: *Its Future Role After Fifty Years*, The Hague; Boston; London: Martinus Nijhoff Publishers, 1997, p. 364.

81 For details about the implication of this advisory opinion see Section 7 in Chapter Six *supra.*

82 See Chapters Four and Five *supra.*

83 Rosenne, *supra* note 4, pp. 355-360.

To be sure, the relationship between the Court and the other UN organs is still characterised by caution. However, new thinking on proper coordination based on the ultimate goal of achieving the interests of the Organisation should be encouraged, even if this goal clashes on occasion with the interests of individual UN organs. This argument is supported by the German doctrine of *Organtreue,* which states that organs of an organisation must exercise their powers with mutual respect for each other and that they must be guided by the purpose and structure of the Organisation.[84]

7 Suggestions for Further Research and Concluding Remarks

This study suggests further areas for research. These include a systemic study of the ICJ's reasoning in advisory cases, which may differ from that in contentious ones. Such studies are much needed to determine how the reasoning of the Court has developed the law through advisory cases and to identify weakness in the reasoning itself. It could be argued that there were many advisory cases where the Court missed the opportunity to clarify some legal concepts that would have been of great help to the international community. An analysis of these cases would be of importance in further development of International Law and would complement the already substantial work that has been done on the ICJ's reasoning in contentious cases.[85]

One of the peculiar features of the ICJ's advisory opinions is that although they are not binding in the strict sense, they carry an authoritativeness which cannot lightly be ignored. Certainly, the prestige of the Court is a contributory factor. However, The quality of the judicial reasoning of the Court in advisory cases plays a dominant role in determining the authoritativeness of opinions and, therefore, the extent to which they meet expectations of the particular advisee.

An advisory opinion, in contrast to a judgment in a contentious case, addresses a wide section of the international community. Therefore the Court in giving an opinion not only must address the advisee directly concerned with the opinion, but also all those parties who may be affected by the Court's clarification of the law. Put differently, the Court must consider the concerns of the international community at large and strive to satisfy "the desire for completely non-political treatment of a matter, and its solution on an articulated basis of law."[86]

---

84 See Malanczuk, "Reconsidering the Relationship Between the ICJ and the Security Council" in: Heere, Wybo p. (ed.), *International Law and the Hague's 750th Anniversary*, The Hague: T.M.C. Asser Press, 1999, p. 91.

85 See Scobbie *supra* note 65; Jennings, *supra* note 17; Prott, Lyndell V., *The Latent Power of Culture and the International Judge*, Abingdon, Oxon: Professional Books Ltd, 1979.

86 Rosenne, *supra* note 4, p. 163.

Selected Bibliography

This selected bibliography contains most of the academic works which appear in the footnotes.

Books

Amerasinghe, Chittharanjan F., Principles of the Institutional Law of International Organizations, Cambridge University Press, 1996.

Amerasinghe, Chittharanjan F., *Jurisdiction of International Tribunals*, The Hague; London: Kluwer Law International, 2003.

Amr, Mohamed S., *The Role of the International Court of Justice as a Principal Judicial Organ of the United Nations*, The Hague: Kluwer Law International, 2003.

Anand, Ram p.°, *Compulsory Jurisdiction of the International Court of Justice*, London: Asia Publishing House, 1961.

Barak, Aharon, *Judicial Discretion*, New Haven: Yale University Press, 1989.

Baxi, Upendra, *The Future of Human Rights*, Oxford University Press, 2002.

Bedeian, Arthur G., *Organizations: Theory and Analysis*, The Dryden Press, 2nd edition, 1984.

Bedjaoui, Mohammed, *The New World Order and the Security Council: Testing the Legality of Its Acts*, Dordrecht; Boston: Martinus Nijhoff Publishers. 1994.

Bentwich, Norman & Martin, Andrew, *A Commentary on the Charter of the United Nations*, 2nd impression, New York: Kraus Reprint Co., 1969.

Berman, Harold J. & Greiner, William R., *The Nature and Functions of Law*, Brooklyn: Foundation Press, 1966.

Blokker, Niels & Muller, Sam (eds.), *Towards More Effective Supervision by International Organizations. Essays in Honour of Henry G. Schermers*, Dordrecht; Boston; London: Martinus Nijhoff Publishers, 1994.

Bodie, Thomas J., *Politics and the Emergence of an Activist International Court of Justice*, Westport, Connecticut; London: Praeger, 1995.

Bowett, Derek W., *The Law of the International Institutions*, London: Stevens and Sons, 4th edition, 1982.

Bowett, Derek W., *The International Court of Justice: Process, Practice and Procedure*, London: British Institute of International and Comparative law, 1997.

Brownlie, Ian, *Principles of Public International Law*, Oxford: Oxford University Press, 6th edition, 2003.

Cassese, Antonio (ed.), *UN Law/ Fundamental Rights: Two Topics in International Law*, Alphen aan den Rijn, the Netherlands: Sijthoff and Noordhoff, 1979.

Castaneda, Jorge, *Legal effects of United Nations Resolutions*, New York: Columbia University, 1969.

Cheng, Bin, *General Principles of Law: As Applied by International Courts and Tribunals*, Cambridge: Grotius Publications limited, 1987.

Ciobanu, Dan, *Preliminary Objections Related to the Jurisdiction of the United Nations Political Organs*, The Hague: Nijhoff, 1975.

Conforti, Benedetto, *The Law and Practice of the United Nations*, The Hague; London: Kluwer Law International, 2nd edition, 2000.

De Visscher, Charles, *Theory and Reality in Public International Law*, Percy E. Corbett (translator), Princeton University Press, Revised Edition, 1968.

Deware, Robert & Aiken, Michael et al., *Coordinating Human Services*, San Francisco; London: Jossey-Bass Publishers, 1975.

De Wet, Erika, *The Chapter VII Powers of the United Nations Security Council*, Oxford; Portland Oregon: Hart Publishing, 2004.

Dijkzeul, Dennis, *The Management of Multilateral Organizations*, Boston: Kluwer Law International, 1997.

Dunne, Michael, *The United States and the World Court, 1920-1935*, London: Pinter, 1988.

Elias, Taslim O., *New Horizons in International Law*, Dobbs Ferry, New York: Oceana Publications Inc., 1979.

El-Rashidy, A., *The Advisory Jurisdiction of the International Court of Justice*, Cairo: Al-Haia Al-Masria Al-Amaa Lelketab, 1992. [in Arabic].

Evans, Malcolm D. (ed.), *International Law*, Oxford: Oxford University Press, 2003.

Eyffinger, Arthur, *The International Court of Justice, 1946-1996*, The Hague; London: Kluwer Law International, 1996.

Falk, Richard, *Reviving the World Court*, Charlottesville: University Press of Virginia, 1986.

Ferencz, Benjamin B., *Enforcing International Law: A Way to World Peace: A Documentary History and Analysis*, London; New York: Oceana Publications, Volume 2, 1983.

Fitzmaurice, Gerald G., *The Law and Procedure of the International Court of Justice*, Cambridge: Grotius Publications limited, 2 Volumes, 1986.

Foda, Ezzeldin, *The Projected Arab Court of Justice. A Study in Regional Jurisdiction with Specific Reference to the Muslim Law of Nations*, The Hague: Martinus Nijhoff, 1957.

Franck, Thomas, *Judging the World Court*, New York: Priority Press Publications, 1986.

Friedmann, Wolfgang G., *The Changing Structure of International Law*, New York: Colombia University Press, 1964.

Fuller, Lon L., *Anatomy of Law*, New York: F. A. Praeger, 1968.

Gamble, John K. & Fischer, Dana D., *The International Court of Justice: An Analysis of a Failure*, Lexington, Massachusetts; London: D.C. Heath and Company, 1976.

Gauthier, David p.°, *Practical Reasoning: The Structure and Foundations of Prudential and Moral Arguments and their Exemplification in Discourse*, Oxford: Oxford University Press, 1963.

Goodrich, Leland & Simon, Anne, *Charter of the United Nations: Commentary and Documents*, New York: Colombia University Press, 1969.

Goodspeed, Stephen S., *The Nature and Functions of International Organizations*, New York: Oxford University Press, 1967.

Gray, Christine D., *Judicial Remedies in International Law*, Oxford: Clarendon Press, 1987.

Gray, Christopher B. (ed.), *The Philosophy of Law: An Encyclopedia*, New York; London: Garland, 2 Volumes, 1999.

Greenberg, Jerald & Baron, Robert A., *Behavior in Organizations*, Prentice-Hall, 8th edition, 2003.

Gross, Leo (ed.), *The future of the International Court of Justice*, Dobbs Ferry, New York: Oceana Publications, 1976.

Halderman, John W., *The United Nations and the Rule of Law: Charter Development Through the Handling of International Disputes and Situations*, Dobbs Ferry, New York: Oceana Publications, 1966.

Hart, Herbert L., *The Concept of Law*, Oxford: Clarendon Press, 1994.

Heere, Wybo p. (ed.), *International law and the Hague's 750th Anniversary*, T.M.C, Asser Press, 1999, p. 405

Higgins, Rosalyn, *The Development of International Law Through the Political Organs of the United Nations*, Oxford University Press, 1963.

Higgins, Rosalyn, *Problem and Process: International Law and How We Use It*, Oxford: Clarendon Press, 1994.

Honoré, Tony, *Making Law Bind: Essays Legal and Philosophical*, Oxford: Clarendon Press, 1987.

Hudson, Manley O., *The Permanent Court of International Justice, 1920-1942*, New York: The Macmillan Company, 1943.

Hudson, Manley O., *International Tribunals: Past and Future*, Washington, [D.C.]: Carnegie Endowment for International Peace and Brookings Institution, 1944.

Jenks, Clarence W., *The Prospects of International Adjudication*, London: Steven and Sons, 1964.

Idris, Kamil & Bartolo, Michael, *A Better United Nations for the New Millennium*, The Hague; London: Kluwer Law Int'l, 2000

Jennings, Sir Robert & Watts, Sir Arthur (eds.), *Oppenheim's International Law*, London: Longman, Volume 1, 9th edition, 1996.

Kaikobad, Kaiyan H., *The International Court of Justice and Judicial Review: A Study of the Court's Powers with Respect to Judgments of the ILO and UN Administrative Tribunals*, The Hague; London: Kluwer Law International, 2000.

Keith, Kenneth, *The Extent of the Advisory Jurisdiction of the International Court of Justice*, Leyden: A.W. Sijthoff, 1971.

Kelsen, Hans, *Peace Through Law*, Chapel Hill: The University of North Carolina Press, 1944.

Kelsen, Hans, *The Law of the United Nations: A Critical Analysis of Its Fundamental Problems*, London: Steven and Sons Ltd, 1951.

Klabbers, Jan, *An Introduction to International Institutional Law*, Cambridge: Cambridge University Press, 2002.

Knop, Karen, *Diversity and Self-Determination in International Law*, Cambridge University Press, 2002.

Lauterpacht, Hersch, *The Function of Law in International Community*, Oxford: Clarendon Press, 1933.

Lauterpacht, Hersch, *The Development of International Law by the International Court*, London: Stevens and Sons Ltd, 1958.

Lewis, David K., *Convention: A Philosophical Study*, Cambridge [Mass.]: Harvard University Press, 1969.

Lissitzyn, Oliver J., *The International Court of Justice: Its Role in the Maintenance of International Peace and Security*, New York: Carnegie Endowment for International Peace, 1951.

Lissitzyn, Oliver J., *International Law Today and Tomorrow*, Dobbs Ferry, New York: Oceana Publication, 1965.

Merrills, John G., *International Dispute Settlement*, Cambridge: Cambridge University Press, 3rd edition, 1998.

Miller, David H., *The Drafting of the Covenant*, New York: G. p. Putnam's Sons, 2 Volumes, 1928.

Mosler, Hermann & Bernhardt, Rudolf (eds.), *International Court of Justice, Other Courts and Tribunals, Arbitration and Conciliation: An International Symposium*, Berlin; Heidelberg; New York: Springer-Verlag, 1974.

Muller, Sam A., *International Organizations and Their Host States: Aspect of Their Legal Relationship*, The Hague; Boston: Kluwer Law International, 1995.

Nantwi, Emmanuel K., *The Enforcement of International Judicial Decisions and Arbitral Awards in Public International Law*, Leyden: A. W. Sijthoff, 2nd printing, 1966.

O'Connell, Mary E. (ed.), *International Disputes Settlement*, Aldershot: Ashgate Dartmouth, 2003.

Oduntan, Gbenga, *The Law and Practice of the International Court of Justice (1945-1996): A Critique of the Contentious and Advisory Jurisdictions*, Enugu: Fourth Dimension, 1999.

Parsons, Talcott, *Structure and Process in Modern Society*, The Free Press of Glencoe, 3rd printing, 1964.

Pasqualucci, Jo M., *The Practice and Procedure of the Inter-American Court of Human Rights*, Cambridge: Cambridge University Press, 2003.

Patel, Bimal N., *The World Court Reference Guide: Judgments, advisory opinions and orders of the Permanent Court of International Justice and the International Court of Justice 1922-2000*, The Hague; London: Kluwer Law International, 2002.

Peck, Connie & Lee, Roy S. (eds.), *Increasing the Effectiveness of the International Court of Justice: Proceedings of the ICJ/UNITAR Colloquium to Celebrate the 50th Anniversary of the Court*, The Hague; Boston; London: Martinus Nijhoff Publishers, 1997.

Peffer, Jefffrey & Salanicik, Gerald R., *The External Control of Organizations: A Resource Dependence Perspective*, Stanford, California: Stanford University Press, 2003.

Perrow, Charles, *Organizational Analysis: A Sociological View*, Great Britain: Tavistock Publications, 1970.

Pogany, Istvan S., *The Security Council and the Arab-Israeli Conflict*, Aldershot: Gower, 1984.

Pogany, Istvan S., *The Arab League and Peacekeeping in the Lebanon*, Aldershot: Gower Publishing, 1987.

Pogany, Istvan S. (ed.), *Nuclear Weapons and International Law*, Aldershot: Gower, 1987.

Pomerance, Michla, *The Advisory Function of the International Court in the League and U.N. Eras*, Baltimore; London: John Hopkins University Press, 1973.

Pratap, Dharma, *The Advisory Jurisdiction of the International Court*, Oxford: Clarendon Press, 1972.

Prott, Lyndell V., *The Latent Power of Culture and the International Judge*, Abingdon, Oxon: Professional Books Ltd, 1979.

Robbins, Stephen p.°, *Organization Theory: Structure, Design, and Applications*, Prentice-Hall International Inc, 3rd edition, 1990.

Rogers, David & Whetten, David et al., *Interorganizational Coordination: Theory, Research, and Implementation*, Ames: Iowa State University, 1982.

Rosenne, Shabtai, *The International Court of Justice. An Essay in Political and Legal Theory*, Leyden: A. W. Sijthoff, 1957.

Rosenne, Shabtai, *The Law and Practice of the International Court*, Leyden: A.W. Sijthoff, 2 Volumes, 1965.

Rosenne, Shabtai (Compiler), *Documents of the International Court of Justice*, Leiden: A.W. Sijthoff, 1974.

Rosenne, Shabtai, *Developments in the Law of Treaties: 1945-1986*, Cambridge: Cambridge University Press, 1989.

Rosenne, Shabtai, *The World Court: What It Is and How It Works*, Dordrecht, London: Martinus Nijhoff Publishers, 1995.

Rosenne, Shabtai, *The Law and Practice of the International Court, 1920-1996*, The Hague; London: Martinus Nijhoff Publishers, 4 Volumes, 1997.

Russell, Ruth A., *A History of the United Nations Charter. The Role of the United States 1940-1945*, Washington: The Brookings Institution, 1958.

Sands, Philippe & Klein, Pierre, *Bowett's Law of International Institutions*, London: Sweet & Maxwell, 2001.

Sands, Philippe, *Principles of International Environmental Law*, Cambridge: Cambridge University Press, 2nd edition, 2003.

Sarooshi, Danesh, *The United Nations and the Development of Collective Security: The Delegation by the UN Security Council of Its Chapter VII Powers*, Oxford: Oxford University Press, 1999.

Schelling, Thomas C., *The Strategy of Conflict*, Cambridge [Mass.]: Harvard University Press, 15th printing, 1995.

Schermers, Henry & Blokker, Niels, *International Institutional Law: Unity Within Diversity*, The Hague; London: M. Nijhoff, 1995.

Scheweble, Stephen M., *Justice in International Law: Selected Writings of Stephen M. Schwebel*, Cambridge: Grotius Publications, 1994.

Schwarzenberger, Georg, *International Law*, London: Stevens and Sons, Volume 1, 1957.

Schweigman, David, *The Authority of the Security Council Under Chapter VII of the UN Charter: Legal Limits and the Role of the International Court of Justice*, The Hague; London; Boston: Kluwer Law International, 2001.

Sharan, Sarojini, *The International Court of Justice. A Study Based on Court's Activities*, Calcutta: New Age Publications, 1971.

Shaw, Malcolm N., *International Law*, Cambridge: Cambridge University Press, 5th edition, 2003.

Shihata, Ibrahim F., *The Power of the International Court to Determine Its Own Jurisdiction*: *Compétence de la Compétence*, The Hague: M. Nijhoff, 1965.

Simma, Bruno et al. (eds.), *The Charter of the United Nations: A Commentary*, Oxford University Press, 2nd edition, 2002.

Singh, Nagendra, *Recent Trends in the Development of International Law and Organisation Promoting Inter-State Co-Operation and World Peace*, Delhi: S. Chand and Co., 1969.

Smuts, Christiaan Jan, *The League of Nations*; *A Practical Suggestion*, London; New York: Hodder and Stoughton, 1918.

Stone, Julius, *Legal Controls of International Conflict*: A Treatise on the Dynamics of Disputes- and War- Law, Sydney: Maitland Publications, 2nd impression, 1959.

Thompson, James D., *Organizations in Action: Social Science Bases of Administrative Theory*, New York: McGraw Hill, 1967.

Ullmann-Margalit, Edna, *The Emergence of Norms*, Oxford: Clarendon Press, 1977.

Verzijl, J.H.W., *The Jurisprudence of the World Court*: *A Case by Case Commentary*, Leyden: A. W. Sijthoff, 2 Volumes, 1965.

Walker, David, *Oxford Companion to Law*, Oxford: Clarendon Press, 1980.

Journal Articles, Chapters in Books, and Lectures

Abi-Saab, Georges, "The International Court as a World Court", in: Lowe, Vaughan and Fitzmaurice, Malgosia (eds.), *Fifty years of the International Court of Justice*: *Essays in Honour of Sir Robert Jennings*, Grotius Publications, Cambridge University Press, 1996, pp. 3-17.

Abi-Saab, Georges, "On Discretion: Reflection on the Nature of the Consultative Function of the International Court of Justice", in: Boisson De Chazournes, Laurence & Sands, Philippe (eds.), *International Law, the International Court of Justice and Nuclear Weapons*, 1999, pp. 36-51.

Ago, Roberto, "Binding Advisory Opinions of the International Court of Justice", 85 *AJIL* 1991, pp. 439-51.

Akande, Dapo, "Nuclear weapons, Unclear Law? Deciphering the Nuclear Weapons Advisory Opinion of the International Court", 68 *BYIL*, 1997, pp. 165-215.

Akande, Dapo, "The International Court of Justice and the Security Council: Is there Room for Judicial Control of Decisions of the Political Organs of the United Nations?" 46 *ICLQ*, 1997, pp. 309-343.

Akande, Dapo, "The Competence of International Organizations and the Advisory Jurisdiction of the International Court of Justice", 9 *EJIL*, No. 3, 1998, pp. 437-467.

Akande, Dapo, "International Organizations", in: Evans, Malcolm D. (ed.), *International Law*, Oxford University Press, 2003, pp. 269-299.

Akehurst, Michael, "The Hierarchy of The Source of International Law", 47 *BYIL*, 1947-75, pp. 273-285.

Alvarez, Jose E., "Judging the Security Council", 90 *AJIL*, 1996, pp. 1-39.

Amerasinghe, C.F., "The Ways and Means of International Organizations", in: Dupuy, René-Jean (ed.), *A Handbook on International Organizations*, Dordrecht; Boston; London: Martinus Nijhoff Publishers, 2nd edition, 1998, pp. 365-373.

Anand, R. p.°, "Attitudes of the 'New' Asian-African Countries Toward the International Court of Justice", in: Snyder, F.E. & Sathirathai, S. (eds.), *Third World Attitudes Toward International Law: An Introduction*, Dordrecht: M. Nijhoff, 1987, pp. 163-177.

Baxter, Richard R., "Introduction", 11 *VJIL*, 1970-71, pp. 291-5.

Beckett, W.E., "Decisions of the Permanent Court of International Justice on Points of Law and Procedure of General Application", 11 *BYIL,* 1930, pp. 1-55.

Bederman, David J., "The Souls International Organizations: Legal Personality and the Lighthouse at Cape Spartel", 36 *VJIL*, 1996, pp. 275-378.

Bedjaoui, Mohammed, "Introduction: On the Efficacy of International Organizations: Some Variations on an Inexhaustable Theme", in: Blokker, Niels & Muller, Sam (eds.), *Towards More Effective Supervision by International Organizations. Essays in Honour of Henry G. Schermers*, Dordrecht; Boston; London: Martinus Nijhoff Publishers, Volume 1, 1994, pp. 7-28.

Bedjaoui, Mohammed, "The *Forum Prorogatum* Before the International Court of Justice: The Resources of an Institution or the Hidden Face of Consensualism", ICJ YearBook, 1996-97, pp. 216-234. (Speech before the Sixth Committee of the UNGA in 1996 as president of the ICJ)

Bedjaoui, Mohammed, "The Contribution of the International Court of Justice Towards Keeping and Restoring Peace", in: Conflict *Resolution*: *New Approaches and Methods*, Paris: UNESCO Publishing, 2000, pp. 9-21.

Bedjaoui, Mohammed, "Expediency in the Decisions of the International Court of Justice", 71 *BYIL*, 2000, pp. 1-28.

Bekker, Peter H., "The 1998 Judicial Activity of the International Court of Justice", 93 *AJIL*, 1999, pp. 534-538.

Bernhardt, Rudolf, "Interpretation in International Law", in: Bernhardt, R. (ed.), *Encyclopedia of Public International Law*, Amsterdam: Elsevier Science B.V., Volume II, 1995, pp. 1416-1427.

Bilder, Richard B., "International Dispute Settlement and The Role of International Adjudication", in: Damrosch, Lori F. (ed.), *The International Court of Justice at a Crossroads*, Dobbs Ferry, New York: Transnational Publishers, Inc., 1987, pp. 155-181.

Bobbitt, Philip, "Public International Law", in: Patterson, Dennis (ed.), *A Companion to Philosophy of Law and Legal Theory*, Blackwell Publishing ltd, 2nd reprint, 2003, p. 96-113.

Bowett, Derek W., "Contemporary Developments in Legal Techniques in the Settlement of Disputes", 180 *RCADI*, 1983, pp. 169-236.

Bowett, Derek W., "The Court's Role in Relation to International Organizations" in: Lowe, Vaughan & Fitzmaurice, Malgosia (eds.), *Fifty Years of the International Court of Justice: Essays in Honour of Sir Robert Jennings*, Cambridge: Grotius Publications, 1996, pp. 181-193.

Brierly, J. L., "The Covenant and the Charter", 22 *BYIL*, 1946, pp. 83-95.

Brownlie, Ian, "The United Nations as a Form of Government", in: Fawcett, J. E. S. & Higgins, Rosalyn (eds.), *International Organization; Law in Movement, Essays in Honour of John McMahon*, London: Oxford University Press, published for The Royal Institute of International Affairs, 1974, pp. 26-37.

Brownlie, Ian, "The Decisions of Political Organs of the United Nations and the Rule of Law", in: Macdonald, Ronald St. J. (ed.), *Essays in Honour of Wang Tieya*, Dordrecht; London: M. Nijhoff Publishers, 1994, pp. 91-102.

Brownlie, Ian, "International Law at the Fiftieth Anniversary of the United Nations", Chapter XV "The Role of the Security Council and the Rule of Law", 255 *RCADI*, 1995, pp. 211-227.

Butcher, Goler T., "The Consonance of U.S. Positions with the International Court's Advisory Opinions", in: Damrosch Lori F. (ed.), *The International Court of Justice at a Crossroads*, Dobbs Ferry, New York: Transnational Publishers Inc., 1987, pp. 423-447.

Chiu, Hungdah, "Succession in International Organizations", 14 *ICLQ*, 1965, pp. 83-121.

Caçado Trindade, A., "Co-existence and Co-ordination of Mechanisms of International Protection of Human Rights (at Global and Regional Levels)", 202 *RCADI*, 1987, pp. 9-436.

Collier, J. G., "The International Court of Justice and the Peaceful Settlement of Disputes", in: Lowe, Vaughan & Fitzmaurice, Malgosia (eds.), *Fifty Years of the International Court of Justice: Essays in Honour of Sir Robert Jennings*, Cambridge: Grotius Publications, Cambridge University Press, 1996, *pp.* 364-373.

Conforti, Benedetto, "Observations on the Advisory Function of the International Court of Justice", in: Cassese, Antonio (ed.), *UN Law/ Fundamental Rights: Two Topics in International Law*, Alphen aan den Rijn, the Netherlands: Sijthoff and Noordhoff, 1979, pp. 85-91.

Couvreur, Philippe, "The Effectiveness of the International Court of Justice in the Peaceful Settlement of International Disputes", in: Muller, Sam A. & Raic, D. et al. (eds.), *The International Court of Justice: Its Future Role After Fifty Years*, The Hague; Boston; London: Martinus Nijhoff Publishers, 1997, pp. 83-117.

Crawford, James, "The General Assembly, the International Court of Justice and Self-Determination", in: Lowe, Vaughan & Fitzmaurice, Malgosia (eds.), *Fifty Years of the International Court of Justice: Essays in Honour of Sir Robert Jennings*, Cambridge: Grotius Publications, Cambridge University Press, 1996, pp. 585-605.

D'Angelo, Deborah, "The 'Check' on International Peace and Security Maintenance: The International Court of Justice and Judicial Review of Security Council Resolutions", 23 *Suffolk Transnational Law Review*, 2000, pp. 561-592.

De Arechaga, Eduardo J., "The Amendments to the Rules of Procedure of the International Court of Justice", 67 *AJIL*, 1973, pp. 1-23.

De Visscher, Charles, "Reflections on the Present Prospects of International Adjudication", 50 *AJIL*, 1956, pp. 467-475.

Ehrlich, Ludwik, "The Development of International Law as a Science", 105 *RCADI*, 1962, pp. 177-260.

Elias, Taslim O., "How the International Court of Justice Deals with Requests for Advisory Opinions", in: Makarczyk, Jerzy (ed.), *Essays in International Law in Honour of Judge Manfred Lachs*, The Hague; Boston; Lancaster: Martinus Nijhoff Publishers, 1984, pp. 355-375

Engel, Salo, "Annual Reports of the International Court of Justice to the General Assembly?", 44 *BYIL*, 1970, pp. 193-200.

Fitzmaurice, Gerald G., "The Law and Procedure of the International Court of Justice: Treaty Interpretation and Certain Other Treaty Points", 28 *BYIL*, 1951, pp. 1-29.

Fitzmaurice, Gerald G., "The Law and Procedure of the International Court of Justice: International Organs and Tribunals", 29 *BYIL*, 1952, pp. 1-63.

Fitzmaurice, Sir Gerald, "The Law and Procedure of the International Court of Justice, 1951-4: Treaty Interpretation and Other Treaty Points", 33 *BYIL*, 1957, pp. 203-294.

Fitzmaurice, Sir Gerald, "Judicial Innovation, Its Uses and its Perils, as Exemplified in Some of the Work of the International Court of Justice During Lord McNair's Period of Office", in: "*Cambridge Essays in International Law: Essays in Honour of Lord McNair*", London: Stevens and Sons, 1965, pp. 24-48

Fox, Hazel, "The Advisory Opinion on the Difference Relating to Immunity from Legal Process of a Special Rapporteur of the Commission of Human Rights: Who has the Last Word on Judicial Independence", 12 *LJIL*, 1999, pp. 889-918.

Goodrich, Leland M., "The Nature of the Advisory Opinions of the Permanent Court of International Justice", 32 *AJIL*, 1938, pp. 738-759.

Gordon, Edward, "Discretion to Decline to Exercise Jurisdiction", 81 *AJIL*, 1987, pp. 129-135.

Gowlland-Debbas, Vera, "The Relationship Between the International Court of Justice and the Security Council in the Light of the Lockerbie Case", 88 *AJIL*, 1994, pp. 643-678.

Gowlland-Debbas, Vera, "Judicial Insights into Fundamental Values and Interests of the International Community", in: Muller, Sam A. & Raic, D. et al. (eds.), *The International Court of Justice: Its Future Role After Fifty Years*, The Hague; Boston; London: Martinus Nijhoff Publishers, 1997, pp. 327-367.

Gowlland-Debbas, Vera, "The Right to Life and Genocide: The Court and an International Public Policy", in: Boisson De Chazournes, Laurence & Sands, Philippe (eds.), *International Law, the International Court Of Justice and Nuclear Weapons*, Cambridge University Press, 1999, pp. 315-338.

Graefrath, B., "Leave to the Court What Belongs to the Court: The Libyan Case", 4 *EJIL*, 1993, pp. 184-205.

Grant, Gilmore, "The International Court of Justice", 55 *YLJ*, 1945-46, pp. 1049-1067.

Gray, Christine, "The Use of Force and the International Legal Order", in: Evans, Malcolm D. (ed.), *International Law*, Oxford University Press, 2003, pp. 589-621.

Greenwood, Christopher, "The Impact of Decisions and Resolutions of the Security Council on the International Court of Justice", in: Heere, Wybo p. (ed.), *International Law And the Hague's 750th Anniversary*, The Hague: T.M.C. Asser Press, 1999, pp. 81-87.

Greenwood, Christopher, "The Law of War (International Humanitarian Law)", in: Evans, Malcolm D. (ed.), *International Law*, Oxford University Press, 2003, pp. 789-824.

Greig, D. W., "The Advisory Jurisdiction of the International Court and the Settlement of Disputes Between States", 15 *ICLQ*, 1966, pp. 325-369.

Grief, Nicholas, "Legality of the Threat or Use of Nuclear Weapons", 46 *ICLQ*, 1997, pp. 681-689.

Gros, A., "Concerning the Advisory Role of the International Court of Justice", in: Friedmann, Wolfgang G., et al., (eds.), *Transnational Law in a Changing Society. Essays in Honour of Philip C. Jessup*, New York: Columbia University Press, 1972.

Gross, Leo, "Participation of Individuals in Advisory Proceedings Before the International Court of Justice", 52 *AJIL*, 1985, pp. 16-41.

Gross, Leo, "Some Observations on the International Court of Justice", 56 *AJIL*, 1962, pp. 33-63.

Gross, Leo, "Limitations upon the Judicial Function", 58 *AJIL*, 1964, pp. 415-432.

Gross, Leo, "The International Court of Justice and the United Nations", 120 *RCADI,* 1967, pp. 312-440.

Gross, Leo, "The International Court of Justice: Consideration of Requirements for Enhancing Its Role in the International Legal Order", 65 *AJIL*, 1971, pp. 253-327.

Gross, Leo, "The International Court of Justice: Consideration of Requirements for Enhancing Its Role in the International Legal Order", in: Gross, Leo (ed.), *The Future of the International Court of Justice*, Dobbs Ferry, New York: Oceana Publications, Volume 1, 1976, pp. 22-104.

Gross, Leo, "Underutilization of the International Court of Justice", 27 *HILJ*, 1986, pp. 571-597.

Guillaume, Gilbert: Speech By the President Of the International Court of Justice, Given at the University of Cambridge, Lauterpacht Research Centre for International Law, 9 November 2001.

Hambro, Edvard, "The Jurisdiction of the International Court of Justice", 76 *RCADI,* 1950, pp. 125-214.

Hambro, Edvard, "The Authority of the Advisory Opinions of the International Court of Justice", 3 *ICLQ*, 1954, pp. 2-23.

Heffernan, Liz, "The Nuclear Weapons Opinions: Reflections on the Advisory Procedure of the International Court of Justice", 28 *Stetson Law Review*, 1998, pp. 134-170.

Hensley, Thomas, "Bloc Voting on the International Court of Justice", 22 *The Journal of Conflict Resolution*, 1978, pp. 39-95.

Higgins, Rosalyn, "Policy Considerations and the International Judicial Process", 17 *ICLQ*, 1968, pp. 58-85.

Higgins, Rosalyn, "The Place of International Law in the Settlement of Disputes by the Security Council", 64 *AJIL*, 1970, pp. 1-19.

Higgins, Rosalyn, "The Advisory Opinion on Namibia: Which UN Resolutions are Binding Under Article 25 of the Charter?", 21 *ICLQ*, 1972, pp. 270-287.

Higgins, Rosalyn, "International Law and the Avoidance, Containment and Resolution of Disputes", 230 *RCADI*, 1991, pp. 9-342.

Higgins, Rosalyn, "A Comment on the Current Health of Advisory Opinions", in: Lowe, Vaughan & Fitzmaurice, Malgosia (eds.), *Fifty Years of the International Court of Justice: Essays in Honour of Sir Robert Jennings*, Cambridge: Grotius Publications, 1996, pp. 567- 581.

Higgins, Rosalyn, "The International Court of Justice and Human Rights", in: Wellens, Karel (ed.), *International Law: Theory and Practice: Essays in Honour of Eric Suy*, The Hague; Boston; London: Martinus Nijhoff Publishers, 1998, pp. 691-706.

Higgins, Judge Rosalyn, "*The Role of the International Court of Justice at the Turn of the Century*", Presidential Address at the Holdsworth Club of the Faculty of Law in the University of Birmingham delivered 19 March 1999, Published by the Holdsworth Club, 1999, pp. 1-11.

Highet, Keith, "Reflections on Jurisprudence for the "Third World": The World Court, the "big case", and the Future", 27 *VJIL*, 1986-87, pp. 287-304.

Highet, Keith, & George Kahale, "International Decisions", (1991), *AJIL*, 85, pp. 680-702.

Hudson, Manley O., "Advisory Opinions of National and International Courts", 37 *HLR*, 1923-24, pp. 970-1002.

Hudson, Manley O., "The Effect of Advisory Opinions of the World Court", 42 *AJIL*, 1948, pp. 630-3.

Jacoby, Sidney B., "Some Aspects of the Jurisdiction of the Permanent Court of International Justice", 30 *AJIL*, 1936, pp. 233-256.

Janis, Mark W., "The International Court", in: Janis, Mark W. (ed.), *International Courts for the Twenty-First Century*, Dordrecht; Boston; London: Martinus Nijhoff Publishers, 1992, pp. 13-42.

Jenks, Wilfred C., "Co-ordination: A New Problem of International Organization. A Preliminary Survey of the Law and Practice of Inter-organizational Relationships", 77 *RCADI*, 1950, pp. 151-302.

Jenks, Wilfred C., "Co-ordination in International Organization: An introductory Survey", 28 *BYIL*, 1951, pp. 29-90.

Jennings, Robert Y., "General Course on Principles of International Law", 121 *RCADI*, 1967, pp. 327-603.

Jennings, Sir Robert Y., "International Courts and International Politics", Josephine Onoh Memorial Lecture, Hull University Press, 21 January 1986, pp. 1-17.

Jennings, Sir Robert Y., "Judicial Reasoning at an International Court", Europa-Institut: Universität Des Saarlandes, 1991.

Jennings, Sir Robert Y., "The International Court of Justice After Fifty Years", 89 *AJIL*, 1995, pp. 493-506.

Jennings, Sir Robert Y., "The Judiciary, International and National, and the Development of International Law", 45 *ICLQ*, 1996, pp. 1-13.

Jennings, Sir Robert Y., "The Role of the International Court of Justice", 68 *BYIL*, 1997, pp. 1-64.

Jennings, Sir Robert Y., "The Proper Work and Purposes of the International Court of Justice", in: Muller, Sam A. & Raic, D. et al. (eds.), *The International Court Of Justice: Its Future Role After Fifty Years*, The Hague; Boston; London: Martinus Nijhoff Publishers, 1997, pp. 33-46.

Jiménez de Aréchaga, Eduardo, "International Law in the Past Third of a Century", 159 *RCADI*, 1978, pp. 1-344.

Joseph, Daly, "Is the International Court of Justice Worth the Effort", 20 *Akron Law Review*, 1987, pp. 391-407.

Keith, Sir Kenneth, "The Advisory Jurisdiction of the International Court of Justice: Some Comparative Reflections", 17 *AYIL*, 1996, pp. 39-59.

Keith, K., "The International Court of Justice Nuclear Weapons", 21 *New Zealand International Review*, 1996, pp. 20-23.

Kelly, Patrick, "The Changing Process of International Law and the Role of the World Court", 11 *Michigan J. Int'l Law*, 1989, pp. 129-166.

Keohane, Robert, "International Institutions: Two Approaches", in: Der Derian, James (ed.) *International Theory: Critical Investigation*, Macmillan Press, 1995, pp. 279- 307

Kerley, Ernest, "Ensuring Compliance with Judgements of the International Court of Justice", in: Gross, Leo (ed.), *The Future of the International Court of Justice*, 1976, pp. 276-286.

Lauterpacht, Hersch, "Decisions of Municipal Courts as a Source of International Law", 10 *BYIL*, 1929, pp. 65-96.

Lauterpacht, Hersch, "Restrictive Interpretation and the Principle of Effectiveness in the Interpretation of Treaties", 26 *BYIL*, 1949, pp. 48-86.

Lauterpacht, Elihu, "The Legal Effect of Illegal Acts of International Organizations", in: *Cambridge Essays in International Law. Essays in Honour of Lord McNair*, London: Stevens and Sons; Dobbs Ferry, New York: Oceana Publications, 1965, pp. 88-121.

Lauterpacht, Elihu, "The Development of the Law of International Organizations by the Decisions of International Tribunals", 152 *RCADI*, 1976, pp. 377- 478.

Lauterpacht, Elihu, "Judicial Review of the Acts of International Organizations", in: Boisson De Chazournes, Laurence & Sands, Philippe (eds.), *International Law, the International Court of Justice and Nuclear Weapons,* Cambridge University Press, 1999, pp. 92-103.

Lawrence, Paul R. & Lorsch, Jay W., "*Organizations and Environment: Managing Differentiation and Integration*", in: Brinkerhoff, Merlin B.; Kunz, Phillip R. (eds.), *Complex Organizations and Their Environments*, Dubuque, Iowa: WM. C. Brown Company Publishers, 1972.

Macdonald, R. St. J., "Changing Relations between the International Court of Justice and The Security Council Of The United Nations", 31 *Canadian Yearbook Of International Law*, 1993, pp. 3-32.

Makarczyk, Jerzy, "The International Court of Justice on the Implied Powers of International Organizations", in: Makarczyk, Jerzy (ed.), *Essays in International Law in Honour of Judge Manfred Lachs*, The Hague; Lancaster: M. Nijhoff, 1984, pp. 501-519.

Malanczuk, Peter, "Reconsidering the Relationship Between the ICJ and the Security Council", in: Heere, Wybo p. (ed.), *International Law and the Hague's 750th Anniversary*, The Hague: T.M.C. Asser Press, 1999, pp. 87-100.

Matheson, Michael J., "The Opinions of The International Court of Justice On The Threat or Use OF Nuclear Weapons", 91 *AJIL*, 1997, pp. 417-436.

McLaughlin, W., "Allowing Federal Courts Access to International Court of Justice Advisory Opinions. Critique and Proposal", 6 *Hastings International and Comparative Law Review*, 1983, pp. 745-772.

McNair, Arnold Duncan, "*The Development of International Justice*", Two Lectures Delivered at the Law Center of New York University, New York: New York University Press, 1954.

McWhinney, Edward, "Judicial Settlement of Disputes: Jurisdiction and Justiciability", Chapter II, "The Contemporary International Judicial Process. Law and Logic, and the "Law"/ "Politics" Dichotomy", 221 *RCADI*, 1990, pp. 36-82.

Mendelson, Maurice, "The International Court of Justice and the Sources of International Law", in: Lowe, Vaughan & Fitzmaurice, Malgosia (eds.), *Fifty years of International Court of Justice*: *Essays in Honour of Sir Robert Jennings,* Grotius Publications, Cambridge University Press", 1996, pp. 63-88.

Merrills, J., "The Justiciablity of International Disputes", 47 *The Canadian Bar Review*, 1969, pp. 241-69.

Oellers-Frahm, Karin, "International Court of Justice", in: Bernhardt, R. (ed.), *Encyclopedia of Public International Law*, Amsterdam: Elsevier Science B.V., Volume II, 1995, pp. 1084-1107.

Oda, Shigeru, "The International Court of Justice Viewed from the Bench (1976-1993)", 244 *RCADI*, 1993, pp. 9-190.

Osieke Ebere, "TheLegal Validity of Ultra Vires Decisions of International Organization", 77 *AJIL,* 1983, pp. 239-256.

Paust, Jordan J., "Domestic Influence of the International Court of Justice", 26 *Denv. J. Int'l L. & Pol'y*, 1998, pp. 787-805.

Pollux, "The Interpretation of the Charter", 23 *BYIL*, 1946, pp. 54-83.

Pomerance, Michla, "The Admission of Judges Ad Hoc in Advisory Proceedings: Some Reflections in the Light of the Namibia Case", 67 *AJIL*, 1973, pp. 446-465.

Pomerance, Michla, "The Advisory Role of the International Court of Justice and its 'Judicial' Character: Past and Future Prisms", in: Muller, Sam A. & Raic, D. et al. (eds.), *The International Court of Justice: Its Future Role After Fifty Years*, The Hague; Boston; London: Martinus Nijhoff Publishers, 1997, pp. 271-323.

Pomerance, Michla, "The Badinter Commission: The Use and Misuse of the International Court of Justice's Jurisprudence", 20 *Mich. J. Int'l L*, 1998, pp. 31-58.

Pomerance, Michla, "The ICJ and South West Africa (Namibia): A Retrospective Legal/Political Assessment", 12 *LJIL*, 1999, pp. 425-436.

Rama-Montaldo, Manuel, "International Legal Personality and Implied Powers of International Organizations", 44 *BYIL*, 1970, pp. 111-155.

Reisman, Michael W., "The Constitutional crises in the United Nations", 87 *AJIL*, 1993, pp. 83-101.

Reisman, Michael W., "Termination of the United States Declaration Under Article 36(2) of the Statute of the International Court", in: Arend, Anthony C. (ed.), *The United States and the Compulsory Jurisdiction of the International Court of Justice*, Lanham: University Press of America, 1986, pp. 71-104.

Reisman, Michael W., "The Supervisory Jurisdiction of the International Court of Justice: International Arbitration and International Adjudication", 258 *RCADI*, 1996, pp. 9-394.

Rosenne, Shabtai, "On the Non-use of the Advisory Competence of the International Court of Justice", 39 *BYIL*, 1963, pp. 1-53.

Rosenne, Shabtai, "Publications of the International Court of Justice", 81 *AJIL*, 1987, pp. 681-697.

Rosenne, Shabtai, "Preliminary Rulings by the International Court of Justice at the Instance of National Courts: A Reply", 83 *AJIL*, 1989, pp. 401-413.

Rosenne, Shabtai, "The Cold War and The International Court of Justice: A Review Essay of Stephen M. Schwebel's Justice in International Law", 35 *VJIL*, 1995, pp. 669-682.

Rosenne, Shabtai, "The Contribution of the International Court of Justice to the United Nations", 35 *Indian Journal of International Law*, 1995, pp. 67-76.

Rosenne, Shabtai, "The Secretary-General of the United Nations and the Advisory Procedure of the International Court of Justice", in: Wellens, Karel (ed.), *International Law: Theory and Practice. Essays in Honour of Eric Suy*, The Hague, Boston, London: Martinus Nijhoff Publishers, 1998, pp. 707-719.

Rosenne, Shabtai, "The Perplexities of Modern International Law", 291 *RCADI*, 2001, pp. 9-472.

Rovine, Arthur, "The National Interest and the World Court", in: Gross, Leo (ed.) *The Future of the International Court of Justice*, 1976, pp. 313-336.

Sarooshi, Danesh, "The Legal Framework Governing United Nations Subsidiary Organs", 67 *BYIL*, 1996, pp. 413-478.

Schachter, Oscar, "International Law in Theory and Practice", 178 *RCADI*, 1982, pp. 9-396.

Schachter, Oscar, "The United Nations Law", 88 *AJIL*, 1994, pp. 1-24.

Schlochauer, Hans-Jurgen, "*International Court of Justice*", in: Bernhardt, R. (ed.), *Encyclopedia of Public International Law*, Amsterdam: Elsevier Science B.V., Volume II, 1995, pp. 1084-1105.

Schwebel, Stephen M., "The Effect of Resolutions of the United Nations General Assembly on Customary Law", (1979), *Proceedings of American Society of International Law*, 1979, pp. 301-304.

Schwebel, Stephen M., "Authorizing the Secretary-General of the United Nations to Request Advisory Opinions of the International Court of Justice", 78 *AJIL*, 1984, pp. 869-879.

Schwebel, Stephen M., "Widening the Advisory Jurisdiction of the International Court of Justice Without Amending Its Statute", 33 *Catholic University Law Review*, 1984, pp. 355-361.

Schwebel, Stephen M., "Reflections on the Role of the International Court of Justice", 61 *Washington Law Review*, 1986, pp. 1061-1072

Schwebel, Stephen, "Preliminary Rulings by the International Court of Justice at the Instance of National Courts", 28 *VJIL*, 1987-88, pp. 495-506.

Schwebel, Stephen M., "Was the Capacity to Request an Advisory Opinion Wider in the Permanent Court of International Justice than it is in the International Court of Justice?", 62 *BYIL*, 1991, pp. 77-118.

Schwebel, Stephen M., "Relations Between the International Court of Justice and the United Nations", in: Virally, Michel (ed.), *Le Droit International Au Service De La Paix, De La Justice: Et Du Développement*, Paris: A. Pedone, 1991, pp. 431-443.

Schwebel, Stephen M., "The Contribution of the International Court of Justice to the Development of International Law", in: Heere, Wybo p. (ed.), *International law and the Hague's 750th Anniversary*, The Hague: T.M.C. Asser Press, 1999, pp. 405-416.

Schwelb, Egon, "The International Court of Justice and the Human Rights Clauses of the Charter", 66 *AJIL*, 1972, pp. 337-352.

Scobbie, Iain, "Reviving the World Court", 58 *BYIL*, 1987, Book Review, pp. 376-378.

Scobbie, Iain, "International Organizations and International Relations", in: Dupuy, René-Jean (ed.), *A Handbook on International Organizations*, 2nd edition, Dordrecht; Boston; London: Martinus Nijhoff Publishers, 1998, pp. 831-897.

Seidl-Hohenveldern, Ignaz, "*Access of International Organizations to the International Court of Justice*", in: Muller, Sam A. & Raic, D. et al. (eds.), *The International Court of Justice: Its Future Role After Fifty Years*, The Hague; Boston; London: Martinus Nijhoff Publishers, 1997, pp. 189-204.

Shaw, Malcolm N., "The Western Sahara Case", 49 *BYIL*, 1978, pp. 119-154.

Shaw, Malcolm N., "The Security Council and the International Court of Justice: Judicial Drift and Judicial Function", in: Muller, Sam A. & Raic, D. et al. (eds.), *The International Court of Justice: Its Future Role After Fifty Years*, The Hague; Boston; London: Martinus Nijhoff Publishers, 1997, pp. 219-259.

Shaw, Malcolm N., "The International Court of Justice: A Practical Perspective", 46 *ICLQ*, 1997, pp. 831-866.

Skubiszewski, Krzysztof "The International Court of Justice and the Security Council", in: Lowe, Vaughan & Fitzmaurice, Malgosia (eds.) *Fifty Years of the International Court of Justice: Essay in Honour of Sir Robert Jennings,* Grotius Publications, Cambridge University Press. 1996, pp. 606-629.

Sohn, Louis B., "The Authority of the United Nations to Establish and Maintain a Permanent United Nations Force", 52 *AJIL*, 1958, pp. 229-241.

Sohn, Louis B., "The Role of International Institutions as a Conflict Adjusting Agencies",

(1960-1961), 28 *University of Chicago Law Review*, 1961 pp. 205-257.

Sohn, Louis B., "Broadening the Advisory Jurisdiction of the International Court of Justice", 77 *AJIL*, 1983, pp. 124-130.

Sohn, Louis B., "Peaceful Settlement of Disputes", in: Janis, Mark W. (ed.), *International Courts for the Twenty-First Century*, Dordrecht; Boston; London: Martinus Nijhoff Publishers, 1992, pp. 3-9.

Sohn, Louis B., "Important Improvements in the Functioning of the Principle Organs of the United Nations that Can Be Made Without Charter Revision", 91 *AJIL*, 1997, pp. 652-663.

Sugihara, Takane, "The Advisory Function of the International Court of Justice", 17 *JAIL*, 1973, pp. 23-50.

Suy, Eric, "Peace-Keeping Operations", in: Dupuy, René-Jean (ed.), *A Handbook on International Organizations*, Dordrecht; Boston; London: Martinus Nijhoff Publishers, 1998, pp. 539-563.

Szasz, Paul C., "Enhancing The Advisory Competence of The World Court", in: Gross, Leo (ed.), *The Future of The International Court of Justice*, 1976, pp. 499-549.

Szasz, Paul C., "Granting International Organizations Ius Standi in the International Court of Justice", in: Muller, Sam A. & Raic, D. et al. (eds.), *The International Court of Justice: Its Future Role After Fifty Years*, The Hague; Boston; London: Martinus Nijhoff Publishers, 1997, pp. 169-189.

Sztucki, Jerzy, "International Organizations as Parties to Contentious Proceedings before the International Court of Justice", in: Muller, Sam A. & Raic, D. et al. (eds.), *The International Court of Justice: Its Future Role After Fifty Years*, The Hague; Boston; London: Martinus Nijhoff Publishers, 1997, pp. 141-168.

Tanzi, Attila, "Problems of Enforcement of Decisions of the International Court of Justice and the Law of the United Nations", 6 *EJIL*, 1995, pp. 539-572.

Thirlway, Hugh, "The Law and Procedure of the International Court of Justice, 1960-1989", 62 *BYIL*, 1991, pp. 1-76.

Thirlway, Hugh, "Advisory Opinions of International Courts", in: Bernhardt, R. (ed.) *Encyclopedia of Public International Law*, Amsterdam: Elsevier Science B.V., Volume I, 1992, pp. 38-42.

Thirlway, Hugh, "Procedural Law and the International Court of Justice", in: Lowe, Vaughan & Fitzmaurice, Malgosia (eds.), *Fifty Years of the International Court of Justice: Essays in Honour of Sir Robert Jennings*, Grotius Publications, Cambridge University Press, 1996, pp. 389-405.

Thirlway, Hugh, "Procedures of International Courts and Tribunals", in: Bernhardt, R. (ed.), *Encyclopedia of Public International Law*, Amsterdam: Elsevier Science B.V., Volume III, 1997, pp. 1128-1133.

Thirlway, Hugh, "The Law and Procedure of the International Court of Justice, 1960- 1989", 71 *BYIL*, 2000, pp. 71-180.

Thirlway, Hugh, "The International Court of Justice and other International Courts", in: Blokker, Neils & Schermers Henry (eds.), *Proliferation of International Organizations: Legal Issues*, The Hague; Boston: Kluwer Law International, 2001, pp. 251-278.

Thirlway, Hugh, "The International Court of Justice", in: Evans, Malcolm D. (ed.), *International law*, Oxford University Press, 2003, pp. 559-589.

Thirlway, Hugh, "The Sources of International Law", in: Evans, Malcolm D. (ed.), *International law*, Oxford University Press, 2003, pp. 117-145.

Thürer, Daniel, "Self Determination", in: Bernhardt, R. (ed.), *Encyclopedia of Public International Law*, Amsterdam: Elsevier Science B.V., Volume IV, 2000, pp. 364-374.

Tiefenbrun, Susan "The Role of The World Court in Settling International Disputes: A Recent Assessment", 20 *Loyola of Los Angeles Int'l & Comparative Law Journal*, 1997, pp. 1-27.

Tomuschat, Christian, "International Law: Ensuring the Survival of Mankind on the Eve of a New Century", 281 *RCADI*, 1999, pp. 9-438.

Treves, Tullio, "Advisory Opinions of the International Court of Justice on Questions Raised by Other International Tribunals", 4 *Max Planck Yearbook of United Nations Law,* 2000, pp. 215-232.

Vallat. F. A., "The General Assembly and the Security Council of the United Nations", 29 *BYIL*, 1952, pp. 63-105.

Vallat. F. A., "The Competence of The United Nations General Assembly", 97 *RCADI*, 1959, pp. 207-293.

Waldock, C.H.M., "The Plea of Domestic Jurisdiction Before International Legal Tribunals", 31 *BYIL*, 1954, pp. 96-143.

Waldock, Sir Humphrey, "General Course on Public International Law", 106 *RCADI*, 1962, pp. 1-251.

Waldock, Sir Humphrey, "*Aspects of the Advisory Jurisdiction of the International Court of Justice*", Lecture delivered on 3rd June 1976, Gilberto Amado memorial lecture

Watson, Geoffrey, "Constitutionalism, Judicial Review, and the World Court", 34 *HILJ*, 1993, pp. 1-46.

Weber, Ludwig, "Cuban Quarantine", in: Bernhardt, R. (ed.), *Encyclopedia of Public International Law*, Amsterdam: Elsevier Science B.V., Volume I, 1992, pp. 882-885.

Wehle, Louis B., "The U.N. By-Passes the International Court as the Council's Advisor, a Study in Contrived Frustration", 98 *UPLR*, 1949-50, pp. 285-320.

Weeramantry, Christopher G., "The Function of the International Court of Justice in the Development of International Law", 10 *LJIL*, 1997, pp. 309-340.

Weiss, Edith B., "Judicial Independence and Impartiality: A Preliminary Inquiry", in: Damrosch. Lori, (ed.), *The International Court of Justice at a Crossroad*, Transnational Publishers Inc., Dobbs Ferry, New York, 1987, pp. 123-154.

Weiss, Edith B., "Opening the Door to the Environment and to Future Generations", in: Boisson De Chazournes, Laurence & Sands, Philippe (eds.), *International Law, The International Court Of Justice and Nuclear Weapons*, Cambridge University Press, 1999, pp. 338-354.

Weissberg, Guenter., "The Role of the International Court of Justice in the United Nations System: the First Quarter Century", in: Gross Leo (ed.), *The Future of the International Court of Justice*, 1976, pp. 131-190.

Werksman, Jacob; Khalastchi, Ruth, "Nuclear Weapons and Jus Cogens: Peremptory Norms and Justice Pre-empted?", in: Boisson De Chazournes, Laurance & Sands, Philippe (eds.), *International Law, the International Court Of Justice and Nuclear Weapons*, Cambridge University Press, 1999, pp. 181-199.

Yee, Sienho, "Forum Prorogatum and the Advisory Proceedings Of The International Court", 95 *AJIL*, 2001, pp. 381-386.

Zacklin, Ralph, "The Problem of Namibia in International Law", 171 *RCADI*, 1981, pp. 233-339.

Zemanek, Karl, "Some Unresolved Questions Concerning Reservations In the Vienna Convention in the Law of Treaties", in: Makarczyk, Jerzy (ed.), *Essays In International Law In Honour of Judge Manfred Lachs,* 1984, pp. 323-337.

Zemanek, Karl, "Peace-keeping or Peace-making?", in: Blokker, Niels & Muller, Sam (eds.), *Towards More Effective Supervision by International Organizations. Essays in Honour of Henry G. Schermers*, Dordrecht; Boston; London: Martinus Nijhoff Publishers, Volume 1, 1994, pp. 29-48.4. Significant Official Reports and Documents

League of Nations

This table lists those official reports and documents which are recurrently referred to throughout the book.

League of Nations Official Journal, Records of the First Assembly, Meeting of Committees (1920); Records of the First Assembly, Plenary; The Permanent Court of International Justice Advisory Committee of Jurists, *Procés-Verbaux* of the Proceedings of the Committee (1920), 27th meeting.

Publications of the Permanent Court of International Justice (PCIJ).

Series B., Advisory Opinions, No. 1 (1922); No. 4 (1923); No. 5 (1923); No. 12 (1925) and No. 16 (1928).

Series C., Acts and Documents relating to judgments and advisory opinions (Pleadings), No. 15 (1926).

Series D., Acts and Documents relating to the organization of the Court, No. 2 (1922) and No. 2 (1936)

Series E., Annual Reports, No. 4 (1927-1928).

World Court Reports: A Collection of the Judgements, Orders and Opinions of the Permanent Court of International Justice, 1922-1926, vol. I and IV.

United Nations

An Agenda for Peace: Preventive diplomacy, peacemaking and peace-keeping, A/47/277- S/24111, 17 June 1992.

Annual Reports of the Secretary-General, UN Doc.A/45/1, part III.

GA Res. 89 (1), 11 December 1946; GA Res. 171(1), 14 November 1947; GA Res. 197(III), 21 November 1947; GA Res. 196(III), 30 December 1948; GA Res. 365(IV), 1 December 1949; GA Res. 338(IV), 6 December 1949; GA Res. 377, 3 November 1950; GA Res. 385(V), 3 November 1950; GA Res. 449 A (V), 13 December 1950; GA Res. 598(VI), 12 January 1952; GA Res. 749 A (VIII), 28 November 1953; GA Res. 957, November 1955; GA Res. 1000(ES-1), 5 November 1956; GA Res. 1001(ES), 7 November 1956; GA Res. 2145(XXI), 27 October 1966.

SC Res. 143, 14 July 1960; SC Res. 145, 22 July 1960; SC Res. 146, 9 August 1960; SC Res. 264, 20 March 1969; SC Res. 284, 29 July 1970; SC Res. 984, 11 April 1995; SC Res. 245, 25 January 1968; SC Res. 264, 20 March 1969.

United Nations Conference on International Organization UNCIO, San Francisco Documents, 1945, Volumes Nos. 9; 12; 13; 14

United Nations Yearbook, 1948; 1950; 1955 and 1995.

United Nations Treaty Series, Nos. 1; 11; 14; 33; 75; 78; 92; 213; 289; 974.

International Court of Justice

Reports of Judgment, Advisory Opinions and Orders, (ICJ Rep), Nos. 1948; 1949; 1950; 1951; 1954; 1955; 1956; 1960; 1962; 1966; 1970; 1971, 1973; 1975; 1980; 1982; 1987; 1988; 1989; 1992; 1996; and 1999.

Pleading, Oral Arguments and Documents (ICJ Pled), Nos. 1948; 1954; 1950; 1961; 1970; 1973; 1947 and 1995.

Yearbook of the International Court of Justice (ICJYB), (1946-1947); (1990-1991); (1991-1992); (1992-1993); (1996-1997) and (2000).

Appendix 1

Rules of Court, Governing the Advisory Procedure (1978) As Amended on 5 December 2000

Part IV

Article 102

1. In the exercise of its advisory functions under Article 65 of the Statute, the Court shall apply, in addition to the provisions of Article 96 of the Charter and Chapter IV of the Statute, the provisions of the present Part of the Rules.
2. The Court shall also be guided by the provisions of the Statute and of these Rules which apply in contentious cases to the extent to which it recognizes them to be applicable. For this purpose, it shall above all consider whether the request for the advisory opinion relates to a legal question actually pending between two or more States.
3. When an advisory opinion is requested upon a legal question actually pending between two or more States, Article 31 of the Statute shall apply, as also the provisions of these Rules concerning the application of that Article.

Article 103

When the body authorized by or in accordance with the Charter of the United Nations to request an advisory opinion informs the Court that its request necessitates an urgent answer, or the Court finds that an early answer would be desirable, the Court shall take all necessary steps to accelerate the procedure, and it shall convene as early as possible for the purpose of proceeding to a hearing and deliberation on the request.

Article 104

All requests for advisory opinions shall be transmitted to the Court by the Secretary General of the United Nations or, as the case may be, the chief administrative officer of the body authorized to make the request. The documents referred to in Article 65, paragraph 2, of the Statute shall be transmitted to the Court at the same time as the request or as soon as possible thereafter, in the number of copies required by the Registry.

Article 105

1. Written statements submitted to the Court shall be communicated by the Registrar to any States and organizations which have submitted such statements.
2. The Court, or the President if the Court is not sitting, shall:
   (a) determine the form in which, and the extent to which, comments permitted under Article 66, paragraph 4, of the Statute shall be received, and fix the time-limit for the submission of any such comments in writing;
   (b) decide whether oral proceedings shall take place at which statements and comments may be submitted to the Court under the provisions of Article 66 of the Statute, and fix the date for the opening of such oral proceedings.

Article 106

The Court, or the President if the Court is not sitting, may decide that the written statements and annexed documents shall be made accessible to the public on or after the opening of the oral proceedings. If the request for advisory opinion relates to a legal question actually pending between two or more States, the views of those States shall first be ascertained.

Article 107

1. When the Court has completed its deliberations and adopted its advisory opinion, the opinion shall be read at a public sitting of the Court.
2. The advisory opinion shall contain:

   the date on which it is delivered;
   the names of the judges participating;
   a summary of the proceedings;
   a statement of the facts;
   the reasons in point of law;
   the reply to the question put to the Court;
   the number and names of the judges constituting the majority;
   a statement as to the text of the opinion which is authoritative.
3. Any judge may, if he so desires, attach his individual opinion to the advisory opinion of the Court, whether he dissents from the majority or not; a judge who wishes to record his concurrence or dissent without stating his reasons may do so in the form of a declaration.

Article 108

The Registrar shall inform the Secretary-General of the United Nations, and, where appropriate, the chief administrative officer of the body which requested the advisory opinion, as to the date and the hour fixed for the public sitting to be held for the reading of the opinion. He shall also inform the representatives of the Members of the United Nations and other States, specialized agencies and public international organizations immediately concerned.

Article 109

One copy of the advisory opinion, duly signed and sealed, shall be placed in the archives of the Court, another shall be sent to the Secretary-General of the United Nations and, where appropriate, a third to the chief administrative officer of the body which requested the opinion of the Court. Copies shall be sent by the Registrar to the Members of the United Nations and to any other States, specialized agencies and public international organizations immediately concerned.

Appendix 2

Provisions for Binding Advisory Opinions

Convention On Privileges and Immunities of the United Nations, Adopted 13 February 1946

Article VIII – Settlement of Disputes
Section 30

All differences arising out of the interpretation or application of the present convention shall be referred to the international Court of Justice, unless in any case it is agreed by the parties to have recourse to another mode of settlement. If a difference arises between the United Nations on the one hand and a Member on the other hand, a request shall be made for an advisory opinion on any legal question involved in accordance with Article 96 of the Charter and Article 65 of the Statute of the Court. The opinion given by the Court shall be accepted as decisive by the parties.

Agreement Between the United Nations and the United States of America Regarding the Headquarters of the United Nations, Signed on 26 June 1947

(a) Any dispute between the United Nations and the United States concerning the interpretation or application of this agreement or of any supplemental agreement, which is not settled by negotiation or other agreed mode of settlement, shall be referred for final decision to a tribunal of three arbitrators, one to be named by the Secretary-General, one to be named by the Secretary of State of the United States, and the third to be chosen by the two, or, if they should fail to agree upon a third, then by the President of the International Court of Justice.

(b) The Secretary -General or the United States may ask the General Assembly to request of the International Court of Justice an advisory opinion on any legal question arising in the course of such proceedings. Pending the receipt of the opinion of the Court, an interim decision of the arbitral tribunal shall be observed by both Parties. thereafter, the arbitral tribunal render a final decision, having regard to the opinion of the Court.

Article XII of the Statute of the I.L.O. Administrative Tribunal as Adopted by the International Labour Conference on 9 October 1946

1. In any case in which the Governing Body of the International Labour Office or the Administrative Board of the Pensions Fund challenges a decision of the Tribunal confirming its jurisdiction, or considers that a decision of the Tribunal is vitiated by a fundamental fault in the procedure followed, the question of the validity of the decision given by the Tribunal shall be submitted by the Governing Body, for an advisory opinion, to the International Court of Justice.
2. The opinion given by the Court shall be binding.

The Previous Article 11 of the Statute UN Administrative Tribunal as Amended by Resolution 957 (X) on 8 November 1955

1. If a Member State, the Secretary-General or a person in respect of whom a judgment has been rendered by the Tribunal (including any one who has succeeded to that person's rights on his death) objects to the judgment on the ground that the Tribunal has exceeded its jurisdiction or competence or that the Tribunal has failed to exercise jurisdiction vested in it, or has erred on a question of law relating to the provisions of the Charter of the United Nations, or has committed a fundamental error in procedure which has occasioned a failure of justice, Such Member State, the Secretary-General or the person concerned may, within thirty days from the date of the judgment, make a written application to the Committee established by paragraph 4 of this article asking the Committee to request an advisory opinion of the International Court of Justice on the matter.
2. Within thirty days from the receipt of an application under paragraph 1 of this article, the Committee shall decide whether or not there is a substantial basis for the application. If the Committee decides that such a basis exists, it shall request an advisory opinion of the Court, and the Secretary-General shall arrange to transmit to the Court the views of the person referred to in paragraph 1.
3. If no application is made under paragraph 1 of this article, or if a decision to request an advisory opinion has not been taken by the Committee, within periods prescribed in this article, the judgment of the Tribunal shall become final. In any case in which a request has been made for an advisory opinion, the Secretary-General shall either give effect to the opinion of the Court, or request the Tribunal to convene specially in order that it shall confirm its original judgment, or give a new judgment, in conformity with the opinion of the Court. if not requested to convene specially, the Tribunal shall at its next session confirm its judgment or bring it into conformity with the opinion of the Court.

4. For the purpose of this article, a Committee is established and authorized under paragraph 2 of Article 96 of the Charter to request advisory opinions of the Court. the Committee shall be composed of the Member States the representative of which have served on the General Committee of the most recent regular session of the General Assembly. The Committee shall meet at United Nations Headquarters and shall establish its own rules.

General Assembly Resolution 50/54, U.N. Doc. A/RES/50/54 (1995 Review of the Procedure Provided for Under Article 11 of the Statute of the Administrative Tribunal of the United Nations, G.A. res. 50/54,).

The General Assembly,

Having considered the report of the Secretary-General, Noting that the procedure provided for under article 11 of the statute of the Administrative Tribunal of the United Nations has not proved to be a constructive or useful element in the adjudication of staff disputes within the Organization, and noting also the views of the Secretary-General to that effect,

1. Decides to amend the statute of the Administrative Tribunal of the United Nations with respect to judgements rendered by the Tribunal after 31 December 1995 as follows:

   (a) Delete article 11;

MIX
Papier aus verantwortungsvollen Quellen
Paper from responsible sources
FSC® C105338

If you have any concerns about our products,
you can contact us on
ProductSafety@springernature.com

In case Publisher is established outside the EU,
the EU authorized representative is:
Springer Nature Customer Service Center GmbH
Europaplatz 3, 69115 Heidelberg, Germany

Printed by Libri Plureos GmbH
in Hamburg, Germany